City, Chant, and the Topography of Early Music

City, Chant, and the Topography of Early Music

edited by

MICHAEL SCOTT CUTHBERT
SEAN GALLAGHER
CHRISTOPH WOLFF

Isham Library Papers 8
Harvard Publications in Music 23
Harvard University Department of Music
2013

Distributed by Harvard University Press
Cambridge, Massachusetts, U.S.A. • London, England

Printed and bound in the United States of America

Typesetting by Hobblebush Books, Brookline, New Hampshire
Printing by Puritan Press, Hollis, New Hampshire

Photograph of Thomas Forrest Kelly by Tony Rinaldo

Library of Congress Cataloging-in-Publication Data

City, chant, and the topography of early music /
edited by Michael Scott Cuthbert, Sean Gallagher, Christoph Wolff.

pages cm.—(Isham library papers ; 8) (Harvard publications in music ; 23)
Includes bibliographical references and index.
ISBN 978-0-9640317-4-6

1. Gregorian chants—History and criticism. 2. Music—History and criticism.
3. Music—Social aspects. I. Cuthbert, Michael Scott, editor of compilation. II. Gallagher, Sean, 1965- editor of compilation. III. Wolff, Christoph, editor of compilation.
ML3082.C55 2013
783.32'22—dc23

2013006259

For Thomas Forrest Kelly

Contents

Preface

ON A BEAUTIFUL New England Indian summer weekend in 2009, some of the world's most distinguished scholars of medieval music gathered on the campus of Harvard University in order to pay tribute to one of their most esteemed colleagues, our own Thomas Forrest Kelly. It also served as a welcome opportunity for the University to draw attention to its strong resources in medieval studies.

An inspiring academic teacher of the history of music and an exemplary scholar of medieval chant, Tom Kelly joined the Harvard faculty as Professor of Music in 1994 and in 2001 was appointed to the Morton B. Knafel chair. He did not come here as a stranger, however, for he had spent his graduate student days at Harvard and obtained the doctorate in 1973 under the tutelage of David G. Hughes. Professor Hughes himself was honored in similar fashion nearly twenty years earlier, in October 1990,[1] and to everyone's delight could be present for the conference honoring his former student.

"City, Chant, and the Topography of Early Music" took place Friday through Sunday, October 2–4, 2009. In all, it attracted some 130 registrants, including musicologists, historians, performers, students, and community members. A Saturday night concert at Adolphus Busch Hall—appropriately under the heading of the Beneventan antiphon "Respondens Thomas ad Dominum"—featured medieval chant and polyphony in performances by two of Europe's most important medieval music groups, the ensemble "Dialogos" under the direction of Katarina Livljanić and the ensemble "Sequentia" under Benjamin Bagby.

[1] See the volume *Essays on Medieval Music in Honor of David G. Hughes*, ed. Graeme M. Boone, Isham Library Papers 4, Harvard University Department of Music (distributed by Harvard University Press, Cambridge, Mass., 1995).

The early planning of the conference settled on the notion of two major centers, Rome and Paris, which had influenced and determined much of the topography of the musical traditions in the European Middle Ages; Tom Kelly has had a very special relationship with both cities for a long time. On the other hand, the concept of topology and chronology had to be sufficiently broad so that it would include other places and regions as well, not only Benevento and the unique tradition so central to Tom's scholarship, but also areas like Dalmatia, Aquitania, and even seventeenth-century Iceland.

The opening session of the conference represented in Part I of the present book set the stage for a broader exploration of the general conference topic with the keynote address by Craig Wright, a fellow graduate student of Tom's at Harvard. At the same time, the opening session expanded the overall historical horizon by playing on the idea of "First Nights"—the subject of Tom's popular General Education course at Harvard, subsequently published in book form, which examines five musical premieres as significant moments of cultural history.[2] Taking up two special examples from Stefano Landi in seventeenth-century Rome and Hector Berlioz in nineteenth-century Paris seemed to be an ideal way to celebrate Tom's often-stated interest in old music not as old, but as new. The subsequent sessions of the international symposium were all devoted to an examination of the various ways in which space, urban life, landscape, and time have revolutionized plainchant (early ritual Christian chanting) and other forms of musical expression.

On behalf of the Department of Music and the organizing committee, we would like to thank the contributors to the conference and to this volume for their participation and unfailing efforts in furthering the cause of medieval musicology and, in a broader sense, the cultural, geographic, and political contexts surrounding early music. This book would not have come about without the tireless dedication, persistence, experience, and editorial fine tuning provided by Lesley Bannatyne in the Department of Music, the expert indexing of Thomas Kozachek, and the superb work of graduate students Emerson Morgan and Matthew Mugmon.

Michael Scott Cuthbert
Sean Gallagher
Christoph Wolff

[2] Thomas Forrest Kelly, *First Nights. Five Musical Premieres* (New Haven: Yale University Press), 2000.

Abbreviations

ParisBN	Paris, Bibliothèque Nationale de France
BAV	Rome, Bibliotheca Apostolica Vaticana
LondonBL	London, British Library, Department of Manuscripts
CAO	René-Jean Hesbert, *Corpus Antiphonalium Officii*, 6 vols. (Rome: Herder, 1963–79)

Part I

First Nights: Early Music in Paris and Rome

Quantification in Medieval Paris and How it Changed Western Music[1]

CRAIG WRIGHT

I FIRST CAME to Harvard in the fall of 1966 with a graduate musicology class of ten students. One, Thomas Forrest Kelly, was distinctive: he was from Chapel Hill, North Carolina, and had an accent. But he also spoke fast, fluent French. Indeed he had just come back from a year in Paris where he had been studying organ on a Fulbright grant. You knew that Tom had been to Paris because he smoked Gauloises Caporal cigarettes. In those days gentleman wore suits and ties to class and everyone smoked, students and instructors alike, if they so chose.

The class around which the lives of Tom and other graduate students gravitated, indeed all fledgling musicologists for several generations, was the famous Music 200, Introduction to Musicology, taught by John M. Ward. John was a remarkable man; he taught us all how to think and how to write. And Tom and others in our class had our first introduction to Gregorian chant in a course taught by David G. Hughes, who forced us to come to terms with primary sources by inventorying chant manuscripts.

So there we were in the fall of 1966 studying chant with David Hughes and flailing away under the tough-love of John Ward. Tom and I took another course together that first year: The Notation of Polyphonic Music. Although a full-year course, it was divided into two semesters. The first was taught by the

[1] This is a revised version of the Keynote Address delivered at the conference honoring Thomas Forrest Kelly.

gentle and very musical Arthur Tillman Merritt (whom Leonard Bernstein acknowledged as his counterpoint teacher), and the second semester—by the second semester Tom and I were the only students left—by the legendary Nino Pirrotta. Nino was a wonderfully idiosyncratic teacher. There was no pedagogical method that I could see, you simply learned through osmosis. And he had quirks. Tom and I waited with great anticipation and a wink for those moments when Nino would inadvertently tumble off the elevated platform-stage in Room 1, and we counted slowly the seconds it would take him to realize, by inhaling, that he had lit the wrong end of his filter cigarette.

But let us focus on the substance of that notation course, for it tells us something about how musicology was viewed in those days, now close to half a century ago. The textbook was Willi Apel's *The Notation of Polyphonic Music: 900–1600*, still the standard text for teaching early musical notation.[2] Because Apel's book covered music 900–1600, the core of our course fell somewhere in the middle, around 1200–1350—the so-called "Notre Dame period" and the "Ars nova." For the most part, we worked in order transcribing the facsimiles in the Apel book.

Let us look at two examples. Figure 1 is a diplomatic facsimile drawn from the so-called Florence manuscript (Florence, Biblioteca Laurenziana, MS Pluteus 29.1), but in truth this is a source compiled in Paris, in the shadow of Notre Dame around 1250.[3] Figure 2 is the motet *Garrit gallus/In nova fert/[Neume]* by Philippe de Vitry from the famous *Roman de Fauvel* as preserved today in ParisBN fr. 146. Both sources, then, emanate from Paris and from a period in which that city was the epicenter of much of the creation, performance, and theoretical discussion of progressive art music in the West.

Our assignment was to convert these medieval documents into equivalents in modern musical notation. At no time did we ask: "Why should we want to do this?" "What might we accomplish?" "What damage might we do through this exercise?" We were students. This was Harvard. It was not our place to challenge the rules of the game; we were simply trying to ascertain what the rules were—how the game was played or the piece transcribed.

More specific questions might have been: "How does this manuscript relate to performance?" "Is this a prescriptive document intending to allow performers to recreate a work of art from these signs? Or is it a descriptive one—does it record for posterity just one of a myriad of performance possibilities?" "Is it

[2] Willi Apel, *The Notation of Polyphonic Music: 900–1600* (Cambridge, Mass.: Medieval Academy of America, 1942, with later revisions).

[3] Rebecca Baltzer, "Thirteenth-Century Illuminated Miniatures and the Date of the Florence Manuscript," *Journal of the American Musicological Society* 25 (1972), 1–18.

Figure 1. Florence, Biblioteca Laurenziana, MS Pluteus 29.1. Reproduced from Willi Apel, The Notation of Polyphonic Music, *Facsimile 46 (1953 edition, 229)*

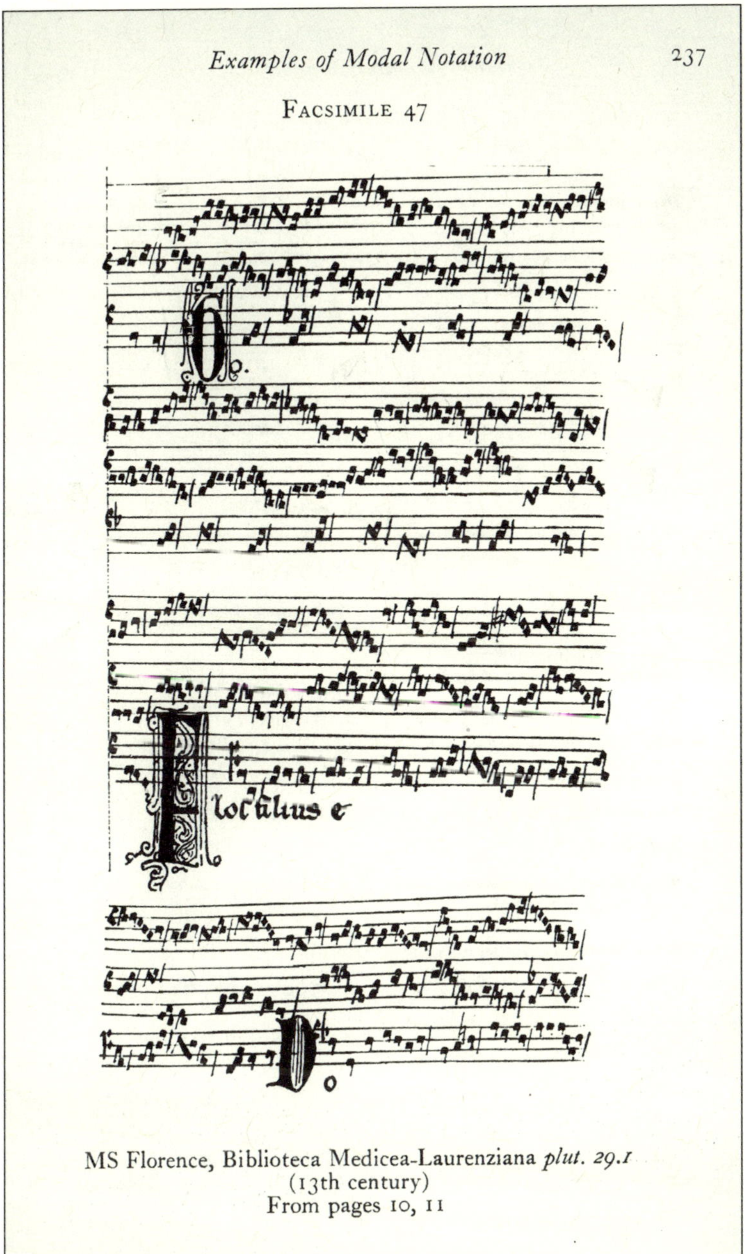

Figure 2. Garrit gallus/In nova fert/[Neume] *by Philippe de Vitry from the famous* Roman de Fauvel. *Preserved ParisBN fr. 146*

The Roman de Fauvel 331

FACSIMILE 67

Roman de Fauvel
Paris, Bibliothèque Nationale *fonds frç. 146* (*ca.* 1310)
Page 48

merely, then, an archival record?" Finally, "Is this document unique to Paris about 1300 or do all other musical cultures around the world have similar sorts of written records of music from that period? If they don't, what might this mean?" Thus we failed to ask—nor were we encouraged to ask—the most basic question: "What *is* this document that we see on the page?" It has taken me, and perhaps Tom, too, a very long time, not to answer this question, but to frame the parameters for a discussion about these issues.

What we see in those pages in the Apel book, or in any facsimile of a medieval polyphonic composition, is a language, a symbolic, binary language. The language is binary because it aims to control phenomena that interact on two axes, pitch (expressed vertically) and duration (expressed horizontally). This notation is very much a two-axis graph, the West's first graph.[4]

Musical notation is, like all written languages, a symbolic language. A language, the Oxford English Dictionary tells us, is a coherent system of "phraseology or terms of a science, art, profession, etc." Was music the first language on this earth, or was that first language a spoken, phonetic one? This is the issue debated most recently by what I call "the four 'Stevens'"—Mithen, Brown, and Harvard's own Gould and Pinker.[5] Spoken or phonetic languages do convey precise semantic meaning, and in some cultures the phonemes have been captured and converted into other symbols, specifically written characters. Obviously in the West we have systems of letter symbols, the main ones being Greek, Cyrillic, and Latin.

But why would any people want to take one symbolic language—speech—and convert it into yet another, written symbols? Why would anyone want to take the more emotive sonic language of music and commit it to a written form? What does this do for the process of communication? To answer these questions, let us think collectively about the symbolic languages used in the Western world and what they do for us. What languages do we have, besides spoken languages such as French, German, and Chinese? Among them are Egyptian hieroglyphics; Arabic and Roman numerals; these same numerals

[4] This point is succinctly made in Alfred Crosby, *The Measure of Reality: Quantification and Western Society, 1250–1600* (Cambridge: Cambridge University Press, 1997), 114. The present author's thinking on many points presented here was first stimulated by Crosby's remarkable book.

[5] Steven Mithen, *The Singing Neanderthals: The Origins of Music, Language, Mind and Body* (Cambridge, Mass.: Harvard University Press, 2006); Steven Brown, "The 'Musilanguage' Model of Human Evolution," in *The Origins of Music*, ed. Nils L. Wallin, Björn Merker, and Steven Brown (Cambridge, Mass.: Harvard University Press, 2000); Steven Pinker, *How the Mind Works* (New York: W. W. Norton, 1997); and Stephen Jay Gould, cited in "Human Evolution: Why Music?" *The Economist*, 18 December 2008, 41–44.

combined with symbols of spatial relationships (pi, "r," and "c," for example) forming the language of geometry; the symbolic, elemental language of chemistry; binary computer code; chess notation (which oddly is similar to musical notation because it involves a binary field (up or across) and also an element of agency or potency depending upon the piece or the note value involved); and Braille, a double symbolic language. Surely there are others.

All of these symbolic languages seem to have two things in common, in addition to the fact that they are found to be useful by a large portion of the population: 1) they are modular—the components (units) of the language can be repositioned to allow for new and different meaning; and 2) they are governed by syntax—in a given context the units must conform to certain rules of sequential order so that the symbols convey meaning (make sense).

As to the reasons why we want these symbolic languages and what they do for us, these can be enumerated as follows: 1) they reduce complex phenomena to simpler units that allow us to work faster and more efficiently with the subject matter at hand; 2) they allow us to stop an action that moves through time (a musical performance, a game of chess, solving a mathematical problem) in order to think, to analyze, and to compare—in brief, notation allows for cogitation; and 3) they permit us to preserve a thought and to hold it in a fixed form in perpetuity. To sum up: speed and efficiency, cogitation, comparison and analysis, and preservation—these are some of the benefits bestowed by symbolic languages, including musical notation. Perhaps that is why we humans invent them when trying to understand the phenomena of this world, including music.

Today musicians around the globe, when performing Western classical music, all use the same symbolic language, the type of notation seen on the page of any Bach fugue, Mozart or Beethoven sonata, or Chopin nocturne. This is the notation of Western classical music. But when and where was it created?

Our Western notation is a direct descendant of the notational system that developed rapidly in Paris between the years 1200–1350. For Western notation, all the fundamental principles were set in place then and there. Everything that has been added since—tempo and expression marks, for example—is simply a refinement already implicit to performers in the score. To repeat, the components of our notational system, a fixed symbolic language expressing pitch and duration, were in place in Paris by no later than 1350 and have remained fundamentally unchanged since that time.

To illustrate what I mean, let us back up and return to the year 1000, allowing a century on either side of that date. How many different symbolic languages intending to represent pitch then existed? At least a half dozen. And it was not initially clear that the method that ultimately won out in thirteenth-century Paris—and that we still use today—would, in fact, be the winner. Let us examine the leading contenders, looking at both performance manuscripts and theoretical sources.[6]

To begin with, systems for notating pitches can be divided into two types: phonetic (or aural) and spatial (or visual). Let's start with the phonetic, which expresses differences in pitch by means of words, or by syllables, or merely by letters. All of the following were "in play" at one time or another during the period 900–1100:

Greek descriptive terms expressing pitch relationships in acoustical space. For example, the lichanos hypaton moving to the hypate meson called for a harmonic ratio of 9:8; from the lichanos hypaton to the lichanos meson the ratio of 4:3.[7]

Greek musical notation (another phonetic language of symbols derived from letters of the Greek alphabet and diacritical marks). It existed in two forms: vocal and instrumental.[8]

Greek and Latin numerical notation, where arithmetic ratios of string lengths were used to set vocal pitch. This in itself is not a phonetic system, but it was combined with phonetic indicators. Thus we Westerners might have had a notational system in which numbers were sung to represent a change of pitch (8216 to 4108 would prescribe an octave leap, for example)—precise in regard to frequencies but not very practical in terms of performance.[9]

The ninth, tenth, and eleventh centuries witnessed a gradual move away from a Greek linguistic basis for expressing pitch relationships toward a Latin-language-based template.[10]

The two languages might be combined as in the didactic poem *Ter tria iunctorum* of Hermannus Contractus. Instead of proslambanomenos proceeding to hypate hypaton, a singer might move by tonus, semitonus, ditonus, and semi-ditonus following a succession of Latin and Greek letters (Figure 3).

[6] In this examination I have greatly benefited from the superb survey of music theory manuscripts of this period presented in Charles Atkinson, *The Critical Nexus: Tone System, Mode, and Notation in Early Medieval Music* (New York: Oxford University Press, 2009).

[7] Anicius Manlius Severinus Boethius, *Fundamentals of Music*, trans. Calvin M. Bower (New Haven: Yale University Press, 1989), 152.

[8] Ibid., 155.

[9] See Atkinson, *Critical Nexus*, 83.

[10] Ibid., 74–75, 160–70, and 214.

Figure 3. Vienna, Österreichische Nationalbibliothek, MS Cpv 2502, f. 27v

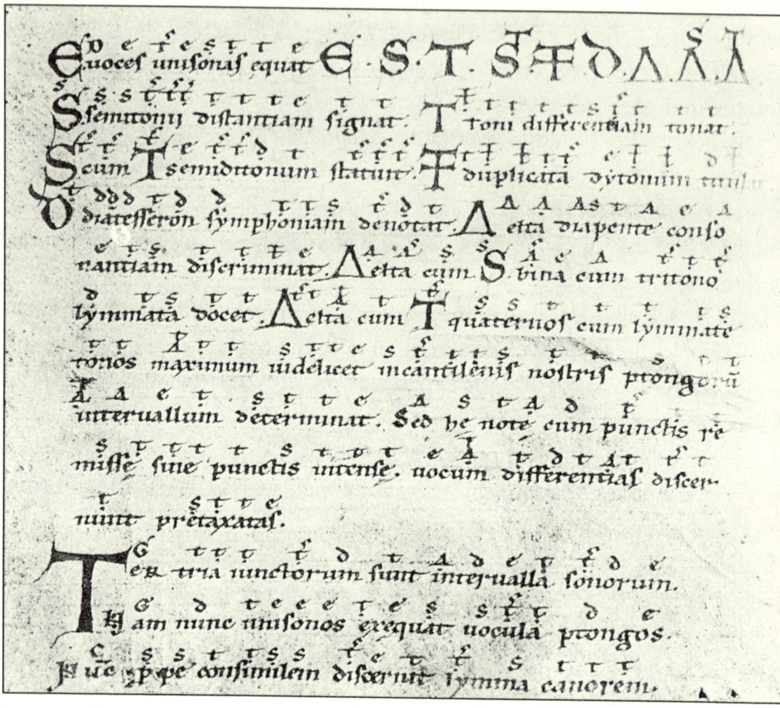

Latin alphabetical names replace Greek letter names with some letters skipped and others doubled.[11]

The Latin alphabet (without omitted letters) could be combined with visual symbols (neumes).[12]

Why then, do we not today sing the notes "p" and "o" or sing the interval "l" to "r," for example? We don't because around 1000 an Italian theorist, identified by Michel Huglo as Pseudo-Odo of Cluny, hit upon a revolutionary idea.[13] Recognizing that the sequence of pitches within one octave constituted a pitch class set that repeated when the scale continued an octave higher, he posited a

[11] Ibid., 75.

[12] As in Montpellier, Bibliothèque de l'École de médecine, H. 159, f. 31r; see Willi Apel, *Gregorian Chant* (Bloomington: Indiana University Press, 1966), pl. VI.

[13] Michel Huglo, "Der Prolog des Odo zugeschriebenen 'Dialogus de Musica,'" *Archiv für Musikwissenschaft* 28 (1971), 134–36. English translation of Pseudo-Odo's writings in *Source Readings in Music History*, ed. Oliver Strunk, revised edition ed. Leo Treitler (New York: W. W. Norton, 1998), 198–210, esp. 203.

Latin alphabet with octave duplication. This seems simple enough to us with a thousand years of hindsight, but music theorists had been grappling with the issue of pitch nomenclature for at least 1400 years before anyone suggested this approach (Figure 4).

Figure 4. Vienna, Österreichische Nationalbibliothek, MS Cpv 55, f. 167v

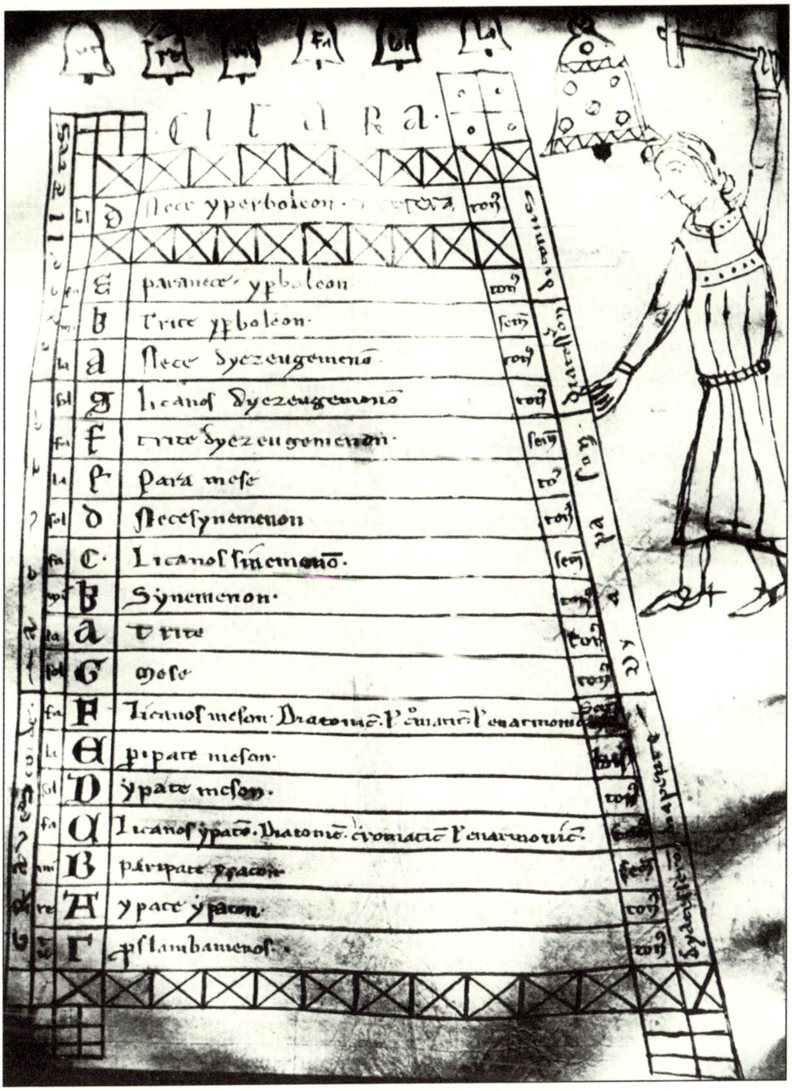

Shortly thereafter, around 1025, Guido of Arezzo proposed another, rather different, phonetic system. He posited what we now call a solfege method by using syllables instead of letters—syllables incorporating vowels drawn from the text of a hymn, *Ut queant laxis,* for St. John the Baptist. But here, as is well-known, instead of an eight-note unit with octave duplication, Guido prescribed a six-note pitch class set TTSTT,[14] which isolated the semitone in the middle and caused less confusion among singers (Figure 5).

By 1025, then, two phonetic systems of aural pitch identification were in play: 1) a fixed and repeating eight-note pitch class using the Latin alphabet running A through G; and 2) a slightly newer moveable six-note system (ut-re-mi-fa-sol-la). And these two systems coexisted for more than five hundred years thereafter.[15]

But "phonetic representation" was just one method for precisely specifying musical pitch. During the years 900–1100 a second, equally important approach emerged: "graphic representation." Scribes placed various kinds of signifiers on a grid of horizontal lines and singers recognized the difference in pitches by the eye, not the ear. The simplest approach was to put the text of a chant across a grid of horizontal lines moving left to right, as Hucbald did in his *De harmonica institutione.*[16] Another method placed a signifier called the dasia (the Greek aspirant) on the grid and turned it forward, backward, upside down, and upside down and backward to show pitch relationships.[17] And a third approach, the one that ultimately won out, was to put neumes on the grid. According to the region of Western Europe in which a manuscript was compiled, these neumes might be shaped in a style now called Paleofrankish, Messine, Mozarabic, Breton, Anglo-Norman, Aquitanian, or Beneventan,

[14] T=tone; S=semitone.

[15] On the coexistence of the two systems, see Stefano Mengozzi, "Virtual Segments: The Hexachordal System in the Late Middle Ages," *Journal of Musicology* 23 (2006), 426–67, and idem, *The Renaissance Reform of Medieval Music Theory: Guido of Arezzo Between Myth and History* (Cambridge: Cambridge University Press, 2010), esp. chapters 2 and 4. Isaac Newton still made use of the Guidonian hexachord in his *Opticks* (London, 1704); see the diagram in Penelope Gouk, "The Harmonic Roots of Newtonian Science," in *Let Newton Be,* ed. John Fauvel et al. (Oxford: Oxford University Press, 1988), 118. A vestige of Guido's system can still be seen in Mozart's symphonic scores when he indicates a horn should sound in "A la-mi-re."

[16] See Atkinson, *Critical Nexus,* 152.

[17] The various positions of the dasia and the scale that results are discussed both in Apel, *Notation,* 204–6 and Atkinson, *Critical Nexus,* 120–32.

Figure 5. Monte Cassino, Archivio dell'Abbazia, MS 318, 291

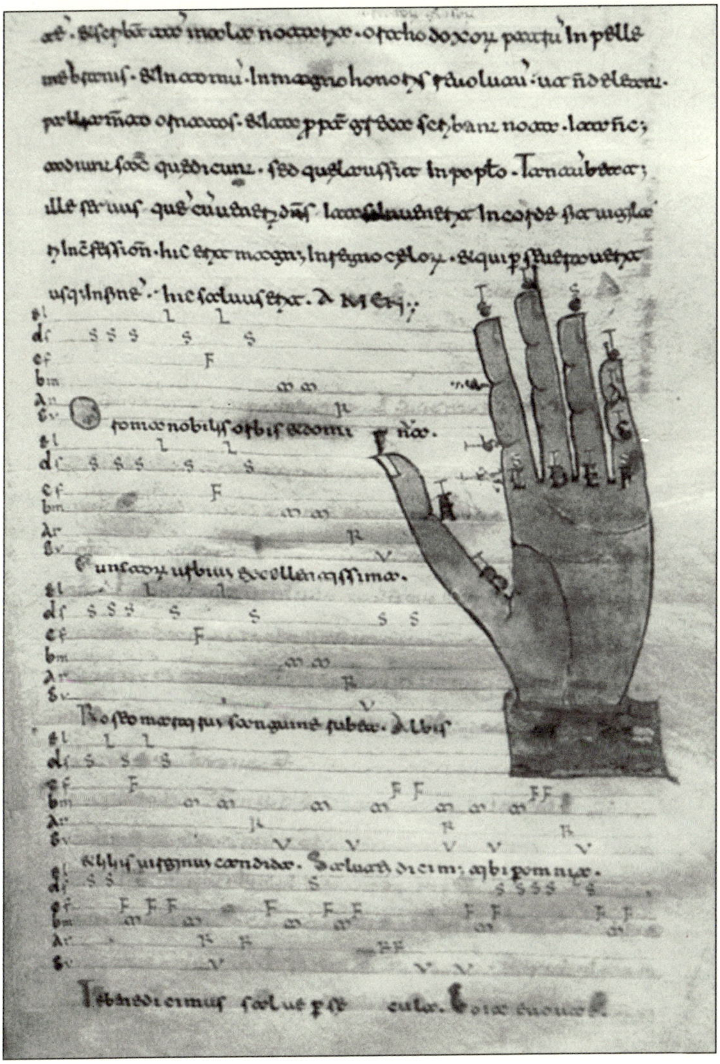

among others.[18] At first the neumes were non-diastematic (did not show pitch relationships). They simply provided mnemonic aids for singers who already knew the chant. But by around 1000 the neumes had come to be heightened—they could show an approximate, relative difference in pitch—a particularly clear instance being those manuscripts from Benevento made known to us by Tom Kelly (Figure 6).[19]

Soon it was recognized that even greater specificity could be attained if the heightened neumes were placed on the horizontal grid—in other words, two visual instruments (grid and neumes) could be combined, and, moreover, the bars of the grid could be color-coded for easy recognition of pitch (Figure 7). But this grid, or template, needed to be activated. Lines and spaces by themselves suggest an equal distance from one line or space to the next. But in music, this is not always true, owing to the half steps of the scale. So to activate or give specific meaning to the grid, the preferred *phonetic* signifiers of the scale, the alphabetical letters of Pseudo-Odo, were superimposed on the grid. One might activate all the lines directly, or indirectly by inference—put a letter name on several lines (Figure 8), or just one, as we do with the letters F (bass clef) or G (treble clef) today. The placement of a single letter provided a key (*claves*, *clé*, or clef) to show how the grid was to be interpreted. Finally, once the template had been activated, visual spatial symbols—neumes or, in more recent Latin parlance, *notae*—could be set upon it.

Thus by the time of Guido around 1025, the axis of pitch was now securely in place, held there by two visual systems (neumes and a grid) and activated by a phonetic system. One could both see the differences in pitch and hear them as pitch letter names. Had not the graphic system been introduced, we likely would have had an exclusively phonetic kind of notation, as sometimes existed in the eleventh and twelfth centuries (the letter C above E, for example, on a page without any grid). In fact, a vestige of this system did survive well into the eighteenth century in the purely phonetic system of keyboard tablature, one which Bach himself sometimes used for the lower lines in organ music. But a visual-spatial system proved more efficient and ultimately it won out as the accepted means by which to notate pitch in the West.

[18] Representative samplings of such neumes are discussed in David Hiley and Janka Szendrei, "Notation III, 1: History of Western Notation: Plainchant," *Grove Music Online;* as well as David Hiley, *Western Plainchant: A Handbook* (Oxford: Oxford University Press, 1993), plates 1–12.

[19] Thomas Forrest Kelly, *The Beneventan Chant* (Cambridge: Cambridge University Press, 1989), plates 5–30.

Figure 6. Benevento, Biblioteca capitolare, MS 40, f. 71r
Reproduced from Thomas F. Kelly, Beneventan Chant, *pl. 12*

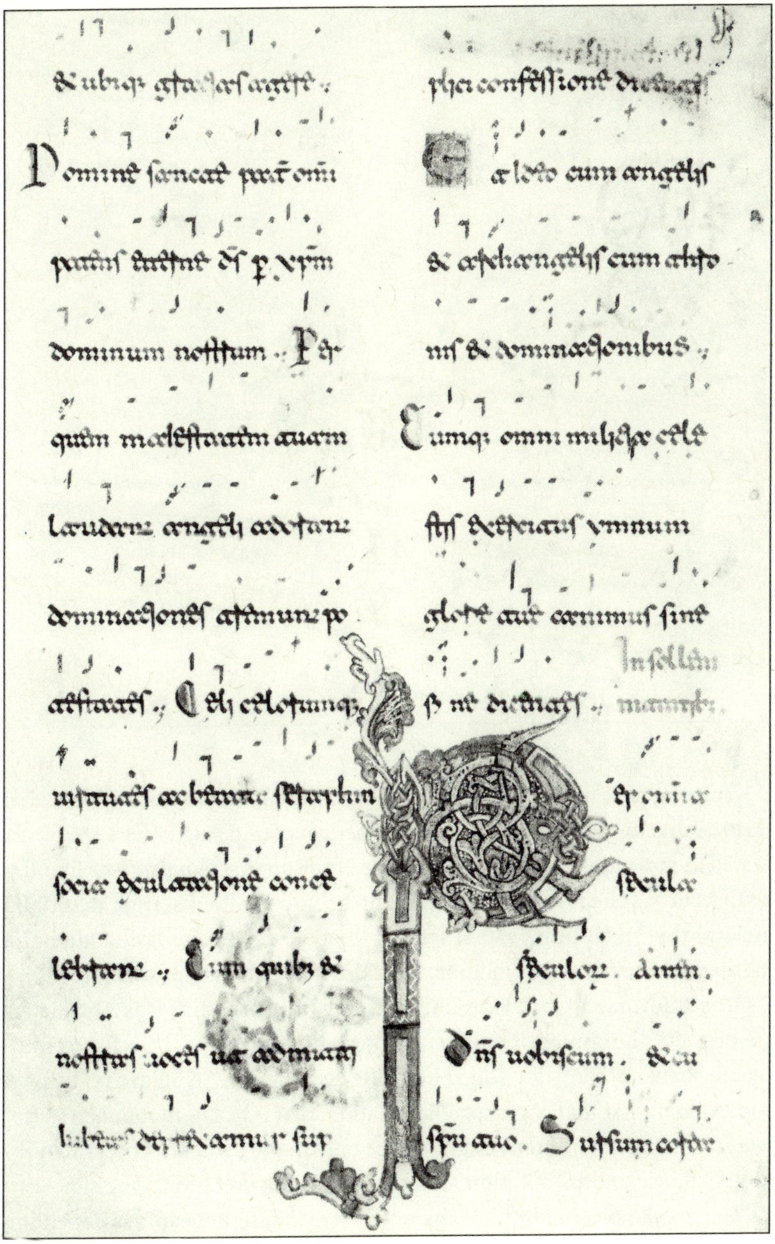

Figure 7. ParisBN lat. 10508, ff. 6rv

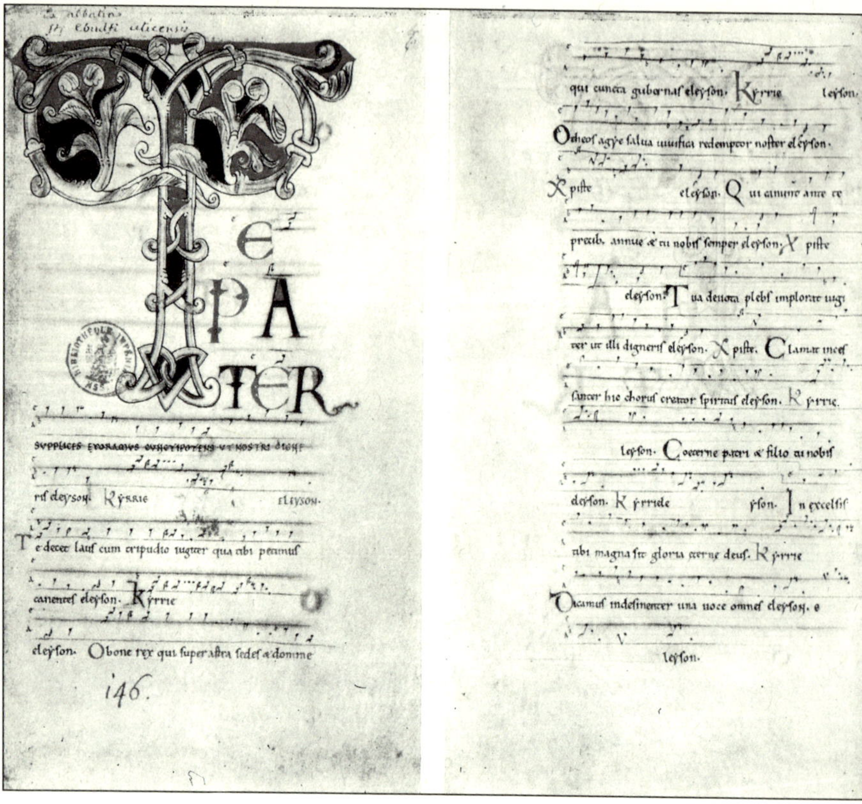

Turning now to the other axis of music: rhythm. If we discard the Greek chronos, the discussion of quantitative poetic meter in Augustine's *De musica*, as well as indications of duration in some of the *litterae significativae* found in tenth-century chant manuscripts, the first self-contained system describing musical rhythm appears rather late, in the theoretical discussion attending the appearance of modal notation, which surfaced in Paris just before 1200.

The information-carrying unit with regard to rhythm was not the single note but the composite neume, expressed in ligatures of twelfth-century square chant notation developed in the Île de France (as in Figure 1). This was contextual rather than sign-specific notation; that is to say, in modal notation neumes assumed durational significance only in the context of other neumes. At first glance, modal notation seems to be lacking precision. One sign, a ternaria, for example, might have any one of five different meanings depending

Figure 8. ParisBN lat. 778, f. 15r

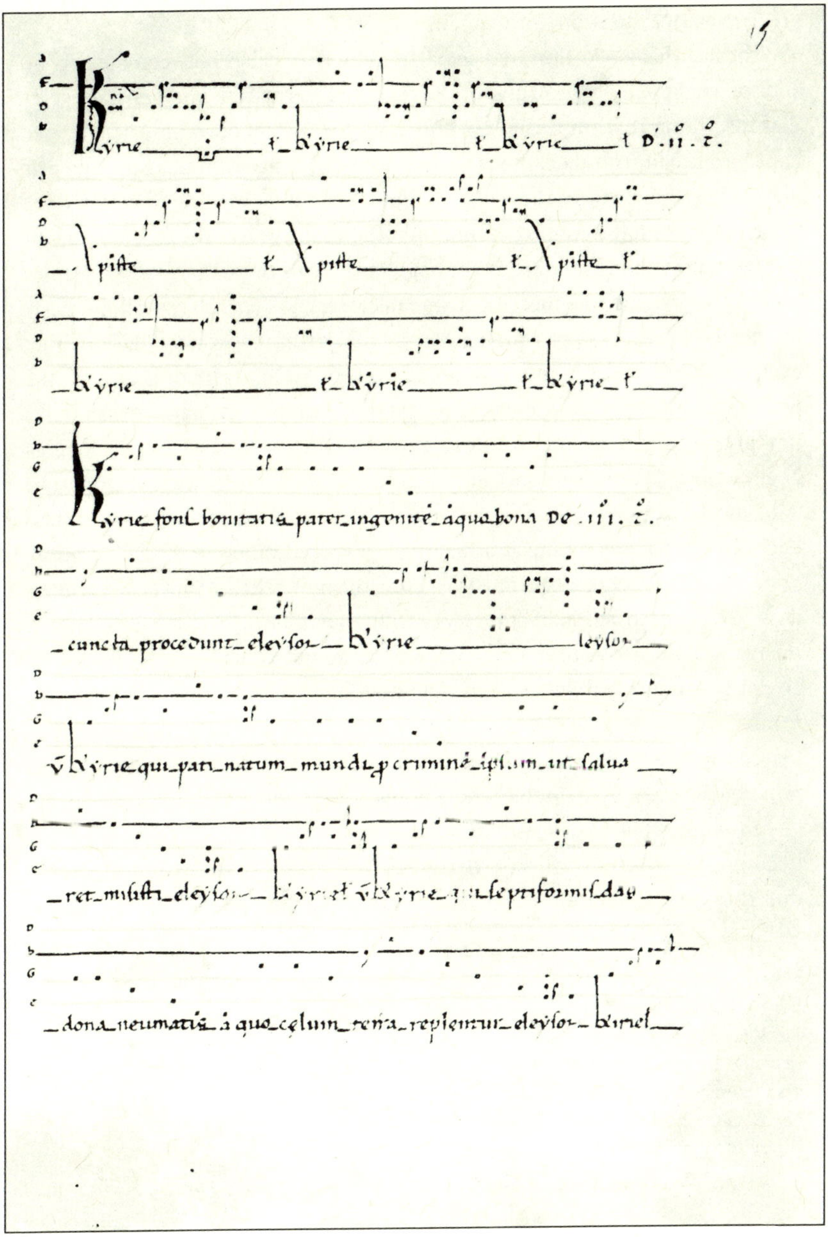

on the context, whereas today a quarter note, for example, has only one relative value. But in modal notation the context, not the symbol itself, indicated the precise relative duration of the pitch.

The fact that a two-hundred year gap (950–1150) exists between the appearance of fixed pitch notation and the advent of fixed rhythmic notation suggests that inscribing rhythm was a less pressing issue for medieval musicians, perhaps because liturgical chant seems to have been sung without a strongly profiled meter and rhythm. Indeed, a system for notating musical duration does not emerge from the context of monophonic chant, as was the case with pitch, but from polyphonic additions to that chant. With two, three, or sometimes four voices singing together, it became necessary to synchronize all the parts by means of precise, prescriptive notation for rhythm.[20] Modal notation, however, could only exist in music that had no text, for an overriding reason: the process of notating vocal music required that each new syllable be assigned a new graphic symbol, either a note or a neume (then as now, each syllable must begin with a separate symbol), and thus texted vocal music was incompatible with modal notation. Texting destroyed the pattern of ligatures, which had been the key to prescribing and reading durational values in modal notation.

The appearance of a new musical genre, the motet, in the thirteenth century hastened the destruction of modal (contextual) notation. In a fully texted motet, the neumes *de jure* were ripped apart and set to individual syllables as notes.[21] To convey durational value, each note now had to be given its own specific meaning, its own shape. By 1300 notational symbols as we now know them had begun to appear (Figure 9). They called them *longae*, *breves*, *semibreves*, and *minimae*; we call them double whole notes, whole notes, half notes, etc.

In sum, what had been contextual neumes on an activated grid had become sign specific notes on that grid. The West's first attempt to specify duration, modal notation, had failed. Within a century a new system replaced

[20] This is the simplest rationale for the emergence of regulated duration. Anna Maria Busse-Berger, however, has recently posited a more intriguing theory in her *Medieval Music and the Art of Memory* (Berkeley: University of California Press, 2005), 188–97. Notated rhythms may also have facilitated memory. Catchy rhythms may have been prescribed to help singers remember long passages of polyphonic music that happened to have no text, just as we can remember a poem more easily by strongly emphasizing the durational stresses of the meter as we say it.

[21] See Apel, *Notation*, Facsimiles 54–58.

Figure 9. Bamberg, Staatsbibliothek, Msc. Lit. 115, f. 11r

it, mensural notation, which we still use today. Thus by 1350 our system for controlling and recording both axes of music was in place, having developed in the context of cutting-edge, high-art church music in high-Gothic Paris.

SCHOLASTICISM AND MUSIC

The musicians of Gothic Paris had found a new toy—rhythm, or at least a way to prescribe rhythmic duration by means of written symbols—and they began to play with it obsessively. Around 1200, judging from the notated works of Leoninus and Perotinus, music was happily thumping along in longs and breves and only in triple meter.[22] By 1350 the note values had grown to include duplex and triplex longs, semibreves, minims and semiminims, and duple meter was placed on a parity with triple. What had been a maximum difference in note values of 1:3 (one long equaled three breves) was now at the most extreme 1:162 (triplex long to semiminim). Rhythmic duration had exploded owing to a contemporary development: quantification.[23] The move to precise measurement, in turn, was being driven by a new kind of philosophy that emerged in Paris at this time, scholastic philosophy, which took the rediscovery of Aristotle as its point of departure.[24]

[22] See *Le Magnus Liber Organi de Notre-Dame de Paris,* ed. Edward H. Roesner, 7 vols. (Monaco: L'Oiseau lyre, 1993–2009).

[23] Alain Boureau, "Jérôme de Moravie et la rationalization dominicaine du XIIIe siècle," in *Jérôme de Moravie: un théoricien de la musique dans le milieu intellectual parisien du XIIIe siècle,* Actes du Colloque de Royaumont–1989, ed. Christian Meyer (Paris : Créaphis, 1992), 43–55, esp. 50–52; David Landes, *Revolution in Time: Clocks and the Making of the Modern World* (Cambridge, Mass.: Harvard University Press, 1983); and especially, Crosby, *Measure of Reality.*

[24] Studies that treat the relationship between philosophy, teaching at the fledgling University of Paris, and the content of music theory treatises in this period include Lawrence Gushee, "Questions of Genre in Medieval Treatises on Music," in *Gattungen der Musik in Einzeldarstellungen: Gedenkschrift Leo Schrade,* ed. Wulf Arlt et al. (Bern: Francke, 1973), 365–433; Max Hass, "Studien zur mittelalterlichen Musiklehre I: Eine Übersicht über die Musiklehre im Kontext der Philosophie des 13. und frühen 14. Jahrhunderts," in *Aktuelle Fragen der musikbezogenen Mittelalterforschung* [*Forum Musicologicum,* III], ed. Hans Oesch and Wulf Arlt, (Winterthur: Amadeus, 1982), 323–456; Jeremy Yudkin, "The Influence of Aristotle on French University Music Texts," in *Music Theory and its Sources: Antiquity and the Middle Ages,* ed. André Barbera (Notre Dame: University of Notre Dame Press, 1990), 173–89; Dorit Tanay, *Noting Music, Marking Culture: The Intellectual Context of Rhythmic Notation, 1250–1400* (Holzgerlingen: Hänssler Verlag; American Institute of Musicology, 1999), esp. 19–29; Pascale Duhamel, "L'Enseignment de la musique à l'Université de Paris d'après le manuscript Bnf lat. 7378A," *Acta musicologica* 79 (2007), 263–89; John Haines, "*Proprietas* and *Perfectio* in Thirteenth-Century Music Theory," *Theoria* 15 (2008), 5–29; Joseph Dyer, "Speculative 'Musica' and the Medieval University of Paris," *Music and Letters* 90 (2009), 177–204; and Laura Weber, "Intellectual Currents in Thirteenth-Century Paris:

In his *Prior Analytics*, Aristotle developed the concept of the syllogism and the notion of a chain of relationships working from the small particular to the ultimate, largest truth.[25] Going one way, toward the large principle, we today call inductive reasoning; working in the other direction, we call deductive. We go from the general to the specific to the particular, but the units are all modular and interrelated. In thirteenth-century Paris, Aristotle's distant disciple, Thomas Aquinas, organized all matters of theological debate into *partes, distinctiones,* and then *articuli* within his great *Summa theologiae.*[26] This penchant for categorization by means of descending subsets, all reciprocal, characterized scholastic thought then and still colors our thinking today; when we tell our students to make an outline, we enjoin them to engage in a scholastic exercise. Thus our chain of reciprocal, interrelating note values ranging large to small (long to minimal) that we meet when transcribing every piece of early polyphonic music involves a scholastic exercise—we embrace a scholastic model used for the organization of musical time. Of course this new reductive method of marking time was not limited to music but was applied to chronological measurement generally. Large municipal clocks appeared in the naves of churches in Strasbourg and Reims, and on the façade of the king's *Palais royal* in Paris at this same time, between 1275–1375.[27] The new clock had wheels and gears of various sizes, but all interconnected and interrelated to show a continuum of time.

Scholastic modes of thought also began to govern thinking about musical harmony at this time. Suppose that in our notation class Tom's transcription or, more likely, mine, went awry. How would we know it was wrong? We would look at the harmonic intervals at the beginnings of units (what we now call downbeats, but in medieval eyes might have conceptually been points where gears meshed). We transcribers had a hierarchy of "good news" and "bad news" when looking at vertical intervals. Good news came in the form of unisons, octaves, fifths and fourths; ambiguous news rested in the thirds and sixths; and bad news sounded, of course, in tritones, seconds, and sevenths. These "rules for correct harmony" also involved a scholastic paradigm of interlocking relationships. They were set forth at this time by Parisian university figures such

A Translation and Commentary on Jerome of Moravia's *Tractatus de musica*" (PhD dissertation, Yale University, 2010).

[25] See particularly Aristotle, *Prior Analytics* II.23 as discussed in Paolo C. Biondi, Aristotle *Posterior Analytics* II.19 (Quebec: Les Presses de l'Université Laval, 2004), 195ff.

[26] English trans. by Fathers of the English Dominican Province, 3 vols. (New York, 1947–48).

[27] On the importance of the appearance of clocks in this period, see Crosby, *Measure of Reality*, 82–86.

as John of Garlandia, Franco of Cologne, and Jerome of Moravia. Franco, for example, leads us along a continuum moving from perfect consonance, intermediate consonance, imperfect consonance, imperfect dissonance, and finally perfect dissonance—each category having its constituent intervals.[28]

The new scholastic mode of thinking, one involving quantification and hierarchical relationships, was sharpened by logical reasoning. To measure and correctly position something along a continuum it was necessary to know what that something was, and this was done in part by Aristotelian dialectics, which sought to determine the essence of things through oxymoronic juxtaposition—opposites. Aristotle had initiated this mode of thought in his *Metaphysics.*[29] Peter Abelard, a famous, indeed infamous, inhabitant of the cloister at Notre Dame of Paris, made this distinctively clear in his *Sic et non.*[30] Aquinas borrowed the method for his *Summa* with his "articles" followed by his "objections" and "to the contrary."

Music theorists, too, adopted this play of opposites, and applied it to both modal notation and later mensural notation; specifically, they used it to describe the basic ligatures (square-note descendents of neumes) in music.[31] The simplest ligature had two notes, the first governed by the condition of propriety and the second by that of perfection; these two notes had two possible durations (a binary code), which could be expressed in terms of positive (*cum*) or negative (*sine*) value. A particular position, or the presence or absence of a particular graphic sign (symbol), would reverse the value of the note, from long to breve or vice versa. The durational values of the archetype (a two-note ligature) consisted of a breve followed by a long. The shortest values (two semibreves) were said to be *cum opposita proprietate*—with opposite propriety.

[28] See Franco's *Ars cantus mensurabilis,* ed. Gilbert Reaney and André Gilles, Corpus Scriptorum de Music, 18 ([Rome]: American Institute of Musicology, 1974); English trans. in Strunk, *Source Readings,* 239.

[29] See, for example, *Metaphysics,* D2, 1004b26–30.

[30] *Sic et non: A Critical Edition,* ed. Blanche Boyer and Richard McKeon (Chicago: University of Chicago Press, 1977).

[31] On this point see Haines, "*Proprietas* and *Perfectio,*" 5–29.

Table 1

cum proprietate et cum perfectione	 B L	 B L
sine proprietate et cum perfectione	 L L	 L L
cum proprietate et sine perfectione	 B B	 B B
sine proprietate et sine perfectione	 L B	 L B
cum opposita et proprietate	 S S	 S S

Using a contraposition of opposites so as to identify the essence of things also extended to musical texts in this period. Consider the mid-thirteenth-century Parisian motet *Ypocrite pseudopontifice/Velut stelle firmamenti/Et gaudebit* (Florence, Biblioteca Laurenziana, MS Pluteus 29.1, ff. 412v–413r; Appendix A). The motetus voice extols the virtues of the clergy, while the triplum excoriates them as vile hypocrites, indeed blood-suckers.[32] This dialectic reflects the pedagogical approach then used at the University of Paris, especially in classes of the Dominicans on the Rue St. Jacques, whose sessions traditionally consisted of a *lectio* (reading and studying the authoritative text) followed by a *disputatio* (a debate).[33] And this dialectical pedagogy continued at the University of Paris at least into the sixteenth century. Humanist music theorist Heinrich Glarean encountered it when he went to Paris in 1516 (he, too,

[32] This sort of musical "play of opposites" continued for centuries, as seen in the Jeu-parti of Philippe de Vitry, the motet *Juvenis qui puellam* of Guillaume Dufay, and the combinative chansons of the late fifteenth century.

[33] Marie-Dominique Chenu, *Toward Understanding Saint Thomas*, trans. Albert M. Landry and Dominic Hughes (Chicago: H. Regnery, 1964), 90; Dyer, "Speculative 'Musica,'" 195–99; *Les Méthodes de travail de Gersonide et le maniement du savoir chez les scolastiques*, ed. Colette Sirat, Sara Klein-Braslavy, and Olga Weijers (Paris: Librairie philosophique J. Vrin, 2003), 61–75 and 239–49, as well as Olga Weijers, *La 'Disputatio' à la Faculté des arts de Paris* (Turnhout: Brepols, 2002), 25–40.

living on the Rue St. Jacques), as he reported back to his mentor Erasmus: "I was lately at a disputation in the Sorbonne, where I heard loud applause as if it had been Pompey's Theatre. I could scarcely restrain my laughter, and yet there was no one laughing there . . . and the supercilious disputants could scarcely restrain their invective . . . I came away myself, after I had heard nonsense enough."[34] Even today a vestige of "Parisian pedagogy by debate" survives in the exercise called "moot court" in law schools around the world.

The type of text that we see in the motet *Ypocrite pseudopontifice* is not the sort of Parisian theological exegesis that we usually encounter in music, where the text of each new voice heaps bit of sacred evidence upon bit of evidence to the point that the opposition crumbles from the weight, but not necessarily the logic, of the argument. What we have in our motet is something very different—sharpening understanding through verbal dialectic—and dialectical disputation comes to the fore precisely during this period. Thus as to the question regarding what it was that Tom and I were transcribing in our notation class, usually it was a symbolic artifact projecting traditional theological exegesis played out in sound. At other times, however, it was the musical counterpart of Aristotelian dialectic. We were transcribing the quantifiable musical equivalent of an exercise in logic as taught in a class at the University of Paris around 1300.

Precise quantitative reasoning permeated most forms of intellectual pursuit at the University of Paris in these years, and it had a transformative effect on music in particular. Quantification changed how musicians (at least "high art" musicians) approached their craft. It marked a change from the oral to the written, and from the heard to the seen. Of course this change was not immediate and total—the oral and written coexisted for centuries in music and still do so to a degree today. But a new course had been set, one that led Western music in a direction very different from that of all other musical cultures around the world. Starting from this point on, Western music became the exception, became unique, the odd culture out, and it was the creation and reliance upon a symbolic, quantitative language—musical notation—that made it so. Although this transformation was long and complex, the main themes may be sketched as follows.

First, a new type of musician now stepped forward, the composer, who produced a written document that the performer executed, in something approaching an "architect-carpenter" relationship with the written score serving as the blueprint. The advent of the composer heralded the decline of the performer-improviser; creation through performance was no longer the only

[34] *The Epistles of Erasmus*, ed. and trans., Francis Morgan Nichols, 3 vols. (New York: Russell & Russell, 1962), II, 602–3, Epistle 592.

mode of creative expression. Similarly, the importance of memory and mnemonic skill decreased as reliance on a visual, written record increased.

From the point of view of the new composer, the written score offered several advantages. The composer could plan (the parameters of music could be manipulated a priori); could think things through in advance; could go back, revise, enjoy an overview without having heard a note, except in his head. In sum, the composer could generate something close to a rational, holistic entity—create something like a composition as we think of it today, a musical work of art. This work of art could be preserved for later re-creation. It could be performed at another time and another place by carpenters who had never met the architect.

Musical notation gave the composer powers of control at all levels. At the macro level, total control was possible, as we see develop in the pan-isorhythmic motet of the late fourteenth century in which the rhythmic values of all notes in all voices is determined in advance (the ultimate in a priori planning, exceeded perhaps only by Anton Webern's serial compositions of the 1920s).[35] Conversely, at the micro level a written prescriptive document allowed for pitch and rhythm to operate tightly and in close harmony. The duration of dissonance (and consonance) could be controlled for expressive purposes. Rules could be established for how these should interact. The discussions found in such landmark counterpoint treatises as Tinctoris's *Liber de arte contrapuncti* as to how suspensions and passing tones and other non-harmonic tones should be prepared, sounded, and departed would not have been possible without the small-level controls allowed by the minutiae of our newly emergent notation. The discipline of music theory, as we presently know it, begins to emerge because these most minute actions are inscribed in the score. They can be studied and the proper syntax (rules) for music extrapolated. Moreover, because it was fixed and visible, one motet or Mass could be studied and set next to another for comparison. Needless to say, present-day musicology and particularly the discipline of music theory would be very different if the artifact under scrutiny existed only in aurally perceived, real-time performance, whether live or recorded, and not in a fixed written score. Musicologists, in effect, would be ethnomusicologists studying an extrinsic, unwritten musical culture.

Finally, owing to the new, rigidly quantified system of notation, musical freedom and spontaneity declined. Pitch notation instructed performers to

[35] See, for example, John Dunstaple's four-voice pan-isorhythmic motet *Veni sancte/Veni creator spiritus* in *Complete Works,* 2nd rev. ed., ed. Manfred Bukofzer et al., Musica Britannica, vol. 8 (London: Stainer and Bell, 1970), 88–91.

move from one discrete frequency on the activated grid to another. In all other musical cultures, however, the most expressive features of the music are found *between* fixed points. And rhythmic rigidity became a hallmark of Western music, for only in the West do we have measure lines or, as we sometimes call them, "bars"—bars that prevent spontaneous expression from breaking out. In this regard it is amusing to note what French jazz pianist Stéphane Mougin said immediately after World War I, when Parisians were trying to comprehend jazz, just then all the rage. "The French have no sense of rhythm. It's probably a consequence of too great a civilization."[36] Perhaps this "too great a civilization"—at least musically—started here, in Paris about 1200 with the advent of rigid and constricting quantification. But quantification changed the very nature of Western music.

This at least is my retrospective interpretation of what Tom Kelly and I were doing in that Harvard course, the Notation of Polyphonic Music, nearly fifty years ago. But needless to say, Tom is entitled to his own views, and indeed he has voiced them in a book tentatively titled *Sounds in Space: The Medieval Technology of Recording Music*,[37] which offers an overview of the development of Western musical notation, particularly from the performer's perspective. By my count, this is Tom's sixth book, to which we should add five others that he has edited. Remarkable productivity! Indeed, Tom has done it all. He has published widely on the subject of medieval music, been a guiding force behind the project Early Music America, lectured extensively for the general public on subjects ranging from Beethoven to Stravinsky, founded a wildly popular Harvard undergraduate course (First Nights), served as chair of the Harvard Department of Music for six years, been a highly valued mentor to many dissertation advisees, and, in his role as music tutor, guided class after class of Harvard music concentrators. Tom Kelly has done it all, and he has done it with a unique vision, unflagging energy, and most important for me, a delightfully sardonic sense of humor. May our harmony and counterpoint continue for years to come!

[36] William H. Kenney III, "Le Hot: The Assimilation of American Jazz in France, 1917–1940," *American Studies* 29 (1988), 13.

[37] To be published by W. W. Norton.

First Nights in Baroque Rome

Stefano Landi's Sant' Alessio

IAIN FENLON

'. . . an imperial city stood,
With towers and temples proudly elevate
On seven small hills, with palaces adorned,
Porches and theatres, baths, aqeducts,
Statues and trophies, and triumphal arcs,
Gardens and groves . . .' (Milton)

PROLOGUE

IN THE SUMMER of 1638, the English poet John Milton arrived in Italy. One of the high points of this, his first experience of the country, was a visit to "the famous Galileo, grown old, a prisner to the Inquisition, for thinking in Astronomy otherwise than the Franciscan and Dominican licencers thought," as he put it in *Areopagitica*.[1] Galileo's treatment at the hands of the Roman Inquisition had inevitably colored Milton's impression of the city, and particularly of the Barberini pope, Urban VIII, as it had for many European intellectuals.[2] The poet's hostile attitude toward Catholicism in general and the Barberini in particular was subsequently strengthened by his two journeys to Rome,

[1] See, most recently, Gordon Campbell and Thomas N. Corns, *John Milton: Life, Works, and Thought* (Oxford: Oxford University Press, 2008), 112.

[2] For Urban's relationship with Galileo, see Sante Pieralisi, *Urban VIII e Galileo Galilei* (Rome, 1875); initially the Pope had supported Galileo, see 14–68.

undertaken shortly afterward, so much so that years later the Dutch philologist, diplomat and writer Nicolaus Heinsius recalled that "The Englishman was hated by the Italians, among whom he lived a long time, on account of his over-strict morals, because he both disputed freely about religion, and on any occasion whatever prated very bitterly against the Roman Pontiff."[3] This engaging insight into Milton's behavior also neatly captures the spirit of the times. Seventeenth-century Rome was both the focus of belief, as well as the principal theater, both symbolic and real, of the doctrinal polemics that divided Catholics and Protestants. If for militant Catholics the Eternal City was the ultimate sacred site, defined and enhanced by its dense accumulation of relics, for the Protestant reformers it was to be roundly denounced as the "Whore of Babylon," the home of idolatry and corruption. Nevertheless, Milton's dislike of Catholic institutions and all that they represented did not prevent him from moving in elevated Catholic circles in the city during his stay; this socializing included dining at the English Jesuit College, and even accepting Barberini hospitality.[4] On one occasion Lukas Holste, a distinguished humanist scholar from Hamburg, secretary to Cardinal Francesco Barberini and librarian of the Vatican collections, invited Milton to attend a performance of the opera *Chi soffre speri*, composed by Virgilio Mazzocchi, who had been *maestro di cappella* to Cardinal Francesco Barberini, with *intermedi* by Marco Marazzoli.[5] This work, which had been commissioned to inaugurate the new Barberini theater, was given before an audience of some four thousand people.[6] Milton, who has nothing to say about the artistic and theatrical aspects of the performance itself, was above all impressed with his reception by Cardinal Francesco, who greeted him warmly. As the poet recalled, the Cardinal himself, "waiting at the door, singled me out in so great a throng and, almost seizing me by the hand, welcomed me in an exceedingly honourable manner."[7] Disapproval of

[3] Barbara Lewalski, *The Life of John Milton: A Critical Biography* (Oxford: Blackwell, 2000), 99.

[4] Campbell and Corns, *John Milton*, 116–18.

[5] Stuart Reiner, "Collaboration in 'Chi soffre speri,'" *Music Review* 22 (1963), 265–82; Margaret Murata, *Operas for the Papal Court in Rome 1631–1668* (Ann Arbor: UMI Research Press, 1981), 32–34 and 258–88. See also Campbell and Corns, *John Milton*, 122–23.

[6] For the capacity of the theater, which no longer exists, see Murata, *Operas for the Papal Court*, 261, document 10, and Davide Daolmi, "La drammaturgia al servizio della scenotecnica. Le 'volubili scene' dell'opera barberiniana," *Il saggiatore musicale* 13 (2006), 5–62 at 43–52. The wing that contained the theater was demolished in 1926 to create the Via Barberini.

[7] Lewalski, *The Life of John Milton*, 100.

decadent spectacle aside, Milton could not disguise his pleasure at being so publicly acknowledged.

Milton's gracious host, Francesco Barberini, was a youthful twenty-six when his uncle Maffeo raised him to the purple in October 1623, the year of his own election as Urban VIII. This was the most recent move in a carefully orchestrated strategy designed to consolidate the power of the family. The son of a Florentine wool merchant, Maffeo Barberini had been sent as papal nuncio to France in 1604, and two years later was elevated to the cardinalate at the request of Henry IV.[8] Once settled in Rome, he set about extending the influence of the Barberini in the upper reaches of the structures of the church. To his elder brother Carlo went riches and the highest secular office of state, that of commander-in-chief of the papal armies. As "cardinal nephew," Francesco, Carlo's eldest son, was to become the principal means through whom all business with the pope was conducted. Astute, learned, and with a keen interest in the arts, Francesco Barberini came to occupy a pivotal position in the political world of Urban VIII's Rome. He was soon joined in the cardinalate by two of his brothers, both named Antonio, while to the third nephew and middle brother, Taddeo, went the task of continuing the dynasty. In late 1627, Taddeo married Anna Colonna, who came from one of the most distinguished and ancient Roman aristocratic families. Following his father's death two years later, he then went on to inherit not only his position as General of the Church, which carried military responsibilities, but his territorial possessions as well, which brought with them the title of Prince of Palestrina. In the following year Taddeo was controversially appointed as "praefectus Urbis" of Rome, in defiance of the general expectation that the title had lapsed with the extinction of the Della Rovere line.[9] This marked a considerable political achievement for the Barberini; since the office was hereditary, it would remain in the family after Urban's death. In terms of status, the significance of Taddeo's attainment was acknowledged in a number of publications including Ottavio Busini's engraving of an idealized version of the Palazzo Barberini, then under construction, which celebrates not only Taddeo's elevation to the prefecture, but also his prestigious marriage, both of which are framed by the overarching

[8] For general studies of the Barberini, see Pio Pecchiai, *I Barberini* (Rome: Biblioteca d'arte editrice, 1959), a largely hostile if entertaining account, and the useful if uncritical sections of Ludwig von Pastor, *The History of the Popes from the Close of the Middle Ages*, ed. Ralph Francis Keir, vols. 28, 29 (London, 1899–1910).

[9] For an impression of the hostility which this generated, see Giacinto Gigli, *Diario romano (1608–1670)*, ed. Giuseppe Ricciotti (Rome: Tumminelli, 1958), 122–23.

theme of divine protection for the papal family.[10] Felice Contelori's treatise on the history and character of the prefecture, published in 1631, is adorned with a title page showing Taddeo, the dedicatee of the volume, on horseback, ceremonially attired.[11] Similarly, Taddeo's investiture in the office, which took place in the Pauline Chapel of the Quirinal Palace, was commemorated in a magisterial painting commissioned by the pope from Agostino Tassi.[12] Consolidation in the interests of continuity and security were the main Barberini preoccupations in these years, and the series of operas produced in the Palazzo Barberini from 1632 onward needs to be read against this policy, aggressively prosecuted through both political and cultural means.

All this constituted an exhilarating rise to power for a Florentine family from merchant stock, though the trajectory was one that had ample precedents among papal lineages in the preceding century. As one historian has eloquently written, "Urban's creative inflation of a moribund title for Taddeo is a telling glimpse of his ambitions for the house of Barberini. Wealth, fiefs, offices of state, even the prestigious marriage alliance with the Colonna were not enough. His sights were set not merely on Rome but on the princely dynasties of Italy; the Medici, and above all, the Farnese."[13] Indeed, Urban VIII's obsessive pursuit of enhanced status, power, and wealth for his clan was the single most important political consideration of his pontificate. Nevertheless, although historians since Leopold von Ranke have associated the family with the most blatant and crude manifestations of papal nepotism, this was not a contemporary perception. The actions of Urban and his nephews, as they pursued an integrated policy of public representation in the pursuit of power, should not be judged as a performance staged merely in the interests of acquiring influence and prosperity, but rather as a conventional and comprehensible response to the pressing political and psychological claims made upon the family by the institution of the papacy itself.

It had been clear from the start of Urban's pontificate that one of its defining characteristics was to be the active encouragement of scholarship and the arts. To some extent this was necessary to fulfill expectations, and to satisfy the requirements of decorum. In addition, as has been claimed, Maffeo

[10] John Beldon Scott,"Patronage and the Visual Encomium during the Pontificate of Urban VIII: The Ideal Palazzo Barberini in a Dedicatory Print," in *Memoirs of the American Academy in Rome* 40 (1995), 197–234.

[11] Felice Contelori, *De Praefecto urbis* (Rome, 1631).

[12] It is now in the Palazzo Braschi (Museo di Roma); see Teresa Pugliatti, *Agostino Tassi tra conformismo e libertà* (Rome: De Luca, 1977), 101–2.

[13] Laurie Nussdorfer, *Civic Politics in the Rome of Urban VIII* (Princeton: Princeton University Press, 1992), 37.

Barberini was conceivably the most sophisticated and civilized man ever to ascend the papal throne. With his passionate interest in classical antiquity, a certain competence as a writer of verse in Italian, Latin, and Greek, and a genuine interest in the arts, Urban was unusually equipped to formulate a style of cultural rhetoric that was capable of projecting, through a variety of media, an image not only of the supremacy of the papacy and of Rome, but also of the Barberini themselves. In this both he and his nephews were encouraged through contacts not only with some of the most important artists and sculptors working in the city, including Andrea Sacchi, Pietro da Cortona, and Gian Lorenzo Bernini, but also with intellectuals and men of letters. The result was an engaged development with cultural life, pursued in the course of a long pontificate, which marked a high point in the evolution of the arts in Rome, exercised through lavish patronage which has been held to be one of the main motors of seventeenth-century Roman Baroque culture.[14] New building projects were the most obvious vehicles for this politically charged enterprise, but also prominent among the fruits of Barberini patronage was the composition of an impressive sequence of operas that were staged at first in the Palazzo ai Giubbonari, and then later in the newly constructed Palazzo Barberini alle Quattro Fontane, the ultimate symbol of Barberini power.

Against this background, the composition and performances of the sacred drama *Sant' Alessio* can be placed in a number of interrelated perspectives.[15] The first is Florentine and familial. Apparently it was Cardinal Francesco Barberini who originally approached Stefano Landi to write an opera, sometime in the late 1620s, evidently influenced by recent developments in Florence. The composer and his work were already well known in Barberini circles. Landi, who had studied at both the German College and the Jesuit Seminario Romano, and had later been attached to the household of the Cardinal of Savoy, had been commissioned early in his career to write a mass setting

[14] See, *inter alia*, Francis Haskell, *Patrons and Painters: A Study in the Relations between Italian Art and Society in the Age of the Baroque* (London: Chatto & Windus, 1963); Judith Hook, "Urban VIII: The Paradox of a Spiritual Monarch," *The Courts of Europe: Politics, Patronage, and Royalty 1400–1800*, ed. A. G. Dickens (London: Thames & Hudson, 1977), 213–32; Marc Fumaroli, "Cicéron Pape: Urban VIII Barberini et la seconde Renaissance romaine," in *idem*, *L'âge de l'eloquence: rhétorique et "res literraria" de la Renaissance au seuil de l'epoque classique* (Geneva: Droz, 2002), 202–26; Peter Rietbergen, *Power and Religion in Baroque Rome: Barberini Cultural Politics* (Leiden: Brill, 2006).

[15] On *Sant' Alessio* see Murata, *Operas for the Papal Court*, 19–23, and 221–48; Frederick Hammond, *Music and Spectacle in Baroque Rome: Barberini Patronage under Urban VIII* (New Haven: Yale University Press, 1994), 199–214; Virginia Christy Lamothe, "The Theater of Piety: Sacred Operas for the Barberini Family (Rome, 1632–1643)" (PhD dissertation, University of North Carolina at Chapel Hill, 2009).

for the wedding of Taddeo Barberini to Anna Colonna, an event that occasioned not only the usual entertainments but also the publication of literary compilations including a number of musical works.[16] Even earlier Landi had also acquired experience of writing for the stage; his first musical drama, *La morte d' Orfeo* of 1619, is firmly set in the tradition of court opera stemming from the first Florentine examples of the genre, and from Monteverdi's two Mantuan works, all of which elaborate subject matter taken from classical mythology.

This was now out of date, and by the 1620s the Medici had turned to religious material for the libretti of their operatic and other staged entertainments. Following the death of Duke Cosimo II in 1621,[17] a regency was formed to govern the Grand Duchy of Tuscany. This placed control of the state in the hands of Catherine de' Medici, the widow of Grand Duke Ferdinando, and Maria Magdalena of Austria, until Ferdinando II succeeded to the Grand Ducal title in July 1628. During this brief period of just over seven years, these two women jointly transformed the traditional rhetoric of Medici public display expressed through cultural means.[18] Traditional interpretations of the economic and political fortunes of the Florentine state during the 1620s have tended to stress their negative aspects, tracing the decline of Tuscany to the policies adopted by the co-regents. In something of a similar vein, and undoubtedly under the influence of this strong historiographical tradition, music historians have generally portrayed Medici interest in music during the period as sterile, with lavish expenditure and religious zeal combining to produce a sequence of newly commissioned theatrical works of slight artistic merit. This view, which has its roots in the late eighteenth century, has been challenged in recent years by a number of writers who have argued that the regents were not as politically inept as they have been conventionally regarded, and that the cultural consequences of their rule were both coherent and effective, particularly in relation

[16] Murata, *Operas for the Papal Court*, 4, 13–15.

[17] For some of the cultural consequences of Caterina de' Medici's regency, see Clare Innocenti [et al.], *Caterina e Maria de' Medici, donne al potere: Firenze celebra il mito di due regine di Francia* (Florence: Mandragora, 2008). [Exhibition catalogue].

[18] Estella Galasso Calderara, *Un'amazzone tedesca nella Firenze medicea del '600: La Granduchessa Maria Maddalena d'Austria* (Genoa: Sagep, 1985); Sheila ffolliott, "Catherine de' Medici as Artemisia: Figuring the Powerful Widow," in *Rewriting the Renaissance: The Discourses of Sexual Difference in Early Modern Europe*, ed. Margaret W. Ferguson, Maureen Quigley, and Nancy Vickers (Chicago: University of Chicago Press, 1986), 227–41.

to their patronage of court spectacle.[19] Taken together, these reevaluations constitute a major reassessment of Medici musical culture during the regency.

In place of the mythological and dynastic themes that had been developed by her male predecessors and their humanist advisors, Maria Magdalena, who seems to have been the more important member of the regency in terms of commissioning new work, made use of material that could both assert her authority while at the same time providing concrete justification for it by referential analogy to the lives of pious women, and in particular to the biographies of female saints.

Some fifteen theatrical spectacles are known to have been performed at court during this period, beginning with *Il martirio di S. Agata della città di Catania*, with music by Marco da Gagliano and Francesca Caccini. In terms of its thematic material (which exalts the virtuous actions of Agatha, a virgin martyr), *Il martirio di S. Agata* set the trend for much of what followed during the remaining years prior to the accession of Ferdinand II, after which court drama took a more secular turn to culminate, in 1637, in the phantasmagorical production of *Le nozze degli dei*, given in the courtyard of the Palazzo Pitti to celebrate the marriage of the new Grand Duke.[20] Of these fifteen substantial works produced at court during the years 1621–27, ten featured female saints or figures taken from the Bible, while the remaining five secular dramas featured female protagonists.

The most significant from the artistic point of view is *La liberazione di Ruggiero dall' isola d'Alcina*, first performed at the Medici villa of Poggio Imperiale in 1625. This was as part of an extensive season of entertainments, which also included a re-staging of *La regina Sant'Orsola* and the musical *barriera, La precedenza delle donne*, which had been devised to celebrate the visits of Maria Magdalena's brother, Archduke Karl of Styria, and their nephew, Crown Prince

[19] Suzanne Cusick, "Of Women, Music and Power: A Model from *Seicento* Florence," in *Musicology and Difference: Gender and Sexuality in Music Scholarship*, ed. Ruth Solie (Berkeley: University of California Press, 1993), 281–304; Kelly Harness, *Echoes of Women's Voices: Music, Art, and Female Patronage in Early Modern Florence* (Chicago: University of Chicago Press, 2006); Suzanne Cusick, *Francesca Caccini at the Medici Court: Music and the Circulation of Power* (Chicago: University of Chicago Press, 2009).

[20] Angelo Solerti, *Musica, ballo e drammatica alla corte medicea dal 1600al 1637. Notizie tratte da un diario con appendice* (Florence, 1905), 197–211; Alois M. Nagler, *Theatre Festivals of the Medici* (New Haven: Yale University Press, 1964), 162–74; Mario Fabbri [et al.], *Il luogo teatrale a Firenze: spettacolo e musica nella Firenze medicea. Documenti e restituzioni* (Milan: Electa, 1975), 140–43; Cesare Molinari, *Le nozze degli dei: un saggio sul grande spettacolo italiano nel Seicento* (Rome: Bulzoni, 1968).

Vladislao, to Florence. In addition to familial motives for the visit, there were also political ones, aimed at securing support for a Catholic League dedicated not only to combating Protestantism, but also to curtailing French influence in Italy. As such, this bold proposal, which sought to forge an alliance between Tuscany, the Papal States, and the Hapsburgs, involved a complete reversal of the policy of alignment with France that the Medici had so actively pursued since the marriage of Grand Duke Ferdinando de' Medici to Christine of Lorraine in 1589.[21]

It was undoubtedly with the Medici precedent in mind that Francesco Barberini, who had been present at the Florentine performance of *Giuditta* with music by Gagliano, turned to one of his uncle's courtiers, Giulio Rospigliosi, an aristocratic member of the Congregation of Rites and one of many literary aspirants in the Barberini circle, to provide a text. It may even have been that Cardinal Francesco was aware of the political context in which the Florentine staging of *La liberazione di Ruggiero*, now published, had taken place. Certainly there are functional similarities and analogous political objectives that link the performances at Poggio Imperiale before influential members of the imperial family, and two of the performances of the work that resulted from Francesco's initiative, the religious melodrama *Sant' Alessio*, given before the imperial ambassador in 1632, and the brother of the King of Poland two years later. Rospigliosi's text also proved to be influential, standing at the head of a specifically Roman sub-tradition of opera libretti based on the lives of saints, which is clearly influenced by Florentine example in both its devotional and political dimensions. Between 1631 and the death of Urban VIII in 1643, Rospigliosi was to write a further four such works for the Barberini, all of which were performed in the newly constructed family palazzo at the Quattro Fontane. They share not only a librettist (it is really Rospigliosi who provides the continuity in the complete series of Barberini operas rather than the composers who set them),[22] but also a concern with ethical and religious ideas skillfully combined with political propaganda. While the latter could change according to circumstance, as we shall see in the case of the changes made to the text of *Sant' Alessio* in the course of its performance history in the 1630s, the former remained constant. From *Sant' Alessio* to *Sant' Eustachio* of 1643, all five works crucially depend upon the theme of sainthood achieved through the rejection of worldly temptations, a topos familiar enough from the *Summa theologica* of Aquinas and its derivatives.

[21] See Furio Diaz, *Il granducato di Toscana: i Medici* (Turin: Unione Tip.-Ed. Torinese, 1976), 363–70.

[22] Hammond, *Music and Spectacle*, 202–3.

* * *

In Rospigliosi's libretto for *Sant' Alessio*, Alexis has returned to Rome without the knowledge of his family and friends, whom he had abandoned in order to live the life of a Christian hermit. Although the Devil tries to tempt him back to his former life, Alexis is able to resist, sustained by his guardian angel who announces his approaching death. Following this event, Alexis is reunited with his family. The allegorical figure of Religion descends from the heavens to underscore the central message of the struggle between human affection and spiritual obligation, and the triumph of the latter. Consolation and support is provided by an angelic chorus. The message, emphatically underscored in the final chorus, is both universal and particular, emphasizing the centrality of Rome itself, which had been visible on the stage since the beginning of the Prologue.

Although tradition has placed the composition of *Sant' Alessio* in the vicinity of 1631, recent research has shown that it was prepared for performance in 1629, two seasons earlier.[23] This places it just one year after the performance of *Marsia*, to a libretto by Ottavio Tronsarelli, the first opera known to have been given in the Palazzo Barberini, which was then still under construction.[24] As for the 1631 performance itself, it is surrounded by a good deal of mythology, some of which argues that it was prepared and rehearsed but then cancelled at the last moment because of the plague. This must be doubted. Firstly there is the general remark of the diarist Giacinto Gigli, who records that although the usual carnival festivities were suspended because of the epidemic, private entertainments in the palaces of the aristocracy continued.[25] Second, an *avviso* of 8 March is quite unambiguous in stating that a performance of "the life of the glorious Roman Saint Alexis" was to be "represented in music" that same evening.[26] A second *avviso* of one week earlier also refers to the intention to mount a "spiritual opera," to be sung by "the singers of the pontifical

[23] Elena Tamburini, "Per uno studio documetario delle forme sceniche. I teatri dei Barberini e gli interventi berniani," in *Tragedie dell' onore nell' Europa barocca*, ed. Maria Chiabò and Federico Doglio (Rome: Torre d'Orfeo, 2003), 255–75.

[24] Ottavio Tronsarelli, *Drammi musicali* (Rome, 1631); See Daolmi, 29–30. Hammond, *Music and Spectacle*, 201, suggests that the music, which is lost, was by Kapsberger.

[25] See Gigli, *Diario romano (1608–1670)*; Murata, *Operas at the Papal Court*, 19.

[26] Murata, *Operas for the Papal Court*, 223, document 1b "Questa sera nel suo palazzo [Taddeo Barberini] fa rappresentare in musica la vita del glorioso santo Alessio romano."

chapel" to which would be invited "cardinals, prelates, and other lords."[27] Some weight must be attached to these notices, social news sheets that could normally be relied upon for their accuracy.[28] In addition, it seems unlikely, given the importance of the occasion, that the performance would have been abandoned a matter of hours before it was due to be given, on account of the plague which, in fact, never reached Rome.[29] The performance itself would have been given in the Palazzo ai Giubbonari, the Barberini palace near the Campo dei Fiori where the family had first established itself in the late sixteenth century.[30] But for more information about the first performances of *Sant' Alessio* it is necessary to turn away from these shadowy speculations, and to examine the evidence for two later productions, both given in the Palazzo Barberini.

In February 1632, Landi's opera was repeated in honor of the visit of the imperial ambassador, Hans Ulrich Fürst von Eggenberg; on this occasion it was presented in the Palazzo Barberini, in part because the old family residence of the Palazzo ai Giubbonari was now rented out.[31] The progress of the preparations can be picked up from documents. Firstly, the nature of the payments to Landi for music paper and writing materials throughout the first three months of the year, "to serve for *Sant' Alessio*," suggest that the work was recomposed during this period.[32] Second, Jean-Jacques Bouchard, ambassador to the King of France, was present at the performance and described some of what he saw in his manuscript journal.[33] He confirms that *Sant' Alessio* was performed in Cardinal Francesco's larger anteroom, now known as the *Sala delle statue* or *dei marmi*, hung for the occasion with yellow, red, and blue satin,

[27] Murata, *Operas for the Papal Court*, 223, document 1a: "Signor Cardinale Barberini in questi giorni di Carnevale vuol far recitare in musica un opera spirituale dalli musici della Cappella pontificia, et altri, con l'intervento de Cardinali, Prelati, et altri Signori."

[28] For the nature and function of the Roman *avvisi*, see Mario Infelise, "Roman *avvisi*: Information and Politics in the Seventeenth Century," in *Court and Politics in Papal Rome 1492–1700*, ed. Gianvittorio Signorotto and Maria Antonietta Visceglia (Cambridge: Cambridge University Press, 2002), 212–28.

[29] See below, page 50.

[30] Murata, *Operas for the Papal Court*, 19.

[31] Ibid., 223, document 2a.

[32] Hammond, *Music and Spectacle*, 202.

[33] Paris, École Nationale des Beaux-Arts, MS 502. Its contents were first published in Lucien Marcheix, *Un Parisien à Rome et à Naples en 1632 d'après un manuscrit inédit de J.-J. Bouchard* (Paris, 1897). Excerpts concerning *Sant' Alessio* are given in Romain Rolland, "La première représentation du Sant' Alessio," *Revue d'histoire et de critique musicale* 2 (1902), 29–36. See now the new edition by Emanuele Kanceff in *Oeuvres de Jean-Jacques Bouchard*, 2 vols. (Turin: G. Giappichelli, 1976–77), I, 137–55.

"with a dais above of the same that covered the whole hall."[34] Bouchard also notes that the work consisted of a prologue and three acts of five, seven, and three scenes respectively. A view of ancient Rome provided the backdrop for the prologue; the other sets showed a cityscape, the mouth of hell, and finally the tomb of the saint. This last scene was the only one to require machinery, which must have been used to part the clouds above to reveal Alexis in Paradise. From payment entries it is known that Pietro da Cortona, who was shortly to be fully occupied in painting the ceiling in the *salone* of the Palazzo, was among those involved in making sets and costumes.[35] Similarly, the performers are known to have included two castrati, one of whom, Angelo Ferrotti, who took the title role, was in the service of Cardinal Francesco.[36] The other was Marc' Antonio Pasqualini, whose seraphic features are familiar from Andrea Sacchi's full-length allegorical portrait in the Metropolitan Museum in New York.[37] The strikingly innovative iconography of Sacchi's painting has been much discussed, earning it a place both in the history of musical portraiture, and for its depiction of the aftermath of pain and its aesthetic consequences.[38] The son of a barber from Imola, Pasqualini had been taken up by Cardinal Antonio Barberini in 1629, and subsequently imposed upon the Cappella Sistina where he remained for the rest of his career. A copyist and composer as well as a singer, at the height of his career he was one of the most sought-after performers in the salons of Rome.[39] For the Barberini he appeared not only in *Sant' Alessio*, but also in *Erminia sul Giordano* (1633), *Didimo e Theodora* (1635 and 1636), *Chi soffre speri* (1637 and 1639), and *Il palazzo incantanto* of 1642. Pasqualini was close to both Sacchi and Cardinal Antonio, and his portrait,

[34] Rolland, "La première représentation," 31.

[35] See Marilyn Aronberg Lavin, *Seventeenth-Century Barberini Documents and Inventories of Art* (New York: New York University Press, 1975), documents 99, 429. Work on the *salone* fresco began in July 1632; see John Beldon Scott, *Images of Nepotism: The Painted Ceilings of the Palazzo Barberini* (Princeton: Princeton University Press, 1991), 130–31.

[36] The documentation is discussed in Murata, *Operas for the Papal Court*, 21–22.

[37] For the portrait, see Terence Ford, "Andrea Sacchi's 'Apollo Crowning the Singer Marc' Antonio Pasqualini," *Early Music* 12 (1984), 79–84.

[38] Franca Trinchieri Camiz, "The Castrato Singer: From Informal to Formal Portraiture," *Artibus et Historiae* 18 (1988), 171–86; Todd P. Olsen, "Long Live the Knife: Andrea Sacchi's Portrait of Marcantonio Pasqualini," *Art History* 27 (2004), 697–722.

[39] See Gloria Rose, "Pasqualini as Copyist," *Analecta musicologica* 14 (1974), 170–75; Margaret Murata, "Further Remarks on Pasqualini and the Music of MAP," *Analecta musicologica* 19 (1980), 125–45. A selection of pieces from one of the manuscripts, Barb. lat. 4223, is presented in facsimile by Margaret Murata in *Cantatas by Marc' Antonio Pasqualini* (New York and London: Garland, 1985).

Andrea Sacchi: Marc' Antonio Pasqualini Crowned by Apollo (New York, The Metropolitan Museum)

thought to date from somewhere between the years 1634–44, is evidence of the high regard in which he was held.[40] By transforming the singer into a classical symbol of virtue through a series of mythological references including the familiar tale of Apollo and Marsyas, Sacchi produced "not a simple portrait, but an extremely beautiful conceit," as Bellori later wrote.[41]

[40] Ann Sutherland Harris, *Andrea Sacchi. Complete Edition of the Paintings with a Critical Catalogue* (Princeton: Princeton University Press, 1991), 83.

[41] "Non è questo un semplice ritratto, a un vaghissimo componimento"; see Giovanni Pietro Bellori, *Vita di Guido Reni, d'Andrea Sacchi e di Carlo Maratti*, ed. Michelangelo Piacentini (Rome: Biblioteca d'arte editrice, 1942), 68. For further on Bellori's *Vite*, see Haskell, *Patrons and Painters*, 158–61.

Two years later *Sant' Alessio* was revived as part of the most dazzling Roman carnival of the entire seventeenth century, which was marked by the visit of Prince Alexander Charles Wasa, the younger brother of King Vladislao of Poland, who had inherited the throne from his father two years earlier. Wasa was a member of the Catholic family that ruled Sweden, and the principal purpose of his visit was to enlist papal support for Polish attempts to negotiate with the Protestant factions who were now gaining the upper hand in the Thirty Years' War. To both entertain and impress his guest through the usual display of conspicuous consumption, Cardinal Antonio Barberini arranged a series of banquets and spectacles in the prince's honor, culminating in a spectacular tournament in the Piazza Navona.[42] Meanwhile, Cardinal Francesco had organized a further reworking of *Sant' Alessio*, which was presented four times in January and a further three times in February.[43] It seems that Landi was excused from duties in the Cappella Sistina in order to work on the new version, which incorporated substantial alterations and additions to the original text.[44]

These alterations are revealing. To start at the beginning, the prologue, which together with the finale was the most obvious place to insert topical and political references, was substantially rewritten for the new production. In the 1634 version, *Sant' Alessio* opens with a chorus of six slaves, who praise the virtues and achievements of both Alexander and his brother, and assert their loyalty to Rome. Among other changes, comic scenes were added, and a pastoral *intermedio* placed between the first and second acts.[45] New spectacular effects provided for both the flight of the angel and the later descent of Religion in Act II and, as in 1632, the final apotheosis. Some of these theatrical *tours de-force* were achieved by reusing machines that had been built for the presentation of another of Rospigliosi's opera libretti, *Erminia sul Giordano*, which is adapted from Tasso's *Gerusalemme liberata*, and was staged for the first time in the Palazzo Barberini in February 1633 to music by Michelangelo Rossi, who also sang in the performance. The determining element of this critical transition to greater technological virtuosity was the arrival in Rome of Francesco Guitti, one of the greatest scenographers of the age, who had previously worked for Giovanni Battista Aleotti in Ferrara and at the famous Farnese theatre in Parma. His translation to Barberini service must have brought particular pleasure to the family, ever-competitive with the Farnese. For the production of

[42] Hammond, *Music and Spectacle*, 208–24, with a detailed discussion of the *giostra*.

[43] Murata, *Operas for the Papal Court*, 224–26, documents 7–14.

[44] For the revisions, see Murata, *Operas for the Papal Court*, 22–23.

[45] Ibid.; Lamothe, "The Theater of Piety," 112.

Sant' Alessio in 1634, Guitti used a variety of stage technologies including rotating flats, flying sets, interchangeable backcloths, and machines. Together with its complicated lighting effects, these caused a sensation. Guitti's "mixed" scenic apparatus, which effectively combined fixed scenery with moveable wings, became the model for the *scena maestra* method later adopted in Venetian stage practice. As such, its influence was to be felt long after the innovations in stage design and scenic effects famously introduced by Giacomo Torelli.[46]

It is probably no accident that both the 1634 version of *Sant' Alessio*, and *Erminia sul Giordano* of the previous year, both experimental in their scenography and lavish in terms of their sets and costumes, were the only two Barberini operas to be published at the time. Both scores were printed by Paolo Masotti, whose model was almost certainly Marco da Gagliano's *La Flora*, published in Florence by Zanobi Pignoni in 1628. For Masotti this marked something of a new departure.[47] Yet while it took *Erminia* four years to arrive in print, the score of *Sant' Alessio*, as it had been given in 1634, was printed in 1635, and was evidently distributed to some of the guests who had attended the Roman performances. Some fifteen copies of this edition are known to have survived. Some of them, and probably originally all, contain tipped-in engravings, signed "J. Collignon," of eight scenes from the opera.[48] A luxurious upright folio, prominently dedicated to the Polish prince before whom it was performed, Masotti's score of *Sant' Alessio* was clearly intended as a propagandistic monument to the virtues of the Barberini, and as a record of the visual appearance of the sets themselves.[49] As such it belongs to a sub-genre that includes the partbooks of the music for the Florentine *intermedi* of 1589, a number of the early Florentine operas, and the two editions of Monteverdi's

[46] Daolmi, "La drammaturgia al servizio della scenotecnica."

[47] See, for an overview of his activity, Claudio Sartori, *Dizionario degli editori musicali italiani (Tipografi, incisori, librai-editori)* (Florence: Leo S. Olschki, 1958), 99–100.

[48] "J. Collignon," presumably Jean-Baptiste (dit François) Collignon, was well established in the Roman publishing and print selling trade within a few years of arriving in the city in about 1630; see Jacques Kuhnmünch, "Un marchand français d'estampes à Rome au XVIIe siècle: François Collignon," *Bulletin de la société de l'histoire de l'art francais* (1978), 79–100. The engravings might have been available separately; see Daolmi, "La drammaturgia al servizio della scenotecnica," 35. Unfortunately neither of the facsimile editions contains a complete set of Collignon's engravings.

[49] It has also been suggested that both the revisions to the score and its publication were intended as a rebuttal to criticisms of Barberini involvement in the Galileo affair; see Frederick Hammond, "The Artistic Patronage of the Barberini and the Galileo Affair," in *Music and Science in the Age of Galileo*, ed. Victor Coelho (Dordrecht: Kluwer Academic Publishers 1992), 67–89, at 82–89.

L'Orfeo, all of which were primarily commemorative publications issued with a propagandistic purpose.

* * *

Reconstruction of the circumstances in which the first performances of *Sant' Alessio* were given, and in particular the questions of where and how it was performed in the Barberini Palace, are not easily resolved. In part this is because the architectural history of the Palazzo Barberini is both complicated and in some respects obscure. Although the earliest phase of its planning, up until the point where construction of the present palace actually began, is reasonably clear, it has proved difficult and in some cases impossible for historians to disentangle the individual contributions of the various architects, beginning with Carlo Maderno, who worked on the project.[50] Pietro da Cortona, who had hoped to be awarded the commission, was responsible for a number of decorative projects including the remarkable doorframe of the Palazzo Barberini and the frescoed ceiling of the main *salone*.[51] Maderno's design of a solid central block flanked by two projecting wings places the building outside the norms of Roman palace construction, which traditionally called for a central courtyard. This is not the only surprise. Instead of the homogeneity and impersonality that characterize many Roman palaces of the time, the Palazzo Barberini has a richly articulated west facade, with a three-story, seven-bay loggia of round-headed arches framed by engaged pilasters, situated between the two strongly projecting wings. In other words, it is more of a villa than a palace, albeit one conceived on a monumental scale. One determining factor may have been the location of the site, which was not in the center of the city but on its eastern edge, in a commanding position on the northern slope of the Quirinal Hill, surrounded by a richly textured assemblage of other buildings of various dates. In Roman architectural terms the immediate model is Baldassare Peruzzi's Farnesina, the most famous of all Roman villas, where two wings branch off from a central hall while the exterior is ornamented with a simple configuration of pilasters and a decorative frieze. But for anyone familiar with Florentine palace construction, the overall design, though not its stylistic clothing, would have immediately recalled the Palazzo Pitti with its two wings projecting into

[50] See Rudolph Wittkower, *Art and Architecture in Italy: 1600–1750* (Harmondsworth: Penguin Books, 1958), 69–73; Anthony Blunt, "The Palazzo Barberini: The Contributions of Maderno, Bernini, and Pietro da Cortona," *Journal of the Warburg and Courtauld Institutes* XXI (1958), 256–87; Patricia Waddy, *Seventeenth-Century Roman Palaces: The Use and the Art of the Plan* (Cambridge Mass.: MIT Press, 1990), 173–290.

[51] For Pietro da Cortona's contribution see now Jörg Martin Merz, *Pietro da Cortona and Roman Baroque Architecture* (New Haven: Yale University Press, 2005), 17–29.

Rome, Palazzo Barberini from the northwest. Engraving by Specchi, courtesy of the MIT Press, Seventeenth-Century Palaces, *by Patricia Waddy*

the Boboli Gardens and, even more so, the newly named Villa Imperiale close to the Porta Romana, which had been recently extensively rebuilt for "the leisure and delight of Tuscany's future grand duchesses."[52] (It was here, it will be recalled, that *La liberazione di Ruggiero* was first performed). The construction, overseen by Giulio Parigi, had taken some two years to complete, had cost around 35,000 *scudi*, and had doubled the size of the original building. The most distinctive feature of its exterior was the large *corps de logis* flanked by two canted lower wings so as to form a *cour d'honneur*, clearly devised with outdoor theatrical performances in mind.[53] In the case of the Palazzo Barberini, the two wings announce the internal functions of the palace and the familial arrangement of the rooms within it; while the northern half was intended for Taddeo Barberini and his family, the southern half was destined for Cardinal Francesco.

The main approach to the palace was originally through the door next to the Quattro Fontane; this brought the visitor to the entrance to the *piano nobile* in the center of the garden facade. From here it was a short step to the

[52] Solerti, *Musica, ballo e drammatica alla corte medicea*, 172.

[53] On the Villa Imperiale see Fiammetta Faini and Anna Maria Puntri, *La villa Mediceo Lorense del Poggio Imperiale* (Florence: Becocci/Scala, 1995).

vestibule (described in the documents as the *sala ovale*), and so on to the *salone*. Between 1632 and 1639, except for an interruption in 1637 when the artist was working on the Palazzo Pitti;[54] that is, during the same years that Barberini enthusiasm for private operatic performance was developing, the vault of the *salone* was being decorated with an immense fresco, the so-called *Gloria dei Barberini*, by Pietro da Cortona. A virtuoso exercise in illusionism, Pietro's conception creates the impression that the coved ceiling of the room has been removed to reveal the sky in which allegorical figures float effortlessly among the clouds above. A minor poet, Francesco Bracciolini, was responsible for the complex program of the composition. At the center of the ceiling, open to the sky, is Divine Providence, mistress of Time and Fate, who can be seen crouching beneath. She gazes upwards toward the Barberini emblem of three bees enclosed in a laurel wreath, which is being supported by the three virtues of Faith, Hope, and Charity, while instructing the nearby figure of Immortality to crown them with a halo of stars. At the top of this central section of the fresco both the Church and the Papacy can be seen, identified by the keys of St. Peter and the papal tiara respectively. Cortona's masterpiece is generally regarded not only as one of the earliest examples of the Baroque decorative ceiling in Rome, but also as the most grandiose. Its central theme of Urban as the embodiment of Holy Wisdom in the guise of Divine Providence proclaims not only the omnipotence of the papacy as an institution, but also the achievements of the Barberini regime. This is clearly signaled through the presence of the family's coat-of-arms.[55]

From the *salone* the visitor would pass into the first anteroom in the south wing, Cardinal Francesco's half of the palace, the large hall C2 (see page 45). This measures fifty-five feet by forty-two and occupies two stories; two windows placed high, just beneath the vault, admit light from a well to the east (D18). It was in this room that the early Barberini operas were presented during the 1620s and 30s, beginning with Tronsarelli's *Marsia*. Although a seventeenth-century reference to the "muro della facciata che divide il salone dal salotto dove si faceva le comedie" was published as long ago as 1928,[56] the myths that would place these performances elsewhere (with the Barberini Theater, that

[54] For which see Malcolm Campbell, *Pietro da Cortona at the Pitti Palace: A Study of the Planetary Rooms and Related Projects* (Princeton: Princeton University Press, 1977).

[55] See Wittkower, *Art and Architecture*, 165–66 and, for a more detailed analysis, Scott, *Images of Nepotism*, Part III, with a detailed analysis of the iconography of the ceiling on 136–45.

[56] Oskar Pollak, *Die Kunsttätigkeit unter Urban VIII*, vol.1 (Vienna: B. Filser, 1928), 187, April 1629 to December 1639, item 886.

Pietro da Cortona: Triumph of the Barberini (Rome, Palazzo Barberini)

was not built until 1639, being a favorite), remains persistent.[57] But there is no doubt about it. Bouchard's description of the 1632 production of *Sant' Alessio* describes a transformed room, not a fixed theater, and a document of 1638 describes Francesco's antechamber as "the big hall where the comedies used to be given." In 1644, five years after the opening of the Barberini Theater, this space is still being referred to as "the hall where the comedies were presented."[58]

How this actually worked in practice can be pieced together from other evidence. The adjoining anteroom on the *piano nobile* [C3] had a lower vault, which allowed for a upper room to be constructed above. This [D1] is referred to in the documents as the "large hall where His Eminence [i.e., Francesco] used to have his *guardaroba* and where they dress for the comedies." After 1632, when Francesco took up residence in the Cancelleria following his

[57] Murata, *Operas for the Papal Court*, 20–21; Hammond, *Music and Spectacle*, 201; 210–12. For the Barberini Theater itself, see Waddy, *Seventeenth-Century Roman Palaces*, 247–48.
[58] Waddy, *Seventeenth-Century Roman Palaces*, 246 and fn. 296.

Palazzo Barberini: piano nobile, *1628–38. Courtesy of the MIT Press,* Seventeenth-Century Palaces, *by Patricia Waddy*

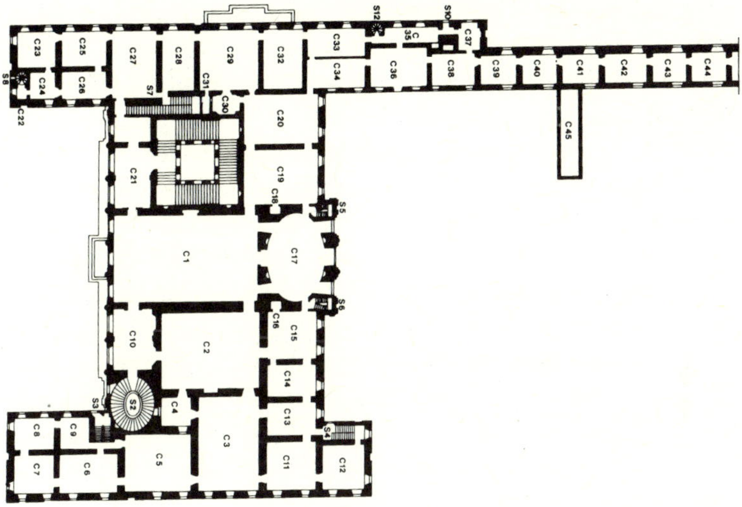

Palazzo Barberini: second floor, 1628–38. Courtesy of the MIT Press, Seventeenth-Century Palaces, *by Patricia Waddy*

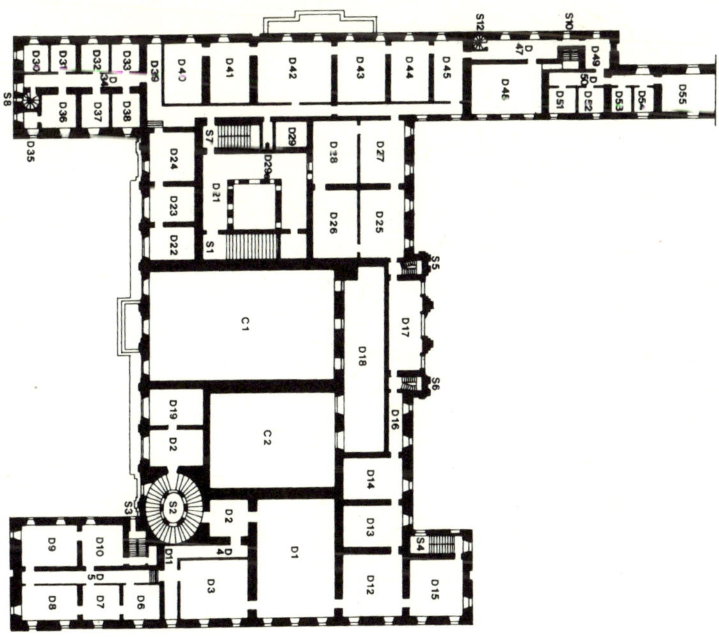

appointment as Vice Chancellor of the Holy Roman Church, this room lost its function as a *guardaroba*; thereafter its only recorded use was as a dressing room for theatrical productions.[59] As can be seen from the two ground plans, by using the staircase [S2], the performers could descend from the dressing room on the second floor to the anteroom [C2] on the *piano nobile*. From here entrances and exits could be made by passing through the adjoining rooms [C4 and C3].

Although it cannot be proved conclusively from the documents, it seems highly likely that the temporary staging used for the performances of the early Barberini operas would have been put up at the eastern end of the anteroom. Firstly, it was only from there that entrances and exits could be made from both the center and both sides of the stage. If Collignon's engravings can be taken as a record of how the sets actually looked, which is not necessarily the case given the opportunity for artistic license, this would have been necessary for the 1634 revival of *Sant' Alessio*. Then there is the question of machinery and scene changes. The Prologue is set against a view of Rome; this was fixed and remained visible until the third scene of Act III, when it was opened to reveal a new structure with three arches to represent a garden. The two scenes in the inferno and the forest were achieved by flying sets.[60] More complicated arrangements were required in the last act, where a cloud bearing Religion in her chariot accompanied by angels and virtues descended to the stage. A cloud machine, which was to become something of a fixture in later Baroque opera, could not be installed in such a narrow room. The only workable solution was to drop it from the flies above the stage, that is, from the vaulted space above the eastern end of the antechamber.[61]

* * *

From this we pass to questions of the social composition of the audience. Contemporary reports claim that 200 people could be accommodated in the antechamber next to the *salone*. Descriptions of different performances of *Sant' Alessio* reveal that the public varied in character from one to the next in accordance with finely tuned conceptions of decorum and status. For the 1634 performance we have information provided by two *avvisi*. The first, from 11 February, reads:

[59] Ibid., 199.

[60] Daolmi, "La drammaturgia al servizio della scenotecnica," 34–35.

[61] See Waddy, *Seventeenth-Century Roman Palaces*, 200, where the vault is illustrated as fig. 119.

> That evening in the palace of the Most Excellent Prefect of Rome at the most important of the residences the *rappresentatione di Santo Alessio* was performed again in the presence of many most eminent prelates and other members of the nobility, and on Wednesday it was also given in the presence of only the principal ladies with their husbands and relatives.[62]

A second, from seven days later, records that:

> On Sunday evening and also on Wednesday the *rappresentatione di Sant' Alessio* in music was performed again in the Palace of the Most Excellent Prefect of Rome for the delight of the gentlemen and other nobility who had been unable to see it previously. It was a most beautiful thing, both because of the actors, each of whom played his part excellently, and also because of the refinement of the costumes, the variety of the scenery, and the *intermedi*.[63]

The production "que faisoit faire le cardinal Francesco Barberino en son nouveau palais,"[64] seen by Bouchard in 1632, was also attended by Cardinals Aldobrandini, Bentivoglio, Brancaccio, and San Giorgio. Bouchard himself was much taken by the courtesy shown to him by Cardinal Francesco, as was Milton some years later. He wrote in his diary:

> The Cardinal himself admitted Orestes [Bouchard's pseudonym] underneath the scaffolding and, leading him by the hand, bade him sit at his feet on a little bench and commanded Luca Holstenius to keep close to Orestes and explain the subject to him.[65]

[62] Murata, *Operas for the Papal Court*, 225, document 11a: "Quella sera nel Palazzo dell' Eccellentissimo Prefetto di Roma a Capo di Case fu di nuovo recitata in musica la rappresentatione di Santo Alessio alla presenza di molti Eminentissimi Prelati, et altra nobilta, e mercordi fu anco recitata con l'intervento solamente di queste principali Dame con li loro mariti e parenti."

[63] Ibid., document 11b: "La sera domenica et anco mercordi fu di nuovo recitata nel Palazzo dell' Eccellentissimo Prefetto di Roma la rappresentatione di Sant' Alessio in musica a compiacenza de' Signori et altra nobilta che per prima non l'havevano potuto vedere, riuscendo cosa bellissima cosi per l'interlocutori che ciascuno fece eccellentemente la parte sua, come per la vaghezza degli habiti, e diversita dell' apparenza delle scene, et intermedii."

[64] *Oeuvres de Jean-Jacques Bouchard*, I, 151.

[65] Piero Weiss, *Opera: A History in Documents* (New York: Oxford University Press, 2002), 33. The original, as given in *Oeuvres de Jean-Jacques Bouchard, op. cit.*, reads: "Le Cardinal luy mesme fit entrer Orestes par dessous l'eschafaut, et le conduisant par la main le fit seoir à ses pieds sur un petit banc, et commanda à Luca Holstenius de se tenir près Orestes et luy expliquer le sujet."

It was said to be, Bouchard remarked, "une des belles representations qui se soit jamais faite à Rome."

The performance that Bouchard attended was also experienced by the diplomat and poet Fulvio Testi:

> Yesterday the Lord Cardinal Barberini invited me to the performance of *Sant' Alessio*, and so I went there this evening. I thought I would have been given a decent place away from all the confusion, but seeing that I was to be put in a seat which did not please me, and which, in my opinion, was not appropriate in view of the duties which I perform, I therefore, under the pretext of a touch of stomach ache, got up with the determination to leave, all of course without making the slightest fuss. The Lord Cardinal took note of it, and sent the Lord Count of Carpegna, brother of the Cardinal, to apologize and beg me to stay, and His Eminence (Cardinal Francesco) himself, after a thousand apologies, led me to a separate box, where there were also the Lord Cardinals Aldobrandini, Bentivoglio, and Brancaccio.[66]

Testi, now in his late thirties, was a learned and distinguished figure, "virtuoso di camera" at the court of the Duke of Modena, with volumes of printed poetry behind him and a career as Ambassador to Spain in front of him. As with Bouchard, it would seem that Testi's main concern was social recognition and, in particular, with being accorded an appropriate status in public by his Barberini hosts. Of Pasqualini's singing we learn nothing.

EPILOGUE

Barberini Rome provides a spectacular example of what Clifford Geertz has termed the "theater-state," a court society that combined many forms of culture in forging a highly individual and immediately recognizable rhetorical

[66] The importance of Testi's account is noted in Lamothe, "The Theater of Piety," 102. The original text, from *Fulvio Testi: Lettere*, ed. Maria Luisa Doglio, vol. 2 (Bari, 1967), 74, reads "Ieri il signor Cardinale Barberini mi fece invitare all rappresentazione di Sant' Alessio, et io questa sera mi sono andato. Supposi che mi fosse per esser dato luogo decente e lontano da tutte le contraversie, ma veggendomi messo in parte che non mi piaceva e che, a giudicio mio, non era di quella riputazione che si cinviene a questa carica che vesto, sotto pretesto d'un poco d'indisposizione di stomaco me non se levato con risoluzione d'andarmene, tutto però con gran modestia e senza farne una minima doglienza. Il signor Cardinale l'hà risaputo e ha mandato il signor conte Carpegna, fratello del cardinale, e farne scuda et a pregarmi che resti; e Sua Eminenza medesima, dopo mille discolpe, m'ha fattocondurre in un palco appartato, dove pur anche sono stati i signori cardinali Aldobrandini, Bentivoglio e Brancaccio."

language that was deployed as a powerful instrument of governance.[67] The grammar of that language, which inevitably incorporated dynastic iconography, was everywhere to be seen, from the facades of palaces to private chapels in churches. Inside Saint Peter's, the ultimate site of sacral authority, Urban VIII famously commissioned the construction of Bernini's visually arresting *baldacchino* over the apostle's tomb, and the same artist's *Cathedra Petri* in the apse of the basilica. These schemes are paralleled in turn by Urban's own tomb, commissioned from Bernini just three years after he became pope. Enthroned at the summit of the monument, Urban raises his hand in benediction. The allegorical figures of Charity and Justice seated below flank a sarcophagus from which Death emerges holding a scroll that reads VRBANVS VIII BARBERINVS PONTIFEX MAXIMVS.

Gian Lorenzo Bernini: Tomb of Pope Urban VIII (Vatican City, St. Peter's Basilica)

[67] Clifford Geertz, *Negara: The Theatre State in Nineteenth-Century Bali* (Princeton: Princeton University Press, 1980).

In the context of self-fashioning and image-building, these grandiloquent statements function not merely as symbols of papal supremacy, but also as expressions of millennial continuity, culminating in the long Barberini pontificate. Perhaps more than any of their immediate predecessors, even the Farnese, the Barberini were keenly aware of the imperative to use the city of Rome as a theater, as a sequence of impressive public spaces and buildings, where their own power could be established, represented, consolidated, and enhanced. In this context, *Sant' Alessio* and the other Barberini operas drew upon evolving metaphors of rule. Yet for all their magnificence, it is also important to recall that they were played out against a background of unease and discontent caused by apprehension in the face of the epidemic that had gripped other parts of Italy, and meteoric increases in the cost of basic essentials. Although plague did not reach Rome during Urban's pontificate, throughout the early 1630s Romans lived in dread that the disease which had swept through Northern Italy and Tuscany would reach the Eternal City.[68] Rome, it was widely believed, was next on the list for Divine Retribution after Florence. Anxieties only increased in the early days of 1630 when, following the example of a number of northern cities as well as that of Florence, the Roman authorities banned all commerce involving the transport of either people or merchandise with the State of Milan, where the epidemic had first taken hold.[69] Against this backdrop of fear, other unpleasant realities, mostly economic, intruded. During the first three decades of the seventeenth century food prices were twice and in some cases three times as high as they had been toward the end of the previous century. In order to augment his revenues, already greatly depleted by his ambitious building programs and his support of the Catholic princes during the Thirty Years' War, Urban was forced to increase old taxes and to impose new ones. For this he was lampooned in prose and verse, the convenient rhyming of his nickname "papa gabella" with "barba bella" providing a convenient rhetorical handle for much ironic comment. Pasquino, famous for his *bon mot* "Quod non fecerunt barbari, fecerunt Barberini" when Urban stripped away the bronze ceiling from the portico of the Pantheon, had plenty of other things to say. Reassurance, conveyed through any means to hand, was required.

[68] See the accounts in Carlo M. Cipolla, *Faith, Reason, and the Plague in Seventeenth-Century Italy* (New York: W. W. Norton and Co., 1981); Giulia Calvi, *Histories of a Plague Year: The Social and the Imaginary in Baroque Florence* (Berkeley: University of California Press, 1989).

[69] Carlo M. Cipolla, *Cristofano and the Plague: A Study in the History of Public Health in the Age of Galileo* (London: Collins, 1973), 20–21.

At one level *Sant' Alessio* retails a standard doctrinal message about constancy of faith and the omnipotence of Rome. To understand its contemporary relevance it needs to be read against the background not only of the possibility of plague and the economic difficulties of the times, but also of the third phase of the Thirty Years' War. This, known as the Swedish War, lasted from 1629 to 1635. Eggenburg's embassy to Rome was designed to gain papal support for the Emperor Ferdinand II after the defeat of the Catholic forces at the hands of Gustavus Adolphus of Sweden, at the battle of Breitenfeld.[70] Similarly, Alexander Wasa's visit in 1634 was made principally so that he could intercede on behalf of his brother, who wished to marry a Protestant princess; this would have allowed him to regain Sweden as part of the ancient Wasa kingdoms.[71] Urban's negative response to this request was underscored by the text of the new Prologue which Landi set to music for the 1634 production. This new version reflects the changed conditions not only of Urban's papacy, now considerably tarnished as a result of the Galileo affair, but of the Catholic world in general. Although Prince Alexander is praised, there is also a thinly disguised admonition of his father, King Ladislao, implicitly criticized for not showing due obedience to Rome. As the chorus of slaves sings in the final paragraph:

> Formerly as a magnificent warrior
> [O Rome] you conquered our hearts;
> Now dedicated to Christ,
> Unfurling the great standard of the Cross,
> In peaceful sovereignty,
> A conqueror worshipped with happy prayers,
> You are the queen of our devoted hearts.

It is hardly accidental that the drama of *Sant' Alessio* is set in Rome itself. With a population that has been estimated at about 115,000, the city consisted of a compact core which, in the decades after the Council of Trent, had been developed as a magnificent sacred site, the ultimate holy city. In this task it had been fortified by the foundation of new religious orders, above all the Jesuits, and strengthened by the many new confraternities that had sprung up in the last decades of the century. Sanctified by its unparalleled collections of relics, and articulated by more than two hundred churches, basilicas, and oratorios,

[70] For this context see Lamothe, "The Theater of Piety," 32–34.

[71] Ibid., 37–38.

the urban fabric of Rome itself proclaimed its indisputable position at the heart of the Christian world, "Roma caput mundi." While Landi's *Sant' Alessio*, together with other works in the sequence of Barberini operas, reiterated that message both for its Roman audience and, through publication, for a wider world, it also served other equally more immediate political purposes, while underlining the authority of Urban's monarchical regime, and the supremacy of the papacy as an institution, in deeply troubled times.

Berlioz's First Nights

PETER BLOOM

TEN YEARS AGO, in 2003, when we celebrated the bicentenary of the birth of Hector Berlioz, I gave a paper in which I said, somewhat hopefully, that Berlioz had now taken his rightful place as one of the B's and one of the best. Confirmation of that hypothesis is offered by the titles of the papers presented in this celebration of the career of Thomas Forrest Kelly whom I came to know in the Middle Ages when he was Kapellmeister at a consortium of five academic institutions in Western Massachusetts, of which mine is one—because, unless I am mistaken, the only modern surname that occurs is that of the composer of the *Symphonie fantastique*.

It was daring of Tom to include the première of the *Fantastique* in his now famous book of famous first nights, because the work was performed during the day.[1] Long synonymous with Berlioz's name and reputation, the composition made no immediate splash—even if, in hindsight, it is the most astonishing first symphony in the history of Western music. Berlioz's second symphony, *Harold en Italie*, likewise caused few critical ripples. The première of his third, *Roméo et Juliette*, did whet the imaginative appetite of the little German fellow in the audience who later became Richard Wagner, as did the first performance of Berlioz's fourth symphony, the *Funèbre et triomphale*, which was a vessel of sound both musical and political that for the first and last time in the author's career poured forth not too much noise but rather too little, because it was performed out of doors—the occasion was the French

[1] Thomas Forrest Kelly, *First Nights: Five Musical Premières* (New Haven: Yale University Press, 2000).

equivalent of the American Fourth of July—and, on the *grands boulevards*, was drowned by indifference.[2]

In these few pages I should like to say, about the première of the *Fantastique*, a few words that you might not have heard. But I begin with a posthumous first night whose resonance is still felt in modern performance. In May 1903, honoring the centenary of Berlioz's birth, Raoul Gunsbourg directed an operatic production of *La Damnation de Faust* at what was then the Théâtre Sarah Bernhardt and what is now the Théâtre de la Ville de Paris. Berlioz had explicitly designated the work a "drame de concert" and an "opéra de concert," and later applied to its genre the expressions "legend" and "légende dramatique." Wishing to justify his decision to put the work on the stage, with costumes and action and dance and *spectacle*, Gunsbourg cited in his program an undated letter in which Berlioz purportedly said this: "I have just written an opera on the work of the immortal Goethe; I don't know if I have done justice to the giant, but I know that no theater director would want to mount it and that I will thus be compelled to have the parts performed in concert in order to hear them."[3] This does not sound like Berlioz to me, because in such instances

[2] Only two of Berlioz's first nights have been studied in particular detail. See Peter Bloom, ed., *Hector Berlioz, Benvenuto Cellini: Dossier de presse parisienne (1838)* (Heilbron: Musik-Edition Lucie Galland, 1995) and Frank Heidlberger, ed., *Hector Berlioz, Les Troyens à Carthage: Dossier de presse parisienne (1863)* (Heilbron: Musik-Edition Lucie Galland, 1995). Using research found in Leslie Horn's Smith College honors thesis (1980), Julian Rushton gives a thorough summary of the reception of the première of *Roméo et Juliette* in *Berlioz, Romeo et Juliette* (Cambridge: Cambridge University Press, 1994), esp. chapters 7 and 8. In "'Politics' and the Musical Press in 1830," *Periodica Musica* 5 (1987), 9–16, I speak about the reviews of the première of the *Fantastique* that I was able to find, of which there are only five. Francesca Brittan, author of "Berlioz and the Pathological Fantastic," *19th-Century Music* 29 (2006), 211–39, is pursuing the ramifications of the *Fantastique* in the nineteenth century. In need of further study, in my view, are the "first nights" of the *Requiem*, *L'Enfance du Christ*, *La Damnation de Faust*, and *Béatrice et Bénédict*.

[3] "Je viens d'écrire un opéra sur l'œuvre de l'immortel Goethe, je ne sais si je me suis approché du géant, mais je sais qu'aucun directeur de théâtre ne voudra le monter et que je serai hélas forcé de faire exécuter des parties en concert afin de pouvoir les entendre." This note is found in the first night program preserved in the *Dossier d'œuvre: La Damnation de Faust* at the Bibliothèque de l'Opéra, Paris. The quotation is followed by an editorial note: "We shall publish in a future program a facsimile of this letter" ("Nous publierons dans un prochain programme un fac-similé de cette lettre"). And indeed, in subsequent printings of the program, the facsimile itself appears. In his articles for the *Journal des débats* of 24 May and 7 June 1903, Adolphe Jullien cast doubt on the authenticity of this fragment, which Gunsbourg claimed was from a letter that Berlioz wrote to his son Louis. But in the autumn of 1846, when "Berlioz" might have written such a letter, Louis Berlioz was only thirteen years old. See my editorial note in Richard Macnutt, "Berlioz Forgeries," in *Berlioz: Past, Present, Future*, ed. Peter Bloom (Rochester: University of Rochester Press, 2003), 192.

of ill feeling Berlioz himself almost always blends irony with ire; here there is none. In point of fact Raoul Gunsbourg invented this text, went so far as to forge an autograph manuscript, and had the audacity to print it in the program booklet sold at the performances, not on the *first night* but on the second and third. The writing is not clear, but it is clearly not Berlioz's.

You have probably enjoyed operatic performances of *La Damnation de Faust*. It is done on the stage of the Metropolitan Opera, in New York, now supervised by an "interactive video designer," and it is done in opera houses round the world. But, fashionable *Regietheater* to the contrary notwithstanding, Berlioz wisely insisted that *mise en scène* is not what is meant. When he invited Baron Taylor to the première, in a letter that has only lately turned up, he said that what would be performed would be "a grand opera with neither action, costumes, nor decorations; the whole enterprise is rather daring, and requires the support of forward-thinking friends of the art of music."[4] When he proposed his candidacy for the Académie des Beaux-Arts of the Institut de France in 1851, he listed the work in his Curriculum Vitae as a *Légende en quatre actes (ou opéra de concert)*."[5] Google and other searches of the term "opéra de concert" lead to references concerning operas performed in concert. But what Berlioz envisioned was something that no one had earlier conceived: an opera destined from the beginning to be seen exclusively in the theater *of the mind*. Thank you, Raoul Gunsbourg . . . *not*.[6]

In beginning, I said that that the first performance of the *Fantastique* made "no splash," and, indeed, it was a very minor event on the cultural calendar of December 1830, even more minor than it might have been a few months later. The reason for this is political. Normally, everyone who was anyone appeared, or read about what was on, at the Académie royale de musique. The news, for example, that French forces had landed at Algiers—in what inaugurated France's second colonial empire but failed to prop up the dying régime of Charles X—was announced at the Opéra, on 18 June 1830, between the second and third acts of *Guillaume Tell*. But on the day of the première of the

[4] "Il s'agit de l'exécution d'un grand opéra sans action, costume ni décors; l'entreprise est presque téméraire, il a besoin de l'appui des amis éclairés de l'art musical." See Berlioz, *Correspondance générale*, ed. Pierre Citron et al., 8 vols. (Paris: Flammarion, 1972–2003) [henceforth *CG*], vol. VIII, 265.

[5] *CG* vol. IV, 36.

[6] *La Damnation de Faust* was first performed under Berlioz's direction in December 1846. The reviews have not been studied in detail but they were numerous—some thirty in all, according to Berlioz—and they were largely positive, as he happily reported to his family (*CG* vol. III, 400). But the cost of the production exceeded the revenues, and Berlioz—who in his *Mémoires* reported only the latter amount—was deeply disappointed.

Symphonie fantastique, 5 December 1830, what was on the mind of those who read the newspapers was not *hearing* scores but *settling* them: the punishment to be attributed, that is, to the four chief ministers of Charles X, who were thrown out of office when he was, during the July Revolution, and who were now on trial for their lives. "Le procès des quatre ministres" was the headline nearly every day in nearly every newspaper in December. The Prince de Polignac and the others had been arrested and imprisoned at Vincennes on 28 August 1830.[7] On 27 and 28 September, the Chambre des députés officially accused them of treason—for having approved the four ordinances in July that had abolished freedom of the press and set off the revolution. In October the judicial matter was settled: the Députés would prosecute the accused in the Chambre des Pairs, which was constituted as a court of law. Between 14 October and 14 December, witnesses gave some eighty-five depositions, and these were printed in the judicial press. They are extensive, wordy, and take a lot of space—which is why a review of a little concert at the Conservatoire, given by a recent graduate of the institution, was hardly material for page one. Or for page two, three, or four, for that matter, as all the papers in those days consisted of one large bifolium.[8] The analogy that comes to mind, for those old enough to remember Richard Milhouse Nixon, is to the Watergate hearings, which mesmerized the American public for four full months. Nixon finally resigned on 8 August 1974. (On 8 September of that year he was pardoned by the new president, Gerald R. Ford.) On 21 December 1830, as the crowd in the street demanded their heads, Charles X's ministers were found guilty and sentenced not to *death* (the penalty was much debated at the time), but to *life*.[9] As Berlioz lamented in a letter of 12 December to his sister, "the damned newspapers are speaking of nothing but politics!"[10]

Still, when you read the papers' fine print, you can find tidbits of musical interest. For example, in one of the extraordinary coincidences that color the

[7] Polignac was président du Conseil. The others were the Garde des sceaux, Jean de Chantelauze, the ministre de l'Intérieur, le comte de Peyronnet, and the ministre de l'Instruction publique, le comte de Guernon-Ranville.

[8] Among the numerous sources of information on the revolutionary year 1830 is the remarkably detailed documentary history in C.L. Lesur, *Annuaire historique universel pour l'année 1830* (Paris: Thoisonier-Desplace, 1832), available on *Gallica*, the public website of the Bibliothèque nationale de France.

[9] For a personal recollection of the behavior of the crowd, see, for example, Mary Summer [Charlotte Filon Foucaux], *La Jeunesse de 1830* (Paris: Dentu, 1885), 16. Six years later (on 23 November 1836) Polignac was freed but banished from France.

[10] "Ces diables de Journaux ne parlent que de politique" (*CG* vol. I, 390).

life of Berlioz, on the same day as the première of the *Fantastique* (5 December), a performance took place at the Opéra for the benefit of Harriet Smithson, the woman who, after years of trials and tribulations, would become Berlioz's first wife. A news item explains that because Smithson's earlier contract at the Opéra-Comique had not been honored—after her Shakespearean triumphs of 1827–1828, she had been engaged for a series of mute roles by the director (since August 1828) of the Opéra-Comique, Paul-Auguste Ducis—and because the Opéra-Comique was a government sponsored theater, her situation was, as the *Journal des débats* reminded readers, a matter of national interest.[11] On 6

[11] This benefit performance, originally scheduled for 20 November 1830, was first noted in the *Journal des débats* of 13 November: "The members of the commission regulating the civil list [the monies set aside by the government for the expenses of the royal household] having decided to put the auditorium of the Opéra at the disposal of Miss Smithson next Saturday, the twentieth of this month, an exceptional benefit performance is now being organized for this exciting artist, whose capacities have grown remarkably under the very eyes of the Parisian public, always quick to discern and to promote merit, even in the case of foreigners. The members of the commission have generously taken advantage of these circumstances to offer partial compensation to Miss Smithson for the considerable losses she suffered during the administration of Monsieur Ducis; and many of the finest artists of the capital have been anxious to lend their support to this act of friendly hospitality, which, under the circumstances, is rather a matter of national interest. On this singular occasion, Miss Smithson will take the title role in *La Muette de Portici*. Immediately afterward she is obliged to return to her native country. The program in its entirety, to be announced shortly, promises to comprise one of the most brilliant soirées that our gifted contributing artists have ever imagined." ("Les membres de la commission de la liste civile ayant bien voulu mettre à la disposition de miss Smithson la salle de l'Opéra pour samedi prochain, 20 de ce mois, on prépare à ce théâtre une représentation extraordinaire au bénéfice de cette intéressante actrice dont le talent s'est agrandi d'une manière remarquable sous les auspices du public parisien, toujours prompte à deviner et à encourager le mérite, même chez les étrangers. Les membres de la commission ont saisi avec un bienveillant empressement, cette occasion de dédommager en partie miss Smithson des pertes considérables qu'elle a éprouvées sous l'administration de M. Ducis, et les premiers artistes de la capitale se sont tous montrés jaloux de concourir pour leurs talents à un acte d'hospitalité qui, dans la circonstance, a quelque chose de national. Le rôle de *La Muette de Portici* sera joué par miss Smithson, cette fois seulement ; elle doit, immédiatement après, se rendre dans son pays. La composition de ce spectacle, que nous ferons bientôt connaître, promet une des plus brillantes soirées qu'aient jusqu'à présent conçues le talent et la généreuse émulation de nos artistes.")

The Commission de la liste civile presumably acted on the recommendation of the crown and in response to the letter that Smithson had addressed to Louis-Philippe himself on 15 August 1830. This letter, written in English and preserved in LondonBL. Add. 33965, f. 89, is mentioned by Peter Raby, *Fair Ophelia: A Life of Harriet Smithson Berlioz* (Cambridge: Cambridge University Press, 1982), 119, but to the best of my knowledge it has not been quoted in full in the modern Berlioz literature.

"Sire, May it please your most gracious majesty to extend your benignity and goodness in behalf of a Female, a foreigner who ventures to make her humble complaint to your Majesty

December the *Débats* reported that her concert had produced receipts of fifteen thousand francs: "a just compensation," said the paper, "for the losses she had suffered."[12]

Berlioz's concert on 5 December took place in the hall at the Conservatoire. At the time it was still called *École royale de musique*, even though it was the sole music school on the European continent which, as a product of the French Revolution, operated as a democratic institution. For example, its library was open to the general public, as Berlioz reminds us, in chapter IX of the *Mémoires*, in his famous description of that day in May 1822 on which Luigi Cherubini, newly appointed as Director, tried to remove him from the premises. Berlioz, then a medical student fascinated by the scores of Gluck, was simply taking advantage of the library's open hours. But Cherubini charged

in the simple words of truth, with the confidence that your Majesty's *heart* will be the best intercessor in her favour.

"Sire, at the repeated salutations of Col. Ducis and Mons. St. Georges, the late directors of the Opéra-Comique, I was induced five months since to accept an engagement to fulfill which I have travelled one thousand miles accompanied by an aged mother and an invalid sister both of whom are, and have been from my very childhood, solely dependent upon my professional exertions for support. After having succeeded in my humble efforts and thereby considerably added to the treasury of the above named Gentlemen on applying for my hard-earned salary I discover'd they had both disappear'd, having spent in the most extravagant luxury the produce of my labours, without paying to me any part of the debt which their own signatures in my possession acknowledge as just. I have been now five months in Paris, I have sought justice in vain until it pleas'd God to give me sufficient courage to implore it at the fountain head, namely Your Majesty, to whom I would not address myself had I ever step'd aside from that path of rectitude which is the best recommendation misfortune can have. May it please Your Majesty I was inform'd on application at the Minister's of the interior by his representative that he would not grant the privilege for reopening the Opéra-Comique until the debts due to the Artists were paid by the new Director. Yet the Theatre has been re-opened, some of the actors have been paid—but I, having no Father or Brother to protect me, am denied my just claim 7000.400 [*recte* 7,400] francs earned at the expense of my health from over exertion, and the loss of my time for five months—one word from your most gracious Majesty to Mons. Guizot, the *present* Minister, who has I am told at his disposal the funds connected with the Theaters, would obtain for me the debt and dry the tears of an afflicted family in a strange Country who would pray to God to give your gracious Majesty that reward which is the brightest hope in this transitory life.

"With the greatest deference I have the honour to subscribe myself / Sire / Your Majesty's / Most humble & obedient Servant / Harriet C. Smithson. / Rue de Rivoli 44 / Hotel du Congrès." See Edward Lockspeiser, "Unpublished Letters of Harriet Smithson and Berlioz," *Musical Times* 79 (December 1938), 894.

[12] "La recette de la représentation donnée hier donnée au bénéfice de miss Smithson s'est élevé à 15,000 fr. C'est un juste dédommagement des pertes qu'elle avait éprouvées" (*Journal des débats*, 6 December 1830). In the letter that she had sent to King Louis-Philippe on 15 August 1830, cited above, she put her claim at 7,400 francs.

him with having entered the building through the newly designated *female* door, not the now consecrated *male* door. So we see that the institution, from the point of view of sex, was not yet democratic in the Woodstock sense of the word.[13]

Berlioz's concert was also a charity performance—not for himself, but for the survivors of the July uprising. At the time many concerts and theatrical entertainments were for the benefit of the widows and children of those who died in the fighting. Berlioz's purpose could be taken as a sign that he, too, was a supporter of the revolution and of Louis Philippe's new regime. However, when he planned a repeat performance, later in December, he remarked dryly that "this time it will not be for the benefit of the wounded."[14] This is a detail in a Berliozian story I have recounted elsewhere that tells of Berlioz's elitism and authoritarianism in politics as in music. It was not for nothing, for example, that Berlioz later dedicated the published score of the *Fantastique* to that great democrat, the tsar Nicholas I of Russia.[15]

Louis-Philippe, especially in the first five years of his eighteen-year reign, was markedly more "liberal" than his predecessor. In the *Fantastique* one might suggest that there are several musical incarnations of this liberalization, of which two are perhaps appropriate to mention here in proximity to chant scholars and men of the cloth. The form of the *Dies irae* as played in the fifth movement—in what I believe is the first *secular* use of the famous old melody—presumably gives the tune as Berlioz would have heard it as an obedient Catholic child in his home town of La Côte-Saint-André.[16] The melody

[13] The new regulation, put in force on 1 May 1822, required that "les élèves hommes entrent par la rue du Faubourg-Poissonnière, et les élèves femmes par la rue Bergère." See Constant Pierre, *Le Conservatoire national de musique et de déclamation* (Paris: Imprimerie nationale, 1900), 244.

[14] *CG* vol. I, 385: "cette fois ce ne sera pas au bénéfice des blessés"

[15] See, for example, my "Berlioz: Reflections on a Nonpolitical Man," *The Yale University Library Gazette* 78 (October 2003), 19–38. Alexandre Dumas, who knew Berlioz as early as 1832 and who lent him assistance at the time of the performance of the *Requiem* in 1837, dedicated his novel *L'Alchimiste* (1839) to tsar Nicholas I, and in September 1839, before leaving for Russia, Adolphe Adam dedicated his opéra comique *Le Brasseur de Preston* (1838) to the same man. These gestures may have inspired Berlioz to dedicate to Nicholas the orchestral score of the *Symphonie fantastique*, which first appeared in the spring of 1845, precisely when the composer, having earlier established contacts with the court, was thinking of making a trip to Russia (*CG* vol. III, 270).

[16] It is sometimes said—as by Robin Gregory, "Dies Irae," *Music & Letters* 34 (1953), 135—that "Berlioz actually introduces the plainsong melody in his *Requiem*." The unison melody at the opening of the *Dies irae* in the *Requiem* is indeed based on plainsong, but not on the *Dies irae*. Berlioz's first thirteen notes rather match those of the opening of the antiphon "Ecce crucem Domine" sung at Vespers on the Feast of the Invention of the Cross (3 May).

is in the "premier mode mixte," as Berlioz's friend the chant scholar Joseph d'Ortigue put it, that is, the Dorian and Hypodorian mode, which Berlioz gives with a *finalis* of C because he is, after all, writing a symphony that follows the quintessential Beethovenian trajectory, from C Minor to C Major.[17] I am not the first person to point out that Berlioz quotes a good deal more of the tune "than has generally been recognized by analysts and commentators."[18] First, the first two phrases: "Dies irae, dies illa, Solvet saeclum in favilla"—"Day of wrath, that day of burning! / Earth shall end, to ashes turning!" (The English rhymes cause us to smile, but the honoree of this volume should know that I use the late-nineteenth-century translation by the Rev. Franklin Johnson, who preached in Harvard University's fair city of Cambridge, Massachusetts.[19]) Then, skipping line 3 (and lines 4 to 6, which repeat lines 1 to 3), he quotes the music for line 7: "Tuba mirum spargens sonum"—"Then is heard a sound of wonder." In the chant, "Tuba mirum" begins a third above the first notes of "Dies irae"; in Berlioz, it begins a fourth below. Then, after presenting once more the eight notes of "Dies irae, dies illa," he quotes line 53: "Qua resurget ex favilla"—"When no more in ashes sleeping," oddly failing to cite the previous line, "Lacrimosa dies illa," "Ah, that day, that day of weeping," which would have rendered the citation whole.[20] Finally—only later in the movement, when he combines the *Dies irae* and the fugue subject of the *Ronde du Sabbat* in what one might wish irreverently to call "counterpoint in the missionary position"—he again quotes line 1 of the *Dies irae* melody, now transposed to fit the context of C Major, followed by line 9, "Coget omnes ante thronum," for which the Reverend Johnson gives: "Rend the sepulchers asunder."[21]

I earlier mentioned Berlioz's friend Joseph d'Ortigue, whose pseudo-modal harmonization of the *Dies irae*, no doubt characteristic of such nineteenth-century ventures, is included in his later *Traité théorique et pratique de*

[17] See Louis Niedermeier and Joseph d'Ortigue, *Traité pratique et théorétique de l'accompagnement du plain-chant* (Paris: Heugel, 1876), 53.

[18] Malcolm Boyd, "'Dies Irae': Some Recent Manifestations," *Music & Letters* 49 (1968), 347–56, here, 347.

[19] Franklin Johnson, *The Dies Irae* (Cambridge, Mass.: [Private printing], 1883).

[20] Elsewhere, too, as in the "Rex tremendae" of the *Requiem*, Berlioz can appear to disregard Latin grammar and sense. See Julian Rushton, *The Music of Berlioz* (Oxford: Oxford University Press, 2001), 212–14.

[21] No one has as yet seriously attempted to find the contemporary sources of the *Dies irae* that Berlioz might conceivably have known. There were several dozen Graduals printed in France during the first two decades of the nineteenth century. These are conveniently catalogued in Theodore Karp, *An Introduction to the Post-Tridentine Mass Proper* (Middleton, Wis.: American Institute of Musicology, 2005), esp. 46–50.

l'accompagnement du plain-chant.[22] Berlioz's harmonization of the tune—in parallel thirds and sixths—is more straightforward. I am informed by my colleague Richard Sherr, expert in music of the Renaissance, that harmonization of the chant in parallel thirds and sixths was the then current improvised practice of the singers in the Sistine Chapel, as documented in an unpublished manuscript, dated 1806, found among the papers of Palestrina's great biographer Giuseppe Baini.[23] Professor Sherr furthermore tells me that not everyone knew this then or knows it now. But could Berlioz have been aware of the practice before leaving for Italy, at the end of 1830, as winner of the Prix de Rome? Perhaps. Because among his acquaintances at the time of the conception of the *Symphonie fantastique* was the composer Hippolyte Chélard, who, during his own sojourn in Italy as winner of the Rome Prize, had studied with, among others, Giuseppe Baini himself.

It happens that at a later point in his career, Berlioz did express himself fully on the question of the harmonization of the chant—in an important document that lies hidden in the archives of the Académie des Beaux-Arts. ("Important," that is, if you will allow for the possibility, as certain specialists will not, that what Berlioz says about the chant might actually be of interest.) The document to which I refer is the report Berlioz drafted for his *confrères* at the Institute on a book submitted for approval to the Academy: a *Répertoire de Plain-chants harmonisés à trois parties . . . composé à l'usage de Paris et de Rome* by the opera singer Fidèle Koenig (1817–86), who was also Maître de chapelle in Paris at the Église Saint-Séverin. Berlioz's report—unsigned, but set down in that unmistakable handwriting of his that allowed me to make the discovery—opens by saying that the introduction of the organ into the church is responsible for the incursion—"l'invasion"—of harmony into religious services, that those who wish to preserve the chant in its original simplicity are battling in vain against the march of science and civilization and against those hell bent upon "embalming" the old melodies in harmony just as the ancient Egyptians embalmed their dead. His sympathies are clear: harmony destroys the character of the various modes and produces a bastardized music ("une musique bâtarde") with a physiognomy that is flat. He goes on to say that to harmonize or not to harmonize is a moral question to be decided not by the Académie des Beaux-Arts but rather by the Church. If one must harmonize, however, and here Berlioz concludes, then one must attempt to preserve the

[22] See note 17.

[23] See Adrien de La Fage, *Essais de Diphthérographie musicale* (1864; repr. Amsterdam: Kunf, 1964), esp. 444.

modal quality of the melodies by avoiding a nineteenth-century sort of *musica ficta* that furnishes leading tones at every possible juncture.[24]

Berlioz's extensive treatment of the *Dies irae* in the *Fantastique*, to return to the symphony, could lead one to ask if he were attempting a programmatical commentary beyond the mere evocation of devilry and witchcraft that are associated with later citations of the famous old tune, but his grab-bag approach to the melody rather suggests purely musical embezzlement. In fact, in the latest book-length contribution to the analytical literature on Berlioz, Stephen Rodgers takes the finale's opening citation of the *Dies irae* as exemplary of his main theoretical point: that form, in Berlioz, is a *metaphor* for non-musical experience.[25] Here, the first twenty notes of the chant are set down in dotted half-notes; then, immediately, in dotted-quarters; then, again immediately, in alternating quarters and eighths—a procedure that constitutes instantaneous strophic variation. This may indeed be a metaphor, but for *what*?

Could it be for the wrong-headedness of the equal-note doctrine in the performance of the Gregorian melodies? I doubt it—although Berlioz was aware of the interest in restoring the chant that, well before 1830, had been publicly expressed in Paris by Alexandre Choron, whom Berlioz admired, and by François-Joseph Fétis, whom he did not. More generally, could such instantaneous strophic variation be a metaphor for the scrambling of *time*? I doubt this, too, although there is a "chronological error" in Berlioz's first, private description of the program of the finale of the *Fantastique*, which no one seems to have noticed: of the appearance in the fifth movement of the melody that links the five movements of the work, the symphony's famous *idée fixe*, Berlioz writes: "it is the once-beloved object who comes to observe the funeral procession of her victim."[26] But that funeral procession, in the fiction of the program, has already taken place: it is the *Marche au supplice* that constitutes the previous movement. Berlioz can be careless about numbers and dates, but this is a truly odd slip of the pen.

In February 1833—to make a last point about Berlioz's use of the chant—Honoré de Balzac published a short story in the *Revue de Paris* called "Ferragus,

[24] I published Berlioz's report in "*Berlioz à l'Institut* Revisited," *Acta Musicologica* 53 (1981), 171–99 (see 187–89). It has never been translated nor is it scheduled for inclusion in Berlioz's collected criticism, the *Critique musicale*, ed. Anne Bongrain and Marie-Hélène Coudroy-Saghaï et al. (Paris: Buchet/Chastel, 1996–), of which six of ten projected volumes have now appeared.

[25] Stephen Rodgers, *Form, Program, and Metaphor in the Music of Berlioz* (Cambridge: Cambridge University Press, 2009), esp. 11–13.

[26] *CG* vol. I, 320 (to Humbert Ferrand; 16 April 1830): "c'est l'objet aimé qui vient au sabbat, pour assister au convoi funèbre de sa victime."

Chef des dévorants," and soon dedicated it, for reasons not immediately obvious, to Berlioz.[27] The story is one of obsessional love for a woman mistakenly accused of infidelity. That could be taken for an allusion to Harriet Smithson. But it is perhaps more likely that Balzac thought of Berlioz when writing near the end a brilliant page on the *Dies irae,* "that terrifying music" which voices "otherworldly sorrows and secret friendships" that weep for the dead. "Never in any human religion," Balzac goes on, "have the terrors of the soul, violently torn from the body and furiously agitated in the presence of the overwhelming majesty of God, been rendered with such power."[28]

Bringing the religious theme to the fore in the *Fantastique* even more forcefully than the plainchant is the daring use of bells. As the historian Alain Corbin reminds us, in *Les Cloches de la terre,* bells for centuries were in some sense heard not only as voices of time, but as voices of God, and in the aftermath of the Revolution, their use was variously prohibited, restricted, and disputed. In one of Corbin's most important sources, we read that bells have always performed the function of tolling the sadness of loss with a "slow, lugubrious, and rhythmic tintinnabulation *on a single note* that announces the agonizing and death of a member of the Christian family."[29]

In his score, which has the instruments play not *une note* but *deux*, Berlioz specifically calls for bells *off-stage.* This prescription is not always followed in modern performance, although the Boston Symphony Orchestra can play

[27] "Ferragus" was first published in 1833, in four issues of the *Revue de Paris* (10, 17, 31 March; 7 April). It then appeared—with the dedication to Berlioz—in his *Scènes de la vie parisienne*, vol. 2 (Paris: Mme Charles-Béchet, 1834). It appeared in a third edition in *La Comédie humaine* (Paris: Furne, Dubochet, Hetzel, 1843).

[28] See Balzac, *Ferragus*, ed. Michel Lichtlé (Paris: Flammarion, 1988), 189: "Jamais, en aucune religion humaine, les frayeurs de l'âme, violemmment arrachée du corps et tempêtueusement agitée en présence de la foudroyante majesté de Dieu." (In fact the description of the *Dies irae* fills several pages.) Another possible reason for the dedication to Berlioz is the repetition of a crucial expression in the epigraph of the first edition: "No one has as yet related one of those Parisian adventures as they actually happen in Paris, with Paris' *fantastical mystery*, and I assure you that in Paris there is indeed a good deal of *fantastical mystery*" ("Personne encore ne nous a raconté quelque aventure parisienne, comme il en arrive dans Paris, avec le *fantastique* de Paris, car je soutiens qu'il y a beaucoup de *fantastique* dans Paris"). This comes from the pen of the aspiring writer Charles Lautour-Mézeray, founder in 1828 of the magazine *Le Voleur* and in 1832 of the *Journal des enfants.* (See Balzac, *Ferragus*, ed. Lichtlé, 307.) In the press at the time, Berlioz was almost *always* associated with the word "fantastique."

[29] "Ce tintement lugubre, lent, mesuré et *sur une note uniforme* qui annonce l'agonie ou la mort d'un membre de la famille Chrétienne." See J. D. Blavignac, *La Cloche: Études sur son histoire et sur ses rapports avec la société aux différents âges* (Geneva: Grosset & Trembley, 1877), 114 (my emphasis).

this shocking page more or less as written, because the orchestra possesses large church bells in C and G cast specifically for the *Fantastique.* I say "more or less" because the actual pitch of bells, with their strike tones, virtual tones, and overtones, is no easy matter to discern or discuss. The weight of a bell producing a real middle C—following the calculations made by Victor-Charles Mahillon, curator of the musical instrument museum at the Brussels Conservatoire at the time that François-Auguste Gevaert wrote his *Nouveau Traité d'instrumentation* (1885) and consulted by Gevaert on the question of bells—would be something on the order of twenty-five tons (*sic*). This is reported by the Flemish conductor Jos van Immerseel, in the informational booklet with his own recent recording of the *Fantastique.*[30] Other orchestras usually use tubular bells, on-stage, to far lesser effect.

In lieu of bells, which Berlioz himself seems to have heard only in his imagination and never in performance, the composer calls for "plusieurs pianos sur l'avant-scène."[31] (On the Immerseel recording, the deep notes C and G are pounded out on two nineteenth-century Érard pianos and make an excellent racket that is enough to scare off the devil himself!) Why pianos on-stage and bells off? Perhaps because the chiming of bells and the naming of those who would chime them was, at the time of the *Fantastique*, highly regulated by law. A decree of the Comité de l'Intérieur, dated 28 August 1822, speaks to the rights of "the local police force" to "regulate the bells of the religious communities authorized to maintain chapels, and the bells installed in public churches."[32] Berlioz's *cloches derrière le théâtre,* like his burlesque parodies of the melody of the *Dies irae*, potentially resonate with sacrilege.[33]

They resonate as well with the "Othello paradigm" that is the subject of a recent and highly perceptive article by Katherine Kolb, who finds echoes of Shakespeare's tragedy in this symphony and throughout Berlioz's life and

[30] Berlioz, *Symphonie fantastique*, with the Anima Eterna Brugge conducted by Jos van Immerseel (Zig-Zag Territoires ZZG 100101; 2008).

[31] Mendelssohn, who was offended by the finale of the *Fantastique*, assumed that the pianos were intended to imitate the sound of bells; he seems not to have been aware of Berlioz's intention to use real bells. See Todd, *Mendelssohn*, 239.

[32] Blavignac, 439: "les droits de la police locale peuvent s'exercer sur les cloches des communautés religieuses autorisées à avoir des chapelles, comme sur les cloches placées dans les églises publiques."

[33] In *Le Figaro* of 4 December 1830, a writer suggested that Berlioz had here invented "irreverent music" ("la musique impie"). Four decades later, in the first edition of Grove, Edward Dannreuther wrote that "bloodthirsty delirious passion such as is here depicted" is more honored "in the breach than in the observance." See *A Dictionary of Music and Musicians*, ed. George Grove (London: Macmillan, 1879), vol. 1, 233.

work.[34] I would add that in Chateaubriand's *Génie du Christianisme* (1802–1803), which we know Berlioz read as a boy, because he copied certain passages of the work into his notebooks, and which we know he was thinking about on writing the *Fantastique*, because in the program he refers explicitly to Chateaubriand's "vague des passions" to describe the narrator's emotional fog, there is a chapter, called " Les Cloches" (part 4, chapter I), which includes a remark that Kolb might have cited to reinforce her point about Berlioz's intoxication with the vengeful Moor of Venice: "How many times, in the calm of the night," writes Chateaubriand, "has the funereal ringing of bells, sounding like the listless beating of a dying heart, not startled and frightened a woman committing adultery?"[35] I mention this sentence, of course, because it suggests to me a primary source for Berlioz's use of bells in the music of a devilish orgy. But I cannot *not* note that Chateaubriand speaks uniquely to the fear of the adulterous *woman*, the man in question presumably having nothing at all to fear, not even fear itself. I leave this subject with the final comment that, later in this section of the *Génie du Christianisme* (part 4, chapter XI), Chateaubriand describes a funeral service that includes the chanting of verses of the "hymne de la colère, *dies irae*"—further evidence that Berlioz's reading of Chateaubriand led to details of the *Fantastique* far more numerous and precise than the vagaries of the *vague des passions*.[36]

Berlioz's symphonic program was conceived, you will remember, on the basis of his passion for a woman whom he had never met, the Shakespearean actress Harriet Smithson, who led him to a senseless jealousy and, in the programmatical fiction, to a murderous revenge. In the symphony she is cast

[34] See Katherine Kolb, "Berlioz's *Othello*," in *The Musical Voyager: Berlioz in Europe*, ed. David Charlton and Katharine Ellis (Frankfurt am Main: Peter Lang, 2007), 241–62.

[35] *Génie du Christianisme*, Quatrième Partie, Livre Premier, Chapitre Premier: *Des cloches*. The entire passage reads as follows: "Et pourtant ce n'était pas là le caractère le plus remarquable du son des cloches; ce son avait mille relations secrètes avec nous. Combien de fois, dans le calme des nuits, les funèbres tintements d'une agonie, semblables aux lentes pulsations d'un cœur expirant, n'ont-ils point surpris l'oreille d'une épouse adultère? Combien de fois ne sont-ils point parvenus jusqu'à l'athée, qui, dans sa veille impie, osait peut-être écrire qu'il n'y a point de Dieu? La plus échappe de sa main; il compte avec effroi les coups de la mort, qui semblent lui dire: *Est-ce qu'il n'y appoint de Dieu?*"

[36] Quatrième Partie, Livre Premier, Chapitre XI: *Funérailles du guerrier, convoi des riches, coutumes, etc.* "Parlerons-nous de ces enterrements faits à la lueur des flambeaux, dans nos villes, de ces chapelles ardentes, de cette file prolongée de chars tendus de noir, de ces chevaux parés de plumes et de draperies funèbres, de ce profond silence, interrompu par les versets de l'hymne de la colère, *dies irae*?" Although he does not mention this detail, David Cairns, in *Berlioz: The Making of an Artist* (London: Penguin, 1999), 55–60, explains at length the tremendous impact Chateaubriand's work had on the young Berlioz.

as a victimizer to whom Berlioz imputes, as does Othello to Desdemona, the virtues of a whore. That Berlioz's jealousy of the real Smithson was unjustified was proven on another Berliozian "First Night"—that of his marriage to the actress in question. On the morrow of which, if I may be permitted to pursue the matter, he wrote to Franz Liszt with what I have always found to be an appallingly indiscrete report: "Vierge, tout ce qu'il y a de plus vierge."[37] What does it mean to tell your best friend that your newly wedded wife was a virgin? Is it innocent, inappropriate, inhumane? Patricia Cohen, professor of history at the University of California at Santa Barbara, who has written on the mistreatment of women in the nineteenth century, has suggested in private correspondence that Berlioz's letter puts an end to what must have been an ongoing conversation between the handsome young pianist, whose conquests would become legendary, and the overemotional composer, whom Hugh Macdonald has dubbed "no Don Juan."[38] Liszt must have argued that Smithson, like others of her profession, had succumbed to the charms of her admirers and leading men. In private, Berlioz, long suffering the pangs of disprized love, had hopefully imagined for her a purity the opposite of which he portrayed in the symphony. His comment to Liszt suggests that he had been right, as he puts it in the same letter, to listen "to the secret voice of his heart," because the prize he sought was pure.[39]

Two years and four days after the première of the *Symphonie fantastique*, Berlioz gave the revised version of the symphony linked to its newly created sequel, *Le Retour à la vie*, later baptized *Lélio*. The first performance of this two-part *Épisode de la vie d'un artiste* had a far greater impact than had the symphony alone in December 1830. For in December 1832 the country was no longer in the throes of revolution; the papers had more room for the arts. The performance of the symphony and the sequel began to generate in France the notion that Berlioz was not only mad but ill-educated—essentially because his melodies were not as symmetrical as the Palais de Versailles: this was a violation of a canon of excellence that had prevailed in French thought from at least François Ier to François Fétis, the latter specifically taken to task in the libretto of *Le Retour à la vie* for his perfectly contemporary views on the nature of beauty in art.

That libretto, which Berlioz called his first serious literary effort, his "coup

[37] *CG* vol. II, 119.

[38] *Selected Letters of Berlioz*, ed. Hugh Macdonald, trans. Roger Nichols (New York: Norton, 1997), x.

[39] In her letter to Louis-Philippe, which we have cited, Smithson, presuming the king might think the opposite, clearly suggests that her virtue is intact.

d'essai en littérature," is marked by several passages that Berlioz had earlier set down in letters—a sign of his self-conscious mixture here, as elsewhere, of life and art, and an instance of his constant habit of self-borrowing. The libretto is also marked by various evocations of Shakespeare, another life-long passion. The libretto, finally, offers a tremendous tirade against those who would edit, alter, or otherwise arrange the works of the masters. It is here that Fétis, who had made an edition of the Beethoven symphonies, comes in for excoriation as a self-centered and prejudiced theorist. Berlioz goes so far as to call him a "vieux libertin"—evidence, I think, for what remains in the literature an otherwise unsubstantiated rumor that Fétis had a hand in the breakup of Berlioz's engagement to the prurient pianist Camille Moke, and his own interest in her talents, musical and other.[40] Fétis is further castigated as one of those "blasphemers who dare to prey upon original works of art and to submit them to horrible mutilations, which they call *corrections* and *improvements*, and for which, they say, one needs an abundance of *good taste*."[41] That was Fétis's catchword, "taste" ("goût"); it is found throughout his widely read book of 1830, *La Musique mise à la portée de tout le monde*, which Berlioz and others ridiculed because its subtitle, "*exposé succinct de tout ce qui est nécessaire pour juger de cet art, et pour en parler sans l'avoir étudié*," in modern terms, was something akin to "music for dummies"—music, that is, for those who want to make pronouncements about it without making an effort to learn what it is *about*.

It took Fétis some twenty years to get over this public slap in the face, which had the effect (like Berlioz's even more vituperative portrait of Cherubini), of minimizing the importance of a musical giant, in some eyes, well into the twentieth century. Berlioz later came to terms with Fétis in mutual admiration of Gluck (and mutual mistrust of Wagner), and the work of Fétis is now well appreciated. But there is still much room for a modern critical study of the life and work of Cherubini, whose *least* important act was chasing Berlioz out of the library at the Conservatoire. In fact Berlioz always admired the Italian composer's sacred music, and it has been suggested to me that Berlioz may

[40] It was Adolphe Boschot who first suggested, I believe, that Fétis had a hand in the breakup of 1831. See Boschot, *Un Romantique sous Louis-Philippe: Hector Berlioz 1831–1842* (Paris: Plon, 1908), 35–36. There is stronger evidence for a later, intimate relationship, when Fétis was director of the Conservatoire de Bruxelles and Madame Pleyel its celebrated professor of piano.

[41] "[C]es profanateurs qui osent porter la main sur les ouvrages originaux, leur font subir d'horribles mutilations qu'ils appellent *corrections* et *perfectionnements*, pour lesquels, disent-ils, il faut *beaucoup de goût*." See *Lélio ou Le Retour à la vie* (*New Berlioz Edition*, vol. 7), ed. Peter Bloom (Kassel: Bärenreiter, 1992), 23.

even have taken over one of Cherubini's work habits, namely his conspicuously finicky way of pasting small sheets, or *collettes*, into manuscripts requiring correction.[42]

Let me make a final point about another first night—that on which the *Fantastique* was done with a revised *Lélio ou Le Retour à la vie* in Weimar, where Liszt held sway, on 21 February 1855. Berlioz was thrilled by that performance, as his letters overflowingly bear witness. He had had the narrator speak to the audience in front of the curtain, which was drawn in order to conceal behind it what he explicitly called the "invisible" orchestra and chorus. This was a graphic representation of the nature of the fiction, in which the narrator *imagines* his nightmarish fixation upon an unattainable woman and his return to life for the sake of his art.

I jump now to a passage from *Cosima Wagner's Diaries*, where Cosima, "the wife of Wagner's old age and the curator of his fame," as Jacques Barzun apostrophized her,[43] quotes the *Meister*'s thoughts about the forthcoming production of *Parsifal*: "Oh, I hate the thought of all those costumes and grease paint! When I think that characters like Kundry will now have to be dressed up, those dreadful artists' balls immediately spring into my mind. Having *created* the invisible orchestra, I now feel like *inventing* the invisible theatre!"[44] Seriously? Wagner did famously put the opera orchestra under the stage, at Bayreuth, where it can be seen by the conductor alone. But it was Berlioz who, in the original and revised versions of *Lélio ou Le Retour à la vie*, insisted that that for the dramatic presentation of his two-part *Épisode de la vie d'un artiste*, the players, the soloists, and the chorus must be *invisible*: seated on the stage, but hidden behind the curtain.[45] So it was *Berlioz* who invented the invisible orchestra, and a bit of the invisible theater as well.[46]

[42] I am grateful to Damien Colas, now studying Cherubini's autograph manuscripts, for suggesting this possibility. Paste-overs, of course, were not new to the nineteenth century.

[43] See Barzun, "Paris in 1830," in *Music in Paris in the Eighteen-Thirties*, ed. Peter Bloom (Stuyvesant, New York: Pendragon, 1987), 17.

[44] *Cosima Wagner's Diaries*, vol. II, ed. Martin Gregor-Dellin and Dietrich Mack, trans. Geoffrey Skelton (New York: Harcourt Brace Jovanovich, 1980), 154 (23 September 1878; my emphasis).

[45] See the stage directions in the 1832 and 1855 versions of the work, printed in the *New Berlioz Edition*, vol. 7 (see note 41), 232.

[46] In fact Wagner was not entirely serious: after saying he wished to invent the invisible theater, he then said (as we know from the same passage in the *Diaries*) that he wanted to invent the *inaudible orchestra* as well! For once we find Berlioz being serious while Wagner was horsing around. Camille Saint-Saëns reminds us, in "Wagner, *L'Anneau du Niebelung*

Richard Wagner was and remains a figure on the world stage far more visible than Berlioz, for reasons that are musical, historical, and political. But on the first night of the Kelly Conference, when this paper was read, it was gratifying that Berlioz had in a sense been seen.

et les Représentations de Bayreuth (août 1876)," reprinted in Saint-Saëns, *Regards sur mes contemporains*, ed. Yves Gérard (Paris: Bernard Coutaz, 1990), 70, that the invisible orchestra had already been imagined if not realized, at the time of the French Revolution, by André Grétry. Indeed, in Grétry's *Mémoires* (nouvelle édition, Liège: Vaillant-Carmanne, 1914), we read this: "Je voudrais que l'orchestre fût voilé et qu'on n'aperçût ni les musiciens, ni les lumières des pupitres du côté des spectateurs" ("I should like that the orchestra be hidden and that from the auditorium one see neither the musicians nor the lamps of their music racks").

Part II

The Musical Traditions and Influence of Benevento

Surge, Petre!

Sets of Chants for St. Peter in Benevento, Peterborough, and Some Places in Between

DAVID HILEY

In the course of some recent work on the antiphoner of the thirteenth century from the Benedictine abbey of Peterborough now kept in Magdalene College, Cambridge,[1] I realized that not only the cycles of chants for the Anglo-Saxon saints represented quite strongly in the Peterborough antiphoner were of interest, but also that the chants in that book for the feast days of St. Peter were relatively little known. It is not surprising that there should be special chants for St. Peter in this antiphoner, given his status as one of the co-patrons of the monastery. Most of the chants for St. Peter that we usually encounter in liturgical books belong to an old established layer or layers, and new sets are quite rare. Nevertheless, new chants were composed not only for saints of only local or regional significance, but also, occasionally, for the great universal saints whose liturgies had been fixed at an earlier period.

On encountering such chants in a later source such as the Peterborough antiphoner, natural curiosity drives one to look further and further along the paths of transmission, and before long one is checking concordances as far back as the record goes. In the present paper I shall follow the path in

[1] David Hiley, "The Saints Venerated in Medieval Peterborough as Reflected in the Antiphoner Cambridge, Magdalene College, F.4.10," in *Essays on the History of English Music in Honour of John Caldwell: Sources, Style, Performance, Historiography*, ed. Emma Hornby and David Maw (Woodbridge: Boydell Press, 2010), 22–46.

reverse, or rather in the proper chronological sequence, starting with Rome and Francia in the ninth century or thereabouts and tracing just one or two of several possible paths, until I arrive at Peterborough in the thirteenth century. In doing so I shall say a little about what sort of melodies were sung, since it is always particularly satisfying to give a musical dimension to a transmission pattern, to find, if possible, features of melodic style that distinguish this group from that one and support what we know of their chronology and geography.

THE THREE FEASTS

There are three feasts of St. Peter whose chants we need to consider. The oldest is that on June 29, for Saints Peter and Paul. The other two feasts, that is, the feast of St. Peter's Chains, "Sancti Petri ad Vincula," on August 1, and the feast of St. Peter's Chair, "Cathedra Sancti Petri," on February 22, were not given proper office chants as early as the main feast. For present purposes it is unnecessary to go into the history of the feasts, and we may simply concentrate on the sets of chants that turn up in books from the ninth century onward. So the two lesser offices will not occupy us at first. In the twelve manuscripts edited by Hesbert in *Corpus Antiphonalium Officii,* only manuscript F (ParisBN lat. 12584) has a proper office for the Cathedra, and only manuscripts L (Biblioteca capitolare, 21) and R (Zurich, Zentralbibliothek, Rh. 28) have a limited number of proper chants for the Vincula feast.[2]

THE MORE COMMON OLD ROMAN AND GREGORIAN ANTIPHONS

The antiphons in the twelve manuscripts of Hesbert's *CAO* fall into some interesting patterns. (The tables I show here are accessible on the internet at the Regensburg chant website, under the rubric "Hesbert at a glance." I have rearranged and supplemented them for this paper). I shall not discuss all items on the tables but concentrate on significant groups and series.

Table 1 sets out the antiphons for Lauds in Hesbert's manuscripts, supplemented by the Albi manuscript (Albi, Bibliothèque municipale Rochegude, MS 14; hereafter Albi 44) and the Old Roman tradition.

As so often, the series in the oldest source, *CAO* C (ParisBN lat. 17436), does not seem representative of a standard exemplar, although the Monza manuscript has the same series, and St.-Denis has most of it. If Lipphardt's reconstruction is correct, then the Metz tonary (Metz, Bibliothèque municipale,

[2] René-Jean Hesbert, *Corpus antiphonalium officii*, vol. 1: *Manuscripti "cursus romanus,"* vol. 2: *Manuscripti "cursus monasticus"* (Rome: Herder, 1963 and 1965).

Table 1. Lauds antiphons for St. Peter in CAO manuscripts, plus Albi (AL) 44 and manuscripts of the Old Roman (OR) use

101	**Petrus & Paulus**	C	G	B	E	M	V	H	R	D	F	S	L	AL	OR
L-A	P. et Iohannes ascendebant	1				1				1				1	1
	Argentum et aurum non est	2				2				2				2	2
	Dixit angelus ad Petrum	3				3				3				3	3
	Misit dnus angelum suum	4				4	4			4				4	4
	Tu es P. et super hanc	5		5	5	5	2	5	5				4	5	5
	P. amas me pasce oves			1	1		5*+	1	1			3	2		
	Symon Iohannis diligis me			2				2	2				1		
	Significavit dnus P.			3	2			3	4				5		
	Ego pro te rogavi P.			4	3		1	4	3						
	Solve iubente deo terrarum				4					5					
	Tu es pastor ovium						3								
	Beatus P. apostolus vidit										1	1			
	Dixit Symon P. dne										2	2			
	Cum respexisset P.										3				
	Cum esset P. in cruce										4				
	Beatus P. dum penderet										5				
	Gloriosi principes terre											4			
	P. apostolus et Paulus doctor											5			
	Caro et sanguis non revelavit												3		

MS 351), a source absent in *CAO*, agrees with *CAO's* manuscripts B (Bamberg, Staatsbibliothek, lit. 23), H (St. Gall, Stiftsbibliothek 390–391), and R.[3] Unfortunately the Mont-Renaud manuscript has a lacuna and cannot be included in this survey. But if we add Albi 44, which is in many ways the most archaic witness of the Frankish office, we find it agrees with *CAO* C.[4] This becomes particularly significant in view of the Old-Roman series.[5]

The patterns among the Matins antiphons are even clearer; see Table 2.

[3] Walter Lipphardt, *Der karolingische Tonar von Metz*, Liturgiewissenschaftliche Quellen und Forschungen 43 (Münster-Westfalen: Aschendorff, 1965).

[4] John A. Emerson, *Albi, Bibliothèque municipale Rochegude, Manuscript 14: A Complete Ninth-Century Gradual and Antiphoner from Southern France*, ed. Lila Collamore, Wissenschaftliche Abhandlungen/Musicological Studies 77 (Ottawa: Institute of Mediaeval Music, 2002).

[5] *Biblioteca Apostolica Vaticana Archivio S. Pietro B 79: Antifonario della Basilica di S. Pietro (Sec. XII)*, ed. Bonifacio Giacomo Baroffio and Soo Jung Kim, Musica Italiae Liturgica 1 (Rome: Torre d'Orfeo, 1995).

Table 2. Matins antiphons for St. Peter in CAO, Albi and Old Roman use

101	Petrus & Paulus	C	G	B	E	M	V	H	R	D	F	S	L	AL	OR
M-A	In omnem terram exivit sonus	1												1	a1*
	Clamaverunt iusti et dnus	2												2	(a2)
	Constitues eos principes	3												3	(a3)
	Principes populorum congre-	4												4	a4
	Dedisti hereditatem timenti-	5												5	a5
	Annuntiaverunt opera dei	6												6	a6
	Exaltabuntur cornua iusti	7												7	a7
	Lux orta est iusto alleluia	8												8	a8
	Custodiebant testimonia eius	9												9	a9
	P. et Iohannes ascendebant			1	1		1	1	1		1		1		
	Claudus quidam cum vidisset			2	2		2	2	2		2		2		
	Argentum et aurum non est			3	3		3	3	3		3		3		
	In nomine Ihesu Christi			4	4		4	4	4		4		4		
	Exiliens claudus et ambulabat			5	5		5	5	5		5		5		
	Vidit populus claudum			6	6		6	6	6		6		6		
	P. autem/quidem servabatur			7	7		7	7	7		7		7		
	Dixit angelus ad P.			8	8		8	8	8		10	11	8		
	Misit dnus angelum suum			9	9			9	9		12	10a	9		
	In plateis ponebantur infirmi					1				1	C1	1			
	Ait P. principibus					2				2	C2	2			
	P. apostolus dixit paralitico					3				3	C3	3			
	Factum est ut quedam					4				4	C4	4			
	Adveniente P. circumstete-					5				5	C5	5			
	Ponens P. genua sua					6				6	C6	6			
	Cornelius centurio vir religiosus					7				7	C7	7			
	Aperiens Petrus os suum dixit					8				8	C8	8			
	Angelus dni astitit					9					9				
	Cum esset P. in cruce						9								
	Solve iubente deo terrarum							10	10			10			
	P. apostolus et Paulus doctor							11	11				c		
	Beatus P. apostolus vidit							12		11			12		
	Quodcumque ligaveris							c			Cc				
	O P. pastor summe et Paule								12						
	Tu es pastor ovium princeps								c				10		b6
	Adhuc loquente P. cecidit									9	C9	9			
	Dixit Symon P. do-									10					
	Dixit Symon P. ad Hie-									12					
	Astiterunt iusti									c					
	Erat P. dormiens inter										8				
	Exiens P. apostolus										11				

Table 2, continued

101 Petrus & Paulus	C	G	B	E	M	V	H	R	D	F	S	L	AL	OR
Gloriosi principes terre										c				
Beatus P. dum penderet											12			
Tu es P. et super hanc											c			
Ego pro te rogavi P.												11		b2
Domine tecum paratus sum										C10				
Felices sancti apostole lacrime										C11				
De tuo principatus										C12				
Si diligis me Symon Petre														b1
Caro et sanguis non revelavit														b3
P. amas me pasce oves														b4
Simon Iohannis diligis me														b5
Tu es Christus filius dei vivi														b7
Dixit Iesus Petro tibi dabo														b8
Cui claves regni ipsi commendat														b9

In a paper read at the meeting of the "Cantus Planus" group in 2009, László Dobszay drew attention to the antiphons common to manuscript C, that is, Hesbert's "Compendiensis," Albi 44, and the Old Roman repertory—he was comparing them globally, not feast by feast—and he concluded, "I think that the bulk of the material common to Albi 44 and the Old Roman manuscript is none other than the basic repertory transmitted from Rome to the Frankish liturgy. This statement is, of course, not equally valid for all individual items. In the common repertory there may be pieces that entered Rome from the Frankish Gregorian tradition, but the proportion of such cases is negligible, and does not negate the general thesis."[6] The Peter antiphons certainly support Dobszay's thesis.

The antiphons in the other Gregorian manuscripts bear striking witness to the high degree of new composition that took place in the ninth and tenth centuries, and sometimes later as well. Exploring the reasons for this, not to mention the ways in which it was done, would take too much space here, but one of the main reasons must have been that the chant texts were felt to be not sufficiently specific. It is the old story of "properization," or, "personalization," as one might say in the case of the Sanctorale. Table 3 gives the texts of three sets of the Lauds antiphons:

[6] László Dobszay, "Comments on Albi 44," paper read at the Fifteenth Meeting of the IMS Study Group "Cantus Planus," Dobogókő, Hungary, August 23–29, 2009.

Table 3. Lauds antiphon texts

C, M, AL, OR
4287 Petrus et Ioannes ascendebant in templum ad horam orationis nonam.
1480 Argentum et aurum non est mihi; quod autem habeo, hoc tibi do.
2268 Dixit angelus ad Petrum: Circumdate vestimentum tuum et sequere me.
3783 Misit Dominus angelum suum, et liberavit me de manu Herodis, alleluia.
5208 Tu es Petrus, et super hanc petram aedificabo Ecclesiam meam.
B, H, R
(5208 Tu es Petrus)
4281 Petre, amas me? Pasce oves meas. Tu scis, Domine, quia amo te.
4960 Simon Ioannis, diligis me plus his? Tu scis, Domine, quia amo te.
4947 Significavit Dominus Petro qua morte clarificaturus esset Deum, alleluia.
2583 Ego pro te rogavi, Petre, ut non deficiat fides tua; et tu aliquando conversus confirma fratres tuos.
F
1656 Beatus Petrus apostolus vidit sibi Christum occurrere; adorans eum et dixit: Domine, quo vadis? Venio Romam iterum crucifigi.
2312 Dixit Simon Petrus: Domine, ad quem ibimus? verba vitae habes; et nos credimus et cognovimus quia tu es Christus Filius Dei, alleluia.
2030 Cum respexisset Petrus crucem, lacrimas fundebat prae gaudio: Non sum dignus caput sursum ponere, sed declinare vultum in terra, alleluia.
2001 Cum esset Petrus in cruce, orabat Dominum dicens: Gratias tibi ago, Pastor bone, qui me ad hanc gloriam perducere dignatus es; peto ergo ut oves quas tradidisti mihi participentur mecum de gratia tua in sempiternum.
1657 Beatus Petrus, dum penderet in cruce, alacri vultu Dominum deprecabuntur: Domine Iesu Christe, commendo tibi oves quas tradidisti mihi.

The set in the Compendiensis, Albi, and Old Roman antiphoners only forms a unit in the sense that its texts refer to Peter, nothing more. The first two texts are from Chapter 3 of the Acts of the Apostles, the healing of the lame man; the third and fourth antiphons spring forward to Chapter 12, where Peter is freed from prison; and the last antiphon is based on the well-known words of Christ in the gospel.

The antiphons in *CAO* manuscripts B, H, and R all refer to the gospel text alone and thus form a quite coherent set.

Manuscript F, from St.-Maur-des-Fossés, goes a different way and takes up the theme of Peter's crucifixion. The first antiphon introduces the theme by paraphrasing the verse from the Gospel of St. John, Chapter 13, verse 36, with

Peter's famous question "Quo vadis?" In the gospel Christ answers, "Whither I go, thou canst not follow me now; but thou shalt follow me afterwards." The chant text refers openly to Christ's crucifixion, which foreshadows the fate of Peter himself. Now this is found not in the New Testament but in the apocryphal Acts of St. Peter.[7] So too is the topic of the third antiphon, Peter's being crucified head downward.[8] It will be noticed how long these texts are in comparison to the previous sets.

Table 4. Matins antiphon texts separated by manuscript tradition, listed with CAO numbers or "CC" if it is absent from CAO

C, AL, OR
3262 In omnem terram exivit sonus eorum, et in fines orbis terrae verba eorum.
1823 Clamaverunt iusti, et Dominus exaudivit eos.
1902 Constitues eos principes super omnem terram; memores erunt nominis tui, Domine.
4379 Principes populorum congregati sunt cum Deo Abraham.
2133 Dedisti haereditatem timentibus nomen tuum, Domine.
1429 Annuntiaverunt opera Dei, et facta eius intellexerunt.
2757 Exaltabuntur cornua iusti, alleluia.
3651 Lux orta est iusto, alleluia, rectis corde laetitia, alleluia.
2083 Custodiebant testimonia eius et praecepta eius, alleluia.
B, E, V, H, R, L
4287 Petrus et Ioannes ascendebant in templum ad horam orationis nonam.
1829 Claudus quidam, cum vidisset Petrum et Ioannem, coepit rogare eos, ut eleemosynam acciperet.
1480 Argentum et aurum non est mihi; quod autem habeo, hoc tibi do.
3260 In nomine Iesu Christi Nazareni: Surge, et ambula in pace.
2803 Exsiliens claudus et ambulabat, et intravit cum illis, ambulans et laudans Deum.
5416 Vidit populus claudum, ambulantem et laudantem Deum; et repleti sunt stupore et extasi in eo quod contigerat illi.
4286 Petrus autem servabatur in carcere, et oratio fiebat pro eo sine intermissione ab ecclesia ad Deum.
2268 Dixit angelus ad Petrum: Circumda te vestimentum tuum et sequere me.
3783 Misit Dominus angelum suum, et liberavit me de manu Herodis, alleluia.

Continued next page

[7] Montague Rhodes James, *The Apocryphal New Testament, Being the Apocryphal Gospels, Acts, Epistles, and Apocalypses* (Oxford: Clarendon Press, 1926), 333.

[8] James, *Apocryphal New Testament*, 334.

Table 4, continued

M, D, F, S
3271 In plateis ponebantur infirmi in lectulis, ut veniente Petro saltem umbra illius obumbraret quem quam illorum, et liberarentur ab infirmitatibus suis.
1317 Ait Petrus principibus sacerdotum: Iesus, quem vos interemistis suspendentes in ligno, hunc Deus suscitavit, et principem ac Salvatorem exaltavit ad dandam paenitentiam in remissionem peccatorum.
4283 Petrus apostolus dixit paralytico: Aenea, sanet te Dominus Iesus Christus; surge et sterne tibi. Qui continuo surrexit, et omnes qui videbant conversi sunt ad Dominum.
2844 Factum est ut quaedam discipula nomine Thabita, plena operibus bonis et eleemosynis, infirmata moreretur. Mierunt autem discipuli ad Petrum, rogantes: Ne pigreteris venire usque ad nos.
1295 Adveniente Petro, circumsteterunt illum omnes viduae, flentes et ostendentes tunicas et vestes quas faciebat illis Dorcas.
4304 Ponens Petrus genua sua oravit, et conversus ad corpus dixit: Tabita, surge. At illa aperuit oculos, et viso Petro resedit; dansque illi manum erexit eam, et sanctis ac viduis assignavit vivam.
1932 Cornelius centurio, vir religiosus ac timens Deum, vidit manifeste angelum Dei dicentem sibi: Corneli, mitte et accersi Simonem qui cognominatur Petrus; hic dicet tibi quid te oporteat facere.
1445 Aperiens Petrus os suum dixit: In veritate comperi, quia non est personarum acceptor Deus, sed in omni gente qui timet Deum et operatur iustitiam acceptus est illi.
1411 Angelus Domini astitit, et lumen refulsit in habitaculo carceris; percussoque latere Petri excitavit eum dicens: Surge velociter. Et ceciderunt catenae de manibus eius.
OR
4885 Si diligis me, Simon Petre, pasce oves meas, alleluia alleluia. (C)
2583 Ego pro te rogavi, Petre, ut non deficiat fides tua; et tu aliquando conversus confirma fratres tuos. *
1774 Caro et sanguis non revelavit tibi, sed Pater meus qui est in caelis.
CC Petre, amas me, pasce oves. Tu scis, Domine, quia amo te.
4960 Simon Ioannis, diligis me plus his? Tu scis, quia amo te, Domine.
1167 Tu es pastor ovium, princeps apostolorum, tibi tradidit Deus claves regni caelorum. *
5202 Tu es Christus, Filius Dei vivi. Et tu beatus, Simon Bar Iona. (C)
CC Dixit Iesus Petro, tibi dabo claves regni caelorum.
CC Cui claves regni, ipsi commendat ovile; sic Dominus curam commendavit Petro, alleluia.

The texts of the Matins antiphons reinforce these points (Table 4).

The first set, in the Compendiensis, Albi, and Old Roman antiphoners, does not refer to Peter at all; in fact, most of the antiphons in the set were used as Commune antiphons. In BAV Archivio San Pietro B79 the first is given as an incipit, with the instruction "*require in plurimorum apostolorum*." London BL Add. 29988 gives all three in full.

The second set, in six of Hesbert's sources (B, E [Ivrea, Biblioteca capitolare 106], V [Verona, Biblioteca capitolare, 98], H, R, and L), has six antiphons about the healing of the lame man and three about Peter's release from prison.

The lengthy texts in *CAO* manuscripts M (Monza, Tesoro della Basilica San Giovanni Battista C.12/75), D (ParisBN lat. 17296), F, and S (LondonBL Add. 30850) have been attributed to Hucbald of St.-Amand.[9] There is some dispute about which feast Hucbald composed them for. In the antiphoner Valenciennes, Bibliothèque municipale, 114, from St.-Amand, they are given on the main feast day, and several other sources follow this practice. The *CAO* manuscripts M, D, and S have them for the main feast, R has them for the Vincula feast, F has them for the Cathedra feast and as incipits ad Vincula.

The antiphons of this *In plateis* set are all paraphrases of the Acts of the Apostles. Antiphons 1 and 3 for the First Nocturn concern Peter's healing of the paralytic Aeneas in Lydda, from Chapter 9, the three for the Second Nocturn relate to later events in Chapter 9, while the centurion Cornelius appears in Chapter 10. The last antiphon is again about Peter's release from prison. The text of the ninth antiphon seems somewhat disconnected but always forms part of the set. These are all fully rounded texts with a narrative purpose, quite different from the pithy statements in the oldest set.

There is one more set of antiphons in Table 4: those found only in the Old Roman manuscripts. These books have a double Matins, with a second set of nine antiphons and eight responsories, divided as usual into three nocturns.[10] This second set in the Old Roman antiphons is unusual. Only two of the texts are found in the wider Gregorian circulation (each marked with an asterisk in Table 4). *Caro et sanguinis* is rare but does turn up elsewhere. Two texts are known otherwise only in *CAO* C (marked with [C] in Table 4), and three are peculiar to the Old Roman books. These texts form a fairly coherent set based on the well-known gospel verses. As such the set resembles the common Gregorian set for Lauds.

[9] Rembert Weakland, "The compositions of Hucbald," *Études grégoriennes* 3 (1959), 155–62. For the wider context in which Hucbald was composing, see Jean-François Goudesenne, "Nouvelles perspectives sur le rôle des abbayes de Saint-Amand, de Saint-Thierry de Reims et de l'oeuvre d'Hucbald dans l'ordonnance régulier des modes dans la composition musicale (850–900)," *Études grégoriennes* 30 (2002), 127–52.

[10] Joseph Dyer, "The Double Office at St. Peter's Basilica on *Dominica de Gaudete*," in *Music in Medieval Europe: Studies in Honour of Bryan Gillingham*, ed. Terence Bailey and Alma Santosuosso (Aldershot: Ashgate, 2007), 200–219.

ANTIPHON MELODIES

The obvious explanation for this state of affairs would be that the Franks first adopted a Roman set of antiphons but then replaced them. The period when this happened seems at first sight to have been quite late. Our two ninth-century sources agree with Rome. It is the tenth-century manuscripts that diverge.

In this situation it is hardly surprising that the melodies of the antiphons also indicate that the Roman example, whatever that was, was altered quite considerably. In fact there is good evidence among the Peter chants for something demonstrated by Edward Nowacki[11] that typical Old Roman melodies had counterparts in typical Gregorian melodies, but that there was no one-to-one correspondence in the texts for which these typical melodies were used.

It is not possible here to give more than a few examples in full. For examples of a match between Old Roman and Gregorian one could point to the mode 7 antiphons *Confortatus es principatus eorum* and *Dirupisti domine vincula mea* in Nowacki's type G.6, which matches type A4 in the classified edition by Dobszay and Szendrei;[12] another pair, *Argentum et aurum* and *Misit dominus angelum suum*, are in Nowacki's type G.4 and Dobszay and Szendrei's type B.

As examples of the differences, one could cite four antiphons that fall under Nowacki's type G.1: *Annunciaverunt opere dei*, *Tu es paster ovium*, *Cui claves regni*, and *Collocet eos dominus*. One of these texts is not encountered in Gregorian sources. The common Gregorian settings of the other three are in mode 8 but fall into different melodic groups. In the edition by Dobszay and Szendrei they are in types B1, D2, and C6 respectively.

The Gregorian melody that corresponds to Nowacki's G.1 is Dobszay and Szendrei's A3, which is used not for *Tu es pastor ovium* but for *Tu es Petrus* (See Example 1).

Conversely, if we look at the Peter antiphons in Dobszay and Szendrei's type D2, they have different Old Roman melodies. The one that corresponds to Gregorian D2 is Nowacki's G.10, which he gives in two variants (Example 2).

The second series of Matins antiphons in the Old Roman sources uses typical melodies in the same way as the first series. It will be recollected that some of the texts were not known in Francia, which suggests that this second series was a later development—though how late, I do not know. But there are no new melodies here.

[11] Edward Nowacki, "The Gregorian Office Antiphons and the Comparative Method," *Journal of Musicology* 4 (1985), 243–75.

[12] László Dobszay and Janka Szendrei, *Antiphonen*, Monumenta Monodica Medii Aevi 5 (Kassel: Bärenreiter, 1999).

Example 1. Tu es pastor *and* Tu es Petrus *in Old Roman and Gregorian versions*

Example 2. OR and Gregorian D2

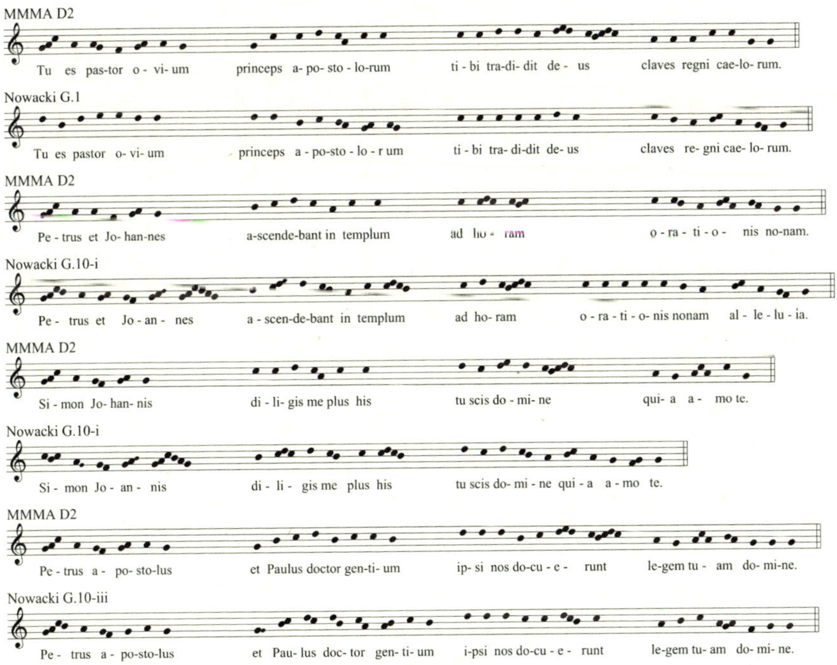

All this corroborates the thesis that the Franks took the Roman tradition, texts, and melodies as a starting point but recast them very substantially, presumably during the ninth century. We have hints of what was going on in Amalar's writings, as has often been discussed.[13] In Rome, too, time did not stand still.

RESPONSORIES

I shall not spend as much time on the responsories, partly because the selection in the early sources does not vary so much (see Table 5).

At the end of the table there are two responsories from the second Matins series in the Old Roman books, which look like a later development. But there is a fairly large common group, even if the order is not constant. Most of the modal assignments are also the same. Among the most commonly found pieces, however, two turn up with different melodies in Old Roman and Gregorian manuscripts. *Ego pro te rogavi Petre* and *Petre amas me tu scis* are both in mode 7 in the Old Roman tradition, but *Ego pro te* is in either mode 3 or 4 and *Petre amas* is in mode 4 in the Gregorian tradition.

In their introduction to the forthcoming edition of responsories for *Monumenta Monodica*, Dobszay and Szendrei have the following to say about *Ego pro te*, "In the OR antiphonary B 79 this very strange piece has a typical 7th-mode melody. Some Gregorian versions start in the middle range and join to it a 3rd-mode verse (Central Europe, Benevento, Piacenza, etc.). Other sources start a fourth lower and combine it with a 4th-mode verse (Franciscans, Cistercians, France, Sarum, Worcester, Utrecht, etc.). These modal variants (also the 5th-mode variant of Aquileia/Kranj) come together at the syllable 'confir*ma*.'"

Example 3 gives a representative German version in mode 3, with most cadences on A. Benevento, Archivio capitolare, 21 has a slightly different opening but understands the modality of the melody in the same way. Other sources in mode 3 make their cadences on G, not A. (I have taken the version in the forthcoming *Monumenta Monodica* edition.) Lucca (Biblioteca capitolare Feliniana e Biblioteca Arcivescovile, 601), pitches most of the piece a fifth lower (or a fourth lower) and has the mode 4 verse tone. None of the typical turns of phrase for responsories in modes 3 or 4 are to be found here.

[13] See, for example, Michel Huglo, "Les Remaniements de l'Antiphonaire grégorien au IXe siècle: Hélisachar, Agobard, Amalaire," in *Culto cristiano, politica imperiale carolingia: XVIII Convegno internazionale di studi sulla spiritualità medievale* (Todi: Presso l'Accademia Tudertina, 1979), 87–120 (reprinted in Michel Huglo, *Les sources du plain-chant et de la musique médiévale* [Aldershot: Ashgate, 2004]).

Table 5. Matins responsories for St. Peter in CAO, Albi, and Old Roman use

101 Petrus & Paulus	C	G	B	E	M	V	H	R	D	F	S	L	AL	OR
M-R Symon Petre antequam de	1		1	1	1	1	1	1	1	1	1	6	1	a2
Si diligis me Symon Petre	2		2	2	2	2	2	2	3	2	2	3	7	al
Tu es Petrus et super hanc	3		3	3	3	3	3	3	5	3	3	5	2	a4
Dne si tu es iube me	4		4	4	4	4	4	5	6	4	4	9	5	a3
Surge P. et indui te	5		6	5	5	5	5	6	7	5	5	10	10	a5
Tu es pastor ovium princeps	6		5	6	6	7	6	8	8	6	6	8	11	a6
Quem dicunt homines esse	7		7	7	7	8	7	9	9	8	9	4	3	a7
Ego pro te rogavi P. non	8		8	8	8	12	8	11	2	7	7	7	6	bl
Beatus es Symon P. quia	9								10				4	b2
P. amas me tu scis	10		9	11	9	9	10	12	4	12	8	2	8	b3
Symon Iohannis diligis me	11											1	9	a8
Solve iubente deo terrarum	12			9		10	9	7	11	9	11	11	12	b4
Qui regni claves et curam	13			10		11	11	10	12	10	12	12		b5
P. et Iohannes ascendebant	14													
Dum esset P. in cruce				12		6				IV		15		
Isti sunt due olive						13	12							b8
Beatus es Symon Bar Iona								4		11				
Cornelius centurio vir									IV			16		
Quodcumque ligaveris									13					
O claviger regni celorum											10			
Hodie Rome duo principes												13		
Ducti sunt P. et Paulus												14		
Isti viventes in carne														b6
Isti sunt duo viri misericordie														b7

Example 3. R. Ego pro te rogavi

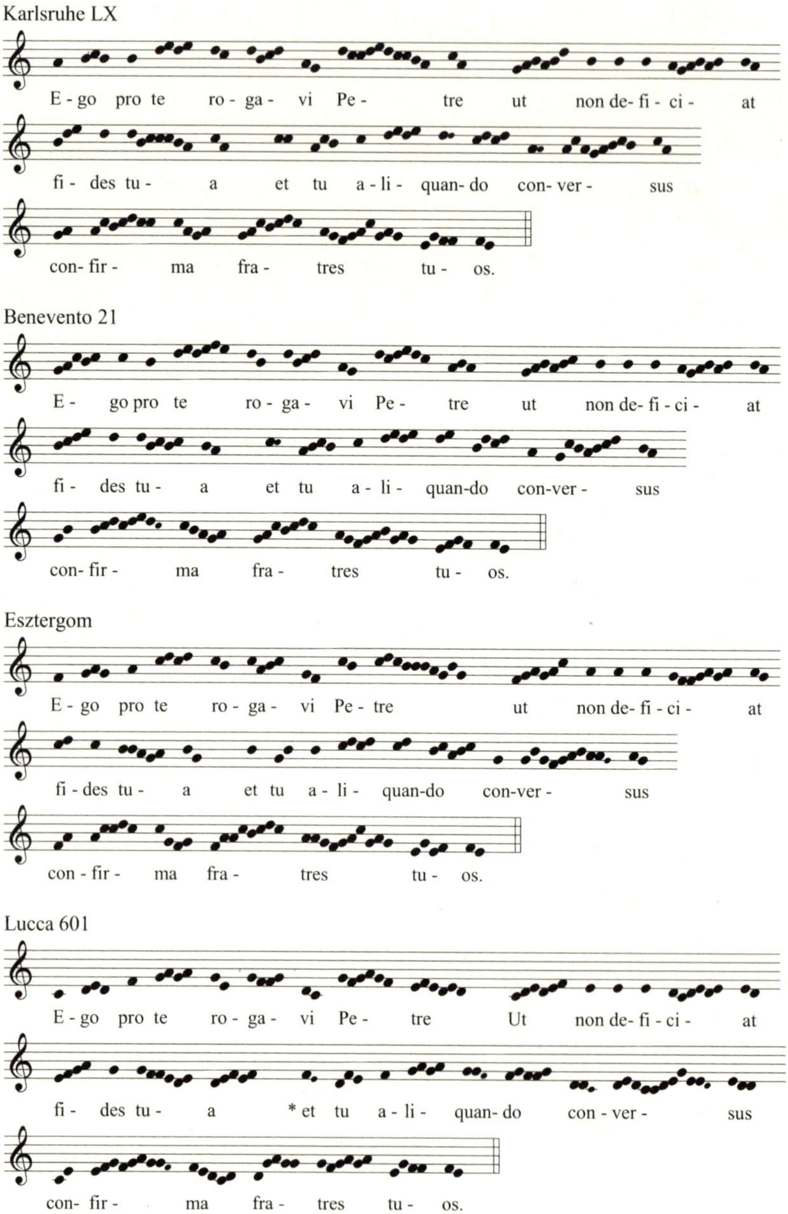

This raises the suspicion that a rather unusual melody which the Franks found difficult to place on the stave was recast in normal 7th-mode fashion in the Old Roman tradition.

On the other hand, there is no obvious problem with the modality of *Petre amas*; they are simply two different melodies. We may understand the situation better when the Old Roman responsories in E mode have been more thoroughly investigated.

Just as two of the Old Roman responsories are unknown elsewhere, so too are a couple of the Beneventan responsories peculiar to Beneventan use. These are *Hodie Rome duo principes* and *Ducti sunt Petrus et Paulus*. What is more, they do not use classical Gregorian turns of phrase. I have not sifted through all the responsories in Beneventan manuscripts and so cannot say if these are typically Beneventan melodies, perhaps from some old local stratum (see Example 4 and, below, Example 5).

Example 4a. Hodie Rome

Continued next page

Example 4a, continued

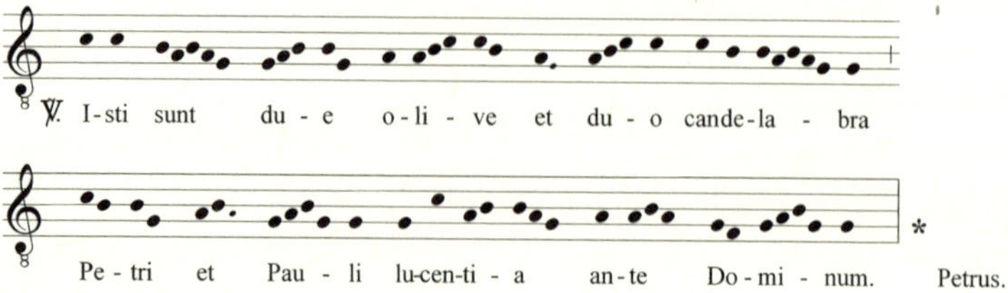

Example 4b. Ducti sunt

It would be interesting to pursue the Beneventan selection further, but space forbids this on the present occasion. At least one may draw attention to the interesting set of chants in Benevento, Biblioteca capitolare, 21 for the Vincula feast. No fewer than five of the responsories are unknown elsewhere. (All but the first use the traditional Gregorian verse tone.) They are *Quid dormis*

Petre vinculatus (mode 3), *Ut placeat* [placeret] *Judeis Herodes* (2), *Cum productus esset Herodes* (1), *Angelus Domini astitit et lumen* (8), and *Reversus ad se Petrus egressus de carcere* (2).

LATER SETS OF ANTIPHONS AND RESPONSORIES

The well-known set of Matins antiphons by Hucbald beginning with the antiphon *In plateis* was seen on Table 4. This set is one of the earliest that is ordered numerically by mode. Musically they are "post-Gregorian" in style. That is a very broad generalization, by which are meant such features as the use of the full modal octave, where antiphons in authentic modes reach the octave above the finalis and antiphons in plagal modes reach both the fourth below and the fifth above the finalis. All but two of Hucbald's antiphons do this. In four of them the ending from below, sometimes called the "Gallican" ending, is employed. This is the oldest set of chants for St. Peter that is numerically ordered. But it is not the only one. Without claiming to have carried out an exhaustive search, I have come across others that are concentrated to some extent in Norman and English sources (see Table 6).

Table 6. New sets of chants for St. Peter

<table>
<tr><td rowspan="3">A. series</td><td>In plateis</td><td>main feast, Matins</td><td>Winchester</td><td>Sarum</td><td>Jumièges</td><td>Worcester</td><td>Peterborough</td></tr>
<tr><td>Pontificalis apex</td><td>Cathedra, Matins</td><td>Winchester</td><td>Sarum</td><td>Jumièges</td><td>Worcester</td><td>Peterborough</td></tr>
<tr><td>Ethereum patrem</td><td>Cathedra, Lauds</td><td>Winchester</td><td></td><td></td><td></td><td>Peterborough</td></tr>
<tr><td rowspan="2">R. series</td><td>Misit impius</td><td>Vincula</td><td>Winchester</td><td>Sarum</td><td>Jumièges</td><td></td><td>Peterborough</td></tr>
<tr><td>Captivare volens (non-numerical)</td><td>Cathedra</td><td>Winchester</td><td></td><td></td><td></td><td>Peterborough</td></tr>
</table>

Winchester — *The Monastic Breviary of Hyde Abbey*, ed. J.B.L. Tolhurst (London: Henry Bradshaw Society), 6 vols. 1932–1942

Sarum — *Antiphonale Sarisburiense*, ed. Frere, etc.

Jumièges — Rouen, Bibl. municipale, 248 (A.339)

Worcester — Worcester Cathedral, Chapter Library, F.160 (*Paleographie Musicale* XII)

Peterborough — Cambridge, Magdalene College, F.4.10

To them should also be added another series of responsories, this time non-numerical, for the Cathedra Petri, beginning with the responsory *Captivare volens*, found only in the Peterborough antiphoner (Cambridge, Magdalene College, F.4.10). So this antiphoner has a particularly rich provision of post-Carolingian chants for the various feasts of St. Peter.

THE ANTIPHON SERIES PONTIFICALIS APEX

The series of antiphons for the Cathedra feast beginning *Pontificalis apex* is in the Hyde breviary (Oxford, Bodleian Library, Rawlinson lit. e. 1* and Gough lit. 8); Sarum books; Rouen, Bibliothèque municipale, 248 from Jumièges; and in the Worcester and Peterborough antiphoners.[14] It begins with a direct reference to Peter's Chair, the *cathedra*:

Pontificalis apex	veneratur iurae cathedrae
quam primum meritis	Petrus conscendit herilis.

(The highest rank of the priesthood [the papacy] is revered by right of the bishop's throne, which Peter, the first of all, ascended as the one worthy to be master.)

Despite the preponderance here of monastic series with thirteen antiphons, it looks as if the original series numbered only eight or nine. The first eight are all in hexameters and follow the order of the modes 1–8. The ninth antiphon breaks this pattern. There is one more verse text in the canticle antiphon found in Hyde and Peterborough. Antiphons 10–12 do not fit the pattern. The Jumièges and Worcester manuscripts have the well-known *Solve iubente deo* as twelfth antiphon, which is in hexameters.

The melodies of these antiphons do not echo traditional melody types. Most are not, however, particularly striking. The sub-tonal endings are not very frequent. Seven of them (nos. 1, 5, 6, 7, 8, 12, and 13) use the whole modal-octave range. The two G-mode melodies are the most ornate, but for the long text of the ninth antiphon a simple syllabic setting is provided. Example 5 gives antiphons 7–9 from the series.

[14] J. B. L. Tolhurst, *The Monastic Breviary of Hyde Abbey, Winchester (mss. Rawlinson Liturg. e. 1*, and Gough Liturg. 8, in the Bodleian Library, Oxford)*, Henry Bradshaw Society 69 (London: Harrison, 1932), 70 (1933), 71 (1934), 76 (1938), 78 (1940), and 80 (1943); Walter Howard Frere, *Antiphonale Sarisburiense: A Reproduction in Facsimile of a Manuscript of the Thirteenth Century* (London, Plainsong and Mediæval Music Society, 1901–24); *Antiphonaire monastique, XIIIe siècle: Codex F. 160 de la Bibliothèque de la Cathédrale de Worcester*, Paléographie musicale I/12 (Tournai: Société Saínt-Jean l'Evangéliste, 1922).

Example 5. Antiphons from the set Pontificalis apex

THE ANTIPHON SERIES ETHEREUM PATREM

The Winchester and Peterborough manuscripts continue the series through Lauds, where Worcester (surprisingly) and the others revert to a better-known set of antiphons. (Unfortunately, Peterborough does not have the more expansive Benedictus antiphon whose text is given in the Hyde breviary.)

THE RESPONSORY SERIES CAPTIVARE VOLENS (NON-NUMERICAL)

Turning to the responsories, we find once again that it is Winchester and Peterborough who have a special series for the Cathedra feast. The series comprises hexameter verses, but the melodies do not follow a numerical modal order. Peterborough has eleven responsories and then gives only the incipit of the well-known *Quodcum ligaveris* for the twelfth responsory. Winchester has *Primatem patrum*, in hexameters. It is just possible that this responsory is a later addition, for whereas the verses of other responsories have prose texts (taken from the psalms, for example), the verse of *Primatem patrum* is another hexameter, *Angelico ductu prodiit de carcere tutus.*

As with the antiphon melodies, these responsory melodies are rather modest in style, while owing rather little to traditional ways of singing responsories. The ninth responsory is a representative example in several ways (see Example 6). There are a few endings from below ("Exiit," "vita," "mittitur," "surgit," and, in the verse "eam"). There are no cadences on D or A, which would be fairly usual in a mode 3 responsory. The melisma in "verbo" is repeated in "vocantis." The move up to the fifth in the second half of the verse is very odd, but this happens in the fourth responsory as well (which is in mode 2).

Altogether we have here a more or less complete new office for the Cathedra feast, perhaps not all created in one sweep but fitting more or less well together and recognizably belonging in the stratum of new offices created in England and Northern France in the eleventh and early twelfth centuries.

Example 6. Captivare *R9*

WINCHESTER AND FLEURY

Of course it would be satisfying to pinpoint the origins of these sets more exactly, and there is a strong temptation to probe further. Is there any trace of these chants among the Winchester organa, for example? No, there is a *vox organalis* only for one of the responsories of the main feast, nothing for the Cathedra or Vincula. However, there is one other office for St. Peter in hexameters, on two leaves in the Vatican manuscript, BAV Reg. lat. 592, which is from Fleury and from the second quarter of the eleventh century. Being in verse, it was edited in *Analecta Hymnica*.[15] There are three sets of three antiphons and three responsories, thus three regular nocturns following the secular cursus. They are followed by what would have been organal voices for all nine responsory verses, but only three were neumed, together with two incipits for the main part, the respond. That is interesting enough, but as far as this paper is concerned, five of the responsories and five of the antiphons are versions of chants I have just been discussing. The concordances are not with the Matins antiphons of the *Pontificalis apex* series, but with the Lauds antiphons in the *Ethereum patrem* series. Table 7 gives parallel texts.

A philologist should be able to say which versions of these texts might claim priority. As to the music, it is suggestive that the antiphons seem to be part of a numerical series. That is, the Peterborough melodies are in modes 1, 2, 4, 5, and 7, and this order corresponds to the position of these antiphons in the Fleury series.

Before leaving the Cathedra feast, mention should be made of one further set of Lauds antiphons in numerical modal order, beginning *Ad speciosa limina*, in the antiphoner of St.-Maur-des-Fossés, ParisBN lat. 12044. The character of these antiphons, in both text and melody, is very like that of Hucbald's *In plateis* antiphons, and it seems possible that they might have been meant to complement that set.[16]

[15] *Analecta Hymnica Medii Aevi* 45a, ed. Clemens Blume and Guido M. Dreves (Leipzig: O. R. Reisland, 1940), no. 67, 168; the facsimile of f. 76v appears in Henry Marriott Bannister, *Monumenti vaticani di paleografia musicale latina*, Codices e vaticanis selecti, phototypice expressi 12 (Leipzig: O. Harrassowitz, 1913 [Reprinted 1969]), no. 230.

[16] The convolutions of transmission are indeed fascinating. The final responsory in the Fleury set, not in Winchester or Peterborough, turns up in a St.-Maur manuscript, ParisBN lat. 12584 (*CAO* F), as an addition to the Cathedra feast, monophonic, not polyphonic, although the manuscript does contain some polyphony.

Table 7. Parallel texts in Fleury, Winchester and Peterborough

Fleury: Matins antiphons		**Winchester, Peterborough: Lauds antiphons**
1. Aethereos patres, divos de lumine soles, Bethsaidae thalamus germano protulit ortu.	1 (mode 1)	Ethereum patrem divo de lumine solem Bethsaide thalamus felice protulit ortu.
2. Hos Iudaea potens, regali germine pompans, Christo sub veteris nutrivit grammate legis.	2 (mode 2)	Hunc synagoga potens, legali dogmate fervens, nutriit ecclesie, censendum nomine Petre.
4. Praescius omnipotens Gallilaeae litora lustrans Sensit in aequoreis splendentia lumina campis.	3 (mode 4)	Prescius omnicreans Galilee litora lustrans, Petrum corripuit, dum verbi rete tetendit.
5. Nec mora, rex reges creat et cognomine ditat Et facit heredes, triplices disponit honores.	4 (mode 5)	Nec mora rex regem creat et cognomine ditat et facit heredem, comendat ovilis honorem.
7. Sed dum multiplices Petrus ferit ore penates, Fascibus ausoniis invictus parcere spernit.	5 (mode 7)	Fascibus ausoniis bellator cedere nescit sed saturnalem deitati vendicat urbem.

Fleury: Matins responsories		**Winchester, Peterborough: Matins responsories**
2. Suscipit ex merito deitatis primus amator Discere amantinos Acherontis frangere traclos Et virtute potens regnorum ferre tridentem. V. *Beatus, quem elegisti* *et assumpsisti, Domine.*	4. (mode 2)	Sumpturus clavem meruit dimittere navem immo quod abiecit melius cum clave recepit Dum datur ecclesia Domino donante regenda. V. *Beatus, quem elegisti* *et assumpsisti Domine.*
3. Errores primae resecat nova gratia culpae, Petrus in hostilem dum vires exserit aurem; Nil minus id pandit medico medicante cicatrix. V. *Hic sanat contritos corde* *et adligat contritiones eorum.*	8. (mode 2)	Errores prime resecat nova gracia culpe. Petrus in hostilem dum vires exerit aurem, Nil minus id pandit medico medicante cicatrix. V. *Hic sanat contritos corde* *et alligat contritiones eorum.*

Table 7, continued

4.	Cedens proposito Petrus fidei pede lapso, Unius allophilae tremefactus voce puellae, Quos ferat, addiscit gratis sibi redditas illi.	7. (mode 6t)	Cedens proposito Petrus fidei pede lapso unius allophile tremefactus voce puelle hac culpa culpis aliorum parcere discit.
V.	*Cuius dum mentis moti sunt pedes* et effusi gressus.	V.	*Cuius dum mentis moti sunt pedes* *et effusi gressus.*
5.	Inter divinae quondam convivia mensae Tres dedit audaces confessio trina timores, Terque regenda Petro traduntur ovilia sancto.	6. (mode 5)	Inter divine quondam convivia mense ter Dominum sese Petrus respondet amare, Terque regenda Petro traduntur ovilia sancto.
V.	*Gloria et honore coronatur* *et constituitur super opera Domini.*	V.	*Gloria et honore coronatur* *et constituitur super opera Domini.*
6.	Sculpsit petra Petrum poliens redditque quadratum Et super hunc locat hos, quos diva litura supernos Mittit in usque polus vitae solidante cemento,	5. (mode 6t)	Sculpsit petra Petrum, polit hunc, quadratque politum; et superedificat, quos diva litura figurat, Quos in regalem componit et ordinat edem.
V.	*Civitatem magni regis montesque Sion* et latera aquilonis.	V.	*Isti sunt lapides vivi,* *ipsi edificium regis eterni.*

THE RESPONSORY SERIES MISIT IMPIUS

For St. Peter ad Vincula we have only a set of responsories, no new antiphons. The series starts with *Misit impius Herodes* and consists of only eight responsories. The ninth responsory is borrowed from elsewhere (as would the tenth through the twelfth in monastic books). The texts are prose that borrow from and paraphrase the Acts of the Apostles, as we would expect. The responds, the first parts of each chant, form a continuous narrative, while the verses sometimes repeat something already said, sometimes add further biblical text. All but the last of these verses are sung to the traditional tone. The eighth responsory is in any case neither clearly in mode 7 nor clearly in mode 8. As to the melodies of the main part, these are not at all conventional, though the occasional traditional cadence can be found. (See the examples discussed later in Example 7.)

In the last decade and a half the tempo of research into saint's offices has accelerated quite noticeably. There is an increased awareness that interesting things are to be found in them, and a significant number of them have been published. Looking at the whole corpus of antiphons and responsories, both old and new, there has been an entirely natural concentration on identifying typical melodies and sets of stock phrases. This identification has now been carried through on a monumental scale by our Hungarian colleagues, editing a very large portion of the repertory, where the melodies are grouped in families—an edition organized according to analytical principles. The antiphons appeared some years ago, and the responsories will follow shortly.[17] Previous studies of responsories—by W. H. Frere, Hans-Jørgen Holman, and, later, Kate Helsen—followed a similar path.[18] This approach, however, leaves a large number of responsories in an analytical limbo. To give just one illustration, there are 778 responsories in Frere's index, of which 460 are assigned to one typical group or another (and sometimes the connections are very slender), leaving 318, or about two-fifths, unclassified.

Quite apart from the question of how these hundreds of more or less individual pieces were remembered—because of course they do not correspond comfortably to the usual model of memorable tunes, where a set of conventional goals is reached along well-known paths—they present us with the considerable challenge of finding ways of adequately describing how their texts are delivered through music. It is true that a number of melodic features characteristic of many chants in the newer saint's offices have been identified—the phrase-endings from below, the concentration on finalis and fifth as cadence points, the full octave range, the running and leaping, and so on—but there is still much work to be done in describing how these features are applied.[19] Example 7 sets out some final examples for discussion.

In the first responsory of Example 7, *Misit impius rex Herodes*, is it significant that the majority of syllables bearing melismas are accented syllables? Is the most striking melisma set on "gladius" because the composer wished to highlight that word for semantic reasons, or because it comes near the end of the respond, or has the word been placed there because a melisma would be

[17] See note 12, above.

[18] Frere, Introduction to *Antiphonale Sarisburiense* (see note 14, above); Hans-Jørgen Holman, "The Responsoria prolixa of the Codex Worcester F 160" (PhD dissertation, Indiana University, 1961); Kate Helsen, "The Great Responsories of the Divine Office: Aspects of Structure and Transmission" (PhD dissertation, Regensburg University, 2008), available online at http://www.opus-bayern.de/uni-regensburg/volltexte/2008/1031/

[19] The literature on the subject has recently become quite extensive. See, for example, the contributions by Dobszay, Hankeln, and Hiley cited in the extensive bibliography in *Political Plainchant? Music, Text and Historical Context of Medieval Saints' Offices*, ed. Roman Hankeln, Wissenschaftliche Abhandlungen/Musicological Studies 111 (Ottawa: Institute of Mediaeval Music, 2009), 201–23.

expected at that point, thus highlighting it by virtue of one of the conventional melodic features of a responsory?

In the sixth responsory of the set, *Ecce angelus domini*, the angel repeats his or her exhortation to Peter three times: "Surge, surge, surge!" Do we hear these three words separately, and should the singers deliver them correspondingly? If we take the melodic line as whole, it moves in much the same way as very many other F-mode phrases. One would not mistake this for a traditional responsory; there are traditional cadences at "carceris" and "eum dicens," but no phrases are traditional throughout. The verse "Et continuo" runs through the traditional two units and then adds on an extra one, which makes a smooth textual transition back into the respond.

The seventh responsory of the set, *Surge Petre*, begins with a rising fifth, "Surge!" But the gesture is repeated for "induete!", and we know it from countless other chants where no semantic intention can be construed. It is simply a double opening gesture (the introit *Puer natus* is perhaps the best-known example). And the imperative "Surge" recurs at the end of the verse, where it is sung to the traditional tone. One notices that the tone is employed in a very flexible way, the first half being stretched all the way to "eum dicens," no restart for the second half of the tone, and then the standard cadence setting the last six syllables. I am sure one cannot attribute the deviations from the normal procedure to incompetence. Singers were using the traditional tones every week of their lives and must have known how to apply them in the conventional way. The postponing of the second half of the tone to the six syllables "Surge velociter" must be deliberate. Why was it done?

The eighth responsory, *Dixit angelus ad Petrum*, sets parts of verses 8–10 of Acts, Chapter 12. The narrative aspect is paramount; there seems to have been no desire to mold the biblical verses to a traditional melody, and traditional turns of phrase are largely abandoned, in the verse as well as in the main part of the responsory.

One might trace the fortunes of many saints along the paths of transmission of office chants. St. Peter's chants offer many illuminating examples of the variable choice of texts and melodies and new composition in new styles. No doubt other saints may provide equally interesting examples and allow us further insights into the history of chants for the office.

Example 7. Responsories from the set Misit impius

1 (Mode 1)

6 (Mode 6)

Example 7, continued

7 (Mode 7)

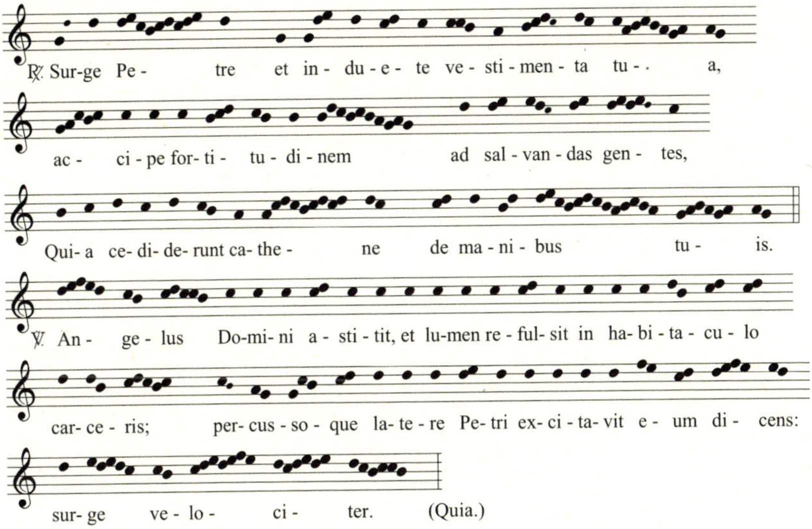

8 (Mode 8)

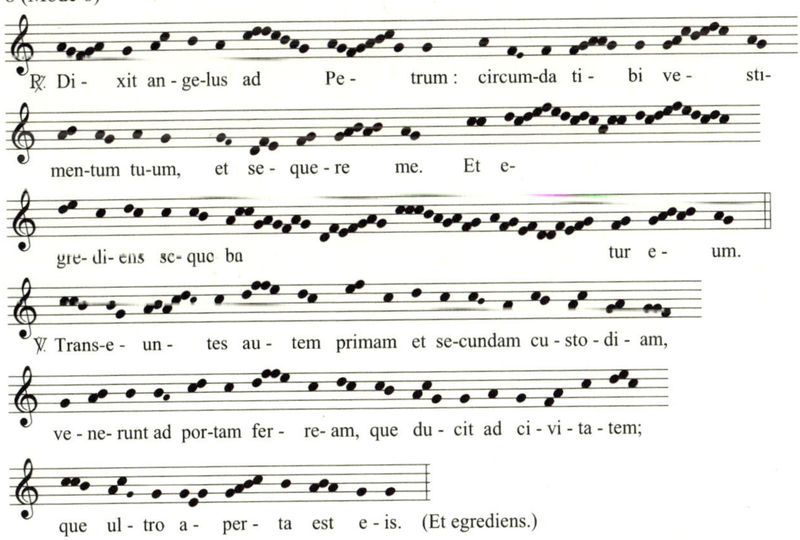

The Genealogy According to St. Luke in Beneventan Dalmatia

Does the Scribe Help the Singer?

KATARINA LIVLJANIĆ

THE GENEALOGY OF Christ according to St. Luke belongs to the category of long narrative readings in the plainchant solo repertoire. It shares performance aspects with the Genealogy according to St. Matthew, the Easter *Exultet*, and the *Lamentations of Jeremiah* sung during Holy Week. All of these pieces are performed generally once a year and represent a high point in the liturgy, anticipated during the entire year. However, their melodic structures do not necessarily always share the virtuoso formulas and features that we encounter, for example, in offertory or gradual verses. The singer of a long reading has a specific task: through the use of repetitive formulas he has to assure an excellent text delivery, using fluid ornamentation to create a concentrated and incantatory—rather than monotonous—atmosphere. In this context, melodies like those of the Genealogy or the *Exultet*[1] present a remarkable domain within which to observe a basic melody structure as used by the "composer" or—to use a more appropriate term—the oral tradition, the scribe and the singer. In the case of medieval chant, our quest is in some ways compromised from the very beginning since it is difficult, if not impossible, for a scholar to assume the responsibility of distinguishing among the roles of the "composer," the scribe, and the singer through the medium of a written manuscript page and in the

[1] On the Beneventan Exultet, see Thomas Forrest Kelly, *The Exultet in Southern Italy* (London: Oxford University Press, 1996).

absence of sound records. We cannot know much about organic modifications in the survival of a melody in an oral tradition several centuries ago, but we can examine written records to see if they give us glimpses of the performance practice of a musical piece over a more or less long period.

With respect to the Genealogy of Luke in Dalmatia we benefit from the existence of several written records from a relatively homogeneous tradition—the tradition of Beneventan Dalmatia between the eleventh and thirteenth centuries. The Genealogy according to Luke (Luke 3:21–38, 4:1) is conserved in a relatively large number of manuscript sources from medieval Dalmatia, a region on the Adriatic coast of Croatia that was heavily influenced by Beneventan medieval culture. This lengthy gospel reading, one of the two Genealogies heard during the Christmas season, is sung by a soloist or several singers (in the case of polyphony, much more common in settings of the Genealogy according to Matthew)[2] in the solemn celebrations for Christmas (Matthew) or Epiphany (Luke). According to Andrew Hughes,[3] the Genealogy of Luke is sung at the end of Matins on the feast of Epiphany in the secular use, and on the Octave of Epiphany in monastic use. The two Genealogies are structured differently: Matthew traces Christ's ancestors forward from Abraham to Jesus, while Luke goes in reverse order from Jesus back to the Creation.

Several versions of the Genealogy of Luke will be compared in this article. Each of the manuscripts contains small variants in the spelling of the Latin text, mostly in the names of Christ's ancestors. It could be interesting, for further research, to compare them carefully and observe possible groupings of manuscripts according to these spelling variants.[4] Since it is neither preferable nor even possible to single out one of the Dalmatian manuscripts as a representative text source, I have chosen to give here the version of the Genealogy from the current edition of the Latin *Biblia Vulgata*,[5] in order to allow the reader to see the entire text, from which examples will be taken later:

[2] Cf. Michel Huglo and James W. McKinnon, "Gospel (i)," in *Grove Music Online*, http://www.oxfordmusiconline.com/subscriber/article/grove/music/11500 (accessed April 18, 2013).

[3] Andrew Hughes, *Medieval Manuscripts for Mass and Office* (Toronto: University of Toronto Press, 1982), 62.

[4] Miho Demović, "Osam varijanti napjeva genealogije po Luki iz neumatskih rukopisa od X. do XII. stoljeća iz Hrvatske," *Dubrovnik* 32 (1989), no. 5–6: 58–114. Demović offers some remarks about this issue, but does not provide a detailed analysis (see 60–61 of his article).

[5] Cf. http://www.vatican.va/archive/bible/nova_vulgata/documents/nova-vulgata_nt_evang-lucam_lt.html#3 (accessed April 18, 2013).

Genealogia Domini nostri Jhesu Christi secundum Lucam.
Factum est autem cum baptizaretur omnis populus et Iesu baptizato et orante apertum est caelum.
Et descendit Spiritus Sanctus corporali specie sicut columba in ipsum et vox de caelo facta est : tu es Filius meus dilectus in te conplacuit mihi.
Et ipse Iesus erat incipiens quasi annorum triginta ut putabatur filius Ioseph

qui fuit Heli qui fuit Matthat qui fuit Levi
qui fuit Melchi qui fuit Iannae qui fuit Ioseph
qui fuit Matthathiae qui fuit Amos qui fuit Naum
qui fuit Esli qui fuit Naggae qui fuit Maath
qui fuit Matthathiae qui fuit Semei qui fuit Iosech
qui fuit Ioda qui fuit Iohanna qui fuit Resa
qui fuit Zorobabel qui fuit Salathihel qui fuit Neri
qui fuit Melchi qui fuit Addi qui fuit Cosam
qui fuit Helmadam qui fuit Her qui fuit Iesu
qui fuit Eliezer qui fuit Iorim qui fuit Matthat
qui fuit Levi qui fuit Symeon qui fuit Iuda
qui fuit Ioseph qui fuit Iona qui fuit Eliachim
qui fuit Melea qui fuit Menna qui fuit Matthata
qui fuit Nathan qui fuit David qui fuit Iesse
qui fuit Obed qui fuit Booz qui fuit Salmon
qui fuit Naasson qui fuit Aminadab qui fuit Aram
qui fuit Esrom qui fuit Phares qui fuit Iudae
qui fuit Iacob qui fuit Isaac qui fuit Abraham
qui fuit Thare qui fuit Nachor qui fuit Seruch
qui fuit Ragau qui fuit Phalec qui fuit Eber
qui fuit Sale qui fuit Cainan qui fuit Arfaxat
qui fuit Sem qui fuit Noe qui fuit Lamech
qui fuit Mathusalae qui fuit Enoch qui fuit Iared
qui fuit Malelehel qui fuit Cainan qui fuit Enos
qui fuit Seth qui fuit Adam qui fuit Dei.

Iesus autem plenus Spiritu Sancto regressus est ab Iordane.

The text is structured in three parts :

1.) introductory section describing the baptism of Jesus in the Jordan.
2.) the longest section, giving the generations of Jesus's ancestors, moving backwards from Joseph to God (*qui fuit Seth, qui fuit Adam, qui fuit Dei*).
3.) conclusion of the scene in the Jordan.

MANUSCRIPT SOURCES FOR THE GENEALOGY ACCORDING TO LUKE IN DALMATIA

The Dalmatian sources of the Genealogy according to Luke were written under Beneventan influence and in Beneventan notation. Some of them also bear witness to Norman influence after the establishment of a Norman presence in southern Italy.[6] The number of sources is relatively large and their dates range from the late eleventh century (the manuscript from Osor, whose dating is unclear) to the late thirteenth (the Dubrovnik *Missale*). They originated in various urban centers along the Adriatic coast. Several authors have already published important articles on the Luke Genealogy in medieval Croatia, establishing the repertory of sources and commenting on the melodic versions.[7] These scholars' works have been crucial to my own research.

> **Osor evangelistary** (hereafter Osor-V): Vatican, BAV, Borg. Lat. 339 (Luke Genealogy: f. 51r–53r);[8] late eleventh century or a later copy of an earlier source (as late as fourteenth c.?).[9]

The evangelistary was written for the diocese of Osor (probably the monastery of St. Nicholas on the island of Susak).[10] The Luke Genealogy is written in Beneventan neumes (Bari type) using a custos, but no clef. [11]

[6] See Richard Gyug, "Innovation, Adaptation and Preservation: The Genealogies of Christ in the Liturgy of Medieval Damatia," in *Zagreb and Music 1094–1994*, ed. Stanislav Tuksar (Zagreb: Hrvatsko Muzikološko Društvo, 1998), 35–55.

[7] Richard Gyug, "Innovation, Adaptation" and Miho Demović, "Osam varijanti."

[8] Select bibliography: Paul Cagin, "Le manuscrit latin—M VI,2—du Musée Borgia," *Revue des Bibliothèques* 12 (1902), 41–73; Henry Marriott Bannister, *Monumenti vaticani di paleografia musicale latina*, 2 vols. (Leipzig, 1913), no. 365, 127–28; Marijan Grgić, "Bogojavljenski navještaj blagdana iz godine 1081," *Arti musices* 1 (1969), 63–74; Elias Avery Loew, *The Beneventan Script: A History of the South Italian Minuscule. Second Edition Prepared and Enlarged by Virginia Brown*, 2 vols., Sussidi eruditi 33–34 (Rome: Edizioni di storia e letteratura, 1980), vol. 2, 163–64; Pierre Salmon, *Les Manuscrits liturgiques latins de la Bibliothèque Vaticane*, 5 vols., Studi e testi 251, 253, 260, 267, 270 (Vatican: Biblioteca Apostolica Vaticana, 1968–72), vol. 2, 43, no. 73; Thomas Forrest Kelly, *The Beneventan Chant* (Cambridge: Cambridge University Press, 1989), 314; Thomas Forrest Kelly, *The Exultet in Southern Italy* (New York: Oxford University Press, 1996), 259; R. Gyug, "Innovation, Adaptation," 50–51; M. Demovć, "Osam varijanti," 59.

[9] Gyug, "Innovation, Adaptation," 50–51.

[10] Ibid., 50.

[11] See Thomas Forrest Kelly, "The Exultet in Dalmatian Manuscripts in Beneventan Script," in *Srednjovjekovne glazbene kulture na istočnoj i zapadnoj obali Jadrana do početka 15. stoljeća / Mediaeval music cultures on the eastern and western shores of the Adriatic until the beginning of the 15th century*, ed. Stanislav Tuksar (Zagreb: Hrvatsko Muzikološko Društvo, 2000), 33.

Kotor lectionary pontifical (hereafter Kotor-P): St Petersburg, Biblioteka Rossiiskoi Akademii Nauk, F. no. 200 (Luke Genealogy: ff. 62r–63v); twelfth century.[12]

This composite manuscript contains a lectionary and a pontifical written in two Beneventan hands. It was used in Kotor in the twelfth century and throughout the Middle Ages (Kotor is now in Montenegro). Some indications (such as the hymn *Te decet laus* after the Matthew Genealogy) suggest a monastic provenance of the manuscript, even if the pontifical part of the manuscript was used by the bishop of Kotor in the cathedral.[13] The Genealogy is notated in Beneventan neumes (Bari type) with custos, but no clef.

Kotor missal (hereafter Kotor-B): Berlin, Staatsbibliothek zu Berlin, Preussischer Kulturbesitz, lat. f. 920 (Luke Genealogy: ff. 20v–21v); twelfth century.[14]

A late twelfth-century missal used in Kotor, with the ex libris "Missale S. Iacobi Catharensis" (f. 6r). The manuscript was modified for local use, which suggests that it was not written in a Kotor scriptorium.[15] The Genealogy is placed before the mass for Epiphany, which suggests secular, not monastic use. It is partially notated, on the last of the three pages: the text without musical notation (though notation was planned to be added later) continues until the section *qui fuit Juda* (ff. 20v–21r). The last short section, starting from *qui fuit Jacob* (begining of f. 21v), has Beneventan notation with custos and no clefs.

[12] Select bibliography: Richard Gyug, *An Edition of Leningrad, BAN, F. no. 200: the Lectionary and Pontifical of Kotor* (Ottawa: National Library of Canada, 1985); Richard Francis Gyug, "From Beneventan to Gregorian Chant in Medieval Dalmatia," in *Srednjovjekovne glazbene kulture na istočnoj i zapadnoj obali Jadrana do početka 15. stoljeća / Mediaeval music cultures on the eastern and western shores of the Adriatic until the beginning of the 15th century*, ed. Stanislav Tuksar (Zagreb: Hrvatsko Muzikološko Društvo, 2000), 41–44; Loew, *The Beneventan Script*, vol. 2, 50; Dušan Sindik, "Pontifikal Kotorske biskupije u Lenjingradu," *Istorijski časopis* 31 (1984), 53–66. An expanded version of Gyug's edition is forthcoming. I am grateful to Prof. Gyug for allowing me to consult parts of his edition prior to publication.

[13] Gyug, "Innovation, Adaptation," 50.

[14] Select bibliography: Lowe, *The Beneventan Script*, vols. 2, 24; Sieghild Rehle, "Missale Beneventanum in Berlin," *Sarcis erudiri* 28 (1985), 469–510; Gyug, "Innovation, Adaptation," 49; Kelly, "The Exultet in Dalmatian Manuscripts," 34; Kelly, *The Exultet in Southern Italy*, 255.

[15] See Gyug, "Innovation, Adaptation," 49.

Rab fragments (hereafter Rab-R): Rab, Nadžupski ured, S.N. (fragments of Luke Genealogy); thirteenth century.[16]

These fragments of a thirteenth-century manuscript were recovered from the bindings of two fifteenth-century graduals. The precise origins are unknown. The manuscript has been identified and assembled by Anđelko Badurina,[17] and Vera Hršak-Flajšman has described the restoration of the fragments.[18] Miho Demović mentions this Rab collection of small fragments as parts of probably two different manuscripts (graduals identified as nos. 3 and 10 in the treasury of Rab Cathedral).[19] This hypothesis seems plausible since the same section in the Luke Genealogy appears twice, on two small pieces of parchment.[20] Nevertheless, the fragments need to be examined more carefully because of other irregularities that appear in the Genealogy, as will be discussed later in this essay. The Beneventan musical notation found here does not use clefs (as far as can be seen in these fragments) but does use the custos. A remarkable feature of this manuscript is the frequent use of a doubled punctum in the unison (cf. Figure 1).

Trogir fragment (hereafter Trogir-V): Vienna, Universität, Institut für Österreichische Geschichtsforschung, no. 4 (no foliation); thirteenth century.[21]

Two bifolia with the two Genealogies (Luke and Matthew). Beneventan notation with no clef, but use of custos.

Trogir evangelistary (hereafter Trogir-T): Trogir, Kaptolski arhiv (Riznica katedrale), 3 (Genealogy of Luke: ff. 13v–15v); thirteenth century.[22]

[16] Select bibliography: Anđelko Badurina, "Fragmenti iluminiranog evanđelistara iz kraja 11. stoljeća u Rabu," *Peristil* 8–9 (1967), 5–12; Vera Hršak-Flajšman, "Restauriranje fragmenata jednog iluminiranog evanđelistara s kraja 11. stoljeća," *Ljetopis JAZU* 73 (Zagreb: Jugoslavenska akademija znanosti i umjetnosti, 1979), 491–94; Virginia Brown, "A Second New List of Beneventan Manuscripts (II)," *Mediaeval Studies* 50 (1988), 611; Demović, "Osam varijanti napjeva genealogije," 80; Gyug, "Innovation, Adaptation," 50.

[17] Badurina, "Fragmenti iluminiranog evanđelistara."

[18] Vera Hršak-Flajšman, "Restauriranje fragmenata."

[19] See Miho Demović, "Osam varijanti napjeva genealogije," 80. Further work on the identification and analysis of these fragments is needed in order to establish their composition and provenance.

[20] See the further analysis of the Rab-R fragments later in this article.

[21] Select bibliography: Loew, *The Beneventan Script*, vol. 2, 172; Demović, "Osam varijanti napjeva genealogije," 59; Gyug, "Innovation, Adaptation," 51.

[22] Select bibliography: *Trogirski evanđelistar*, 2 vols., ed. Josip Bratulić and Miho Demović

Figure 1. Rab-R, no foliation. Reproduced with the kind permission of the parish priest in Rab, Father Anton Depikolozvane.

Beautifully illuminated and notated source with Beneventan musical notation, no clefs, one red line and custos. The manuscript was made for secular use. The Genealogy according to Luke is sung in the night of Epiphany.

Dubrovnik missal (hereafter Dubrovnik-O): Oxford, Bodleian Library, Canon. Lit. 342 (Genealogy of Luke: ff. 7r–9r); late thirteenth century.[23]

A fragmentary missal from Dubrovnik, judging from the sanctorale. The Luke Genealogy precedes the Epiphany mass, followed by the *Te Deum*, a sign of secular use. Beneventan notation with clefs, line, and custos. The Dubrovnik missal has the most ornate melody of the Luke Genealogies. In his article on the *Exultet* in Beneventan Dalmatia, Thomas Kelly mentions its ornate character in this manuscript as well.[24] Both the *Exultet* and the melody of the Genealogy have here an almost improvisatory quality.

MELODIC TYPES

The Genealogy melodies can be divided into two main groups. Fortunately there are sources with diastematic notation for both melodic types (in Trogir-T and Dubrovnik-O, even using clefs and a colored line), and therefore we can ascribe the melodies in this group of sources to the D mode, with a more or

(Split: Književni krug, 1997); Loew, *The Beneventan Script*, vol. 2, 140; Demović, "Osam varijanti napjeva genealogije," 80–1; Gyug, "Innovation, Adaptation," 50.

[23] Select bibliography: Richard Francis Gyug, *Missale Ragusinum. The Missal of Dubrovnik (Oxford, Bodlean Library, Canon. Liturg. 342)*, Studies and Texts 103; Monumenta Liturgica Beneventana I (Toronto: Pontifical Institute of Mediaeval Studies, 1990); Loew, *The Beneventan Script*, vol. 2, 111; Kelly, *The Beneventan Chant*, 309–10; Kelly, *The Exultet in Southern Italy*, 257; Kelly, "The Exultet in Dalmatian Manuscripts," 34; R. Gyug, "From Beneventan to Gregorian," 44–45; Demović, "Osam varijanti napjeva genealogije," 81; Gyug, "Innovation, Adaptation," 50.

[24] Kelly, "The Exultet in Dalmatian Manuscripts," 29.

less developed ambitus, varying from simple melodies with limited ambitus (in Trogir-V) to more ornate and larger range melodies (Dubrovnik-O). The melodies for the Luke Genealogy tend to be more complex than those for Matthew. The second section of the reading (with the names of Christ's ancestors) will be the focus of our analysis.

Nine-part structure

The most frequently encountered structure has nine parts: it is composed of three sections, each having three short phrases : B1+B2+B3 / B4+B5+B6 / B7+B8+B9 (see Example 1). This general structure with nine phrases is repeated eight times. At the very end, three more names need to be recited to complete the genealogical tree (*qui fuit Seth, qui fuit Adam, qui fuit Dei*): the first three-fold section (B1+B2+B3) is repeated one more time for this final sequence of names.

The following Dalmatian sources make use of this nine-part structure: Kotor-P, Kotor-B, Trogir-T, Dubrovnik-O, and Rab-R (this manuscript has a special status, see below).

Example 1. Luke Genealogy with nine-part structure (Kotor-P, f. 62v)

Three-part structure

One also finds another, much simpler structure: the list of Christ's ancestors is divided into groups of three names (A1+A2+A3), with each three-fold group repeated twenty-five times (Example 2).

Example 2. Luke Genealogy with three-part structure (Osor-V, f. 51v)

The only Dalmatian source that uses this three-part structure is Osor-V.

A subspecies of this melodic type is a very simple two-part melodic structure:

A1+A1+A3 (Example 3). Trogir-V is the only Dalmatian source to use this two-part structure.

Example 3. Luke Genealogy with two-part structure (Trogir-V, no pagination)

The use of formulas

A complete transcription and detailed analysis of all the melodies of the Genealogy of Luke in Dalmatian manuscripts would exceed the space and purpose of this essay. Given the melody's extremely repetitive quality, it seems more logical to isolate some concrete examples and use them in the observation of this melody in one particular context. Since the relationship between the written document and its performance is central to this study, I will choose some examples from the Dalmatian sources in order to concentrate on the following questions:

- Does the scribe reflect the practice of a performer?
- Does he help the singer, and if so, how?
- Might the scribe actually *be* the singer?
- Can we discern relationships between written and oral traditions as reflected in the Dalmatian sources?

Naturally I do not pretend to offer definite answers to these questions, but will examine the following cases in this particular light.

Manuscripts with the nine-part melodic type

This melodic type is found in most Dalmatian sources. It is composed of nine short sections articulated in groups of three: each three-fold group explores a higher melodic ambitus, but every third section (i.e., B3, B6, B9) always comes back to the ending on D (*finalis*), thus providing a more symmetrical general frame (see Example 1). The melody reaches the ambitus of an octave plus a third: in order to enunciate the text efficiently and intelligibly, the singer performing the Genealogy according to this melodic structure needs to be skillful and possess not only very good breath control but also a focused voice capable of singing very *legato*.

Let us observe a few examples, chosen from some of the sources that might reflect a relation between manuscripts and performance practice. The scribe of Trogir-T shows an interesting tendency: the B1-B2-B3 formulas are written rather simply at the beginning of the list of names. As the piece progresses, however, they contain more and more details and ornaments written out (see Example 4. Liquescent neumes are indicated by "x."). Might this notational practice reflect an actual performance practice in which the singer ornamented the pattern in an increasingly more flexible way as he went on?

Example 4. Ornamented repetitions of sections B1–B2–B3 (Trogir-T)

In Dubrovnik-O, the scribe uses liquescent forms more frequently than in the other manuscripts: in the list of Christ's ancestors, liquescent neumes are used also for the end of the word *fuit*,[25] a practice seen much less often in the other sources. The final syllables of the names themselves are also often liquescent (*Zorobabel, Salathiel*,[26] *Symeon, Booz, Salmon, Naason*, etc.),[27] regardless of their position in the middle sections or in the ending sections of the three groups (B3, B6 or B9). In the ending sections of the groups we would expect the singer to make a longer break, breathe and therefore not make the connection between the last syllable of one section and the first syllable of the next (a connection expressed by the use of liquescent neumes). It is not quite clear what the scribe wants to tell us with this notational gesture. Either he is reflecting the practice of an unusually skillful and virtuosic singer capable of very long and nuanced phrases without breathing, or he is suggesting the need for such a singer, or perhaps he is displaying his own notational skills, showing his virtuosic hand in the frequent usage of various liquescent neumes.

Faithful to his tendency of almost a *horror vacui*, this scribe also writes out more detailed ornaments in the melody. The Trogir-T scribe also generously decorates the melody, although slightly differently from the version of Dubrovnik-O (see Example 5). Are these two scribes notating a more virtuosic version of the melody, or are they merely "transcribing" an oral tradition of individual singers that existed also in the other locations, only without being written down?

In Kotor B, musical notation is found only in the rather short final part of the Genealogy (f. 22r), a fact that raises questions concerning the performance. The notated part starts in the middle section of the melodic phrase (B7) and therefore does not provide the singer with the entire formula he could use as a mnemonic tool for singing this repetitive melody. It would have been much more logical to expect the notation at the beginning of the piece, since the singer could then use the pattern for the following phrases. Perhaps the lack of musical notation on the first two (of three) pages of the Genealogy indicates that the piece might not have been performed from this manuscript; or if the manuscript was used, the singer needed only the text, since he already knew the melody and did not need the notation.

[25] Cf. Dubrovnik-O, f. 7v (*fuit Ioda, fuit Iohanna, fuit Neri, fuit Elmodan*).

[26] Ibid.

[27] Ibid., f. 8r.

Example 5. Excerpt from the comparative table of manuscripts

In the case of the Rab-R Genealogy, a detailed analysis would be too complex and would exceed the purpose of this article.[28] This fragment is likely composed from two separate manuscripts (see Example 6),[29] since on two different pieces of parchment one can identify the same section of the Genealogy twice (*qui fuit Iamne*).

It is equally difficult to speak about a clear melodic structure here. As can be seen in Examples 6 and 7, both parts of this fragment mix elements from the nine-part (sections B1, B3, B4) and the three/two-part melodic type

[28] This collection of small fragments needs further investigation and will be the subject of a forthcoming article. I express my gratitude to Ms. Saša Lajšić, who helped me in identifying this source, which for a time was impossible to locate, in the collection of the parish church of Rab. This analysis is based on the microfilm, for which I am grateful to Prof. Richard Gyug.

[29] Cf. Demović, "Osam varijanti," 80.

Example 6. Rab fragment

Example 7. Rab fragment

(sections A1, A3). Since the source is incomplete, it is even more difficult to draw any definite conclusions. Nevertheless, it should be noted that Rab R is generally more oriented toward the nine-part melodic type (as we shall see in Examples 7 and 8).

This source contains several irregularities. The main difficulty in the analysis comes not from the number of small pieces of parchment, since a knowledge of the whole Genealogy can help us in connecting the pieces of puzzle. Rather, problems arise on a single piece of parchment, as we encounter melodic inconsistencies or even breaks in the sequence of names that do not follow the order of the gospel. For instance, on the same piece of parchment, the sequence is broken and then continues with a text that should properly be situated several pages later: the names *Mathathie* and *Ihesu* come one after another (see Figure 2, end of the first line and beginning of the second).

Figure 2. Rab-R fragments

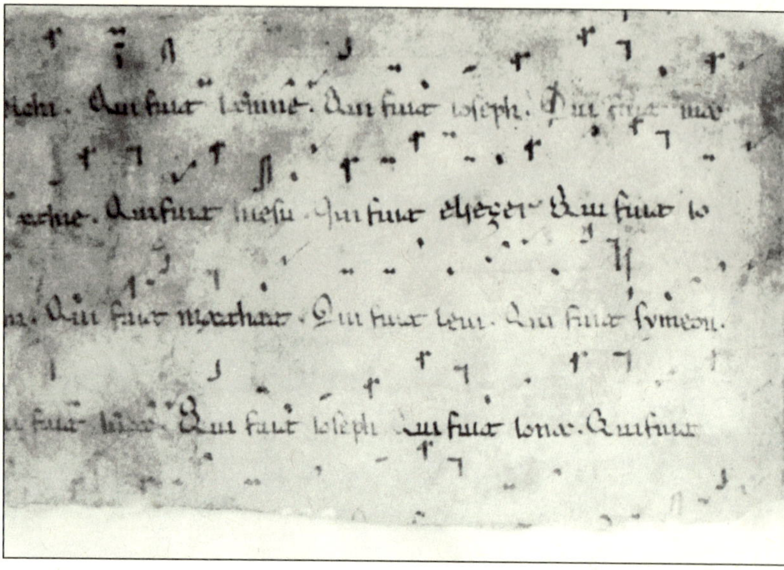

The sequence of melodic formulas corresponding to these names is equally disturbed by this "jump": the two names go melodically from B2 to B3, whereas in the other manuscripts the name *Ihesu* corresponds to B9. After this piece of parchment, we are confronted with only very short sections, where one can read only parts of a name or two. Nevertheless, the sequence of melodic formulas seems to follow a path that starts with *Ihesu*, at least until the section *qui fuit Esrom*, which corresponds to the section B7 (according to the sequence established after *qui fuit Ihesu*). From this section onward it becomes more difficult to put together the "puzzle" pieces, since there are more missing sections and more names that depart from the melodic sequence. If we wish to follow the melodic sequence established with *qui fuit Jhesu*, then the section *qui fuit Seruch* should be sung to the formula B5, but it comes with B4. *Qui fuit Arfaxat* should correspond to B1 and come after *qui fuit Caynan*. Instead, the list omits one name and gives *Arfaxat* with the formula B8, directly on the same piece of parchment after *qui fuit Sale*, resulting in one more irregularity (see Example 8). Furthermore, it is equally obvious that after the first major break (*qui fuit Ihesu*) the sequence found in the other nine-part type manuscripts does not correspond at any moment to these irregularities in the Rab-R fragments.

Example 8. Rab fragments

Clearly, further research needs to be done on the Rab fragments, a manuscript (or rather, a group of manuscripts) with many inconsistencies. It is not impossible that more fragments might be found that help us to better understand this source. Nevertheless, one thing seems clear: some names have been omitted and the melody does not follow the usual pattern. It seems unlikely that a source such as this might have been used for performance even when (or if) it was an entire manuscript. Could the Rab-R fragments come from parchment leaves that the scribe started to use for the Genealogy, but made too many mistakes for the manuscript to be finished and used? Was it for this reason that the leaves were relegated to the binding of a later choir book in Rab, where the fragments were found?

Manuscripts with two-part and three-part melodic types

According to Richard Gyug, this melody might be the last vestige of an older Beneventan version, supplanted elsewhere by the nine-part melody that is more likely of Norman origin.[30] In Dalmatia it is conserved in two sources that come from different regions: Osor-V (an island in the northern region of the Adriatic coast) and Trogir-V (southern Dalmatia).

Let us examine some details that might give us glimpses of performance practice as reflected in these two manuscripts. In Osor-V, the melodic formula for the list of Christ's ancestors is established according to the pattern A1+A2+A3 (see Example 2). On folio 52v, after a long sequence of regularly repeated patterns, the formula A1+A2+A3 suddenly changes: the scribe omits section A2 and writes A1+A3+A1 on the sequence *qui fuit Esrom, qui fuit Phares, qui fuit Iude* (see Example 9).

[30] Gyug, "Innovation, Adaptation," 47.

Example 9. Osor-V, f. 52v, alteration of A1+A2+A3 sequence

After this moment, which might well be a scribal mistake (not surprising in such a repetitive formula that has to be written out many times during the piece), the pattern A1+A2+A3 continues, but this causes the whole three-part sequence to be "displaced" into A2+A3+A1 (see Example 10).

Example 10. Osor-V, f. 52v, "displaced" A1+A2+A3 sequence

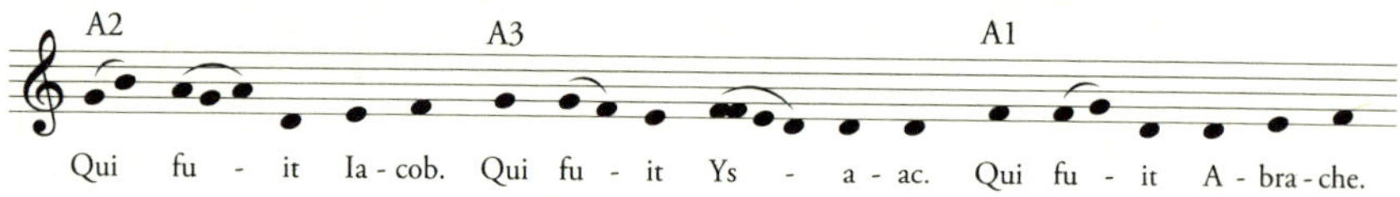

The scribe eventually returns to the A1+A2+A3 pattern on the last set of names (*Qui fuit Seth, qui fuit Adam, qui fuit Dei*). In order to do that he is obliged to repeat A1 twice in a row, which sounds, for a moment, like Trogir-V (which uses the two-part formula with A1 repeated twice; see Example 3). The list of names therefore ends with the usual regular pattern, but with a larger ornament on *qui fuit Dei* (see Example 11).

Example 11. Osor-V, ff. 52v–53r, "realigned" A1+A2+A3 sequence

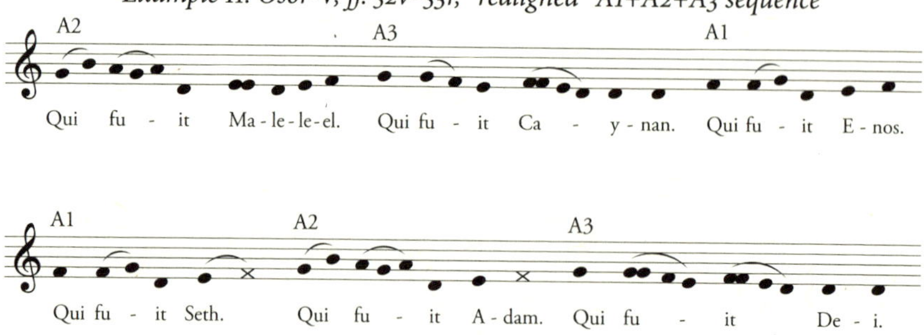

We might wonder whether this scribal error was followed by the singer in practice. The repetitive three-fold melodic pattern seems quite difficult to break once the singer is in the middle of this part of the Genealogy, and it seems possible this manuscript might have been used by the singer more as a text support.

On the other hand, the manuscript might contain some small signals (in the liquescent neumes) that reflect fine details of performance which the scribe might have had in mind as he was notating the Genealogy. It is impossible to know whether he was copying another manuscript and following the models in it, or whether he was remembering the articulations of a singer he had heard previously. Or, was he trying to inform and influence the singers for whom he was copying the manuscript?

The use of liquescent neumes should be noted. In the list of Jesus's ancestors the liquescence is never used at the end of the word *fuit* (even when followed by names like *Nagge* or *Matath*, where one would expect liquescent neumes).[31] On the contrary, liquescence is used rather on the names themselves (*Zorobabel, Salathiel)*,[32] perhaps to underline the necessity of careful text articulation in these places. Since the role of liquescence is to link one syllable to the next, rather then to separate them, its usage at the end of these phrases could inform us equally about the articulation of the phrases and the choices the scribe (or the singer?) made concerning the length of sections that can be sung without breathing.

The other source in this group uses the simplest, two-clause melodic pattern. It is the Trogir-V. The sequence is very stable and consistent.

The page layout in the second section of the Genealogy shows a clear organization: each sequence of three names fits on one line and the initial Q (*Qui fuit . . .*) of every group comes at the beginning of a line, thus facilitating the singer's orientation on the page while he is performing.[33]

Still, the scribe of Trogir-V makes one very significant and revealing "mistake": in the section *qui fuit Aminadab* he abandons for a moment his two-part pattern A1+A1+A3 and changes the melody. Instead of a usual A1, he writes a more developed A2 melodic formula, which never appears in this manuscript, but does belong to the three-part melodic type found in the Osor-V manuscript (see Example 12).

[31] Osor-V, f. 51v.

[32] Ibid.

[33] See Mary Carruthers, *The Book of Memory: A Study of Memory in Medieval Culture* (Cambridge: Cambridge University Press, 1990), 250–51 concerning written mnemonic devices for memorizing and transmitting Christ's genealogical tree.

Example 12. Excerpt from the comparative table of manuscripts

A correction is then made in red ink (see Figure 3) to change the melody back into the expected A1 formula. Did this scribe know the more developed melody? Was he a cantor whose writing was a process combining copying from an older book and copying from his own memory of the other melody (known in Osor)? Could we also suppose that the simple musical formulaic material in this manuscript might represent a canvas that could be ornamented by the singer?

We should remember that the scribe of Trogir-T, a manuscript from the same city, uses a nine-part Genealogy melodic type. In the moment when the scribe of our Trogir-V deviates from its habitual scheme and writes the A2 instead of A1 formula, he does not follow the equivalent formula from Trogir-T, but the three-part formula as in Osor-V. This might indicate several different possibilities:

- All these different melodic types might have been known in Trogir.

- The (more Norman-influenced) nine-part melody could have been introduced after the older (Beneventan) two-part melody was less in use.
- The scribe of Trogir-V, in his revealing "mistake," remembered a melodic type that he himself knew from a place other than Trogir.

Figure 3. Trogir-V, no pagination

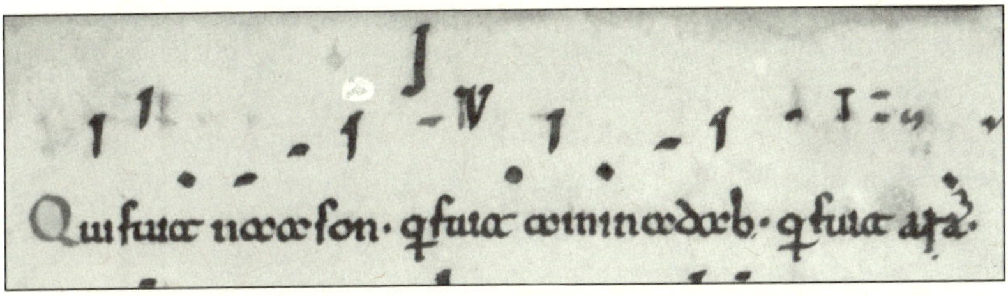

Reproduced with the kind permission of the Institut für Österreichische Geschichtsforschung (I am particularly grateful to Dr. Paul Herold for allowing me to include a fragment from this source here)

We should notice one more detail about the notation in this manuscript: the first Genealogy part (introduction) and the third part (conclusion after the list of Jesus's ancestors) display a more copious use of liquescent neumes and of *acuasta*-type neumes (especially in the descending formulas; cf. Figure 4).

Figure 4. Trogir-V, no pagination

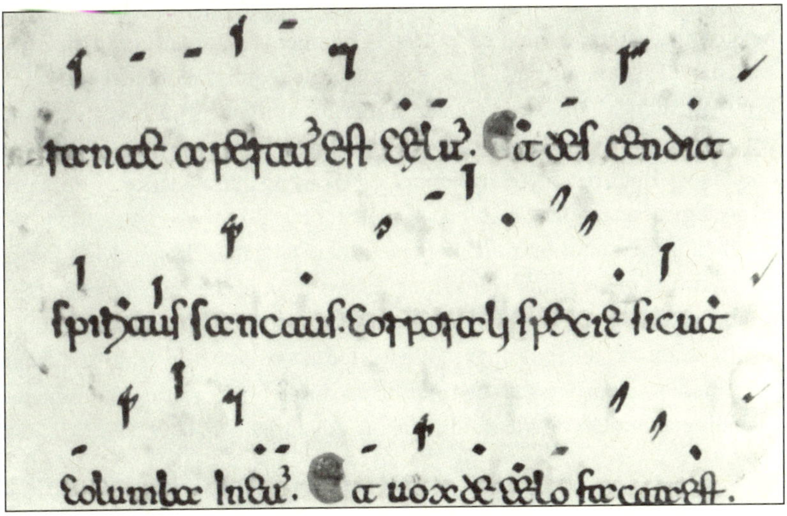

The second section of the Genealogy (the list of names) seems to be notated more "routinely," with fewer liquescent neumes. Could we suppose that the reason for this scribal decision might be the formulaic, repetitive structure of this section, which relies less on the written page and more on oral tradition and the singer's ability to ornament the basic pattern?

CONCLUSION

These examples prompt us to consider that the various Dalmatian sources of the Genealogy according to Luke might have been made with different purposes in mind: some of them describe more accurately the performing reality; some of them seem to be suggesting performing options to the singer; some of them may reflect the fact that oral and written traditions might not have overlapped entirely.

It seems that the written Genealogy in some cases represents a sort of canvas for the singer's general orientation without writing out all the details of ornamentation and liquescence (as in the case of Trogir-V). On the other hand, some scribes seem to be describing more of what the singer *could* do, by adding more small ornaments as the piece progresses (as in Trogir-T). The manuscript Dubrovnik-O reflects performance practice in more detail. Nevertheless, it remains unknown whether this scribe describes the vocal gestures from a singer he heard before writing this manuscript, from an earlier book he was copying, or whether he was prescribing ornaments for the singer who was to use this manuscript. Trogir-V and Osor-V seem to reflect a more archaic melodic tradition that may have disappeared in favor of a more developed nine-part structure, as adopted by a larger number of manuscripts on the Adriatic coast. Two manuscripts from Kotor (Kotor-P and the notated section of Kotor-B) show a rather remarkable similarity in their melodic gestures and seem to confirm a more homogeneous tradition there, while the Rab-R fragments may not even be really connected with the performance of the Luke Genealogy as a complete reading.

In his article on the *Exultet* in Beneventan Dalmatia, Thomas Kelly makes an important observation concerning the notation of these melodies in relation to performance, and he clearly summarizes the problems also noticed in this study of the Genealogy: "What we can say is that in Dalmatia, as in Italy, there was a process in the twelfth and thirteenth centuries of producing melodic elaboration on the traditional melody of the *Exultet*."[34]

[34] Kelly, "The Exultet in Dalmatian Manuscripts," 29.

In the case of the Luke Genealogy, we face a complex situation, since two different melodic types exist in Dalmatian manuscripts, but it is true that Trogir-T and Dubrovnik-O, likely the latest among the sources, use the most elaborately ornamented nine-part melody. These two manuscripts also have the most precise diastematic staff notation (with a colored line). Kelly continues: "These ornamented melodies suggest a process that might almost represent extemporization . . . It might be that other melodies, particularly repetitive formulaic ones, were sometimes sung in ways that we can only guess from the notation. The older notation is preserved, but the newer version is sung . . . But why should the older notation be preserved? Why not write what will be sung? . . . The most practical way of providing notation would be to provide just the framework. It might be a change of writing style, not a change of performance habit, that gives us our few ornamented *Exultet* melodies."[35]

As we examine manuscript sources from medieval Dalmatia it is impossible to neglect the other side of liturgical musical reality—the oral tradition of Glagolitic chant in Dalmatia.[36] In the case of another recitative solo chant, the *Lamentations of Jeremiah*, as sung in Dalmatia, I recently studied three locations on the island of Hvar (in the Split archipelago) and observed the same lamentation as it was transmitted in oral tradition and as it relates to the written tradition of that same melody (the melodic origin being clearly the Gregorian Latin version).[37] The comparison showed how surprisingly weak the connection is between written and oral traditions, and how substantial the variants are among villages.[38] Each singer is remarkably consistent and sings every year in a very stable style that he does not change much, but his style

[35] Ibid., 29–32.

[36] For summary surveys of Glagolitic chant heritage in Croatia, see Jerko Bezić, "Le chant glagolitique," in *La Croatie et l' Europe*, vol. 1: *Croatie, Trésors de la Croatie ancienne des origines a la fin du XIIe siecle*, ed. Ivo Supičić (Paris: Somogy Éditions d'Art; Académie Croate des Sciences et des Arts; AGM, 1999), 570; Hana Breko-Kustura, "Glagolitic Singing, An Inheritance of the Croatian Middle Ages" in *Discovering the Glagolitic Script of Croatia: Catalogue of the Exhibition, Trinity College Library Dublin (November 2000–February 2001)* (Zagreb: Erasmus, 2000), 118–21; Geoffrey Chew, "Glagolitic Mass, Glagolitic chant," in Grove Music Online http://www.oxfordmusiconline.com/subscriber/article/grove/music/45440 (accessed 6 November 2012); Jerko Martinić, *Glagolitische Gesänge Mitteldalmatiens*, 2 vols. (Regensburg: G. Bosse Verlag, 1981).

[37] *Liber Usualis Missae et Officii* (Tournai: Desclée & Socii, 1958), 631–33.

[38] See Katarina Livljanić, "Lamentations de Jérémie glagolitiques sur l'île de Hvar en Croatie: peut-on 'traduire' le chant?" in *Lingua mea calamus scribae. Mélanges en l'honneur de Marie-Noël Colette*, ed. Daniel Saulnier, Katarina Livljanić, and Christelle Cazaux-Kowalski (Solesmes: Editions de Solesmes, 2009), 253–73.

may be radically different from that of other local singers, even from those of the neighboring parish church.[39]

Would any of these singers need to see changes being made in the written documents that contain the melodies they perform in order to reflect more accurately what each of them actually sings? Probably not. In many cases these singers simply ignore that there *is* an existing written record of their chant, and if they use it (which in the case of the Genealogy might be rather useful, given the length of the list of Christ's ancestors to be sung) they would need only—the *text*. I once asked a Glagolitic singer to sing a rather long and elaborate saint's life for me and I wondered if he needed written support for what he was going to sing. He answered: "Let me just find the text. Of course, I don't care about the written music, I know it."[40]

[39] Short audio excerpts of three singers from Hvar performing the first Jeremiah's Lamentation can be heard on: http://www.ensemble-dialogos.org/samples. I am grateful to Ivan Lozica of the Institute for Ethnology and Folklore in Zagreb, as well as to Giovanni Sgaria from the Arcana record company for allowing me to use these short musical examples.

[40] Matko Franetović, Glagolitic traditional singer from Stari Grad on the island of Hvar, in a working session in August 2007.

Beneventan Music and Gregorian Modality

Evidence of Modal Change in the Melodic Fund of the Old Beneventan Chant

MATTHEW G. PEATTIE

THIS ESSAY IS about a meeting between two repertories that work under different conceptions of mode and melodic construction. The Beneventan chant was the liturgical repertory of southern Italy at the time of the arrival of the Romano-Frankish or Gregorian chant in the region. Like most regional repertories, the Beneventan chant was replaced by the Gregorian repertory as a result of the Carolingian drive for liturgical uniformity. Although the Beneventan chant was replaced by the central Frankish dialect and eventually suppressed entirely, the two repertories did coexist for a time, and examples of the Beneventan repertory are partially preserved in sources dating from the eleventh to thirteenth centuries.

The remnants of the Beneventan chant are preserved for the most part in Gregorian antiphoners and graduals—books whose primary purpose was to record the central Frankish liturgy. The central sources of the music of the Old Beneventan rite are the two Gregorian graduals—Benevento, Biblioteca capitolare, MS 38 and Benevento, Biblioteca capitolare, MS 40 (hereafter Ben38 and Ben40).[1] These sources preserve twenty-one doublet Masses—sets of Beneventan Mass Propers placed next to the Gregorian material for the same feast.

[1] *Benevento Biblioteca capitolare 40 Graduale.*, facsimile edition edited by Nino Albarosa and Alberto Turco (Padua: La linea, 1991). The sections containing Beneventan doublet Masses in both manuscripts are identified and reproduced in Thomas F. Kelly, *Les témoins manuscrits du chant Bénéventain*, Paléographie musicale XXI (Solesmes: Abbaye Saint-Pierre, 1992).

These doublet Masses preserve a textual and musical tradition distinct from the Gregorian Mass Propers with which they are juxtaposed.

Although the doublet Masses appear to record a stylistically uniform (and, perhaps we can conclude, a relatively pure) form of the Beneventan repertory, many of the later sources show evidence of a mixture of local and imported forms. In several of the late sources of Beneventan chant, particularly manuscripts for the office, it appears that Beneventan music has been transformed by Gregorian modality and its system of four finals—a modal system that, as I will explain, adapts uneasily to the formulaic melodic fabric of the Beneventan chant. I will argue that the contact with Gregorian modality (and the process of making the Beneventan melodies conform to the particularities of the octoechos) precipitated changes in the melodic fund of the Beneventan chant. This paper will discuss several examples of Beneventan music that appear to have been significantly altered by their contact with the Frankish-Roman repertory. To put these examples in context, it will be useful to provide a brief introduction to the Beneventan repertory and its unique system of melodic construction.

PITCH AND MODE IN THE BENEVENTAN CHANT

Beneventan musical style

The music of the Beneventan rite has a highly unified, characteristic musical style, one distinguished by numerous distinctive melodic phrases that recur throughout the repertory with a formulaic regularity. Example 1 illustrates some common figures in an excerpt from the Beneventan Mass Propers. The Beneventan style is characterized by a remarkable interconnectedness of musical material, and the melodic material in almost every phrase in the Beneventan Mass Propers can be identified in multiple places in the repertory. Example 1 shows only a few of these melodic figures, but when the study of formulas is expanded across the repertory, we can identify well over 100 recurrent figures. Because of the regularity and distinctive character of the melodic formulas, Beneventan music is immediately recognizable. Although there are occasional minor differences among sources, the scribes are generally consistent in the calligraphic rendering of the formulas. The formulaic patterns and the unique complex neume groups mark a style that is uniquely *Beneventan*—a unified musical repertory that is readily identifiable and obviously distinct from the Gregorian, Old Roman, and Ambrosian repertories. This formulaic style is built on a common fund of melodic material that is shared by all genres of the Beneventan Mass Propers.[2]

[2] Beneventan musical style is treated in some detail in Thomas F. Kelly, *The Beneventan Chant* (Cambridge: Cambridge University Press, 1989), Chapter 4.

Example 1

1a) Maria vidit angelum *(ingressa): Benevento, Biblioteca capitolare, MS 40, f. 187v*

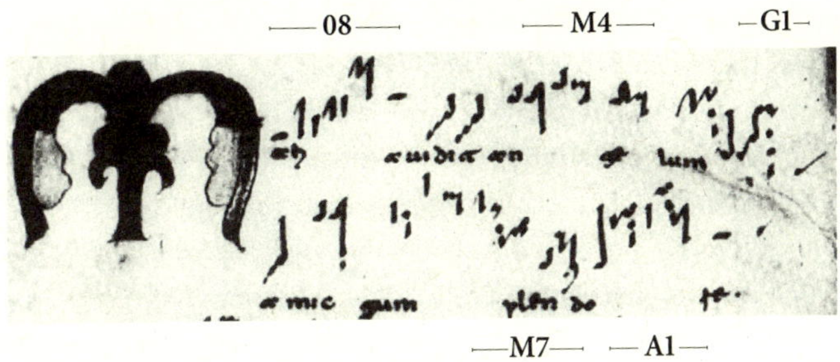

1b) Postquam surrexit *(ingressa): Benevento, Biblioteca capitolare, MS 40, f. 4v*

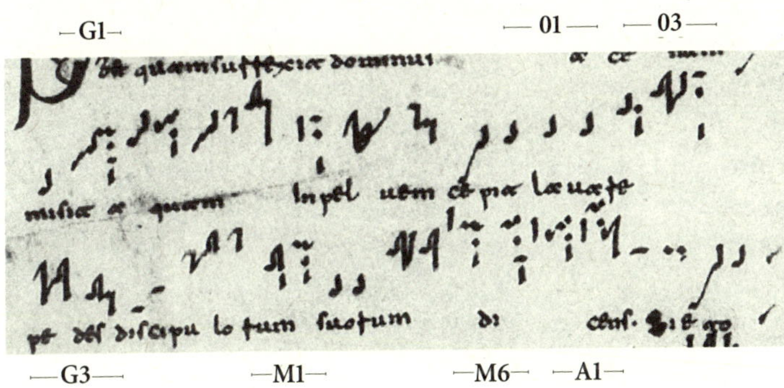

1c) Milia Milium *(offertory): Benevento, Biblioteca capitolare, MS 40, f. 61*

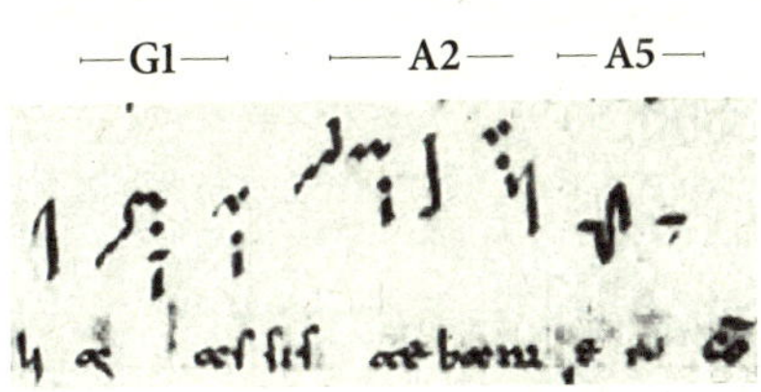

1d) Martinus abrahe *(offertory): Benevento, Biblioteca capitolare, MS 40, f. 139*

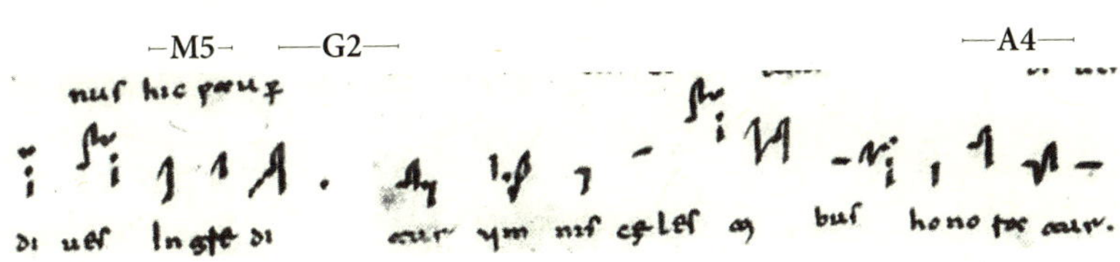

The pitch of the Beneventan repertory

The pitch of the Beneventan repertory also requires a brief introduction. Virtually the entire repertory is notated *in campo aperto* without lines or clefs to indicate the placement of the semitone. Despite the limitations of the notation, we are nonetheless able to determine a great deal about the pitch placement of Beneventan melodies. The following overview of pitch and modality is based on the observation and study of pieces that we know to be part of the Old Beneventan liturgy, a corpus of melodies that I will refer to as the *core repertory*. The core repertory includes two main categories of music: 1) pieces that can be identified as Beneventan by the facts of their transmission (for example, several antiphons for Holy Week are preceded in the sources by a rubric indicating that they belong to the local rite),[3] and 2) pieces that are preserved in "doublet Masses" in the Graduals, Ben38, and Ben40. Although the music in the doublets is not identified explicitly as Beneventan, they preserve a distinctive and stylistically unified repertory of chant. They also contain several liturgical features that identify them with the Old Beneventan rite, most notably the opening chant of each Mass, which is labeled with the rubric "ingressa" rather than "introit" as found in the Romano-Frankish liturgy.[4] These two sources preserve twenty-one doublet Masses and together form the principal record of the Beneventan repertory.[5]

[3] Beneventan manuscripts refer to this local rite as "Ambrosian," a reflection of the historical link with the Lombard north and the liturgy of Milan. For example, the Beneventan ordo for Good Friday in Rome, BAV, MS Vat. lat. 10673 f. 33r is prefaced by the rubric "officium sexta feria in Parsceben secundum Ambrosianum." Although this southern Lombard repertory appears to share an ancient lineage with the liturgy of Milan, it sustained an independent liturgical and musical development and became a repertory in its own right that for convenience is referred to as "Beneventan." Other examples of the Beneventan chant labeled as "Ambrosian" are discussed in Kelly, *Beneventan Chant*, 181–83.

[4] The use of the term "ingressa" rather than "introit" is a testament to the shared Lombard heritage with the Ambrosian chant of Milan. See Kelly, *Beneventan Chant*, 184.

[5] In addition to the twenty-one doublet Masses, the extant Beneventan repertory includes music for Holy Week, two doublet Offices, and a substantial amount of music in Beneventan style preserved in late antiphoners. For this study I will privilege the doublets and music for Holy Week as the core repertory of the Beneventan chant. This core repertory is comprised for the most part of self-contained sections of music of the old Beneventan rite in a distinct and unified style, and can be identified as belonging to the old Beneventan rite by the facts of its transmission or liturgical placement. While the Beneventan-style music in the late antiphoners provides an important perspective on the repertory, it appears at times to be mixed with the imported Frankish-Roman repertory and is not always in a style wholly consistent with the music of the Mass Propers and doublet Offices. A methodology for identifying a core repertory of Beneventan chant is discussed in more detail in Matthew G. Peattie, *The Beneventan Antiphon and the Influence of Beneventan Style in the South Italian Office* (PhD dissertation, Harvard University, 2005), 96–104.

The principal sources of the core repertory preserve the melodies with more or less accurate heightening, and a careful comparative study of the heightening allows us to establish the diastematic relationship of the formulas at a local level and ultimately over large stretches of music. The solution to the problem of pitch and transcription in the Beneventan chant was first discussed by Thomas F. Kelly in *The Beneventan Chant.* In his study of the repertory, Kelly made a number of important observations concerning Beneventan style and modality. His summary of the pitch of the repertory is an elegant and economical way of describing a system that is cumbersome to demonstrate and relies on diastematic evidence that is sometimes intractable. Kelly's findings can be summarized in three main points: First, that "the Beneventan chant generally employs a single pitch level for a recurrent formula or phrase"; second, that "we can by experimentation discover that there is only one pitch level that accounts for virtually the entire repertory"; and finally, that "when the repertory is considered in this fashion, it becomes apparent that all the pieces share the same general range and they conclude either on A or a step lower on G."[6]

This system of recurrent figures, each operating at a single pitch level, forms a stable fund of material that defines the melodic surface and modal character of the repertory. Some examples of the pitches of common Beneventan formulas are illustrated in Example 2 on the next page. The cadences to A and a tone lower on G are among the most common figures in chant, and because one or more of these cadence figures occurs regularly in almost every Beneventan melody, the cadences become the most useful practical reference points for establishing the pitch of a given chant.

A small number of exemplars of the Beneventan Mass Propers are preserved in pitch specific notation (sources notated with a staff line, or to which a staff line has been added by a later scribe).[7] Although relatively few of the Mass Propers are preserved in pitch specific notation, the few exemplars generally

[6] Kelly, *Beneventan Chant,* 154.

[7] These include nine alleluias (which share a common melody), three communions, one tract, and one offertory. These are: *Alleluia: Hodie natus est* (Cologny-Geneva, Bibliotheca Bodmeriana MS 74, f. 12v); *Alleluia: Hodie baptizatus est,* (Cologny, Bodmer 74, f. 19v); *Alleluia: Hodie migravit,* (Ben39, f. 121v); *Alleluia: Hodie transfiguratus,* (Ben39, f. 140v); *Alleluia: Resurrexit,* (Ben30, f. 75v; Ben34, f. 126r; Ben35, f. 68r; Ben39, f. 27v; Cologny, Bodmer 74, f. 80v); Offertory: *Omnes qui in Christo,* (Ben35, f. 68r); Communion: *Ymnum canite,* (Ben35, f. 68rv); Tract: *Sicut cervus* (Salerno, Archivio del Museo del Duomo, ms. 3, f. 142v / Salerno, Archivio del Museo del Duomo, ms. 4, f. 153v); Communion: *Pascha yeron (palimpsest)* (Florence, Biblioteca Medicea-Laurenziana MS 33.31, f. 45); Communion: *Hos duodecim,* (Ben21, f. 236r; preserved in this source as an antiphon).

Example 2

2a) Opening Figures

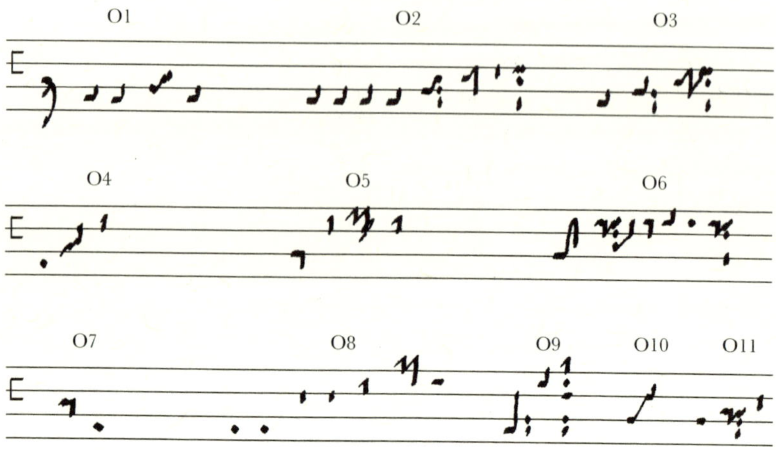

2b) Mid-phrase Figures

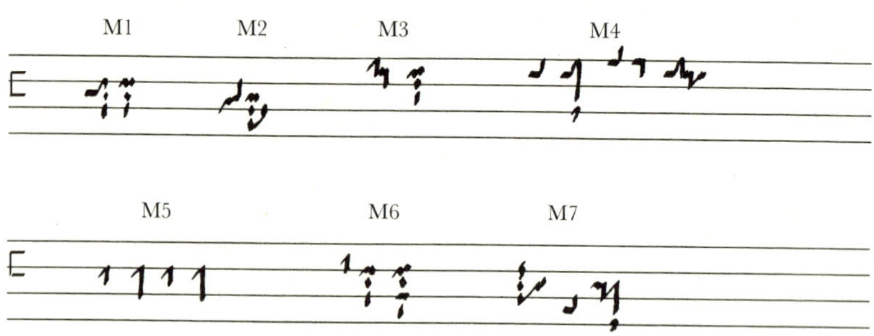

2c) Cadential Figures

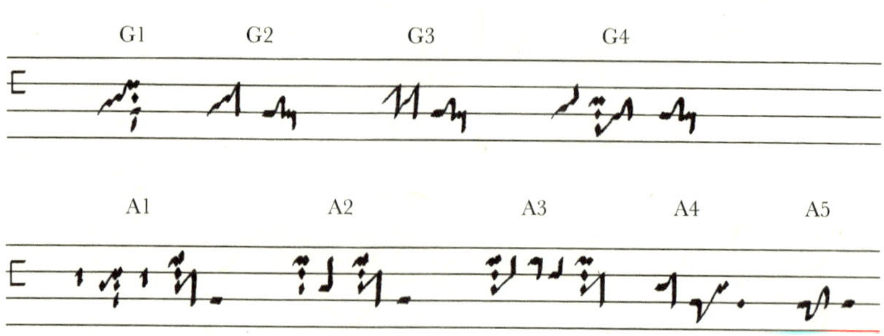

confirm the understanding of pitch proposed above. Example 3 shows the Beneventan offertory for Holy Saturday, *Omnes qui in xpisto*, notated on a staff line with F and C clefs in a source from the early twelfth century (Benevento, Biblioteca capitolare, MS 35, f. 68r).The example illustrates four common Beneventan figures that can be compared to the figures in the previous example. Note especially Figure A1, the most common cadence figure in the Beneventan repertory. This cadence figure is the higher of the two common cadence notes (A and G) and this example confirms the cadence note as A.

Example 3. Common Beneventan formulas with F and C clefs
Omnes qui in xpisto *(offertory): Benevento, Biblioteca capitolare, MS 35, f. 68*

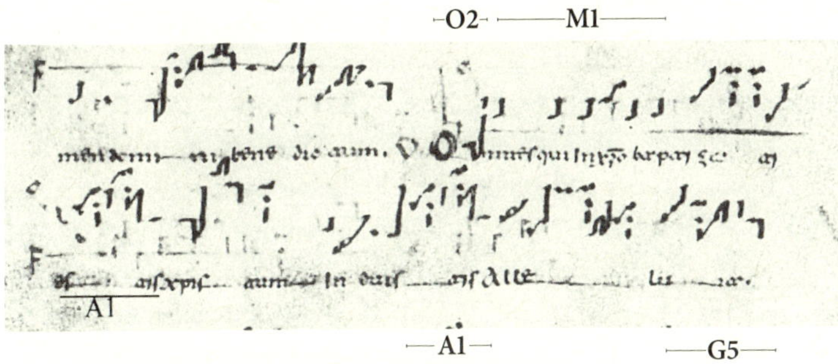

THE WITNESS OF THE LATE ANTIPHONERS

In addition to the core repertory, there exists a modest repertory of office music (mostly antiphons) that can be identified as Beneventan on the basis of musical style. Although these antiphons are not distinguished liturgically from the Gregorian music alongside which they are preserved (i.e., they are not preserved as "doublets" nor are they identified as Beneventan by rubrics), they share the distinctive formulaic structure and melodic shapes of the Beneventan repertory. The Beneventan-style pieces are found in offices of saints unique to southern Italy, such as the Holy Twelve Brothers of Benevento, St. Mercurius, and Saint Barbatus of Benevento. Consideration of their musical style and their provenience allows us to include them with some confidence in the corpus of Beneventan chant.[8] Many of these Beneventan-style antiphons are preserved in fully heightened pitch-specific sources with a staff line and clef

[8] Antiphons from the Holy Twelve Brothers and Barbatus are included by Kelly in the corpus of Beneventan music preserved in manuscripts for the Office; Kelly, *Les témoins manuscrits*, 421–24. Beneventan-style antiphons for Mercurius can be found in Naples, Archivio storico diocesano, Fondo Ebdomadari, Cod. Misc. 1 fasc VII. Several antiphons for Mercurius not included in Pal. Mus. XXI can be added to the corpus of Beneventan music on the basis of musical style.

and are therefore of great relevance to the study of the pitch and modality of the Beneventan repertory.

In the study of early chant repertories, the emergence of pitch-specific notation (in this instance a staff line and clef) usually heralds an important breakthrough in our access to the musical material. Lined and fully heightened sources reveal the intervallic content obscured by the notation *in campo aperto* and allow us to interpret the nuances of the notation in the context of pitch-specific passages. Most important, sources that provide an accurate record of pitch allow us to engage with the melodic material, addressing questions of melodic construction and mode. We would hope that in their pitch-specific guise, the melodies of the late office repertory operate exactly like the notation of *Omnes qui in xpisto* (Example 3 above) and confirm all we know, or think we know, about the pitch of the Beneventan repertory.

Unfortunately, it is not that simple. While the system of formulas that makes up the Beneventan melodic fund operates with great consistency in the core repertory, the late antiphoners preserve what appears to be a garbled record of the repertory. The pitch-specific witnesses of Beneventan-style office music are the source of much confusion and contradiction. It is by no means clear that the pitches indicated in these sources accurately reflect the melodic and modal fund of the old Beneventan repertory. In a few instances the pitch-specific sources confirm what we know about the system of formulaic construction, yet in other instances they do not. Cadences that we expect to find on A are written on G, and in some cases entire pieces seem to have been placed at a pitch level that is inconsistent with our understanding of the Beneventan melodic/modal system. The problem is as follows: in several sources of Beneventan-style antiphons, the system of diastematic relationships between figures seems to have broken down, particularly at cadence points. Figures are notated a tone lower or higher than we might expect relative to another figure. Cadence shapes in particular seem to be the source of some confusion, with similar shapes ending on G in one source, on A in another. The cadence figures in Example 4 illustrate one such inconsistency in which a common Beneventan cadence figure (A1) has been notated at three different apparent pitches.

MODAL CHANGE IN THE MELODIC FUND OF THE BENEVENTAN CHANT

The contradictory nature of the pitch-specific sources poses a difficult question for the Beneventanist. Should the sources notated with a staff line and clef be viewed as accurate records of a practice or disregarded as late corruptions or

Example 4. Contradictory Pitch Indications in the Late Sources: Cadence Figure A1 notated at three different pitches

4a) Cadence to A: Benevento, Biblioteca capitolare, MS 35, f. 15v

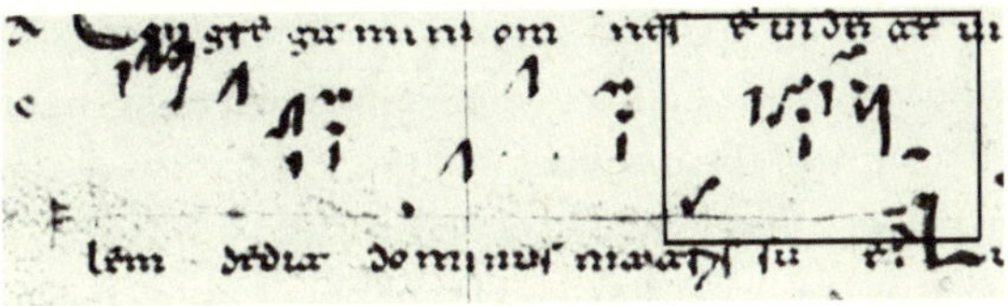

4b) Cadence to G: Naples, Archivio Storico Diocesano, Fondo Ebdomadari, Cod. Misc. 1 fasc. VIII, f. 42

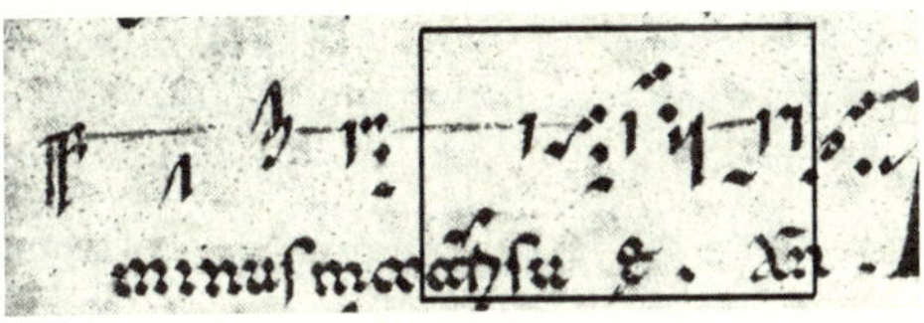

4c) Cadence to D: BAV Reg. lat. 334, f. 57

notational errors? The answer to this question depends on one's perspective. For the scholar interested in the core repertory of the Beneventan chant, the central question is whether the late sources, even if they are corrupted records of a repertory in decline, contain information that can inform our understanding of the pitch of the repertory. (If we are proposing transcriptions of the chant, we must at least be able to explain why some of the sources of Beneventan-style music are at odds with our understanding of the core repertory.)

For the scholar of later medieval chant, this perspective is reversed: What can these records tell us about the continuing practice of Beneventan chant in the twelfth and thirteenth centuries? In comparing the pitch and relative diastematic relationship of formulaic material in the core repertory with that of the late office sources, it becomes apparent that the late sources preserve a modified (or muddled) record of the pitch of many common melodic formulas. Why do the sources of office music preserve what appears to be a modified or contradictory record of the pitch of many common Beneventan formulas, and what has caused the apparent shifts in the modal structure of these antiphons? Do the differences of pitch in these sources represent a transformation in the pitch structure of the melodies and the way they were sung, or simply differences in the way they have been notated?

In the repertory of Beneventan-style antiphons in pitch-specific sources, we find the melodic and modal fund of the Beneventan chant in various states of preservation and disrepair. In some instances, the Beneventan chant appears to continue in its archaic modes, transcribed onto the staff line in a manner wholly consistent with the Beneventan modal system. Where we find evidence of change or modernization I believe this reflects the imposing influence of the Frankish-Roman repertory on the music of the region. I will argue that many of the inconsistencies in the late sources appear to be the result of various attempts to render Beneventan music in a notational/theoretical system that adapts uneasily to its melodic/modal fabric. While several of these examples seem to represent notational solutions to the problem of writing archaic melodies within the confines of the octoechos, others examples appear to record evidence of change and transformation in the modal properties of the Beneventan formulaic system. In the examples below, I outline several categories of modal change that I believe represent stages in the dissolution of Beneventan modality.

1) Pure Beneventan modality: An antiphon notated in pitch specific notation in a manner wholly consistent with the modal system of the Beneventan chant.

The notation of an antiphon for the Purification, *Congregamini omnes* (Benevento, Biblioteca capitolare, MS 35, f. 15v), provides a remarkable record of consistency with the melodic and modal fund of the Beneventan chant. This antiphon employs numerous melodic elements that have corollaries in the core repertory of the Beneventan chant (the Beneventan figures are illustrated in Example 5 below). Each of these figures is notated at a relative pitch level consistent with the diastematic relationships that have been observed in the core repertory. The placement on the staff line is also perfectly consistent with the pitch of the Beneventan core repertory. This can be illustrated by the pitch placement of figure A1, the most common cadence figure in the Beneventan Mass Propers. This cadence represents the higher of the two modal finals in the Beneventan melodic system (G and A), and in this recension it is clearly notated as a cadence to A. Except as a transposition, the A final does not normally exist among the tones of the octoechos, and in this example, the scribe has made no attempt to conform to the precepts of Gregorian modality. It should be noted that the scribe omits the psalm tone after this antiphon (and the Beneventan-style antiphon that follows), so the evidence of the differentia is not available to us as a record of the scribe's understanding of the mode. (It is tempting to imagine that the scribe was unsure of which reciting tone and differentia to apply to an antiphon with an anomalous final and avoided the difficulty by simply omitting it.)

This example reflects the purest level of the Beneventan modal system; both the melodic material and the notational realization reflect a system that exists apart from the norms of Gregorian modality.

Example 5. Benevento, Biblioteca capitolare, MS 35, f. 15v

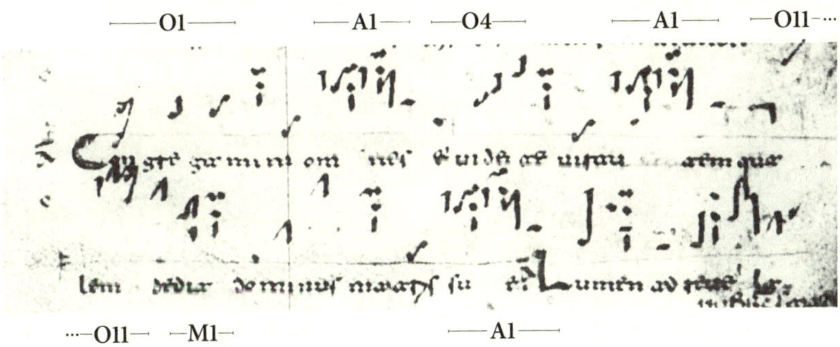

2) *An antiphon in which the diastematic relationships of the Beneventan modal system are internally consistent, but a Beneventan final on A is notated transposed to D.*

An alternate pitch-specific reading of *Congregamini omnes* is preserved in a twelfth-century processional (BAV MS Reg. lat. 334, f. 57r). In this source the melody has been transposed a fifth lower than the version discussed above (see Example 6 below). While all of the formulaic material is notated at a *relative* pitch level consistent with the diastematic relationships that have been observed in the core repertory, the antiphon has been notated with a final on D and a mode 2 differentia. The transposition to D avoids the A final, and in this instance it appears the scribe had no problem supplying the appropriate psalm tone.

Example 6. BAV Reg. lat. 334, f. 57

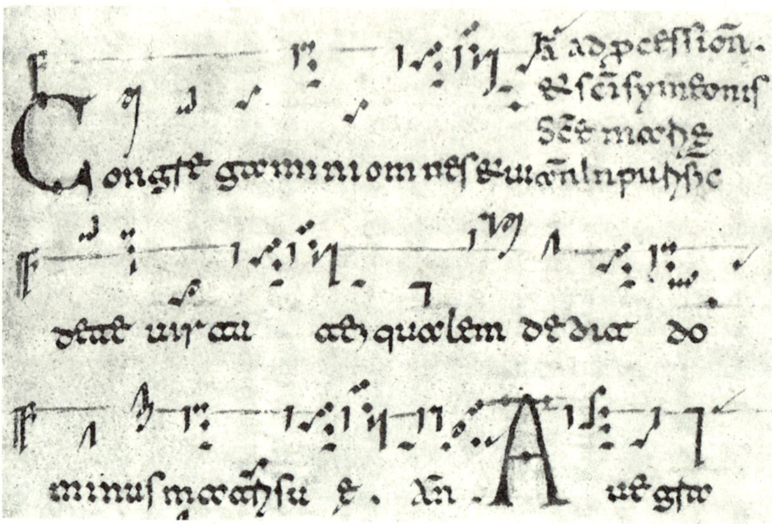

This example represents a relatively simple solution to the problem of reconciling the Beneventan finals with the precepts of Gregorian modality. By notating the antiphon in transposition with a D final, the scribe fits the melody neatly into the octoechos and its system of four finals. Taken at face value, the transposition leads to some minor variation in the pitch structure of the antiphon. Although the relative diastematy of the melodic figures remains wholly consistent with what we have observed in the core repertory, the system can only be maintained by the addition of a B-flat. In this example, the pitch structure of the Beneventan modal system (and consistency with the reading of this same melody in Ben35) necessitates the addition of a B-flat on the podatus that begins figure A1. Given the paucity of notated B-flats in south Italian sources it is unlikely that this detail would have been notated even if it were normally sung. The range of this particular antiphon, which does not reach above A, precludes the need for any chromatic alteration in the upper range. Despite the minor adjustments necessitated by moving an A final to D, this transposition appears to be the preferred solution for notating antiphons having an A final in the Beneventan system. Table 1 lists several other antiphons in which formulaic material normally associated with the A final (or the higher of the two Beneventan finals) is notated in "transposition" on a D final.

Table 1. Beneventan style antiphons notated in "transposition" on a D final

Cum recubuisset	Benevento, Biblioteca capitolare, MS 35, f. 62v
Laudamus te Christe	Benevento, Biblioteca capitolare, MS 35, f. 65v
Inclinato capite	Benevento, Biblioteca capitolare, MS 39, f. 25v
Mercurrii meritum	Naples, Archivio storico diocesano, Fondo Ebdomadari, Cod. Misc. 1 fasc VII, f. 60v
Armenia felix	Naples, Archivio storico diocesano, Fondo Ebdomadari, Cod. Misc. 1 fasc VII, f. 60v
Beatus Honoratus	Naples, Archivio storico diocesano, Fondo Ebdomadari, Cod. Misc. 1 fasc VII, f. 47v.
Beatum Vitalum	Naples, Archivio storico diocesano, Fondo Ebdomadari, Cod. Misc. 1 fasc VII, f. 47v
Beatus Donatus	Naples, Archivio storico diocesano, Fondo Ebdomadari, Cod. Misc. 1 fasc VII, f. 47v

3) An antiphon in which the diastematic relationships of the Beneventan modal system are internally consistent, but the melody is transposed downward by one tone.

A less obvious solution to the problem of the A final can be observed in Example 7 (next page), the antiphon *Sancti vero uno ore* from the office of the Holy Twelve Brothers of Benevento (Ben21, f. 236r). Here the entire antiphon has been notated one tone lower than it would sound in the Beneventan modal system. The relative diastematy of the Beneventan formulas is entirely consistent within the piece, but on the surface the pitch structure has been radically altered. The final on A becomes a final on G, but in the process every other recognizable Beneventan formula is subjected to the same downward transposition. It seems implausible that the antiphon was meant to be sung as written (note especially the melodic tritones between F and B in the opening phrase).

In the case of *Sancti vero*, it appears that the solution for avoiding an A final was to notate the antiphon in its entirety one tone lower than expected, a notational solution which, if taken at face value, has serious implications for the pitch structure of the melody. Perhaps this notational solution is purely cosmetic to give the appearance of a final on G. (The choice of a mode 8 differentia indicates that the scribe did conceive of this antiphon as having a final on G). The pitch structure of the Beneventan formulas can be restored quite easily with the hypothetical addition of a B-flat throughout, and while this is

Example 7. Sancti vero uno ore*: An Antiphon from the Office of the Holy Twelve Brothers of Benevento (Beneventan modal system transposed downward by a tone)*

7a) Sancti vero uno ore *Benevento, Biblioteca capitolare, MS 21, f. 236r*

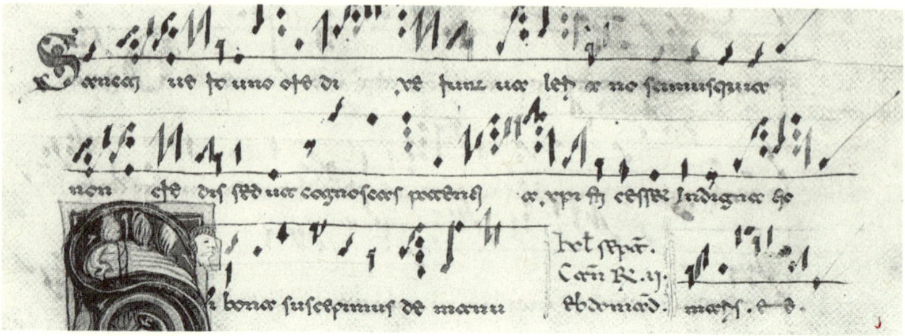

7b) Beneventan shapes in Sancte vero uno ore, *Ben 20, f. 278*

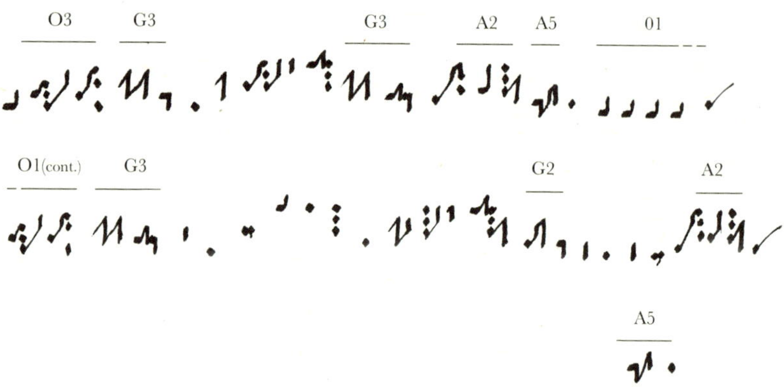

an unusual solution to the problem of transposition, it is easily manageable since the range of the melody does not extend beyond the sixth above the final. A similar phenomenon has been discussed by Katarina Livljanić in her study of modality in practical and theoretical sources from Montecassino. Livljanić discusses several examples of conflicting modal attribution in which a given antiphon is notated at differing pitch levels in several south Italian sources. She concludes that the apparent differences in mode between several of these examples (differences that can be adjusted to indicate the correct placement of the semitone by the addition of a B-flat) do not signify a difference in the pitch structure of the melody, but in the manner of notating the melody.[9] It

[9] Katarina Livljanić, "Modalité orale et modalité écrite: Attribution modale des antiennes dans le tonaire de Monte Cassino," *Études Grégoriennes* 30 (2002), 34, 39.

seems likely that this is the case here as well and that the notational solution is simply a result of writing a melody known aurally in a system of Gregorian finals. It is probable that this piece was still sung with the pitch structure of the Beneventan system even though the notation indicates a modification of pitch.

4) Antiphons in which the Beneventan and Gregorian modal spaces have become mixed

In *Sanctissimus arontius*, an antiphon for the Holy Twelve Brothers of Benevento (Ben21, f. 236r), we find a number of common Beneventan formulas at a pitch level consistent with the Beneventan core repertory (see figures G2 and M6 in Example 8). The second cadence (figures A2 and A5 in the example) appears to be comprised of two characteristic melodic shapes that are associated with cadences to A in the core repertory. In *Sanctissimus arontius*, these figures are used for a cadence to G. It appears the scribe has made some adjustments to the pitch of some characteristic Beneventan cadence formulas. The formulaic melodic material at the cadence is still recognizable as Beneventan, but the pitch structure has been altered.

In this antiphon, the desire to conform to the precepts of the Gregorian modal system appears to have altered the modal fabric of the piece; while many melodic shapes are placed where we might expect them, the cadence figures have been altered to assure adherence to the Gregorian system of finals. Material commonly found in cadence formulas to A appears to have been adapted

Example 8. An Antiphon from the Office of the Holy Twelve Brothers of Benevento (Antiphon with mixed modal space)

8a) Benevento, Biblioteca capitolare, MS 21, f. 236r/v

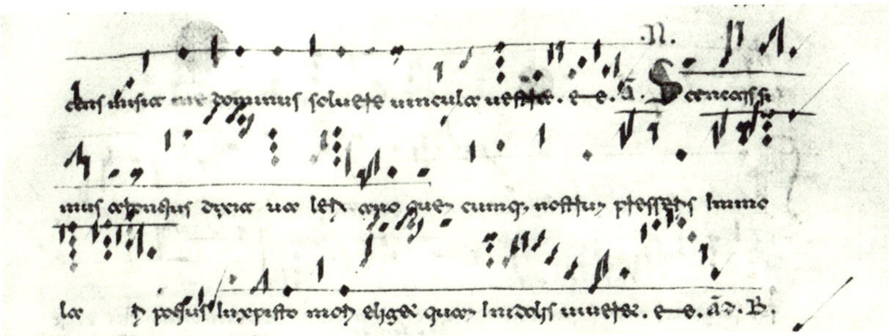

8b) Beneventan shapes in Sanctissimus arontius

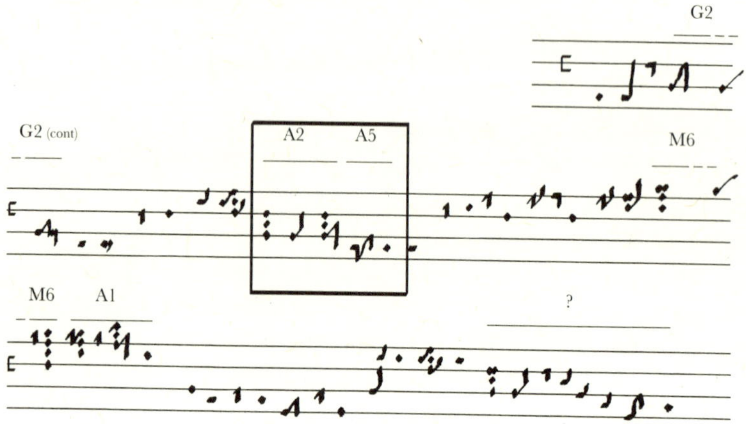

to a G cadence, and for a short span the characteristic Beneventan melodic space is brought into conformity with the Gregorian finals.[10]

5) Usque in senectam: Notational inconsistency or modal change?

A further example of the conflict between Beneventan and Gregorian modality can be seen in Example 9, a Beneventan-style antiphon for St. Xistus, *Usque in senectam* (Ben21, f. 236rv). The first part of this antiphon contains several common Beneventan formulas notated at a pitch level consistent with the Beneventan modal system. The Beneventan modality then appears to break down in the last phrase of the antiphon. Beginning at the text *domine deus*, a number of common Beneventan formulas appear to have been shifted downward by one step. This sudden transposition is particularly striking in that a single formula (figure G2) appears successively in the same line at two different pitches.

In the example, a smooth arrival on a G final seems to have been achieved by simply shifting the final phrase of the antiphon down a tone. This sequential modulation is inconsistent with our understanding of the relative diastematy

[10] Livljanić also observed a related example of the phenomenon of modal change in the final note or cadence pattern in a manuscript from Montecassino. Livljanić discusses an example in which a transposed melody is brought back to its correct final only by the final cadential formula; Livljanić, "Modalité orale et modalité écrite," 31. Although the context is different (Livljanić's example involves a conflict of modal assignment between the plagal and authentic modes), the phenomenon of modifying cadence material to bring the piece to a close on the appropriate final is analogous to the example presented here.

Example 9. Usque in senectam: *An Antiphon from the Office of St. Xistus (Antiphon with mixed modal space)*

Benevento, Biblioteca capitolare 21, f. 216r/v

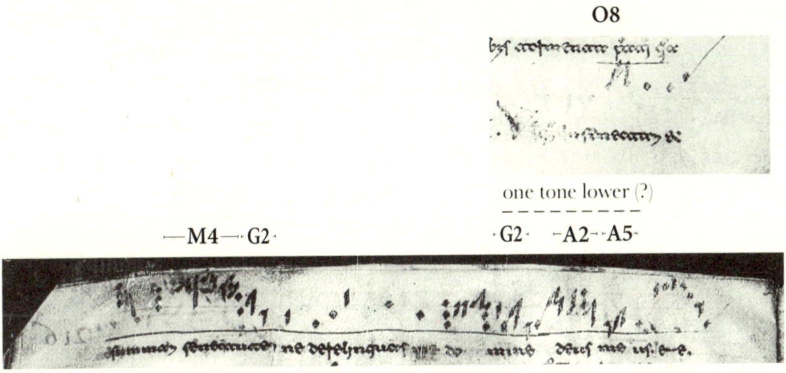

of the Beneventan melodic fund, and while the resulting melody is uncharacteristic of the modality of the Beneventan Mass Propers, it is not wholly implausible that the melody could be sung as written.

In *Sanctissimus arontius* and *Usque in senectam* we find many of the common Beneventan formulas at a pitch level consistent with the Beneventan modal system, while cadence formulas appear to have been transposed without regard for the relative diastematy of the Beneventan musical language. Although these sudden transpositions make little sense within the context of an archaic Beneventan modality, they work comfortably in a Gregorian context, and it is fully plausible that these notations represent the way these antiphons were sung. The phenomenon of adjusting a melody (via the cadence) to fit the strictures of the octoechos has been presented as part of the process of change between archaic and Gregorian modality. I believe these examples represent a lowering of the A final of the archaic Beneventan modality to fit the norms of the Gregorian books in which these antiphons were preserved.

6) Psallite Domino omnes: An antiphon for the Dedication of a Church in a transformed modal space

A final example is drawn from a Beneventan-style melody from an office for the Dedication of a Church, *Psallite Domino* (Ben21, f. 274v). This antiphon is part of a series of antiphons in Beneventan style preserved in a south Italian office for the Dedication of a Church.[11] The melody of *Psallite domino* shares

[11] The inclusion of these antiphons in the corpus of Beneventan office music is discussed in Peattie, "Beneventan Antiphon," 115–20.

melodic figures from several sources in the old Beneventan liturgy and is related to a larger complex of Beneventan material for the Mass and office. In this antiphon, it appears that the melody, which makes use of significant Beneventan melodic material and structural processes, exists in a modal space that has been completely transformed. The Dedication antiphon is illustrated in Example 10, alongside the opening section of the Beneventan communion for Ascension, *Psallite domino quis ascendit* (Ben40, f. 71v).

The Dedication Antiphon and the Beneventan Communion share a melodic and structural outline, including an opening figure (figure x), the melodic outline of a melisma (figure y), and a cadence (figure z). This musical parallel is likely inspired by the text incipit. The second phrases of both the communion and the antiphon are comprised of a recitation.[12] While the melodic shapes and structural processes of the antiphon are clearly related to the Beneventan melodic fund, the characteristic melodic material has been notated at a pitch inconsistent with our understanding of the core repertory; the pitch of the antiphon is notated one tone lower than the understood pitch of the communion. The pitch placement of the communion and the antiphon are illustrated in Example 11. The hypothetical placement of the communion *Psallite domino quis ascendit* on the staff line has been reconstructed according to the principles outlined earlier in this article.

Unlike in *Usque in senectam* and *Sanctissimus arontius* it is not only cadences that have been adjusted, and unlike in *Sancti vero uno ore* both redactions of the melody are arguably plausible. Is it possible that this piece was written entirely in a transformed modality, a modality in which some common Beneventan material associated with pieces with an A final in the Beneventan Mass Propers was thoroughly assimilated into a Gregorian modality with a G final?

BENEVENTAN AND GREGORIAN MODALITY

The manuscripts of the Beneventan zone are a melting pot of musical styles of diverse chronological and regional provenance. These musical styles range from the archaic melodies of the old Beneventan liturgy to the historically significant south Italian recensions of the central Frankish repertory. Between these distinct repertories there is a significant tradition of unique south Italian

[12] This is part of a larger complex of related material; the material in the second phrase can also be found in the Beneventan antiphons *Ad vesperum* from the Vigil of Holy Saturday (Ben33, f. 73r; Ben35, f. 66v; Ben39, f. 25v; and others) and *Ipse super* from the Vigil of Pentecost (Ben33, f. 97v; Ben35 f. 110v; Ben39, f. 92v; BAV Vat. Lat. 10645, f. 4v).

Example 10

10a) Psallite domino *(antiphon): Benevento, Bibioteca capitolare, MS 21, f. 274v*

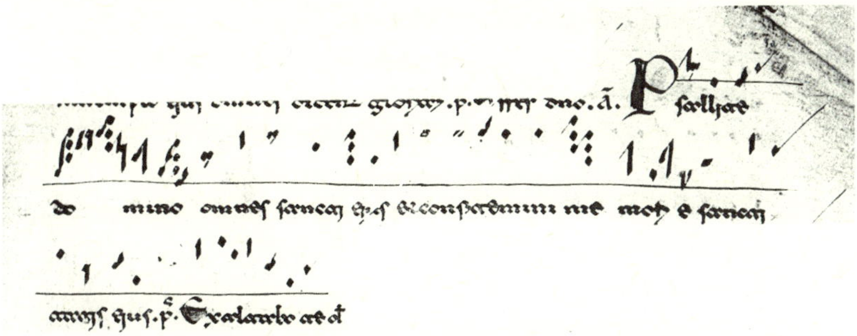

10b) Psallite domino *(communion): Benevento, Biblioteca capitolare, MS 40 f, 71v*

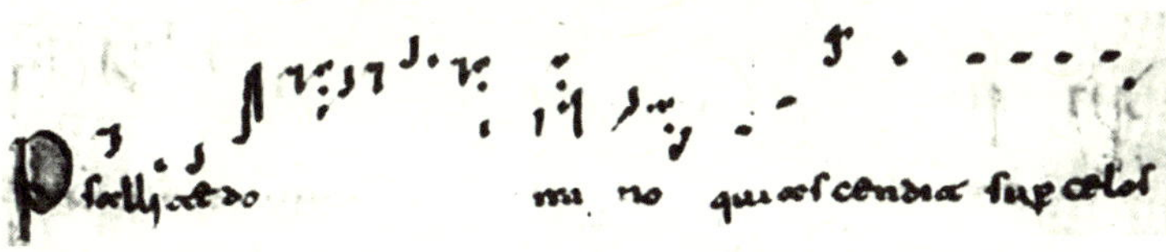

Example 11

a) Ben 21, f. 274v

b) Ben 40, f. 71v

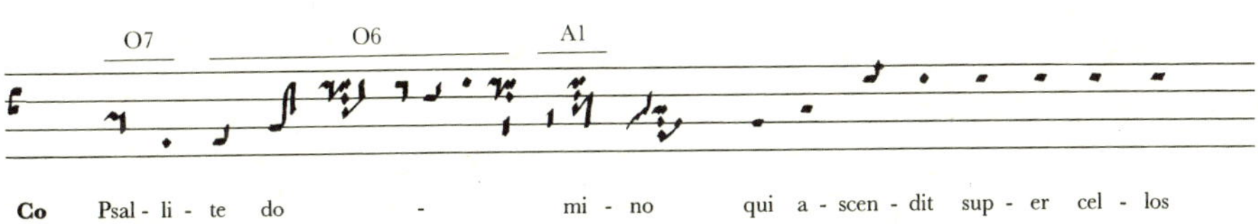

composition that includes pieces written in a musical style modeled after the Gregorian melodic tradition (the Romano-Beneventan or Neo-Gregorian repertory),[13] and others in a style that retains significant elements of the Beneventan melodic fund. The examples discussed reflect this variety, and illustrate diverse responses to the competing repertories and changing musical landscape.

I believe that the changes of mode and pitch structure discussed above are the result of a confrontation between two repertories that work under very different premises of melodic construction and mode. The Beneventan chant was a pre-octoechos repertory that made use of two distinct finals, A and G. Pieces ending on either final made use of the same formulas and fund of melodic material. The Gregorian, on the other hand, had four finals—D, E, F, and G. This is of particular importance in the office, where the system of modal classification had its greatest practical use in guiding the singer to the correct psalm tone.

Most of the inconsistencies in the late sources appear to be the result of various attempts to make the Beneventan melodies fit the notational/theoretical system of the Gregorian repertory and the octoechos. When Beneventan music is notated in Gregorian books with lines and clefs, it appears in some instances that adjustments were made to make pieces cohere to the Gregorian system of finals. In one single example (*Congregamini omnes*, Ben35), the scribes simply maintained the Beneventan system, notating a Beneventan piece on an A final. The notation of this example represents the Beneventan modality that we have observed in the core repertory of the doublet Mass Propers. I believe that this writing of the melody reflects an understanding of the Beneventan melodic fund as it was sung in the pieces of the Beneventan Mass Propers.

In many instances scribes appear to have gone to great lengths to avoid the A final. Transposition appears to be the most common solution to the problem of reconciling Beneventan music with the precepts of the octoechos and its system of finals. There are various attempts at notating antiphons so that they end on one of the four finals; the most obvious is simply to notate a piece with

[13] The terms Romano-Beneventan and Neo-Gregorian have been used to describe a variety of non-Gregorian music in south Italian manuscripts. The term Romano-Beneventan was first proposed in *Paléographie musicale* XIV to describe Gregorian-style composition in the sources of the Beneventan zone. More recently, Luisa Nardini has proposed the term Neo-Gregorian to describe pieces of local manufacture related to the Gregorian style. Luisa Nardini, "Il repertorio neo-Gregoriano del proprium missae in area Beneventana" (PhD dissertation, Universita degli Studi di Roma, 2001), 3–5.

an A final transposed to D. This transposition requires either the addition of a B-flat or a minor melodic adjustment to avoid this note.

Another, less consistent, solution, seen in the example of *Sancti vero uno ore*, was to notate the piece one tone lower than its placement in the Beneventan system, a notational solution which, if it is to be believed, would have serious implications for the pitch structure of the antiphon. It seems unlikely that these were meant to be sung as notated, and since the correct placement of the semitone can be restored quite easily with the hypothetical addition of a B-flat throughout, I believe this notational solution is purely cosmetic to give the appearance of a final on G. The apparent contradictions in pitch structure of this antiphon are a matter of notational convenience, not of any change in the way they were sung or heard. This example illustrates a collision of aural and written modality caused by a desire to give the appearance of a final on G.[14]

In other instances the changes were not entirely cosmetic. The various attempts at making Beneventan music conform to the precepts of Gregorian modality evidently began to have an effect on the melodic and modal palate of the Beneventan-style melodies. We find evidence of change in the modal fund—pieces in lined sources that insert G cadences where we might expect to find a cadence a tone higher, and some pieces that appear to have been completely transformed by Gregorian modality.

Several examples (such as *Sanctissimus arontius* and *Usque in senectam*) preserve notations where the modal space has become mixed. In these examples we find some Beneventan melodic shapes (formulas) at a pitch level that is consistent with the Beneventan system, while other shapes appear to have been transposed without regard for the relative diastematy of the Beneventan musical language. I believe these examples represent a lowering of the A final of the archaic Beneventan modality to fit the norms of the Gregorian books in which the antiphons were preserved. It is plausible that these adjusted finals were sung and that they represent Beneventan music transformed by Gregorian modality.

A final category includes pieces with Beneventan shapes that exist only in the late lined sources. In a series of antiphons from an office for the Dedication of a Church, it appears that the music, which makes significant use of

[14] In an analogous example from Montecassino, Livljanić concludes that although the same melody is sometimes notated at two different pitch levels this does not mean that they were sung differently in their practical usage in the liturgy. It shows only that they were notated differently (Livljanić, "Modalité orale et modalité écrite," 34).

Beneventan melodic material and structural processes, exists in a modal space that has been completely transformed.

The Beneventan modality adapts uneasily to the theoretical precepts of Gregorian modality, and the contradictions in the late sources appear to be the result of a struggle to render the Beneventan melodic system in a foreign notational/theoretical system. The influence of Gregorian modality precipitated change in the melodic and modal fund of the Beneventan chant, and, indeed, some of the later examples of Beneventan style music appear to have been radically altered by their contact with the Frankish-Roman chant.

Easter Vigil Canticles from Italy

ANDREAS PFISTERER

ROME

AT THE OUTSET I should mention one place in Italy that will not be discussed in this essay: Rome. There is a certain consensus that the transmitted melodies of the Roman Easter Vigil Canticles are of Carolingian origin and that the original Roman way of performing them was probably some recitation formula suitable for a lector not specializing in music.[1] At any rate, the Roman canticles seem to be independent from those to be presented here.

"VERONA"

The first tradition to be discussed here will be called (for the sake of simplicity) "Verona." The main witness for that tradition is a splendid Carolingian lectionary from around 800, written somewhere in Northern Italy, perhaps at Monza (ParisBN lat. 9451). It includes neither musical notation nor extensive rubrics, but the texts in themselves provide much useful information.

[1] Cf. Philippe Bernard, *Du chant romain au chant grégorien (IVe-XIIIe siècle)* (Paris: Les Editions du Cerf, 1996), 110 and 126–30; James McKinnon, "The Gregorian Canticle-Tracts of the Old Roman Easter Vigil," in *Festschrift Walter Wiora zum 90. Geburtstag*, ed. Christoph-Hellmut Mahling and Ruth Seiberts (Tutzing: Schneider, 1997), 254–69; Andreas Pfisterer, *Cantilena Romana: Untersuchungen zur Überlieferung des gregorianischen Chorals* (Paderborn: Schöningh, 2002), 205–6; Joseph Dyer, "The Eleventh-Century Epistolary of Santa Cecilia in Trastevere," *Archiv für Liturgiewissenschaft* 46 (2004), 311–50. For the texts of the Roman canticles, see Bonifatius Fischer, "Die Lesungen der römischen Ostervigil unter Gregor d. Gr.," in *Colligere Fragmenta*, ed. Bonifatius Fischer and Virgil Fiala (Beuron: Beuroner Kunstverlag, 1952), 144–59 (repr. in *idem*, *Beiträge zur Geschichte der lateinischen Bibel* [Freiburg: Herder, 1986], 18–50).

Table 1. Canticle texts in ParisBN lat. 9451

f. 83–83v: **Canticum Exodi**	f. 85: **Canticum Isaiae**	f. 86: **Canticum Habacuc**
Cante- mus domino gloriose enim honorificatus est. equum et ascensore de- gecit in mare. cantemus. fortitudo mea $^{\text{et laus mea}}$ dominus et factus est mihi in salu- te. cantemus. iste deus meus et glorificabo eum deus patris mei et exalta- bo eum. cantemus. dominus quasi uir pugnator omnipotens nomen eius. cantemus. electi principes ^{eis} submersi sunt in mari rubro. cante- mus. dominus regnauit in ae- ternum et ultra. cante- mus. filii autem israhel ambu- lauerunt [su]per siccum in medio eius cantemus.	uinea domini spetiosa facta est. Cantabo nunc dilecto can- ticum dilectae uineae meae. uinea facta est di- lecta in cornu in loco ube- ri. et edificaui turrem in medio eius. et torcolar fodi in ea. et macheria[m] circumdedi et circumfo- di et plantaui uineam so- rech. nunc homo qui ha- bitas in hierosalem. iu- dica inter me et uineam meam. debuerat enim fa- cere uuas fecit autem labrus- cas. sustinui ut facere ius- titiam fecit iniquitatem. diruam maceriam eius non plantabitur neque fodietur. uae qui con- iungitis domum ad domum et agrum et ad agrum copo- latis usque ad terminum loci. numquid habitabi- tis soli uos in medio ter- rae. in auribus meis sunt haec. dicit dominus exercituum.	gaudebo in deo salutari meo domine deus uirtus mea. Domine audiui auditionem tuam et timui. domine opus tuum in medio an- norum *uiuifica*[bo] illud domine deus uirtus mea. in medio annorum notum facies. cum iratus fue- ris misericordia re^{cor}- *daueris domine deus.* deus ab austro ueniet et sanctus de monte umbroso. domine deus. ope- ruit caelos gloria eius. et laudes eius plena est terra. domine deus. splen- dor eius ut lux erit. cor- nua in manibus eius. domine deus. suscitans sus- citabis arcum tuum iura- menta tribus quam lo- cutus es. domine deus. egres- sus es in salute populi tui. in salute cum christo tuo. domine deus. uiam fecis- ti in mari. equis tuis in lutum aquarum multarum. domine deus. ego autem in domino gau- debo. et exultabo in deo ihesu meo. domine deus. et po- net pedes meos quasi ceruorum. et super ex- celsa mea deducit me in psalmis canentem. domine deus. gaudebo in deo salutare meo domine deus uir- tus mea.

[letters deleted by points] | *written on erasure* | $^{\text{interlinear addition}}$

The texts of the three Easter Vigil Canticles were published by Klaus Gamber in 1961.[2] A quasi-diplomatic transcription appears in Table 1. All three Canticles have a refrain; in the Canticum Exodi and the Canticum Habacuc,

[2] Klaus Gamber, "Die Lesungen und Cantica an der Ostervigil im 'Comes Parisinus'," *Revue Bénédictine* 71 (1961), 125–34, especially 128–29. This article was the starting point for my research presented here. The edition of the lectionary by Robert Amiet ("Un 'comes' carolingien inédit de la Haute-Italie," *Ephemerides Liturgicae* 73 (1959), 335–67) includes no hint as to the existence of these canticles.

these are marked by a cue after each verse (*Cantemus, Domine Deus*). In the Canticum Isaiae there is no cue, but the first sentence does not belong to the biblical text (Is. 5:1–9) and the best justification for a textual addition is a refrain. This interpretation is reinforced by the extra-large initial letter at the beginning of the biblical text. Why does the scribe use two different ways of notating a refrain—with and without cue? Perhaps because he (or one of his predecessors) used two different exemplars.

This explanation becomes even more plausible when we look at the biblical texts. *Cantemus Domino* and *Gaudebo* use the Vulgate version for the verses, but an Old Latin version for the refrain. This can be seen easily in *Gaudebo*, where the text of the refrain is partly repeated in the ninth verse—it begins in the longest line of the third column of Table 1 (*ego autem in domino gaudebo*). There we find the very characteristic Vulgate reading *in deo ihesu meo* instead of *in deo salutari meo* of the refrain. It was Jerome who inserted the name of Jesus in the place of its presumed etymological meaning.[3] This sort of discrepancy between refrain and verse is a typical phenomenon in chant texts. Often it is easy to modernize the text of verses sung to a psalmodic formula, while it is difficult to modernize a refrain text connected with an individual melody. So we may assume that at some point before our manuscript was copied the original Old Latin texts had been replaced by their Vulgate equivalents without changing the refrains. And we may assume that the verses were sung to some sort of psalmodic formula.

Vinea Domini, however, has preserved its Old Latin text. It is another type of revision that we can detect here. Almost all Old Latin versions of this canticle end with verse seven of the biblical text.[4] The Verona canticle adds parts of verses eight and nine (*uae qui coniungitis*)—in the Vulgate version. So there was a redaction using the Vulgate, but it worked differently from the redaction that introduced the Vulgate version into the other two canticles. The best solution for that situation is to assume two different traditions of Easter Vigil Canticles that have been united in our manuscript (or one of its predecessors).

Another suspicious point is the placement of *Gaudebo*, the Canticum Habacuc. It is preceded not by a reading from the book of Habacuc, but by the introductory verses of the song of Moses from Deuteronomy. That is, it is introduced as if it were the Canticum Deuteronomii that is actually sung

[3] Heinrich Schneider, *Die altlateinischen biblischen Cantica* (Beuron: Beuroner Kunstverlag, 1938), 82–83.

[4] Jean-Claude Haelewyck, "Le cantique de la vigne: Histoire du texte vieux latin d'Is 5,1–7(9a)," *Ephemerides Theologicae Lovanienses* 65 (1989), 257–79.

in other traditions at that place. So we have to assume again the combination of two different traditions, a set of readings without Habacuc and a set of canticles with Habacuc and probably without a Canticum Deuteronomii. The redactor obviously could not find a better place for the orphaned canticle than to dress it up as the song of Moses.

The series of ten readings as contained in our lectionary is identical to that of the Old Gelasian Sacramentary,[5] wherever it comes from originally. A series of readings including Habacuc is attested in Spain by the Missale Mixtum[6] and in Gaul by the palimpsest lectionary of Weissenburg.[7] For Italy, I know of only two manuscripts that include a Habacuc reading: the central Italian missal BAV Vat. lat. 4770 from the tenth/eleventh century and the eleventh-century missal and breviary Rome, Biblioteca Casanatense 1907 from Monte Amiata. Both integrate the Habacuc reading into a modified version of the Frankish Gelasian series. Vat. lat. 4770 represents a colorful mixture of material from the standard tradition, Benevento, Rome, and elsewhere. It contains, furthermore, a late Beneventan series of Gregorian tracts and canticles, including the Habacuc canticle *Domine audiui*, to be sung after the narration of the Creation, but no trace of a suitable canticle connected with the Habacuc reading.

* * *

We should now turn to the lesser witnesses. First, there is another lectionary, Verona, Biblioteca capitolare, LXXXII (77), written in the ninth century, probably in Verona. It includes identical texts for *Cantemus Domino* and *Vinea Domini*, but no canticle after the introduction to the Canticum Deuteronomii.[8] Obviously someone deleted the disguised Canticum Habacuc without replacing it by a real Canticum Deuteronomii. Then there is the fragment of a lectionary from Regensburg (Munich BSB, clm 7678) from the eighth century, which includes the beginning of *Vinea Domini*. Klaus Gamber, who published

[5] *Liber Sacramentorum Romanae aeclesiae ordinis anni circuli*, ed. Leo Cunibert Mohlberg (Rome: Herder, 1960), 70–72.

[6] *Missale mixtum*, ed. Alfonso Ortiz, Alexander Lesley, Jacques-Paul Migne, Patrologia latina 85 (Paris 1850), 446–61.

[7] *Das älteste Liturgiebuch der lateinischen Kirche: Ein altgallikanisches Lektionar des 5./6. Jhs aus dem Wolfenbütteler Palimpsest-Codex Weissenburgensis 76*, ed. Alban Dold (Beuron: Beuroner Kunstverlag, 1936), 7–8.

[8] Sieghild Rehle, "Lectionarium Plenarium Veronense (Bibl. Cap., Cod. LXXXII)," *Sacris Erudiri* 22 (1974–75), 321–76, especially 339–40.

it, thought it was a relative of the Verona lectionary.[9] I would prefer to place its exemplar in central Italy.[10]

A second complete witness is the famous Missal of San Eutizio near Norcia (Rome, Biblioteca Vallicelliana, B 8) from the eleventh century, unfortunately without musical notation.[11] Here the Easter Vigil includes the normal Gregorian canticles, but the Vigil of Pentecost includes our three canticle texts. In the Roman liturgy, the Vigil of Pentecost is mainly a shortened copy of the Easter Vigil, so it is possible for it to function as an area of retreat for older uses. Two points are significant in this witness. First, the way of notating the refrain is identical to that in our lectionaries; thus, the difference between the notation with and without cues is not owing to the fancy of a single scribe, but is part of the written transmission of these texts. Second, in the San Eutizio manuscript, the canticle texts are given as part of the reading, marked by an enlarged capital and in one case by the rubric *Lectio abbacuc prophetae*; and after each there follows the cue for the respective Gregorian canticle. Obviously the scribe did not recognize these texts as chants; he simply copied them from his exemplar. Perhaps he intended to preserve as much material as he could from older books, even when he did not know what to do with it. This observation shows that our canticles were no longer actually sung in the liturgy. It is not surprising that other manuscripts from that area, for example the missal BAV Barb. lat. 560, dispense with them altogether.

I have found only two missals that include further traces of our canticles. The most interesting is Benevento, Biblioteca capitolare, 33 (tenth/eleventh century). It includes the canticle texts *Cantemus Domino* and *Vinea Domini*. In the first case the cues for the repetition of the refrain have been omitted; one can recognize the prehistory of that part of the reading as a chant only from

[9] Klaus Gamber, "Fragmenta Liturgica III," *Sacris Erudiri* 18 (1967–68), 306–32, especially 328–32.

[10] Gamber based his claim on the series of readings in the Easter Vigil. Since this series of ten readings reached the Roman Old Gelasian Sacramentary as well as a Northern Italian lectionary, it cannot be used for a narrow localization. The other indicative point is the position of the gospel Luke 14:16–24 directly before the Vigil of John Baptist. The "Verona" lectionaries have that gospel at the second Sunday after the octave of Pentecost; it is followed by three Sundays and the Ember Days before John Baptist. There are, however, manuscripts that have Luke 14:16–24 on the fourth Sunday after Pentecost, directly before John Baptist; these include the Missal of San Eutizio and the Beneventan tradition. Thus the Regensburg fragment should be grouped with these.

[11] Facsimile edition: *Missale Antiquum Plenarium: Ex Gelasiano, et Gregoriano codice conflatum . . .* (Spoleto: Tipolitografia Nuova Eliografica, 2006).

the Old Latin reading *honorificatus est* instead of *magnificatus est* in the former refrain and from its selection of verses, which is identical with the Verona canticle. In the second case the text of the verses has been replaced by the plain Vulgate text, but the non-biblical refrain has been preserved at the end.

The tenth/eleventh century missal BAV Vat. lat. 4770 from central Italy has no canticle texts within the readings, but at the end of the Isaiah reading it gives the former refrain *Vinea enim Domini speciosa facta est*. This seems to be the last remnant of the canticle.

The Old Gelasian Sacramentary has already been mentioned, its series of ten readings is identical with that of the "Verona" lectionary. The Old Gelasian Sacramentary and some of its descendants do include the cue *Vinea Domini* or even *Vinea Domini speciosa*.[12] This is clearly not the Roman canticle *Vinea facta est*. Therefore, it seems probable that *Vinea Domini speciosa* was originally connected with that series of ten readings, whatever its origins before it came to Rome and northern Italy.

Another Roman witness for *Vinea Domini* is the Epistolary of Alcuin which is based on a seventh-century Roman book. Here again we get only a cue within a series of six readings.[13] These cues in liturgical books do not necessarily correspond to actual practice at the time of the writing of the manuscripts. Often they are copied without being updated. So it is difficult to say for which time and for which place their testimony is valid.

"PISTOIA"

The next tradition may be called "Pistoia". It is represented by two graduals with musical notation from the eleventh/twelfth century. Pistoia C 119 is probably from Pistoia itself; Rome, Biblioteca Vallicelliana, C 52 was in the library of San Eutizio, but was surely not written there (probably it, too, is from Tuscany).[14] These manuscripts contain the normal Gregorian canticles

[12] *Vinea Domini spet* is found in an isolated descendant: *Das Prager Sakramentar [Cod. O.83 (fol. 1–120) der Bibliothek des Metropolitankapitels] II: Prolegomena und Textausgabe*, ed. Alban Dold and Leo Eizenhöfer (Beuron: Beuroner Kunstverlag, 1949), 59*. *Vinia/Vinea Domini* is preserved in some of the principal witnesses of the Frankish Gelasian Sacramentary: *Das fränkische Sacramentarium Gelasianum in alamannischer Überlieferung (Codex Sangall. No. 348)*, ed. Kunibert Mohlberg (Münster in Westfalen: Aschendorff, 1918), 85; *Liber sacramentorum Augustodunensis*, ed. Odilo Heiming (Turnhout: Brepols, 1984), 65; *Liber sacramentorum Engolismensis*, ed. Patrick Saint-Roch (Turnhout: Brepols, 1987), 112.

[13] André Wilmart, "Le lectionnaire d'Alcuin," *Ephemerides Liturgicae* 51 (1937), 136–97, especially 156.

[14] Paola Supino Martini, *Roma e l'area grafica romanesca (secoli X–XII)* (Alessandria: Edizioni dell'orso, 1987), 335.

Table 2. Canticum Isaiae (Is. 5, 1–9)

"Verona"	**"Pistoia"**
P – Paris, BnF lat. 9451 V – Verona, BC LXXXII (77) N – Rome, Bibl. Vall. B 8	P – Pistoia, BC 119 V – Rome, Bibl. Vall. C 52
R. Vinea domini speciosa facta est.	R. Vinea enim domini sabaoth domus israhel.
1 Cantabo nunc dilecto canticum dilectae uineae meae.	1 Cantabo nunc dilecto canticum / dilectae uineae meae. Domus.
2 Vinea facta est dilecta in cornu in loco uberi.	2 Vinea facta est dilecta / in cornu in loco uberi. Domus.
3 Et aedificaui turrem in medio eius et torcolar fodi in ea.	3 Et aedificaui turrem in medio eius / et torcular fodi in ea. Domus.
4 Et maceria circumdedi et circumfodi et plantaui uineam sorech.	4 Et maceria circumdedi et circumfodi / et plantaui uineam sorech. Domus.
5 Nunc homo qui habitas in hierusalem. iudica inter me et uineam meam.	5 Et nunc homo qui habitas in hierusalem / iudica inter me et uineam meam. Domus.
6 Debuerat enim facere uuas fecit autem spinas.	6 Debuerat enim facere uuas / fecit autem spinas. Domus.
7 Sustinui ut faceret iustitiam fecit autem iniquitatem.	7 Sustinui ut faceret iustitiam / fecit autem iniquitatem. Domus.
8 Diruam maceriam eius. non plantabitur neque fodietur.	8 Diruam maceriam eius / non plantabitur neque fodietur. Domus.
9 Vae qui coniungitis domum ad domum et agrum ad agrum copulatis usque ad terminum loci.	9 Vae qui coniungitis domum ad domum / et agrum ad agrum copulatis / usque ad terminum loci. Domus.
10 Numquid habitabitis soli uos in medio terrae.	10 Numquid habitabitis soli uos / in medio terrae. Domus.
11 In auribus meis sunt haec. dicit dominus exercituum.	11 In auribus meis sunt haec / domini exercituum. Domus. Vinea.
3 aedificauit N | eam V 6 spinas] labruscas P (= Vulgata) 7 sustinuit V | facere P | autem] *om.* P 8 et non N 9 ad agrum] et ad agrum P agro N (= Vulgata) 11 dicit dominus] domini V (= Vulgata) | sunt. haec dicit N post 11 Vinea domini speciosa *ad.* N	1 cantico P 2 aedificauit PV | turrim V | fodit P 3 maceriam circumdedit et circumfodit P | soretht P soreph V 5 et nunc] et tu V 7 sustinuit V 8 non] neque P | potabitur V (= putabitur Vulgata) | fodetur P (*sed cum quatuor notis!*) 9 us usque V

and additionally another Canticum Isaiae with the refrain *Vinea enim Domini Sabaoth domus Israhel*. This piece has been published several times in transcription and facsimile.[15] The text can be found in normalized form in Table 2. As may be seen there, the text of the verses is practically identical to that of

[15] Peter Wagner, *Einführung in die Gregorianischen Melodien III: Gregorianische Formenlehre: Eine choralische Stilkunde* (Leipzig, 1921; repr. Hildesheim – Wiesbaden: G. Olms, 1962), 360–61; Michel Huglo, "Notes historiques à propos du second Décret sur la Vigile Paschale," *Revue grégorienne* 31 (1952), 121–36, especially 131; Bruno Stäblein, "Psalm: B. Lat. Ps.-Gesang im MA," *MGG* 10 (1962), 1676–90, especially 1689; *idem*, *Schriftbild der einstimmigen Musik* (Leipzig: Deutscher Verlag für Musik, 1975), 138–39.

the "Verona" canticle; the variants between the two texts are roughly the same or of the same sort as the variants within the texts. The significant difference is the text of the refrain and the cues for the repetition of the second half of the refrain after each verse.

Since the text of the verses is a reordered collection of elements of the biblical text, one cannot explain the correspondence between Verona and Pistoia as due to chance. Thus we have to assume another redaction that exchanged the refrain text. The Pistoia refrain is biblical, the Verona refrain is not; therefore priority belongs very probably to the Verona version.

On the other hand, the Pistoia melody may give us an indirect impression of the lost Verona melody. The two manuscripts show some variants (see Example 1), especially on the word *Sabaoth*; the Vallicelliana manuscript turns into the final melisma of the verse a bit earlier than the Pistoia manuscript. From the point of view of a normalizing transmission, the Pistoia version would be judged as the more conservative one. It would be possible with a bit of conjecture to re-exchange the refrain text as I have done in the third line of the example. The psalm tone used for the verses is close to the Gregorian seventh psalm tone for the introit and communion. The middle cadence and the re-intonation correspond exactly to the seventh psalm tone as found in the Pistoia gradual, the end of the final cadence corresponds to the medial caesura of the refrain as is typical for responsorial chants with a shortened repetenda. So either this psalm tone is the result of a mixture of Gregorian and local traditions or it represents a tradition that is musically close to the Gregorian.

Example 1. Canticum Isaiae, refrain and verse tone

Table 3. Stemma Canticum Isaiae

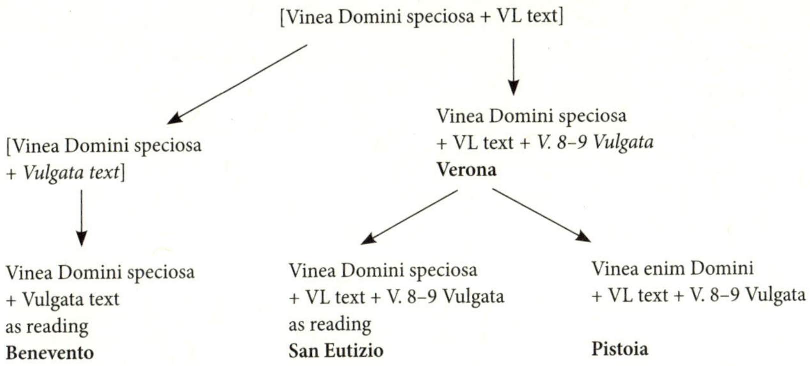

For this canticle to have been preserved alongside the respective Gregorian canticle, there must have been a strong local tradition, perhaps even involving the people singing the refrain. But why only one canticle? The simplest explanation would be that only one canticle had its own melody; perhaps the other canticles were sung to a recitation formula (i.e., without refrain). This would at least explain why the redactor of the Verona lectionary had to rely on different traditions for his series of Easter Vigil Canticles. The relations between the versions of this canticle are summarized in Table 3.

MILAN

Before traveling to Benevento we have to make a little detour to Milan. The liturgical structure of the Milanese Easter Vigil is a bit confused, and the manuscripts disagree about the order of the six readings.[16] A short version of

[16] The earliest witness seems to be the Sacramentary of Bergamo from the 9th century (*Sacramentarium Bergomense*, ed. Angelo Paredi [Bergamo: Edizioni Monumenta Bergomensia, 1962], 163–64) with the order: Gen. 1–2, Gen. 22, Ex. 13–14, Ex. 12, Is. 54–55, Is. 1. The eleventh-century Manuale (*Manuale Ambrosianum ex codice saec. XI olim in usum canonicae Vallis Travaliae*, ed. Marcus Magistretti, 2 vols. [Milan, 1904–05], 2:202–4) gives the order: Gen. 1–2, Gen. 22, Ex. 12 (+Deut. 3), Is. 54–55 (+Ex. 15), Ex. 13–14, Is. 1. The twelfth-century liturgist Beroldus (*Beroldus sive Ecclesiae Ambrosianae Mediolanensis kalendarium et ordines saec. XII*, ed. Marcus Magistretti [Milan, 1894], 110) corrects this order to: Gen. 1–2, Gen. 22, Ex. 12 (+Deut. 3), Ex. 13–14 (+Ex. 15), Is. 54–55, Is. 1. The exact length of the readings can be found in a twelfth-century Old Testament Lectionary (*Auctarium Solesmense, series liturgica 1: Veterum Ambrosianae liturgiae monumentorum absoluta collectio 1,1: Codex sacramentorum Bergomensis: Accedunt tres Indiculi sive Capitularia Lectionum, Epistolarum et Evangeliorum antiqua* [Solesmes, 1900], 199).

the canticle of the Three Men in the Fiery Furnace is sung after the reading from Exodus 12 (the Passover lamb). The corresponding reading of the Three Men has its place together with the long version of the same canticle on Good Friday, which seems to be the original place; therefore I exclude this canticle from our investigation.

The Exodus canticle,[17] which is clearly at home in the Easter Vigil, has a corresponding reading from Exodus 13 and 14, but this breaks off before reaching the Red Sea. Thus, it is necessary to introduce the canticle proper with a phrase from the reading *Tunc cantabat moyses et filii israhel canticum hoc deo et dixerunt*, sung to a recitation formula. This is a peculiarity of Milan, but another feature reappears in some manuscripts we already know: after the canticle proper the reading continues with the same recitation formula for the narration of Miriam leading the women in dancing and singing the same refrain as Moses had before. This final part of the reading is missing in the older Verona lectionary, but it is present in the younger one as well as in the missal of San Eutizio and in Benevento 33, so it was probably an original part of the Verona tradition (see Table 4).

The Milanese canticle has preserved an Old Latin text version, in contrast to the Verona tradition, but its selection of verses is almost the same. The beginning of the canticle corresponds to the first three verses of the biblical text, so it is not significant, but the following verses (from *Electi principes*, verse five in my numbering) are selected from the nineteen biblical verses (Ex. 15:1–19). The Milanese version omits one of the selected verses present in Verona, but includes the other two. This seems to be enough to propose a distant connection between the two traditions.

The Milanese manuscripts give no hint of responsorial performance of the Canticum Exodi. Nevertheless, it seems possible that the first verse was sung originally as a refrain, as in the Verona version. The verse melodies are formulaic in the way that there are several options for the beginning, two options for the medial caesura, and an identical final phrase. The melody of the first verse, however, is more individual.[18] We shall find even clearer examples of this

[17] Editions: *Antiphonarium Ambrosianum du Musée Britannique (XIIe siècle), codex additional 34 209: Transcription*, Paléographie musicale 6 (Solesmes, 1900), 308–9; Terence Bailey, *The Ambrosian Cantus*, (Ottawa: Institute of Mediaeval Music, 1987), 226–37 (comparative edition of four manuscript versions).

[18] Cf. Bailey, *Ambrosian Cantus*, 64.

Table 4. Canticum Exodi (Ex. 15, 1–21)

"Verona"	**Benevento**	**Milan**
P – ParisBN lat. 9451 V – Verona, BC LXXXII (77) N – Rome, Bibl. Vall. B 8	Benevento, Biblioteca capitolare, 33	LondonBL Add. 34209
	... Tunc cecinit moyses et filii israhel. carmen hoc domino et dixerunt	Tunc cantabant moyses et filii israhel canticum hoc deo et dixerunt
R. Cantemus domino gloriose enim honorificatus est.	cantemus domino gloriose enim honorificatus est.	cantemus domino gloriose enim honorificatus est.
1 Equum et ascensorem deiecit in mare. Cantemus.	equum et ascensorem deiecit in mare.	1 Equum et ascensorem proiecit in mare.
2 Fortitudo mea et laus mea dominus et factus est mihi in salutem. Cantemus.	2 Fortitudo mea et laus mea dominus. et factus est mihi in salutem.	2 Adiutor et protector factus est mihi in salutem.
3 Iste deus meus et glorificabo eum. deus patris mei et exaltabo eum. Cantemus.	3 Iste deus meus et honorabo eum. deus patris mei et exaltabo eum.	3 Hic deus meus et honorificabo eum deus patris mei et exaltabo eum.
4 Dominus quasi uir pugnator. omnipotens nomen eius. Cantemus.	4 Dominus quasi uir pugnator. omnipotens nomen eius.	4 Dominus conterens bella dominus nomen est ei.
5 Electi principes eius submersi sunt in mari rubro. Cantemus.	5 Electos principes eius submersi sunt in mari rubro.	
6 Dominus regnauit in aeternum et ultra. Cantemus.	dominus regnauit in aeternum et ultra.	6 Dominus regnans in aeternum et super saeculum et adhuc.
7 Filii autem israhel ambulauerunt per siccum in medio eius. Cantemus.	7 Filii autem israhel ambulauerunt per siccum in medio maris.	7 Filii autem israhel ambulauerunt per aridam in medio maris.
X Sumpsit ergo maria prophetissa soror aaron tympanum in manu. egressaeque sunt omnes mulieres post eam. cum tympanis et choris quibus praecinebat dicens. Cantemus domino gloriose enim honorificatus est. equum et ascensorem deiecit in mare.	X Sumpsit autem maria prophetissa soror aaron tympanum in manu. egressaeque sunt omnes mulieres post eam. cum tympanis et choris. quibus praecinebat dicens. cantemus domino gloriose enim honorificatus est equum et ascensorem deiecit in mare.	X Sumpsit autem maria prophetissa soror aaron tympanum in manu sua et exierunt omnes mulieres post eam cum tympanis et choris praecedebat autem eas maria dicens cantemus domino.
1 Cantemus] *om.* VN | *V. 1 pars responsorii* VN (*ut uidetur*) 2 et laus mea] *s.l.* P | est] es V | Cantemus] *om.* V 5 eius] eis *s.l.* P | submersi sunt] sunt V | mari rubro] mare rubrum V 7 per] *corr. e* super P | in medio] immedio N X *om.* P | honorificatus] magnificatus V (= Vulgata)	filiis | hoc] oc *s.l.* X praeinebat	

situation in Benevento, so I defer discussion for the moment. Table 5 gives a stemma for the versions of this canticle.

Table 5. Stemma Canticum Exodi

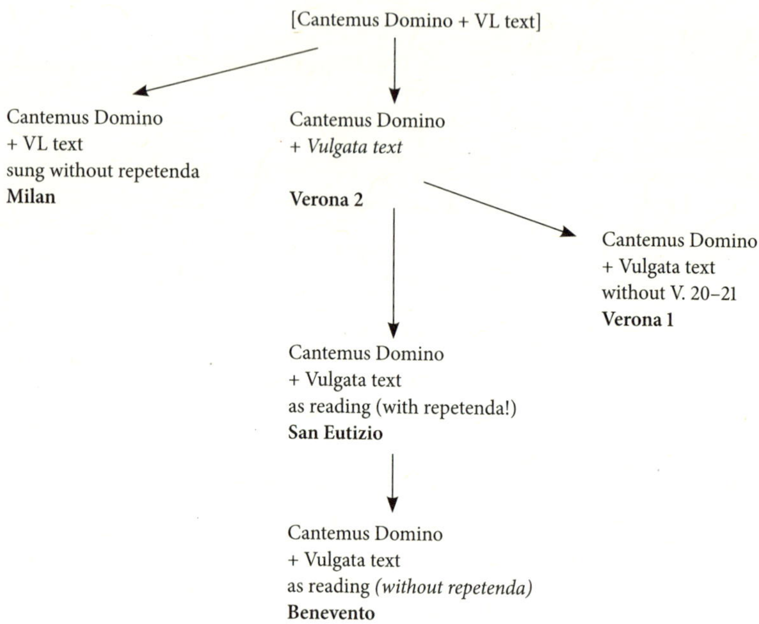

BENEVENTO

In Benevento the situation is more complicated, or at least we can recognize that it is more complicated owing to a broader transmission. The liturgy of Benevento as we know it is heavily contaminated with Roman influences, and the manuscripts show different degrees and varieties of contamination. Concerning the Easter Vigil, the different series of readings derive either from the Gregorian Sacramentary or from the Gelasian Sacramentary; there are some local peculiarities, but they are not sufficient to reconstruct an original Beneventan series.

The Beneventan chant manuscripts give us a tract or canticle after each reading—a convention known only in Benevento and its neighborhood and in Milan—but the material is completely Gregorian. Some of the manuscripts, especially two eleventh-century graduals, Benevento 38 and 40, notate additional canticles in Old Beneventan style; and as we have already seen, Benevento 33 includes former canticle texts within the readings. So at least two non-Roman traditions of Easter Vigil Canticles are attested in Benevento.

Furthermore, the Beneventan canticle melodies can be divided into four stylistic levels. Is this the result of indigenous differentiation or decadence, or of foreign influence? Some points become clearer when we take a closer look at those melodies.

On the lowest stylistic level, there is a well-known recitation formula used for the canticles of Jonah and of Azariah.[19] In some manuscripts from Benevento and Central Italy, these canticles are notated in the Easter Vigil together with the respective readings. In the more conservative Beneventan manuscripts, however, there is no hint of their being used in the Easter Vigil; instead, their place is in the Beneventan services for Maundy Thursday and Good Friday. So they probably never had a place in the Old Beneventan Easter Vigil.

The same can be said about the piece at the highest stylistic level, the Canticle of the Three Men in the Fiery Furnace sung in responsorial manner and in melismatic style. This canticle has its place in the Beneventan service for Good Friday.[20]

If we remove these pieces from the Easter Vigil, four canticles with proper melodies remain.[21] Two of them (*Attende caelum*, *Sicut ceruus*) are sung to psalmodic melodies repeated for each verse. The other two (*Domine audiui*, *Cantabo nunc*) have additionally an individual melody for the first verse. René-Jean Hesbert proposed a responsorial way of performance with the first verse as a refrain.[22] This seems in fact to be the only reasonable explanation for the individuality of the first verses in contrast to the other ones. But our eleventh-century manuscripts give no cues for the repetition of the first verse, while they do so consistently in the Canticle of the Three Men. Thus we should assume that an original responsorial performance had been lost in the case of *Domine audiui* and *Cantabo nunc* by the eleventh century.

The assumption of a development from responsorial to soloistic psalmody is at first sight contrary to the general picture of the development of psalmody drawn by Jean Claire.[23] But on closer inspection it seems quite comprehensible. The main objective of the antique responsorial psalmody was the participation

[19] Dyer, "The Eleventh-Century Epistolary," 337–42.

[20] Thomas Forrest Kelly, *The Beneventan Chant* (Cambridge: Cambridge University Press, 1989), 156–60; Dyer, "The Eleventh-Century Epistolary," 333–37.

[21] Texts and melodies are edited in [René-Jean Hesbert,] "La tradition bénéventaine dans la tradition manuscrite," *Paléographie musicale* 14 (1931), 60–465, especially 362–72.

[22] Ibid., 368, n. 2.

[23] See the recent summary in Jean Claire, "Modality in Western Chant: An Overview," *Plainsong and Medieval Music* 17 (2008), 101–27, especially 109–13.

of the people in singing. During the Middle Ages the participation of the people quickly diminished, its role in singing taken over by a clerical community. In the case of the Mass chants this led to an expansion of the melodies and to a shortening of the chant texts. In the case of chants that were regarded as parts of a reading, shortening of the text may have been problematic, whereas the omission of the repetition of a refrain seems to have been the better way of saving time. An exception, of course, is the Canticle of the Three Men where the responsorial structure is part of the biblical text itself.

The difference between two canticles with a special first verse and two without is explained by Hesbert as a response to the text structure.[24] This seems a weak argument. In one case, the Canticum Habacuc, we are now able to disentangle the foreign influences that led to the Beneventan version. We again find a refrain with Old Latin text combined with verses with Vulgate text.

But there is more: The text of the verses corresponds almost exactly to the Verona canticle (see Table 6); only verse five is missing in Benevento. This correspondence is significant since the canticle text is a selection out of the eighteen verses of the biblical text. As can be seen in the table, the Beneventan text is even closer to the Verona lectionary than is the San Eutizio missal (called N in the critical apparatus), which omits two verses and has a little addition in the tenth verse. The tenth verse is in fact the decisive point. Verses nine and ten of the canticle text follow each other directly in the biblical text, except for a gap of four words between those verses. This gap is easily explained: those four words are the text of the Verona repetenda *domine deus uirtus mea* (or *dominus deus fortitudo mea* in the Vulgate version). Since the repetenda is sung at this place, they need not be repeated. Thus the gap is reasonable in the Verona version, but arbitrary in the Beneventan version (with a different refrain). As a consequence, we should regard the Beneventan canticle as a descendant of the Verona canticle, its original refrain having been lost and replaced by a refrain taken from the beginning of the canticle text.

As Thomas Kelly demonstrated in his book on Beneventan chant, the first verse of the Beneventan canticle corresponds closely to the first verse of the Roman tract for Good Friday, textually as well as melodically.[25] Thus there can be no doubt that the source for the new refrain was Rome. The question

[24] [Hesbert], "La tradition bénéventaine," 368–69, n. 2.

[25] Kelly, *The Beneventan Chant*, 171–76.

Table 6. Canticum Habacuc (Hab. 3, 2–19)

"Verona"	**Benevento**
P – ParisBN lat. 9451 N – Rome, Bibl. Vall. B 8	A – Benevento, Biblioteca capitolare, 38 B – Benevento, Biblioteca capitolare, 40
R. Gaudebo in deo salutari meo domine deus uirtus mea.	
1 Domine audiui auditionem tuam et timui. domine opus tuum in medio annorum uiuifica illud. Domine deus.	*Domine audiui auditum tuum et timui consideraui opera tua et expaui.*
2 In medio annorum notum facies. cum iratus fueris misericordia recordaueris. Domine deus.	2 In medio annorum notum facies / cum iratus fueris misericordiae recordaueris.
3 Deus ab austro ueniet. et sanctus de monte umbroso. Domine deus.	3 Deus ab austro ueniet / et sanctus de monte umbroso.
4 Operuit caelos gloria eius. et laude eius plena est terra. Domine deus.	4 Operuit caelos gloria eius / et laude eius repletur terra.
5 Splendor eius ut lux erit. cornua in manibus eius. Domine deus.	
6 Suscitans suscitabis arcum tuum iuramenta tribubus quae locutus es. Domine deus.	6 Suscitans suscitabis arcum tuum / iuramenta tribus quae locutus es.
7 Egressus es in salute populi tui. in salute cum christo tuo. Domine deus.	7 Egressus es in salutem populi tui / in salutem cum christo tuo.
8 Viam fecisti in mari. equis tuis in luto aquarum multarum. Domine deus.	8 Viam fecisti in mare equis tuis / in luto aquarum multarum.
9 Ego autem in domino gaudebo. et exultabo in deo ihesu meo. Domine deus.	9 Ego autem in domino gaudebo / et exsultabo in deo ihesu meo.
10 Et ponet pedes meos quasi ceruorum. et super excelsa mea deducit me in psalmis canentem. Domine deus.	10 Et ponam pedes meos quasi ceruorum / et super excelsa mea deducet me uictor in psalmis canentem.
R. Gaudebo in deo salutari meo domine deus uirtus mea.	
V deest R1 gaudens gaudebo N 2 misericordiam recordaberis N 4 *om.* N laudes P 6 iuramenti N | tribus P | quam P 8 mare N | lutum P 9 *om.* N 10 et[1]] Deus dominus fortitudo mea et N | deducit me] deducet me uictor N | Domine deus] *om.* N R2 salutare P	2 medio-o A | motum A 4 laudes A 6 suscitaui B | tribus] patribus B (*cum notis duarum syllabarum*) 7 es] *om.* A (*notae adsunt*) | tui A 10 meos] meo A | deducit A

Example 2. Canticum Habacuc (beginning) in Old Roman, Beneventan, and Gregorian version

is, when and how did this verse come to Benevento? Example 2 shows the beginning of the three melodic versions of this verse, the so-called Old Roman, Beneventan, and Gregorian. The Gregorian version is included in the Beneventan manuscripts on Good Friday with only minimal variants; obviously they were able to reproduce the Gregorian melody correctly. The Beneventan version, however, is melodically adapted to the Old Beneventan style; the melisma marked by a circle in the example is a standard formula called "A" by Kelly.[26] Why should the Beneventan singers adapt it thus, and why should they continue to use two different versions of the same Roman piece side by side? There seems to be no reasonable answer except that these two versions represent two different stages of reception of Roman material in Benevento. They arrived at different times and probably by different routes. For the Gregorian version it is sufficiently clear that it came within the complete chant repertory, probably around the year 800, and surely not directly from Rome, but via Francia. After that complete reception of the Roman chant, it would be strange to receive another version of a piece already present. It is much more probable that the Beneventan version goes back to pre-Carolingian times and that it came more or less directly from Rome. That would mean that we possess here a small remnant of the pre-Carolingian chant of Rome. Table 7 gives a stemma of the versions of this canticle.

The other three Beneventan canticles show a certain textual correspondence to the Roman ones, but this may be due to the use of similar Old Latin text versions. At any rate, they contrast with the Vulgate text of the Habacuc canticle and of the two canticles within the readings of Benevento 33. The three Vulgate texts form a group that corresponds to the series of canticles in the Verona lectionary, so it seems possible that they came to Benevento as a group. Perhaps we should regard the transmission of the Beneventan Easter Vigil

[26] Kelly, *The Beneventan Chant*, 97–100. See also the contribution of Matthew Peattie to this volume.

Table 7. Stemma Canticum Habacuc

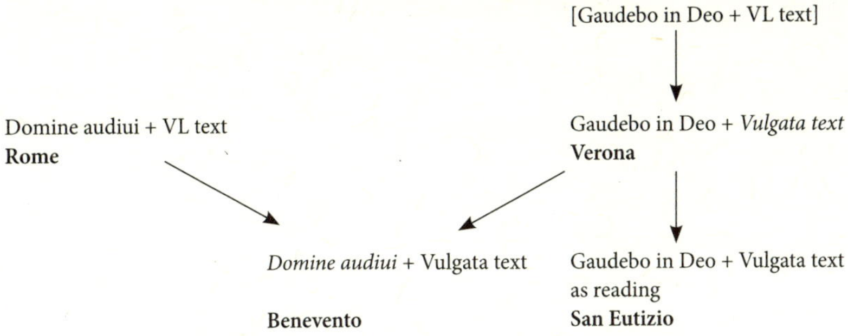

Table 8. Beneventan canticles

Canticum Habacuc	**Domine audiui** Vulgata with melody	Ben 38/40		
Canticum Exodi	**Cantemus Domino** Vulgata as reading	Ben 33	??	
Canticum Isaiae	**Vinea Domini speciosa** Vulgata as reading	Ben 33	**Cantabo nunc** VL with melody	Ben 38/40
Cant. Deuteronomii			**Attende caelum** VL with melody	Ben 38/40
Cant. Psalmi XLI			**Sicut ceruus** VL with melody	Ben 38/40, ..

Canticles as the result of a collision between two different groups or traditions of canticles (see Table 8).

The absence of the Habacuc canticle from Benevento 33 is not surprising, since there is neither a Habacuc reading nor a Deuteronomy reading in that manuscript. The absence of the Isaiah canticle *Vinea Domini speciosa* from the graduals Benevento 38 and 40 may be the result of its being replaced by a competitor from the other group. The most surprising point, however, is the absence of a Canticum Exodi from the musical tradition of the Old Beneventan chant. Can we imagine an Old Beneventan Easter Vigil without that canticle, which is sung in almost every Christian rite? Or is it probable that it got lost while the other canticles have been preserved? I have no convincing answer to these questions. They remind us that a much more complicated state of affairs may once have existed, just beyond the presently visible horizon.

CONCLUSION

The case of the Easter Vigil Canticles is a special one, as is also, for example, that of the proper chants for the Vigil Mass studied by Kenneth Levy many years ago.[27] Each of these cases opens a small window into the largely unknown chant topography of pre-Carolingian Italy. But there is a methodological peculiarity of the canticles: it is the simple text transmission in lectionaries and missals that gives us the clue to a better understanding of the few fragments of musical transmission.

For each of the Verona canticles we have found one distantly related version with a melody. Unfortunately, we never find two melodic versions for the same canticle. So it is hardly possible to judge how these melodies changed during their travels through the Italian peninsula. Even if we assume that the three Verona canticles had similar melodies (this is in no way necessary), it is difficult to argue which of the three melodies from Pistoia, Milan, and Benevento is closer to the eighth-century original. Perhaps we can exclude the Milanese canticle, for we observed that the Verona canticles require a psalmodic formula for the verses, but that will not help us very much.

On the other hand we can detect a net of connections that seems to include almost all Italian chant traditions of which we have some record. And we can see again that the musical tradition of Benevento, so comprehensively researched by Thomas Kelly, is a precious treasure; it contains many strange and difficult things that might begin to speak to us if we can find the proper context for them.

[27] Kenneth Levy, "The Italian Neophytes' Chants," *Journal of the American Musicological Society* 23 (1970), 181–227. Other studies of Italian chant include: Egon Wellesz, *Eastern Elements in Western Chant: Studies in the Early History of Ecclesiastical Music* (Oxford: Oxford University Press, 1947), 68–77, 105–10; James Borders, "The Northern Italian Antiphons ante evangelium and the Gallican Connection," *The Journal of Musicological Research* 8 (1988), 1–53.

Part III

The Persistence of Chant and of "Medieval" Music

Echoes from the Periphery

Rask 98, Modal Change, and Oral Transmission in Seventeenth-Century Iceland

ÁRNI HEIMIR INGÓLFSSON

In his epic novel *Independent People*, or *Sjálfstætt fólk*, Halldór Laxness memorably describes an ailing old woman on a small, isolated farm in the Western fjords of Iceland, "like a candle the Lord had forgotten to snuff." She spends her days reciting, in a trembling voice, the hymns she had learned in her youth, among them a bungled version of the well-known Christmas hymn *In dulci jubilo*, in which some of the Latin-texted lines are transformed into the closest sounding equivalent in the Icelandic language. Her intimacy with these songs is described as follows:

> In these pious old verses, age-hallowed and Latin-sprinkled, which the old woman had learned from her grandmother, in these lay hidden her other world; their rhythm in time with the regular pressure of the treadle was her music, to which she surrendered herself till the walls of the narrow room had floated out to the horizons of eternity and she was sitting with her hands fallen in her lap, the thread snapped, the wheel silent.[1]

In Laxness's novel, a story of one cantankerous farmer's heart-rending struggle for independence, the old woman's singing serves to remind us of

[1] Halldór Laxness, *Independent People*, trans. J. A. Thompson (New York: Alfred A. Knopf, 1946), 152.

how this isolated family has been largely unaffected by the passing of time. Accompanied by the tapping of the treadle, her grandmother's songs have been handed down from one generation to another, among the rare pastimes afforded a household living literally on the edge of civilization, on the brink of survival.

Laxness does not describe her singing in detail, but presumably it would have borne the hallmarks of the so-called "old style" of hymn-singing common in Iceland in the nineteenth century and into the early twentieth, the period in which the novel takes place. Like her treatment of the Latin-texted lines, the old woman's music-making may have been similar to what Leo Treitler has termed the Marylebone or Pettycoat-Tail phenomenon, when, as in the case of *Marie le bonne* or *Petit gateau taillé*, an unfamiliar string of sounds is assimilated into a familiar code. As Treitler explains, this phenomenon is apparent in medieval music whenever a song of one tradition has been assimilated into another, taking on the characteristics of the host tradition in the process. In such cases the foreign material, "even if it arrived by way of written books, has been transformed by local habits of hearing and performing and then newly transcribed in writing."[2] It is to such transformations of music through the fusion of oral and written processes that the present study will be devoted.

RASK 98: A SEVENTEENTH-CENTURY ICELANDIC SONGBOOK

Until the second half of the twentieth century, Iceland belonged to the European periphery both culturally and economically. An impoverished Danish colony for centuries, it is one place to which the English historian G. M. Trevelyan's notion of the "long Middle Ages," extending to the Industrial Revolution, certainly applies.[3] In a sense, Iceland was doubly peripheral, a colonial outpost of a country itself on the fringe of central European culture. It was mostly through its religious institutions that Iceland managed to stay abreast of the main cultural currents. Schools and monasteries were founded soon after the country's conversion to Christianity in the year 1000, and attempts to introduce the European musical traditions to this "insula maris in finibus mundi"—to quote Pope John XXIII from a letter of 1413—were successful

[2] Leo Treitler, *With Voice and Pen* (Oxford: Oxford University Press, 2003), 248.

[3] Ernst Robert Curtius, *European Literature in the Latin Middle Ages*, trans. Willard R. Trask (New York: Harper & Row, 1963), quoted in Karol Berger, *Bach's Circle, Mozart's Arrow* (Berkeley: University of California Press, 2007), 3.

to a certain degree.[4] The surviving manuscript sources for music in Iceland consist of hundreds of fragments of chant manuscripts written prior to the Reformation, and roughly 140 manuscript songbooks and hymnals written between 1550 and 1800. Standing worlds apart from the grand choirbooks used in English and continental cathedrals, the Icelandic sources offer instead a glimpse into Europe at the boundaries: a world both provincial and isolated, one in which familiar traditions sometimes become strangely skewed. They are remnants of what Nino Pirrotta famously called the "submerged and invisible" iceberg, as opposed to the visible tip, "the music from which we make history."[5]

It is worth noting, as both Pirrotta and Jacques Handschin have done, that the kinds of music referred to as "archaic" or "peripheral" belonged to the normal practice in "most churches, large and small, of the Western world."[6] Leo Treitler has recently raised doubts as to the usefulness of the familiar concept-pair of center and periphery, suggesting that it largely serves to preserve an overall conception of the history of art as a continuous progression to higher stages of development, the main line constantly being one that moves through centers.[7] The Icelandic sources are certainly both peripheral and archaic. Still, one would do well to keep in mind that the music they roughly suggest may not only have been confined to the farthest reaches of European civilization. Each cathedral, city, and state was encircled by its own periphery: rural areas whose music may have differed more in degree than in kind from that found in Iceland.

The Reformation transformed the nation's religious and cultural landscape. Achieved only after a decade of religious turmoil, the transition was completed with the beheading in 1550 of Jón Arason, the tenacious Roman Catholic bishop of Hólar, the Northern diocese to which roughly a quarter of the country belonged. Relics of popery were abolished with such force that of the chant manuscripts belonging to hundreds of churches and seven monasteries, none survives in its entirety, and only substantial fragments of three

[4] *Diplomatarium Islandicum* (Reykjavík: Hið íslenska bókmenntafélag, 1857–1972) vol. 8, 23.

[5] Nino Pirrotta, "The Oral and Written Traditions of Music," in *Music and Culture in Italy from the Middle Ages to the Baroque: A Collection of Essays* (Cambridge, Mass.: Harvard University Press, 1984), quoted in Treitler, *With Voice and Pen*, 11.

[6] Nino Pirrotta, "Church Polyphony apropos of a new fragment at Foligno," in *Music and Culture in Italy*, 124–25, quoted in Treitler, *With Voice and Pen*, 85.

[7] Treitler, *With Voice and Pen*, 85.

remain.[8] A Protestant church ordinance issued by King Christian III had wide-ranging consequences for musical education. It prescribed the foundation of a Latin school in every town within the Danish realm, but since Iceland had no towns, schools were established instead at the rural cathedrals of Skálholt in the south and Hólar in the north.[9] These would remain the centers of higher learning in Iceland until the late eighteenth century, when a series of natural disasters threatened to obliterate the Icelandic schools altogether.

Despite the enormous influence of the Reformation, the musical changes it entailed proved difficult to achieve. An Icelandic missal was published only in 1594, following an extended period of discord between the two episcopal sees regarding the precise formulation of the new liturgy.[10] Thus, for a period of forty-four years, no printed music was available to aid in the inculcation of the new German hymn repertoire. It is certainly plausible that native singers, learning the melodies by ear (if at all), found ways to adapt them to their own local traditions.[11] Incidentally, this was also true in the nineteenth century. Although the last edition of the missal known as *Graduale* was printed in 1779, its songs were transformed into an oral tradition, the remnants of which were still being collected and transcribed a century and a half later.

* * *

Among the Icelandic manuscripts at the Arnamagnaean Institute in Copenhagen is a songbook written around 1660 and known by its shelfmark, Rask 98. It is the largest Icelandic music manuscript of the seventeenth century

[8] Inventories of church holdings, including manuscripts, are published in *Diplomatarium Islandicum, passim.* Hundreds of small fragments used as binding material have survived; these are mostly now collected as "Accessoria 7" at the Arnamagnæan Institute in Copenhagen, with additional fragments in the National and University Library of Iceland, and the National Archives in Reykjavík. Three larger, partially complete sources survive from the Roman Catholic era: a fourteenth-century office for St. Thorlak (Reykjavík, Stofnun Árna Magnússonar í íslenskum fræðum, AM 241a fol.), and two manuscripts in the hand of the fifteenth-century scribe Jón Þorláksson (a "Missale Scardense," and a "Graduale Gufudalense"). See Róbert A. Ottósson, *Sancti Thorlaci episcopi officia rhythmica et proprium missae in AM 241 A folio* (Copenhagen: E. Munksgaard, 1959), and Lilli Gjerlow, *Liturgica Islandica* (Copenhagen: C. A. Reitzel, 1980).

[9] Loftur Guttormsson, "Siðaskipti – siðbreyting í samtíma," *Kristni á Íslandi* (Reykjavík: Alþingi, 2000) vol. 3, 44–46.

[10] In his preface to the 1594 *Graduale*, Bishop Oddur Einarsson expresses his hope that the new publication will put an end to the "long-standing strife" ("langa Tuidrægne") between the Icelandic parishes. The collaboration of the two Icelandic bishops in this volume, published at Hólar but with a preface written by the bishop of Skálholt, must have been intended as a mark of reconciliation.

[11] Njáll Sigurðsson, "Kirkjusöngur í kjölfar siðaskipta," *Kristni á Íslandi*, vol. 3, 70.

to have survived, and contains a total of 223 songs, many of them unique to this source. Rask 98 is a notably eclectic manuscript, bearing witness to the variety of music making in seventeenth-century Iceland. It contains hymns from Icelandic, Danish, and German hymnals, folk songs to secular texts, chant in Latin as well as in Icelandic translations, archaic two-part polyphony, and single as well as multiple parts from four-part chansons and *Tenorlieder* by continental composers such as Ludwig Senfl, Paul Hofhaimer, Francesco Corteccia, and Didier Lupi. In Rask 98, the melodies bear neither titles nor attributions, making the search for concordances a rather arduous task. Thus far, roughly a quarter of the songs have been traced to manuscripts and printed sources originating in Denmark, Germany, Austria, Switzerland, France, Italy, and Spain, suggesting that although they were situated on the edge of the European cultural sphere, Icelandic singers were to some extent able to keep abreast of the main currents in continental music making.

Rask 98 is in oblong octavo format (11.3 x 16.4 cm) and its physical appearance suggests that it was an informal manuscript. The notation is fluent and casual, consisting of virga and compound neumes without mensural meaning. One might even regard the manuscript as a kind of seventeenth-century iPod: a collection of favorite songs handily compiled in a single volume for the scribe's own use. Its planning is rather haphazard; while the first sixteen songs are arranged in alphabetical order, this system subsequently breaks down. The contents are divided into six large sections, to which two songs are appended at the end, the elevation hymn *Discubuit Jesus* from the Danish gradual of 1573, and the sequence *In sapientia disponens omnia* in Icelandic translation (see Table 1). The manuscript's archaic notational features are obviously ill suited to the later chanson repertoire that it partly contains. Yet Rask 98 also contains music that by 1660 would have been hopelessly out of date in the musical centers of Europe; a two-part *Ave regina coelorum* is similar to a setting found in a French manuscript from the late twelfth or early thirteenth century, and another two-part song (on which more below) is found in the fourteenth-century Catalan manuscript known as *Llibre vermell*.[12] For such pieces, the archaic notation of Rask 98 served as well as any other. The repertoire of music in Iceland, like the old woman in Laxness's novel, often seems in its own way like a candle the Lord had forgotten to snuff.

[12] The French manuscript is Sélestat, Bibliothèque de la Ville, 22, see *Manuscripts of Polyphonic Music, 11th–early 14th Century*, ed. Gilbert Reaney (Munich: G. Henle Verlag, 1966), 448.

Another two-part setting of the same chant is found in fascicle 11 of W1 (Wolfenbüttel, Herzog August Bibliothek, Cod. Guelf. 628 [*olim* Helmstadiensis 677]), which dates from the thirteenth century.

Table 1. Rask 98—Outline of contents

Section/fol.	Content	Songs	Of which Lydian	%
1 (1r-20r)	Various [local?] hymns	68	41	60
2 (20v-26v)	Secular songs	21	19	90
3 (26v-27v)	Miscellany	4	2	50
4 (28r-43r)	Ólafur Jónsson's songbook	46	16	35
5 (43r-78r)	Miscellany	64	8	12,5
6 (78v-88v)	From the Icelandic Hymnal	21	1	5
+ no. 225: Discubuit Jesus; no. 226: In sapientia; Register of songs 1-92				

Rask 98, 61v (Úr djúpum mjög, *a contrafactum of Paul Hofhaimer's* Meins Traurens ist)

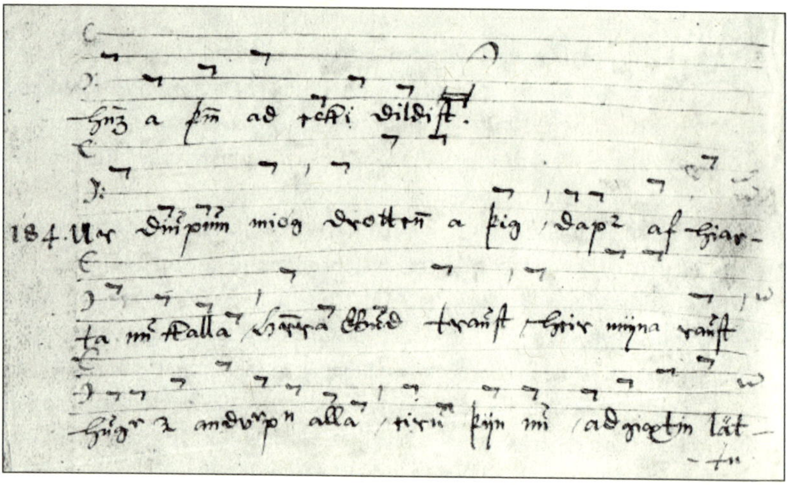

The origins of Rask 98 remain frustratingly elusive. The scribe's identity is unknown, as is the manuscript's history until the Danish linguist Rasmus Rask acquired it presumably during his travels in Iceland in 1813–15.[13] The contents of Rask 98 may yield some clues as to where it might have originated. Among the sacred repertoire in the fifth section one finds, curiously, tenor and bass parts from *Psalmorum Davidis paraphrasis poetica*, Latin psalm paraphrases in classical meters by George Buchanan, to four-part homophonic settings largely composed by the Rostock cantor Statius Olthof and first published in

[13] Rask had a musical background, played violin and piano, and learned to play the Icelandic *langspil* (a bowed dulcimer) during his stay in Iceland. See Louis Hjelmslev, *Breve fra og til Rasmus Rask*, (Copenhagen: Munksgaard, 1941), vol. 1, 87 and 296.

1585.[14] Such pedagogical pieces were part of the curriculum at the Latin school at Skálholt, the only site in Iceland where four-part singing seems to have been common. Yet even there, singing simple homophony could stretch the limits of the school community, as is suggested by the inclusion in Rask 98 of only the lower two parts for the six pieces in question. The manuscript transmits two single tenor lines, a single bass line, and both tenor and bass parts for three songs, but with individual numbering, as if to suggest that each part could be sung on its own as well as in a two-part version. Presumably the upper parts of the original arrangements would have been sung by boys as they were on the continent, but since Icelandic students began their schooling considerably later than their German counterparts, a shortage of pre-pubescent boys for the soprano and alto parts seems to have been largely unavoidable.[15] Still, these songs, along with the several Latin-texted pieces found toward the end of the manuscript—e.g. *Ave regina caelorum*, *Ad cantus leticie*, and *Victimae paschali laudes*, all in two-part polyphony—plausibly suggest that Rask 98 was prepared by someone connected with the Latin school at Skálholt.

These were heady times for the Skálholt community. In 1638 King Christian IV had appointed Brynjólfur Sveinsson, renowned for his knowledge of ancient languages and assistant dean of the Latin school in Roskilde, Denmark, as Bishop of Skálholt. Sveinsson had his eyes set on a career as an academic on the continent, and initially declined the offer, but the king persevered and coaxed the Icelandic scholar into swearing his oath the following year.[16] During Sveinsson's thirty-five-year reign, he had the church and school refurbished to great expense, collected valuable manuscripts that he later presented to King Frederick III—including the aptly named Codex Regius, the sole source for much of the Poetic Edda—and attracted intellectuals to the school in greater numbers than before. In 1643, the Skálholt community numbered 108, including the bishop and his family, teachers, farm workers, and thirty students.[17] Whether Rask 98 was actually written at Skálholt is a matter of speculation, but

[14] Walter Blankenburg, "Statius Olthof," *The New Grove Dictionary of Music and Musicians*, second edition, ed. Stanley Sadie and John Tyrell (London: Macmillan, 2001), vol. 18, 402.

[15] Only two Icelandic sources preserve the original four-part settings: Reykjavík, Stofnun Árna Magnússsonar í íslenskum fræðum AM 102 8vo (*ca.* 1680) and ReykjavíkNUL Lbs 508 8vo (*ca.* 1750).

[16] Guðrún Ása Grímsdóttir, "Biskupsstóll í Skálholti," in *Saga biskupsstólanna*, ed. Gunnar Kristjánsson (Reykjavík: Bókaútgáfan Hólar, 2006), 55.

[17] Ibid., 135. Few accounts have survived of instruments in Iceland in the seventeenth and eighteenth centuries. Þórður Þorláksson, bishop at Skálholt (r. 1672–97), acquired a "clavichordium, symphonie et regal," but it seems that these were already in a state of disrepair by 1690.

given that its contents include Latin-texted pieces, homophonic ode settings, and *binatim* polyphony, it seems that the scribe must at least have had some connections to the place.

Uniquely among Icelandic manuscripts from this period, Rask 98 transmits twenty-one pieces with secular texts. These are collected in the manuscript's second large section, which bears the heading, "Now the matter turns to a different subject, to which the reader or singer should not take offense."[18] Yet even with such a caveat, the most salacious material was nonetheless omitted. Song no. 70, *Bóndans dóttirin*, consists of six phrases of music, yet the scribe only wrote the text to the first three: "The farmer's daughter / the lovely bride / if you knew what I'd like to do *etcetera*."[19] If the manuscript was primarily intended for the scribe's own use, this act of self-editing indicates that some things were considered altogether inappropriate for the written page. At a small community like Skálholt, students probably thought it wise not to commit anything to paper that might create trouble with the church or school authorities.

We do not know whether the anonymous scribe of Rask 98 was responsible for transcribing these secular songs or if he relied on another source, now lost. Viewed as a group, one is struck primarily by the uniformity of mode: nineteen are in the Lydian mode while only two are not. Example 1a shows a typical song from the second section of the manuscript; it is in the Lydian mode, to a secular text in an irregular poetic meter, which includes several short, repeated phrases toward the middle of the song (here, the repeated C-E-C figure for "mitt hjarta/má kvarta"). The concluding phrase appears to be a stock melodic formula and is found in many of the Lydian songs in the manuscript's first two sections. Example 1b gives several examples of typical concluding phrases found in Rask 98. These often take the form of a scalar descent from B♮ to F, generally consisting of six or seven notes, one for each syllable of the final poetic line; somewhat less common is a similar figure but with a leap from B♮ down to G (Example 1c). That these songs are, at least in part, variants on a basic formula seems quite clear. Whether this formula was characteristic of native singing in general at the time Rask 98 was committed to paper, or whether it reflects local or even personal preference, cannot be answered with any certainty given the lack of other secular sources from this period.

[18] Rask 98, 20v: "Hier tekur efnid ad snuast til annars efnis sem lesarinn edur søngvarinn lati sig ei hneixla."

[19] Rask 98, 21r: "Böndans dötturin / brudurinn amorlig / ef þu visser vilian minn etc."

Example 1a. Amors bönd og byrði þung, no. 69 from Rask 98 (65v)

Example 1b. Typical concluding phrase from first and second sections of Rask 98: descending scalar pattern

Example 1c. Typical concluding phrase from first and second sections of Rask 98: descending pattern

The Lydian mode predominates not just in the secular portion of the manuscript. Of the 223 songs of all types in Rask 98, a total of eighty-seven are in the Lydian mode on F. One might at first be tempted to speculate whether this might be nothing more than a scribal quirk; that possibly B♭s might have been intended but not written, or that the absence of B♭s might reflect some native performing tradition that did not rely on written accidentals, a kind of home-grown *musica ficta*. Yet the scribe of Rask 98 knew perfectly well how to write flats and notate songs in F major: a total of forty-one songs employ B♭. However, nearly all of these occur in sections five and six of the manuscript, where the scribe was more consistently copying songs that originated in foreign sources. The first two sections of the manuscript contain the largest number of songs in the Lydian mode; perhaps not coincidentally, here the scribe also seems to be mostly documenting a native tradition of both sacred and secular song.

MODAL SHIFTS AND ORAL TRANSMISSION

Other songs in Rask 98 also appear to retain elements of oral transmission and performance. *Sorg er sárleg pína*, for which no other source is known, is copied twice, as no. 39 and 79, with small melodic and textual variants in virtually each phrase. That this song occurs twice may tell us something of the scribe's casual approach to planning the manuscript as a whole, but it also raises the more fundamental question of to what extent the second, variant reading, would have counted as "the same" song. That the scribe would, consciously or not, have copied the song from two different sources seems unlikely. To slightly modify Leo Treitler's felicitous phrase, it seems more plausible that the two "versions" were individual products of the scribe's own mind; they suggest that the manuscript was not made strictly by copying, but by remembering, composing, and performing, all at once.[20]

The scribe of Rask 98 copied two other songs in multiple versions. Since each of these versions is notated to a different text, they do not share the "sameness" of *Sorg er sárleg pína*, and here the melodies differ to a far greater extent than in the previous example. There are three variants on Jakob Regnart's well-known hymn tune *Auf meinen lieben Gott* (songs no. 33, 122, and 172), and though all are clearly derived from the German melody, each has quite specific variants. Perhaps most interestingly, though all these songs share the same general melodic contour, they are notated in different modes: F Lydian, D Dorian, and G Dorian, respectively (see Example 2). Two Icelandic forms of the melody *Allein auf Gott setz dein Vertraun* are notated in Rask 98, as no. 14 (*Xerxes treysti á sína makt*) and no. 99 (*Alleina til Guðs set trausta trú*). The former is notated in F Lydian while the latter is in F major, suggesting that even when dealing with a single manuscript written by one scribe, the modal categories existed in a highly fluid state.

Two items from the manuscript's fourth section, containing melodies to sacred as well as secular texts by the sixteenth-century reverend Ólafur Jónsson, are found in several manuscripts in relatively standardized form except for the execution of their melismas. Both melodies are in F Lydian, and in

[20] Cf. Leo Treitler, "The Transmission of Medieval Music," *Speculum* 56 (1981), 482.

Example 2. Opening phrases of Auf meinen lieben Gott variants in Rask 98 (nos. 33, 122, and 172)

Example 3. Syng mín sál, opening phrases from (a) ReykjavíkNUL JS 73 4to, (b) ReykjavíkSÁM, NKS 139b 4to, (c) Rask 98

both cases Rask 98 preserves more ornate forms of embellishment than the other sources. *Syng, mín sál* appears in a rather plain form in Reykjavík, Landsbókasafn Íslands—Háskólabókasafn (National and University Library, hereafter ReykjavíkNUL, JS 73 4to), a 1727 manuscript hymnal (Example 3a), but is somewhat more embellished in Reykjavík, Stofnun Árna Magnússonar í íslenskum fræðum (hereafter ReykjavíkSÁM, Ny kgl. Saml. 139b 4to), a songbook roughly coeval with Rask 98 (Example 3b). Rask 98 is the only source of the three whose second phrase repeats the music of the first phrase note for note, with melismas that are somewhat more elaborate than the others (Example 3c).[21] Another song, *Framorðið er*, concludes in one manuscript from

[21] Other manuscripts also transmit the music to *Syng, mín sál*, but these seem not to be independent versions but rather copies related to the three manuscripts discussed here: ReykjavíkNUL ÍB 70 4to and ReykjavíkNUL Lbs 1516 4to (both 1693), ReykjavíkSÁM AM 240 8vo (1704), and ReykjavíkNUL JS 264 4to (1740).

Example 4. Framorðið er og meir en mál, concluding phrase from (a) Reykavík ÍBR 86 4to, (b) Rask 98

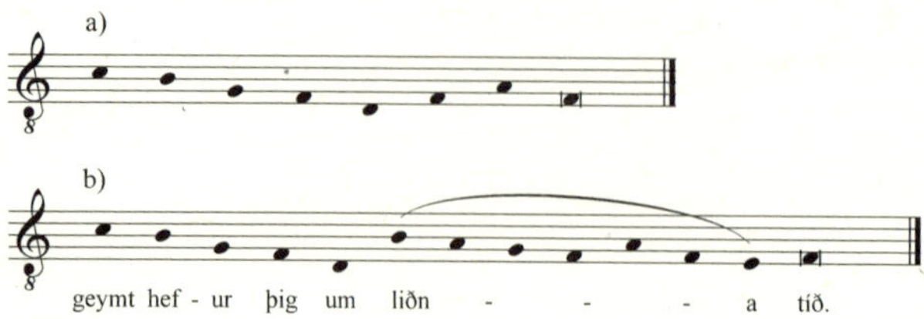

around 1680 (ReykjavíkNUL, ÍBR 86 4to, shown in Example 4a) with a simple, syllabic cadence that circles around the final on F, reaching first down a third to D, then up a third to A. In Rask 98, this basic pattern is considerably extended through a four-note descending scalar pattern followed by a lower-neighbor figure at the end, transforming the four-note syllabic version into a nine-note melismatic one (Example 4b).

Such variant readings are akin to performances frozen in time: one recognizes the same general pattern although the details are not quite the same. It would seem that the Icelandic scribes each had their own way of singing and writing typical F-mode formulas, and more often than not the scribe of Rask 98 chose to render such phrases in a relatively elaborate manner. Considering the Icelandic sources of the post-Reformation period, one is reminded of Treitler's description of the transmission of medieval music as "a process of repeated and successive re-creation," or, elsewhere, of "music whose composition coincided with its performance."[22]

Though it contains a miscellany of items of a mostly theological nature, the *Llibre vermell* (Montserrat, Biblioteca de l'Abadia, MS 1), or Red book, compiled at the monastery of Montserrat no later than 1399, is known to most students of medieval music for the ten songs to Latin and Catalan texts found on six of its 137 pages. Three of the songs bear the rubric "Caça de duobus vel tribus," indicating that they can be sung as canons in two or three parts. These are simple tunes, with a comfortable range and easily committed to memory, and thus well suited to the music-making that was part of the pilgrims' vigils described on folio 22r of the manuscript.[23] Most of the songs from the *Llibre vermell* have not survived in other sources. In written form they seem to have been unique to the repertory of this particular place, although they may well have travelled far and wide in orally transmitted versions. After all,

[22] Treitler, *With Voice and Pen*, 13.

[23] *Llibre vermell de Montserrat*, ed. Dom Francesc Xavier Altés i Aguiló (Barcelona: Fundació Revista de Catalunya, 1989).

Example 5. Laudemus virginem, from Llibre vermell

Montserrat, one of the most revered pilgrimage sites of the Middle Ages, was described in 1342 by Pedro of Aragon as a place in which "the diverse climates of the world converged."[24]

Such seems at least to have been the case with *Laudemus virginem*, until recently believed to be unique to the *Llibre vermell* but which also survives with notation in five Icelandic sources from the seventeenth century, including Rask 98.[25] In the original version, *Laudemus virginem* is a simple first-mode canon, consisting of three short phrases (see Example 5). The three-note descent of the first phrase is mirrored by an ascending second phrase; the third reaches higher than the other two before coming to rest on the cofinal. The Catalan manuscript indicates that when sung "de duobus vel tribus," each part should enter as the preceding one begins a new phrase. In such a performance, the voices come together to create a simple yet effective harmonic mirage; the

[24] "a diversis mundi climatibus confluentes," quoted in Higinio Anglés, "El 'Llibre Vermell' de Montserrat y los cantos y la danza sacra de los peregrinos durante el siglo XIV," *Anuario musical* 10 (1955), 52. The only musical concordance previously known is the virelai *Inperayritz—Verges ses par* (also in Montserrat, Biblioteca del Monestir, MS 1 and Tarragona, Archivo Histórico Archidiocesano, MS s.s. [1]); see Giulio Cattin, Francesco Facchin, and Maria del Carmen Gómez, *Polyphonic Music of the Fourteenth Century*, vol. 23B (Monaco: Éditions de L'oiseau-lyre, 1991), 501. *Ad mortem festinamus* is also found in another source as a contrafactum, see Maricarmen Gómez Muntané, *La música medieval en España* (Kassel: Reichenberger, 2001), 272.

[25] Two-part versions are also found in ReykjavíkSÁM AM 102 8vo and ReykjavíkNUL Lbs 496 8vo; a single part is transmitted in Boreal 113 and also in ReykjavíkNUL Lbs 1055 4to to a different text attributed to Guðmundur Erlendsson, "Það stillir sturlanir / styggð og neyð." At least eight Icelandic manuscripts transmit texts intended to be sung to this melody, without notation but with a rubric indicating the tune. They are Lbs 495 8vo (to the text *Ó Jesú, sjálfs Guðs son*); JS 232 4to, Lbs 1568 8vo, Lbs 237 8vo (all to the text *Það stillir sturlanir*); JS 138 8vo, Lbs 736 8vo, ÍB 380 8vo (all in ReykjavíkNUL), and Oxford, Bodleian Library, MS Boreal 113 (all to a third text, *Salve þér sorgfull tér*). That at least twelve Icelandic sources transmit music, or related texts, originally derived from *Laudemus virginem*, suggests that this song enjoyed considerable popularity in seventeenth-century Iceland.

melodic movement appears to dissolve in a perpetual cycle of three harmonies built on F, E, and D, respectively.

Certain features distinguish the Icelandic versions from their Catalan predecessor. The Icelandic text is considerably longer than the Latin quatrain found in *Llibre vermell*, and is not a translation but a newly composed poem in praise of Christ; twenty-two lines in a longer version but eight lines in Rask 98. The Icelandic two-part versions are not canons. Instead, both voices sing throughout but exchange parts between the first and second phrases in a manner reminiscent of continental *Stimmtausch*-pieces. That this is so is no doubt due to the long-standing tradition in Iceland of the form of polyphony referred to as *cantus planus binatim* or doubled plainchant, widely practiced at institutions throughout Europe that were geographically peripheral, provincial, rural, or, in some cases, urban yet inclined to austerity. The earliest such manuscript source from Iceland is a single leaf from a missal written in 1473 for the monastery at Munkaþverá, containing fragments of a troped *Agnus Dei* and the *Credo cardinalis*, but a ban on two- and three-part singing by Bishop Lárentíus Kálfsson (r. 1324–30) suggests that *binatim* singing was already well established by the early fourteenth century.[26] Adding a second voice to a known chant melody did not depend entirely on written notation, but led a fluid existence between the improvised/variable and written/fixed, as also seems to be the case with the Icelandic versions of *Laudemus virginem*.

The transformation of this simple song from canon to a two-part *Stimmtausch*-piece presented the scribes with some difficulties. Each of the three Icelandic versions retains elements of the original, yet each also finds its own solution to the problem of how to create/represent the song in a closed, noncanonic form. None of the versions are identical; both music and texts suggest that the Icelandic scribes were not copying from an existing source, relying instead on their own memory and imagination. ReykjavíkNUL Lbs 496 8vo, a hymnal written around 1750, comes closest to the Spanish original. It retains the melodic shape of the upper part, while the lower part requires a small adjustment toward the end of the third phrase. This results in a somewhat unusual cadence, a fifth followed by a fourth followed by a major third (Example 6a). This same phrase seems also to have given considerable trouble to the scribe of ReykjavíkSÁM AM 102 8vo, a hymnal dating from the second half of the seventeenth century. Here, the upper part avoids a strict voice-exchange in the second phrase; things seem to go smoothly until the penultimate note of the third phrase, when the two voices sound the unlikely interval of a ninth (Example 6b).

[26] ReykjavíkSÁM AM 80b 8vo; see also *Laurentius saga biskups*, ed. Árni Björnsson (Reykjavík: Handritastofnun Íslands, 1969), 99.

Example 6a. Ó Jesú, sjálfs Guðs son, from ReykjavíkNUL Lbs 496 8vo (ca. *1750*)

Example 6b. Ó Jesú, sjálfs Guðs son, from ReykjavíkSÁM, AM 102 8vo (ca. *1650*)

Example 6c. Ó Jesú, sjálfs Guðs son, from Rask 98 (ca. *1660*)

Ó Jesú, sjálfs Guðs son, sé þér lof,
hjálpa nú, náðar von, neyð er of
þung og stór, þar fyrir þig biðjum,
græðari vor, gef að vér gott iðjum,
miskunn þín mestu nauð mœðu af,
sál var mín syndum dauð, sælu gaf
hann sem ráð hefur á himni og jörð,
því skal tjá þeim allt má þakkargjörð.

Glory be to Jesus, God's own son,
help us, hope of grace, we are undone
by heavy hardship, so we pray to you,
our healer, grant that we do good deeds,
with your mercy ease my greatest need.
To my soul, dead in sin, you brought joy,
so to him who rules over heaven and earth
let us make our thanksgiving heard.

trans. Bernard Scudder

Rask 98 preserves yet another version of the song (Example 6c). Here the most striking features are the transposition and change of mode to F Lydian, along with a different solution to the ending than in the preceding manuscripts. By copying the three short phrases twice in succession, the scribe creates a voice exchange on two levels: between the first and second phrase of each half, and again between the complete first and complete second half. Instead of repeating the earlier ending, the concluding phrase is the only one not to end on an F-C sonority; here the scribe opts for a major third, C-E, with one last voice-crossing on the last two notes.

Among Spanish pilgrimage sites, Montserrat was surpassed in veneration only by Santiago de Compostela. Only one Icelandic pilgrim is known to have visited Spain around the time the *Libre vermell* came into existence: Björn Einarsson, a wealthy chieftain who sailed from Iceland to Venice and onward to Jerusalem in 1406. Upon his return to Italy from the Holy Land, he appears to have travelled by foot to Santiago, thus quite possibly taking the popular pilgrim route that led through both Barcelona and Montserrat.[27] Of course, a simple song such as *Laudemus virginem* could have made its journey to the far North via any number of intermediary routes, but the travels of an Icelandic pilgrim to Montserrat within a decade of the writing of *Llibre vermell* at least make for an intriguing conjecture.

Laudemus virginem is not the only case in which Rask 98 differs from other sources in matters of mode. Table 2 lists eighteen songs that appear in other Icelandic manuscripts in conflicting modes. It seems clear that of the Icelandic manuscripts, three are mostly in agreement—Rask 98, Reykjavík-SÁM, AM 240 8vo, and ReykjavíkSÁM, NKS 139b 4to—while at least ten others contain significant differences. Of the presumably local songs found in conflicting modes, the scribe of Rask 98 seems most likely to use Phrygian where others employ Dorian, and also to prefer Dorian to Lydian. Some of the Icelandic manuscripts seem to have a distinct "modal profile," presumably reflecting the preference (or unconscious style, or geographic location) of the scribe in question. Two manuscripts also written in the second half of the seventeenth century, ReykjavíkNUL ÍB 70 4to and Reykjavík SÁM, NKS 139b 4to, use Phrygian in at least seven cases where Rask 98 employs Dorian, Lydian, or Mixolydian. Table 3 lists ten songs found in continental sources in different modes than notated in Rask 98. Here the changes are more varied and the evidence less conclusive than in the presumably local repertoire, yet there is some duplication of the modal processes involved in the former. For example, the Phrygian *Meins Traurens ist* becomes Dorian in Rask 98, while the Dorian (minor)-to-Lydian transformation is found not only in *Laudemus virginem* but also in the hymn tunes *Auf meinen lieben Gott* and *Allein auf Gott setz dein Vertraun*.

[27] Einarsson's travels are described in the so-called "Nýi annáll" (New Annal) for the year 1406, in *Annálar 1400–1800* (Reykjavík: Félagsprentsmiðjan, 1922–27) vol. 1, 14; see also Björn Þorsteinsson and Guðrún Ása Grímsdóttir, "Norska öldin," in *Saga Íslands*, vol. 4, ed. Sigurður Líndal (Reykjavík: Sögufélag, 1989), 208.

Table 2. Songs found in conflicting modes in Rask 98 and other Icelandic manuscripts, 1650–1780

Title	Mode in Rask 98	Conflicting MSS
Alleina til Guðs	F major (+ AM 240 8vo)	Lydian (ÍB 70 4to); Phrygian (JS 264 4to)
Dýr fæðingin drottins vors	Lydian (+ AM 240 8vo, NKS 139b 4to)	Mixolydian (ÍB 70 4to, JS 264 4to, Lbs 837 4to)
Enn vil ég einu sinni	Lydian (+AM 240 8vo, NKS 139b 4to)	Phrygian (ÍBR 86 4to, ÍB 70 4to, JS 264 4to)
Ég hef upp til þín	Lydian (+ AM 240 8vo)	Phrygian (NKS 139b 4to)
Framorðið er og meir en mál	Lydian (+ NKS 139b 4to, ÍBR 86 4to)	Dorian (AM 240 8vo, *ending only*)
Gaumgæfið kristnir	Dorian (+ AM 240 8vo, NKS 139b 4to et al.)	Phrygian (Lbs 1516 8vo), Aeolian (Lbs 837 4to)
Landið guðs barna	Lydian	Aeolian (JS 138 8vo)
Minn guð, minn guð	Lydian (+ AM 240 8vo, NKS 139b 4to)	Phrygian (ÍB 70 4to, Lbs 837 8vo, JS 264); Mixolydian (ÍB 380, Lbs 830 8vo)
Ó ég manneskjan auma	Lydian (+ AM 240 8vo, NKS 139b 4to, ÍBR 86 4to)	Phrygian (ÍB 70 4to, *ending only*); F major (ÍBR 7 8vo)
Ó herra guð mín heilsa er rýr	Lydian (+ AM 240 8vo, NKS 139b 4to)	F major (ÍB 70 4to, Lbs 837 8vo)
Ó Jesú elsku hreinn	Dorian (+ÍBR 7 8vo, ÍB 669 8vo)	Phrygian (NKS 139b 4to); Aeolian (Lbs 399 4to); Mixolydian (JS 264 4to)
Ó Jesú, sjálfs Guðs son	Lydian	Dorian (AM 102 8vo, Lbs 496 8vo, Lbs 1055 4to, Boreal 113)
Sjálf ritningin sælan prísar	Dorian (+ AM 240 8vo)	Phrygian (NKS 139b 4to)
Sjálfur guð drottinn sannleikans	Mixolydian (+ AM 240 8vo, NKS 139b 4to)	Phrygian (ÍB 70 4to)
Upp líttu sál mín	Lydian (+ NKS 139b 4to et al.)	Dorian (Lbs 399 4to)
Vel eg þér ráðin vinsamlig	Dorian (+AM 240 8vo)	Mixolydian (Boreal 113)
Vígð náttin	C major	Mixolydian (Lbs 1927 4to); Dorian (Lbs 1422 8vo, Lbs 1435 8vo, Lbs 1536 8vo)
Víst er nú manni	C major	Mixolydian (AM 240 8vo)

Table 3. Songs found in conflicting modes in Rask 98 and original sources

Title in Rask 98	Mode in Rask 98	Original source	Mode in original
Úr djúpum mjög	Dorian	Meins Traurens ist (Paul Hofhaimer)	Phrygian
Lávarður vor	Dorian	O nostre Dieu et Seigneur (Geneva Psalter)	Dorian/minor
Öll jörð frammi fyrir drottni	Dorian	Secum insania (Statius Olthof)	Aeolian
Patientia er sögð urt	Phrygian	Patientiam mueß ich han (Ludwig Senfl)	Aeolian
Himnar er hver má sjá	Phrygian	Les cieux en chacun lieu (Geneva Psalter)	Major
Ó Jesú, sjálfs guðs son	Lydian	Laudemus virginem (Llibre vermell)	Dorian
Herra, þín heilög verk	Lydian	Auf meinen lieben Gott (Jacob Regnart, 1574)	Minor
Alleina til Guðs set trausta trú	Lydian	Allein auf Gott setz dein Vertraun	Dorian
Viljir þú varast hér	Lydian	Si vitare velis (Statius Olthof)	Aeolian
Heiður lof og dýrð	Lydian	Priss oc ære oc dyd (Thomissøn Hymnal, 1569)	Major

It has long been known that music instruction in post-Reformation Iceland often left much to be desired. The Danish Erasmus Villatsson (d. 1591) taught singing at Skálholt and was said to have introduced "discant-singing" at the Latin school—presumably the four-part homophonic ode settings mentioned above. His efforts seem to have been largely successful, but by 1647 the situation had deteriorated to such an extent that an Icelandic scholar, Gísli Magnússon, wrote a document addressed to King Christian IV asking for, among other things, a learned musician to be sent to the island to improve the situation of music, which he regarded as "wholly decayed" and neglected.[28]

[28] "Olim fuit in usu et admiratione, unde magno studio a permultis exercebatur; hodie prorsus exoleta negligitur," quoted in Jakob Benediktsson, *Gísli Magnússon (Vísi-Gísli) - ævisaga, ritgerðir, bréf* (Reykjavík: Fræðafélagið, 1939), 83–84.

This situation appears to have improved somewhat in the second half of the seventeenth century, though not because of royal intervention, but the general situation still raises the question whether the degree of modal variance found in the Icelandic sources could be the result of scribal ineptness or confusion rather than deliberate revision. It is worth noting that of the nineteen manuscripts listed in Table 2, not a single one is written by a professional musician. These are the work of amateurs, mostly local priests whose studies were by and large limited to the Icelandic Latin schools. Yet the scribe of Rask 98 seems to have been musically intelligent; the writing is confident and carefully executed, with only a few corrections in what is a considerable amount of music by any standard. Most of the other manuscripts cited in Table 2 also appear to be reliable, and in any case some of the modal fluctuations are of a kind that would seem unlikely to arise as scribal errors. It seems wise to evaluate each individual manuscript on its own terms, keeping in mind Margaret Bent's advice—with regard to simple polyphony—that the simplicity of the repertory is "neither the simplicity of condescension nor that of incompetence."[29]

MODALITY AND THE NINETEENTH-CENTURY TRADITION

The evidence for modal change in seventeenth-century Iceland is further corroborated by younger sources, both written and oral, which suggest that modal fluidity continued to shape Icelandic singing as late as the nineteenth and early twentieth centuries. A recent study by Ingibjörg Eyþórsdóttir focused on transcriptions made in the early twentieth century by Sigtryggur Guðlaugsson (1862–1959), an Icelandic schoolmaster and amateur of music, of hymns he had heard in his youth when the "old way of singing" was still a living tradition.[30] Of forty-six melodies, thirty-five also appear in continental hymnals of the sixteenth and seventeenth centuries, and are verifiably not of Icelandic origin. Of these, only a handful had remained in the same mode. Interestingly, the most prevalent modal changes in the late nineteenth century seem to be for Dorian to become Lydian—as in Rask 98—and for Mixolydian to become Phrygian; i.e. for "major-third" pieces to become identified with "minor

[29] Bent, "The Definition of Simple Polyphony," in *Le polifonie primitive di Cividale*, ed. Pierluigi Petrobelli (Cividale: Associazione per lo Sviluppo degli Studi Storici ed Artistici di Cividale del Friuli, 1980), 33–34.

[30] The manuscript is ReykjavíkNUL Lbs 2848 4to; see Ingibjörg Eyþórsdóttir, "Með sínum tón: Tóntegundabreytingar í íslenskum sálmalögum" (B.A. thesis, Iceland Academy of the Arts, 2005).

Example 7. Melodic comparison of Vater unser im Himmelreich from Geistliche Lieder (Leipzig 1539), and Faðir vor sem á himnum ert from ReykjavíkNUL Lbs 2848 4to)

third" and viceversa.[31] Example 7 shows the opening phrases of the melody to Luther's well-known hymn *Vater unser im Himmelreich*, and Guðlaugsson's transcription of the Icelandic variant as sung in the last decades of the nineteenth century. Here we find the Dorian melody notated in the Lydian mode on C, with some of the ornamentation typical for Icelandic hymn singing at this time, yet the basic outlines are clearly those of the original hymn tune.[32]

Other evidence from the nineteenth- and twentieth-century oral traditions suggests that modal shifts were of a varied and somewhat unpredictable nature, in some cases associated with particular locations or individuals. In 1909, Bjarni Þorsteinsson, a priest and amateur composer, published a mammoth volume of Icelandic folk music, mostly collected by himself during the preceding two decades. This collection remains an indispensable tool for any

[31] This tendency was first noted by Róbert A. Ottósson in the 1970s; see his "Tvesang" in *Kulturhistorisk leksikon for nordisk middelalder* (Copenhagen: Rosenkilde og Bagger, 1956–78) vol. 19, cols. 83–86, and "Iceland," *The New Grove Dictionary of Music and Musicians*, ed. Stanley Sadie (London: Macmillan, 1980) vol. 9, 8.

[32] Another transcription of an Icelandic version of *Vater unser im Himmelreich*, also in the Lydian mode, is found in Bjarni Þorsteinsson's *Íslenzk þjóðlög* (Copenhagen: S.L. Møller, 1906–09), 727.

Example 8. Opt vindar eik þjá, transcription by Bjarni Þorsteinsson (from Íslenzk þjóðlög, 541)

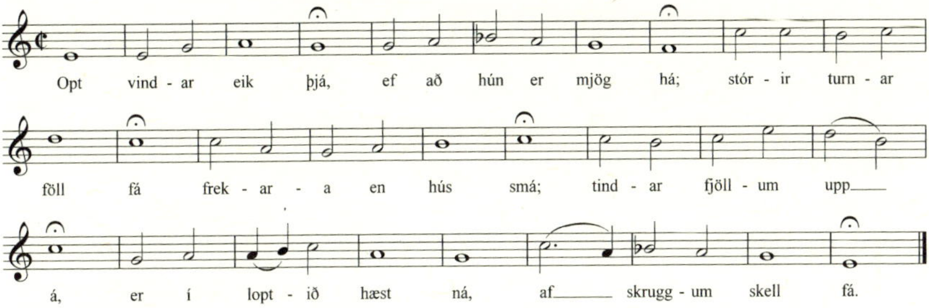

research on Icelandic folk music, and it includes eight songs transcribed after a performance by an elderly man whom the author describes as follows:

> During the winter of 1887–88, one of my neighbors in Reykjavík was an old and quite peculiar man by the name of Hans Wiingaard, who made his living as a carpenter and by sharpening barber knives. . . . he was quite fond of singing and came to visit me on occasion, whereupon I would write down all the old songs he knew.[33]

One of Þorsteinsson's transcriptions is of a song whose text holds the key to its origins. *Opt vindar eik þjá* is an Icelandic translation of *Saepius ventis*, from the second book of Horace's Odes. The melody was common in nineteenth century Iceland; it appeared in the 1801 Hymnal and was still being sung to various sapphic poems by students at the Icelandic Latin school in the 1830s (see Example 8). It is ultimately derived from the tenor voice of a four-part setting by Petrus Tritonius of Horace's *Iam satis terris*, published in 1507.[34] Transcribing the song as performed by old Wiingaard caused Þorsteinsson considerable trouble. In his commentary on the song, he wrote:

> As far as I can recall, Lárus [Blöndal, Þorsteinsson's father-in-law] sang the first and last note F, but dean Björn Ólsen, who is quite a good tvísöngur singer, told me in 1893 that he had heard many old

[33] Þorsteinsson, *Íslenzk þjóðlög*, 541.

[34] Petrus Tritonius, *Melopoiae, sive Harmoniae tetracenticae* (Augsburg, 1507). Tritonius's *Iam satis terris* is widely reproduced in the modern literature; see for example Allan W. Atlas, *Renaissance Music* (New York: W.W. Norton, 1998), 621–22.

> men sing the last note E (not F) both in this song and others in the same mode. Old Hans Wiingaard sang it thus, and therefore I wanted to keep it this way, and emphasize that this song was actually sung like this, and that it isn't a misprint.[35]

Þorsteinsson's original manuscript, written in 1889, shows the collector grappling with whether to notate this song as he himself had learned it or in the performance of old Wiingaard. His first substantial attempt at transcribing folk music was made in 1889 and consisted of thirty-one songs, most of them in two-part polyphony, headed "Nokkur tvísöngslög [A few songs in two parts] ex memoria et ex auditu conscripsit."[36] He first notated the song as he knew it, in F major; the tonality reinforced throughout the song by the frequent emphasis on both F and C, tonic and dominant. Toward the end of the manuscript, almost like an afterthought, Þorsteinsson decided to write out the melody as sung by the old carpenter, with E replacing F as both first and last note, while the remainder still strongly suggests the original tonality.[37]

The opposite phenomenon to Wiingaard's flattened final is documented in a more recent example. Þórður Guðbjartsson (1891–1982) was a fisherman from Western Iceland whose unique style of singing was documented in several recordings made between 1958 and 1974. Among his peculiar characteristics was to sing the final note of each verse half a step higher than one would expect (see Example 9).[38]

[35] Þorsteinsson, *Íslenzk þjóðlög*, 541–42. Hans Wiingaard Einarsson was born in 1821 and was thus sixty-six years old when Þorsteinsson made his transcription. He may have learned the song from his father, Einar Sæmundsson Einarsen (1792–1866), who had studied at the Latin school at Bessastaðir and was a respected priest in his day.

[36] ReykjavíkSÁM Bjarni Þorsteinsson collection, folder 8.

[37] We may never know for certain, but it is possible that some notated songs in seventeenth- and eighteenth-century Icelandic manuscripts reflect a similar tradition. For example, *Ó ég manneskjan auma* (no. 95 in Rask 98), is notated in the Lydian mode in virtually all the surviving manuscripts except ReykjavíkNUL ÍB 70 4to (1693), which gives the final note a step lower, E instead of F. Another song in Rask 98, *Voldugur herra, vertu mér hjá* (no. 59) is also notated in the F mode but with a flattened final on E. This suggests that the performance practice documented in Þorsteinsson's folk transcriptions may date back several centuries.

[38] Stephen L. Mosko, preface to Hreinn Steingrímsson, *Kvæðaskapur* (Reykjavík: Mál og mynd, 2000), 17. In Guðbjartsson's performances, the melody is never quite the same from one verse to the next. During one recording session for a disc of Icelandic folk music, Guðbjartsson was interrupted by the foreign producer, who complained that he was forgetting the melody and changing it constantly. The disgruntled singer performed the melody "exactly the same several times and then left." (Ibid., 26).

Example 9. Þórður Guðbjartsson (1891–1982), from Rhymes of Þórður hreða, to a poem by Hallgrímur Jónsson (1787–1860). Recorded in 1965 (ReykjavíkSÁM).

Such a cultivation of an individual style of singing, characterized by distinctive vocal ornaments and inflections, seems to have been highly prized by the performers themselves; Guðbjartsson himself told the story of having practiced his songs in solitude until he felt had found his own, original, way.[39] In his study of Icelandic epic song, the ethnomusicologist Hreinn Steingrímsson remarks that the finest singers were considered those who sang "not like anyone else," even though sometimes the overall contour of a melody might be recognizable from one singer to the next. Singers would have their own so-called "stemma" or basic melody that would then be associated with them; the most popular of these might be taken up by others after the singer had passed away. Melody types and ways of singing could also be particular to specific regions; it was often possible to determine the geographic origins of singers by the melodies they employed.[40]

One can only speculate as to possible connections between such localized, individual modes of late nineteenth-century performance and the songs found in the earlier manuscript sources. What seems clear is that the seventeenth-century manuscript Rask 98 documents an ingrained local tradition of singing, and that it also holds clues as to how native practice was capable of adapting, even transforming, music that travelled from warmer climes to the "insula maris in finibus mundi," as was the case with *Laudemus virginem*. Under circumstances far removed from those that brought such songs into existence, the European tradition in Iceland was indeed akin to a candle's faint gleam, an unexpected, hidden world hardly touched by the passing of time.

[39] Steingrímsson, *Kvæðaskapur*, 111.

[40] Þorsteinsson, *Íslenzk þjóðlög*, 810.

Reproducing the Middle Ages in Eighteenth-Century Toledo

SUSAN BOYNTON

> Some professors of music, both of the holy Church of Toledo (where there are and have always been excellent ones) and of this court, to whom I showed the musical points of the Goths, confess openly that they do not understand them, and thus one from Toledo, [who] consulted them [as he] heard the Mozarabic Chaplains sing, and not finding any correspondence, or not understanding what the notes had to do with the letters for lack of clefs and lines, were left more doubtful and confused than before carrying out this observation.[1]

THIS PASSAGE FROM an eighteenth-century treatise on the Visigothic script appears to be the earliest explicit acknowledgment of the difference between the early sources of the Mozarabic chant and the contemporary rite practiced in the Mozarabic chapel of Toledo cathedral. The author of the treatise was not a musician or music historian, or even a university-trained scholar, but rather a professional scribe and calligrapher, Francisco Xavier Santiago y

[1] Francisco Xavier de Santiago y Palomares, *Polygraphia Gothico-Española* (Madrid, Real Academia de la Historia, MS 9/4752), 21: "Algunos profesores de la Musica, assi de la Santa Iglesia de Toledo en donde los hay, y ha havido siempre muy excelentes, como de esta Corte, à quienes he mostrado los puntos de la Musica de los Godos confiessan llanamente, que no los entienden, siendo assi que uno de Toledo, teniendolos presentes oyò cantar à los Capellanes Muzaraves, y no hallando corespondencia, o no entendiendo la que tenian las notas con las voces por falta de claves y de rayas, se quedò mas dudoso y confuso que antes de hacer esta observacion."

Palomares (1728–96).[2] Although a layman, Palomares acquired a familiarity with the Toledan codices of the Old Hispanic rite that enabled him to carry out the musical experiment described above, and thereby to observe with rare immediacy the gulf between the medieval manuscripts and the living tradition of the Mozarabic rite.

Palomares's unusual interest in the neumes grew out of his work for the Spanish government in the early 1750s, when he took part in the most important of the research initiatives begun in the reign of Ferdinand VI (1746–59), the Royal Commission on the Archives.[3] Created in 1749 with the prominent Jesuit scholar Andrés Marcos Burriel at its head, the Commission was charged with locating medieval archival documents in support of ongoing negotiations with the Vatican over the *patronato real*, meaning in this context the jurisdiction of the Crown over ecclesiastical property in Spain. This was just one dimension of the policies pursued by Ferdinand's government to consolidate the power of the monarchy in relation to the national church.[4]

In 1750 Burriel began work in the library and archives of Toledo Cathedral, assisted by the philologist Francisco Pérez Bayer and a group of amanuenses. The archival inventories and transcriptions required by the government were almost finished about a year later, and the team soon moved on to investigate the manuscripts of literature, history, theology, patristics, and canon law in the cathedral library. At the center of this endeavor stood the medieval liturgical manuscripts, particularly the codices of the Old Hispanic rite, which Burriel came to study more closely than any of his contemporaries. These manuscripts were the neglected vestiges of Toledo's Mozarabic liturgical tradition. After King Alfonso VI of León captured the city in 1085, the Roman rite was established in the cathedral, in conformity with the liturgical reform Alfonso had initiated in his kingdom already in 1076.[5] The community of Arabized Christians in

[2] On Palomares's biography, see the introduction to *Francisco Javier de Santiago y Palomares: Selected Writings, 1776–95*, ed. Dennis P. Seniff (Exeter: University of Exeter Press, 1984).

[3] For an overview of the Commission, see José Simón Díaz, "El reconocimiento de los archivos españoles en 1750-1756," *Revista bibliográfica y documental* 4 (1950), 131–70.

[4] On the regalist policies of Ferdinand VI's first government and the Concordat of 1753, see Rafael Olaechea, "La Politíca eclesiástica del gobierno de Fernando VI," in *La época de Fernando VI: Ponencias leídas en el coloquo conmemorativo de los 25 años de la fundación de la Cátedra Feijoo* (Oviedo: Facultad de filosofía y letras, Universidad de Oviedo, 1981), 139–226, at 142–81.

[5] On the liturgical reform in Toledo see three recent publications by Juan Pablo Rubio Sadia: "La introducción del rito romano en la Iglesia de Toledo," *Toletana* 10 (2004), 151–77; *Las órdenes religiosas y la introducción del rito romano en la Iglesia de Toledo. Una aportación desde las fuentes litúrgicas* (Toledo: Instituto de Estudios Visigóticos-Mozárabes, 2004); *La*

Toledo (known as Mozarabs), who had maintained the practice of their religion under Muslim rule, was allowed to continue celebrating its customary liturgy.[6] By the late Middle Ages, this practice came to be the most distinctive feature of the Toledan Mozarabic community; their rite outlived other aspects of their common cultural heritage, such as the use of the Arabic language.[7]

Of several efforts in the fifteenth century to consolidate the dwindling cultural legacy of the Mozarabic community in Toledo, the most consequential were the actions of Francisco Ximénez de Cisneros, Archbishop of Toledo from 1495 to 1517 and the founder of the Mozarabic chapel in Toledo cathedral.[8] Cisneros appointed a commission directed by one of the cathedral canons, Ortiz, to publish editions of the Mozarabic rite for the use of the Mozarabic parishes.[9] These editions do not consistently reproduce the texts of the medieval liturgical books; they include many elements from the Roman rite, which supply services and parts of formularies that were needed in the early modern period but had not existed in the Old Hispanic rite.[10] Thus the Ortiz editions can be designated "neo-Mozarabic."[11]

Likewise, the cantorales prepared under Archbishop Cisneros for the use of the Mozarabic chaplains in Toledo Cathedral contain melodies that were either adapted from Gregorian chant or newly composed for the restored services in the Mozarabic chapel.[12] They do not correspond to those in the Old

recepción del rito francorromano en Castilla, ss. XI-XII: las tradiciones litúrgicas locales a través del Responsorial del Proprium de tempore (Vatican City: Libreria editrice vaticana, 2011).

[6] Ramón Gonzálvez, "The Persistence of the Mozarabic Liturgy in Toledo after A.D. 1080," in *Santiago, Saint-Denis and Saint Peter: The Reception of the Roman Liturgy in León Castile in 1080*, ed. Bernard F. Reilly (New York: Fordham University Press, 1985), 157–85.

[7] Francisco J. Hernández, "Language and Cultural Identity: The Mozarabs of Toledo," *Boletín Burriel* 1 (1989), 29 48. I am grateful to Peter Linehan for giving me a copy of this publication.

[8] On attempts to secure the Mozarabic liturgical legacy earlier in the fifteenth century (in addition to those carried out by Cisneros), see Lynette Bosch, *Art, Liturgy, and Legend in Renaissance Toledo: The Mendoza and the Iglesia Primada* (University Park, Penn.: Penn State University Press, 2000), 60–64.

[9] *Missale mixtum secundum regulam Beati Isidori, dictum Mozarabes* (Toledo, 1500); *Breviarium secundum regulam Beati Isidori* (Toledo, 1502).

[10] Louis Brou, "Etudes sur le Missel et le Bréviaire 'mozarabes' imprimés," *Hispania Sacra* 11 (1958), 349–98.

[11] For a recent discussion of the Ortiz editions and their early historiography see Susan Boynton, "Restoration or Invention? Archbishop Cisneros and the Mozarabic Rite in Toledo," forthcoming in the *Yale Institute of Sacred Music Colloquium Journal.*

[12] The cantorales have been published in facsimile editions as *Los Cantorales Mozárabes de Cisneros*, ed. Férnandez Collado, Alfredo Rodríguez González, and Isidoro Castañeda Tordera, 2 vols. (Toledo: Cabildo de la Catedral Primada de Toledo, 2011).

Hispanic sources, as far as one can judge from the adiastematic neumes.[13] All the evidence suggests that the oral melodic tradition of the Toledan Mozarabs had died out long before 1500, when the cantorales were compiled. This apparent lack of continuity does not seem to have been a concern at the time; as Vito Imbasciani points out, the preface that Ortiz wrote for the *Missale Mixtum* does not refer to melodies at all.[14]

The contrast between the medieval Mozarabic manuscripts and the neo-Mozarabic editions was widely overlooked. Many assumed that Ortiz had simply printed the contents of the Old Hispanic liturgical books. Thus the reinvention of medieval liturgy accomplished under Cisneros created an enduring myth of ancient and coherent ritual tradition. In this way the history of the neo-Mozarabic rite is an example of the process Eric Hobsbawm has termed "the invention of tradition."[15] Although the early modern Mozarabic liturgy originated in the Ortiz editions, its practitioners, adherents, and supporters could claim continuity with a remote past. By the eighteenth century, the rite celebrated in the Mozarabic chapel of Toledo Cathedral was widely understood as a living artifact of early Hispanic practice that had somehow survived intact until the present day. One of the most eloquent affirmations of this continuity appears in a plea from the Mozarabic clergy of Toledo to Ferdinand VI requesting that he place the Mozarabs under the *patronato real*:

> The Holy Gothic-Mozarabic Office was known in the first centuries of the Law of Grace by the venerable name of Apostolic, because it owed its origin to the Apostolic See and it was made known and established in Spain by the seven Apostolic Bishops, Disciples of our Patron St. James. When they were sent to this Province by the Apostle St. Peter, they planted it in the Faith of Jesus Christ. And afterwards it acquired the name of Gothic, since it is known to have been taught by Saints Leander, Isidore, Eugenius, Ildephonse, and Julian, Archbishops of Toledo and Seville, all from the Gothic Nation. And finally that of Mozarabic, because in the prolonged period of the tyrannical Domination of the Saracen Arabs, the Catholic Faithful, who lived mixed with them conserved it in the aforementioned seven churches, despite their tyranny, unhurt and pure. And they practiced it always constant and steady in the Faith, and they used it during almost four centuries in the same form, method, and rule

[13] Herminio González Barrionuevo, "La música litúrgica de los mozárabes," in *Los mozárabes: una minoría olvidada*, ed. Manuel González Jiménez and Juan del Río Martín (Seville: Fundación "El Monte," 1998), 182–85; Vito Imbasciani, "Cisneros and the Restoration of the Mozarabic Rite" (PhD dissertation, Cornell University, 1979), 12.

[14] See Imbasciani, "Cisneros," 6; for the preface to the *Missale Mixtum* of 1500, see ibid., 187–88.

[15] Eric Hobsbawm, "Introduction: Inventing Traditions," in *The Invention of Tradition*, ed. Eric Hobsbawm and Terence Ranger (Cambridge: Cambridge University Press, 1983), 1–14.

> in which they had received it from the Apostolic See. Because of these things, it has been and today is known, famous, laudable, and respected in the entire Catholic world.[16]

The mythology surrounding the Ortiz editions were not the only reason that almost no one before Burriel had consulted the manuscripts of the Old Hispanic rite in Toledo Cathedral. Access was limited for those from outside the cathedral chapter, and few had the ability to read the Visigothic script fluently enough to undertake extensive research.[17] Even those who did see the early manuscripts did not study them closely. For instance, the Bollandist Pinius (Jean Pien, 1678–1749) went to Toledo in 1721 in preparation for the *Acta Sanctorum*, but evidence that he worked directly with the early liturgical manuscripts is scant. In his treatise on the Mozarabic rite, first published in 1729, the summary description of the relevant codices in Toledo Cathedral's library was provided by the librarian Pedro Camino Velasco, a canon who had regular access to the collection for almost thirty years but was not a scholar of the liturgy.[18] Pinius pointed out that many elements in the Mozarabic missal of Ortiz derived from the "Gallic" liturgical books introduced into the Iberian Peninsula in the eleventh century, but this observation was based on the analysis of the edition rather than comparison with early Toledan books.[19]

In the early modern period, most scholarship on the Old Hispanic rite relied on previously published material such as the acts of church councils and the Ortiz editions, which were often reprinted but fundamentally unrevised.

[16] Madrid, Biblioteca Nacional de España, MS 13059, f. 204r: "Que el Oficio Sancto Gothico-Mozarabe conocido en los primero siglos de la Ley de Gracia con el renombre venerable desde Apostolico, por que debio su origen a la silla Apostolica, y le publicaron, y establecieron en España los siete Santos Apostolicos Obispos Discipulos de nuestro Patron Santiago, que embiados a esta Provincia de los Apostoles San Pedro plantaron en ella la Fee de Jesu Christo. Y que despues adquirio el de Gothico, por saberle illustrado los santos Leandro, Isidoro, Eugenio, Ildephonso y Jullian, Arzobispos de Toledo y Sevilla, todos de lo Nacion Goda. Y ultimamente el de Mozarabe, porque en el dilatado tiempo de la tyrana Dominacion de los Arabas Sarracenos, los Fieles Catholicos, que vivieron mezclados con ellos, le conservaron en dichas seis iglesias, a pesar de su tyrania, indemne y puro; y le practicaron tambien constantes y firmes en la Fee, y exercieron por casi quarto Siglos en la misma forma, method y regal que le recibieron de la Apostolica Silla. En cuyo supuesto, ha sido, y hoi es, conocido famoso, plausible, y respetado en todo el Orbe Catholico." Translation by Liam Moore.

[17] The Benedictine Martín Sarmiento prepared an inventory of the library's collection in 1727, now Madrid, Biblioteca Nacional de España, MS 13413 (*olim* Toledo, Biblioteca Capitular, MS 42.35), but he did not study the manuscripts closely.

[18] He became Mozarabic Chaplain in 1731 and stepped down in 1753, was president of the Mozarabic congregation in 1754, and remained active until his death in 1761. Mario Arellano Garcia, *La Capilla Mozárabe o del Corpus Christi* (Toledo: Instituto de Estudios Visigoticos-Mozarabes de San Eugenio, 1980), 81.

[19] Joannes Pinius, *Liturgia Mozarabica. Tractatus historico-chronologicus de liturgia antiqua Hispanica, Gothica, Isidoriana, Mozarabica, Toletana, mixta* (Antwerp, 1729), 102.

Burriel alone was able to demonstrate specifically that the Ortiz editions significantly rearranged and altered the texts in the medieval manuscripts. In the twentieth century, liturgists carried out the same comparisons, reaching similar conclusions.[20] The republication of the Ortiz editions with some of the Roman-rite elements excised by Cardinal Lorenzana, Archbishop of Toledo, shows no awareness of Burriel's findings (even though Lorenzana was a canon at Toledo in the same years Burriel was working there).[21] Indeed, Burriel's results went essentially unnoticed in the intervening two hundred years because he was prevented from completing his work in Toledo Cathedral's Library when the Commission on the Archives ended prematurely in the wake of dramatic political upheaval.

In 1753, a concordat between Spain and the Holy See restored tens of thousands of benefices to the Spanish Crown, alleviating the government's need for the Commission on the Archives. The king's most powerful minister, the Marques de la Ensenada, saw his downfall in 1754. The secretary of state who had hired Burriel, Joseph de Carvajal, died in the same year. Burriel's other patron, the royal confessor and Jesuit Francisco de Ravago, was removed from government in 1755.[22] The new, anti-Jesuit secretary of state, Ricardo Wall, ordered Burriel to finish his work in Toledo. Only in 1756, at the order of the new Inquisitor General, Manuel Quintano y Bonifaz, did Burriel finally abandon his projects for the Commission on the Archives. Despite repeated orders to turn his papers over to the Crown, Burriel maintained possession of almost all his manuscript materials until his death in 1762, and they are now preserved in the Biblioteca Nacional in Madrid.[23]

[20] See for instance, José Janini, "La peculiar edición del breviario mozárabe de Cisneros," in *Liber misticus de cuaresma (Cod. Toled. 35.2, hoy en Madrid, Bibl. Nac. 10.110)*, ed. José Janini (Toledo: Instituto de Estudios Visigótico-Mozárabes, 1979), xxxi–xliii; Janini, "Las piezas litúrgicas del Toledo 35.7 editadas por Ortiz," *Escritos del Vedat* 8 (1978), 161–77; Janini, "La reforma cisneriana de la liturgia mozárabe," in the introduction to Janini and Gonzálvez, *Catálogo de los Manuscritos litúrgicos de la Catedral de Toledo* (Toledo: Diputación Provincial, 1977), 39–49; and José Maria Martín Patino, "El Breviarium Mozárabe de Ortiz: su valor documental para la historia del oficio catedralicio hispánico," *Miscelánea Comillas* 50 (1963), 207–97.

[21] *Breviarium Gothicum Secundum Regulam Beatissimi Isidori* (Madrid, 1775); *Missale Gothicum* (Rome, 1804).

[22] On these events, see John Lynch, *Bourbon Spain 1700–1808* (Oxford: Basil Blackwell, 1989), 182–89.

[23] For an inventory of Burriel's library based on the list compiled by the Jesuits upon his death, see Juan Carlos Galende Diaz, "Repertorio bibliográfico de la biblioteca del Padre Burriel," *Espacio, Tiempo y Forma, Revista de la Facultad de Geografía y Historia*, Serie IV. Historia moderna 8 (1994), 241–68. The manuscripts of the papers related to liturgy appear in José Janini and José Serrano, *Manuscritos litúrgicos de la Biblioteca Nacional* (Madrid: Dirección General de Archivos y Bibliotecas, 1969).

Analysis of this legacy reveals that much of Burriel's research in the early 1750s was greatly facilitated by Palomares, a native of Toledo in his early twenties, who was one of the only calligraphers in the eighteenth century with a profound knowledge of the Visigothic script. It seems that Palomares became acquainted with the Visigothic script at an early age, perhaps through the fragments owned by his father, who was an avid amateur historian.[24] There were no formal channels in Spain at the time for learning the script. Even authoritative and widely read works such as Mabillon's *De re diplomatica* did not include examples of Visigothic script.[25] Instead, just one faulty reproduction appeared in the first major book on Spanish paleography, the *Bibliotheca Universal de la Poligraphia Espanola* by Cristóbal Rodríguez (as published by the royal librarian Blas Nassarre in 1738).[26] Palomares mocked this treatise mercilessly in his own manuscript treatise, the *Polygraphia Gothico-Española*, in which each stage of handwriting in Iberia is illustrated meticulously in a hand-drawn plate. The sources of these images were Palomares's own drawings of manuscripts in Toledo or the Escorial, where he was working on an inventory of the collection in the early 1760s.[27]

Although Palomares is best known for his contributions to handwriting in Spain,[28] his ability to reproduce medieval musical notation is just as impressive. He seems to have learned to copy neumes while assisting Burriel in Toledo. Palomares's engagement with medieval notation is all the more remarkable for its precocity. He became an expert copyist of neumes long before the music historians of the later eighteenth century would take an interest in early notations; while some earlier writers addressed chant notation, they were not aware of the Old Hispanic manuscripts.[29] The complex, highly calligraphic shapes of the neumes in the Old Hispanic chant manuscripts appear to have intrigued

[24] See Susan Boynton, *Silent Music: Medieval Song and the Construction of History in Eighteenth-Century Spain* (New York: Oxford University Press, 2011), xix.

[25] Jean Mabillon, *De re diplomatica libri VI in quibus quidquid ad veterum instrumentorum antiquitatem, materiam, scripturam, et stilum; quidquid ad sigilla, monogrammata, subscriptiones, ac notas chronologicas; quidquid inde ad antiquiariam, historicam, forensemque disciplinam pertinet, explicatur et illustratur* (Paris: Louis Billaine, 1681).

[26] Cristóbal Rodríguez, *Bibliotheca Universal de la Poligraphia Española publicada por D. Blas Nassarre* (Madrid, 1738).

[27] Palomares, *Polygraphia Gothico-Española*, vi–vii and plate 61.

[28] He wrote the influential handwriting manual *Arte nueva de escribir* (Madrid, 1776).

[29] On the study of medieval chant notation in the seventeenth and eighteenth centuries see Eduardo Henrik Aubert, "Historicizing Neumatic Notation: Medieval Neumes as Cultural Artifacts of Early Modern Times," *Studies in medievalism* 21 (2012), 65–87. Aubert has kindly shared with me his forthcoming monograph, *The Modern Life of 'Medieval Neumes': An Archeology of Medieval Notation.*

him throughout his career.[30] In the *Polygraphia Gothico-Española*, he wrote that copying the neumes was the only way to make the melodies available to future generations.[31] Their very inscrutability demanded faithful reproduction. This combination of historical consciousness with visual acuity endowed his work with exceptional accuracy.

Palomares executed many single-page copies to accompany the textual transcriptions produced by Burriel's associates in Toledo. In some cases, he copied all the musical notation in a manuscript. The earliest example of this procedure is a hybrid copy with neumes (in the style characteristic of northern Spain) carefully drawn in black pen over texts transcribed in modern script; for a few chants Palomares produced a likeness of the Visigothic script and the neumes together.[32] The original manuscript, now in the New York Hispanic Society of America, as MS B.2916, was produced in the Rioja and became part of Toledo Cathedral's library sometime in the late Middle Ages. I identified this book in 2001 as the manuscript formerly known as Toledo, Biblioteca Capitular, MS 33.2 (considered lost for a century) and attributed it to the abbey of San Millan de la Çogolla.[33] Palomares's approach to the manuscript suggests that he was experimenting with methods for reproducing the melodies while conveying the substance of the text through transcription. Such close attention to the appearance of medieval music was otherwise unknown in Spain at this time.

The most remarkable products of the collaboration between Burriel and Palomares are two handwritten copies of musical manuscripts, each dedicated to a royal patron. These manuscripts reflect Burriel's wish to convey directly to the monarchs the importance of his work in the context of waning support for the Commission on the Archives. The first is Palomares's complete copy of the Toledo codex of the Cantigas de Santa Maria. Although it is dedicated to Barbara de Braganza, the Portuguese-born consort of Ferdinand VI, it remained in Burriel's papers until his death and is more likely to be a draft than a presentation copy. Palomares transcribed the texts into modern script but painstakingly copied the original musical notation.[34] This hybrid copy con-

[30] On Palomares's study of neumes after the Commission on the Archives, see Boynton, *Silent Music*, 151–64.

[31] See Susan Boynton, "An Early Notated Song of the Sibyl," in *Hortus troporum. Florilegium in honorem Gunillae Iversen*, ed. Alexander Andrée and Erika Kihlman (Stockholm: Almqvist & Wiksell, 2008), 54–56, and Boynton, *Silent Music*.

[32] Madrid, Biblioteca Nacional de España, MS 13060, ff. 120–200.

[33] See Susan Boynton, "A Lost Mozarabic Liturgical Manuscript Rediscovered: New York, Hispanic Society of America, B2916, olim Toledo, Biblioteca Capitular, 33.2," *Traditio* 57 (2002), 189–219.

[34] See Susan Boynton, "Reconsidering the Toledo Codex of the Cantigas de Santa Maria in the Eighteenth Century," in *Quomodo Cantabimus Canticum? Studies in Honor of Edward*

stituted a dual homage to the queen; Barbara's native language was close to that of the Cantigas, and she was an avid, highly accomplished musician (as well as a renowned patron of music). Neither Burriel nor Palomares could interpret the musical notation, but they both apparently considered it to be integral to the work as a whole.

In 1755, the Duke of Alba presented to Ferdinand VI the most extraordinary of all the Commission's artifacts, a facsimile of Toledo, Biblioteca Capitular, MS 35.7, which Burriel believed to be the earliest Toledan liturgical book, dating it to the late eleventh century, specifically the period around 1085 when Toledo was conquered by Alfonso VI.[35] The full-size, full-color reproduction had taken Palomares six months to create, apparently in 1752, and he later wrote that the script, neumes, decoration, and binding were all so accurately rendered that the dean and canons of the cathedral thought that the copy would be confused with the original later on, once the parchment had become worn.[36] The inks in the Toledo manuscript have faded, but the resemblance is still clear. Palomares left out some late-medieval additions to the manuscript, but otherwise the copy is remarkably faithful to the original, incorporating subtle details such as the different shade of ink in which a slightly later hand added a second layer of musical notation to the first. A few elements in the facsimile call attention to its status as a modern copy, such as the foliation added in the upper margins, and the hand calling attention to a lacuna caused by the loss of a leaf in the original. The addition of the hand pointing to the annotation recalls the *maniculae* inserted into manuscripts by medieval readers. The reproduction of Toledo, Biblioteca Capitular, MS 35.7 was accompanied by a separate transcription of the text into modern script, rendering the contents of the manuscript accessible to Ferdinand VI.[37]

H. Roesner, ed. Rena Charnin Mueller, John Nádas, David Cannata, and Gabriela Ilnitchi (Stuttgart: American Institute of Musicology, 2008), 209–22, and Boynton, *Silent Music*.

[35] Burriel's opinion appears in his notes on the transcription: Madrid, Biblioteca Nacional de España, MS 13060, f. 31v.

[36] LondonBL, MS Egerton 588, f. 159rv ("Relacion breve de los servicios hechos por Don Francisco Xavier de Santiago Palomares, natural de la Ciudad de Toledo"): "hizo una copia al vivo de todo un Missal Gothico Muzarabe en pergamino de los que se conservan en aquella Bibliotheca, en que trabajo incesantemente cerca de seis meses, y saliò tan parecido al Original, no solo en lo raro de los Caracteres Gothicos, notas particulares de la Musica (que hasta ahora ninguno ha entendido) sino aun en lo material de su enquadernacion, y circunstancias, que haviendolo visto el Dean, y otros Canonigos de aquella Santa Iglesia, mereciò la aprobacion de identica con el original, y aun pensaron algunos en que se dejase Certificacion de haver hecho el Suplicante esta Copia, para que en lo subcesivo no se equivocase con los originales."

[37] Madrid, Biblioteca del Palacio Real, II/482.

Figure 1. Toledo, Biblioteca Capitular, 35.7, f. 41r, compared to Madrid, Palacio Real, Biblioteca, II/483, f. 81r

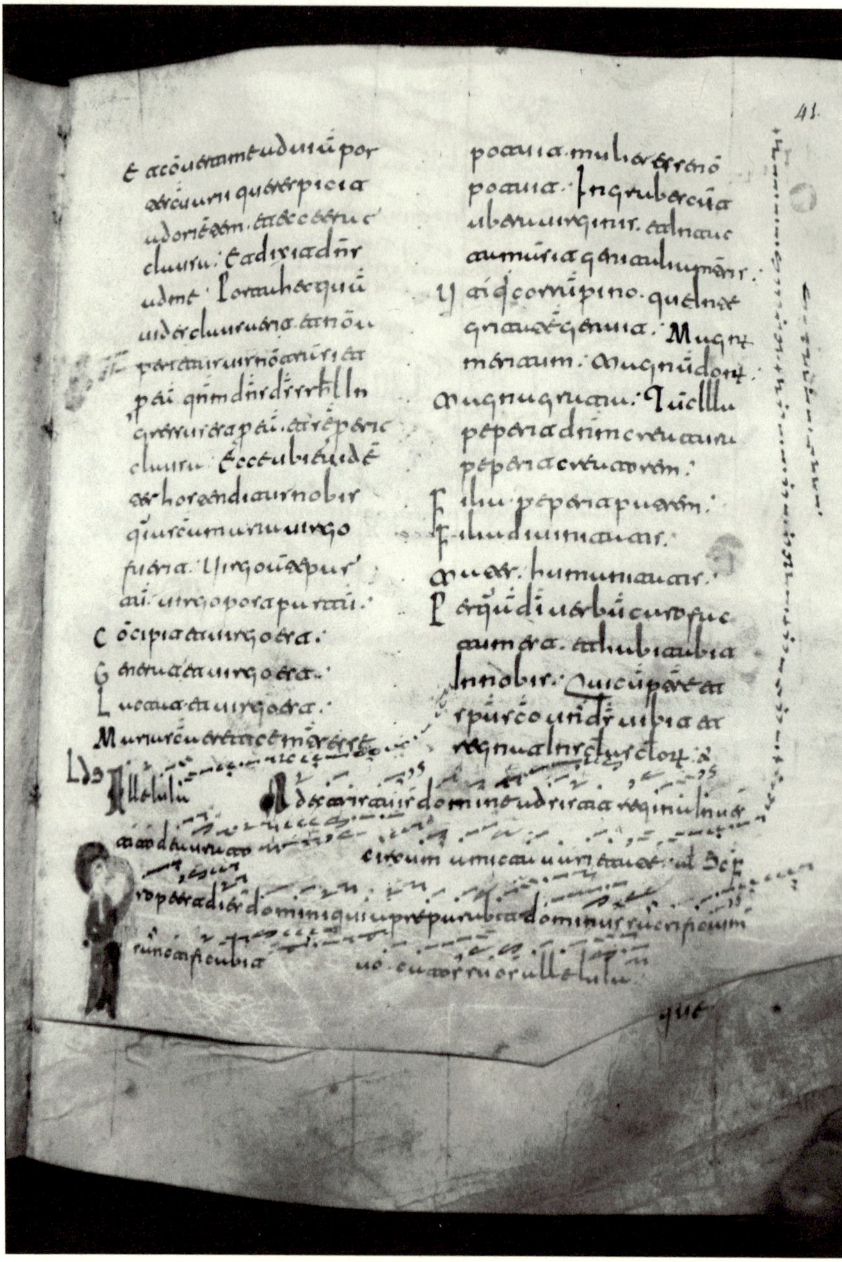

Figure 1, continued

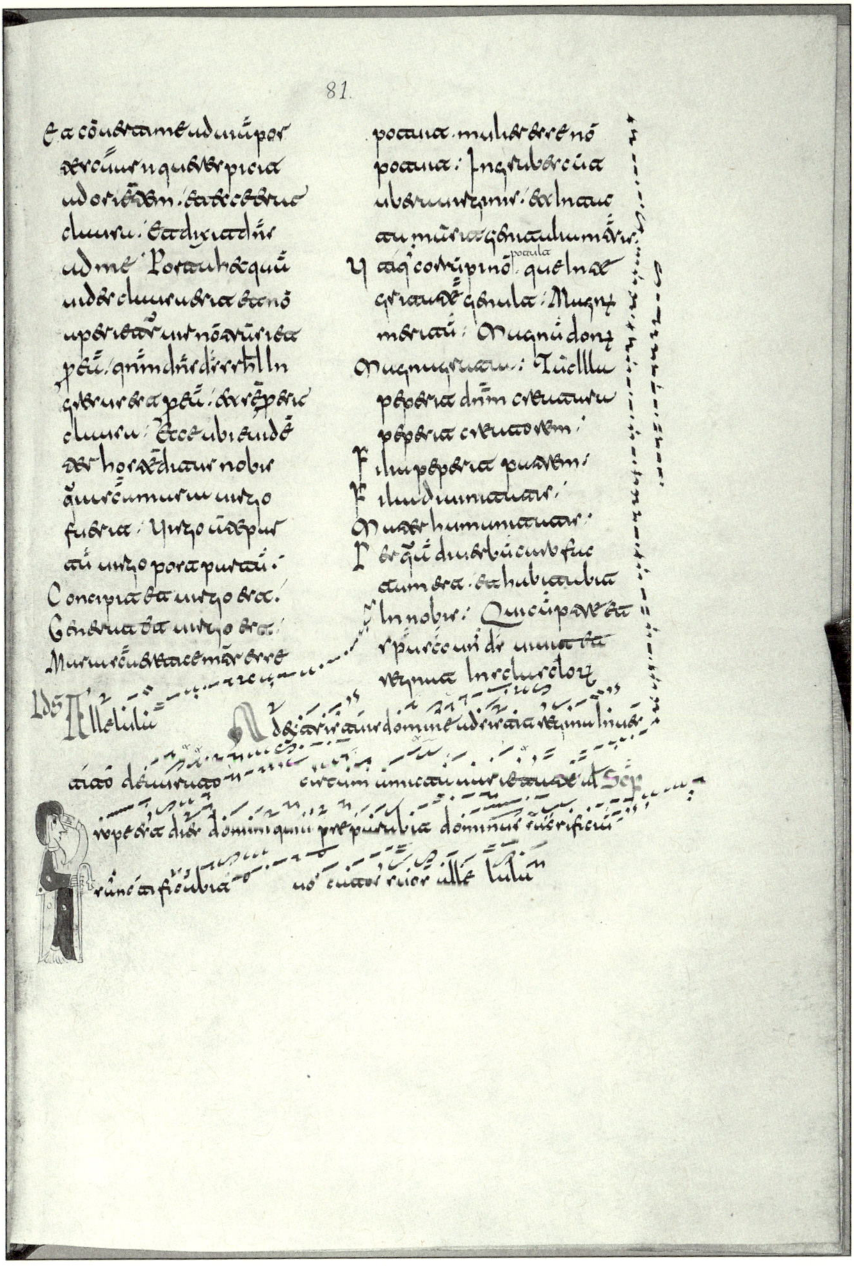

Figure 2. A hand pointing out a lacuna in Madrid, Palacio Real, Biblioteca, II/483, f. 142r

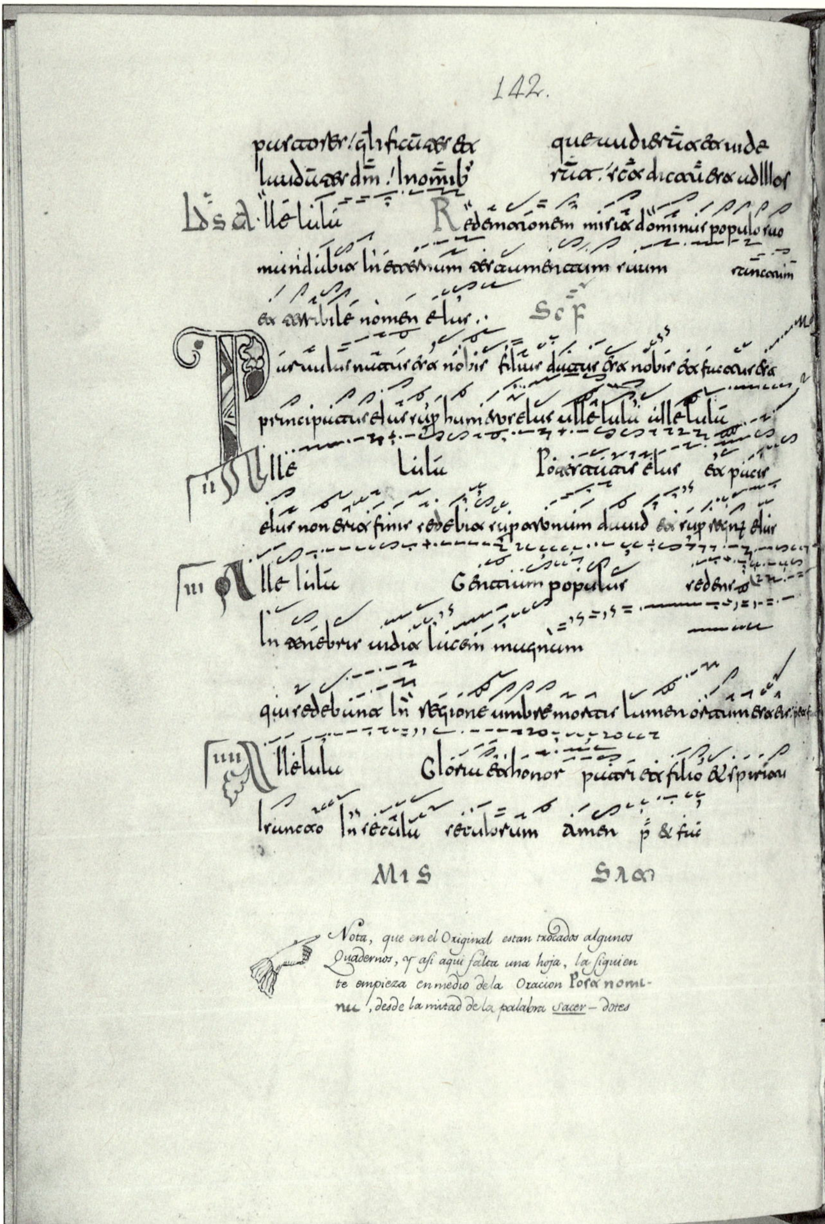

At the beginning of the facsimile volume, Burriel inserted a preface that he wrote especially for the king. This text presents the historical significance of the liturgy as a marker of Spanish national identity, construed here as an unbroken ritual tradition that, like Ferdinand's own religious beliefs, represented a continuous tradition inherited from the Visigothic kings. This was a common historiographical strategy in Bourbon Spain; also in the 1750s, Martín Sarmiento juxtaposed the Visigoths and the Bourbons in his treatise proposing a program of decoration for the new Royal Palace in Madrid.[38]

In his preface to the facsimile Burriel described the books in Toledo Cathedral library as the embodiment of the venerable Visigothic legacy going back to Ildefonsus of Toledo, the theologian and bishop of Toledo who died in 657.[39] The manuscript itself constitutes a kind of link to Ildefonsus, for it begins with his treatise on the perpetual virginity of the Virgin Mary, divided into seven sections for reading as prayers during Mass.[40] The connection to Ildefonsus is made even more explicit in the facsimile by the addition of an author portrait that depicts the bishop writing while gazing raptly upon the Virgin and Child. An image of Toledo can be seen in the background.[41] Ildefonsus, who was venerated as a saint, had long functioned as a symbol of Toledo, which had been the capital of the Visigothic kingdom as well as the primatial see of the Visigothic church.[42] Burriel studied Ildefonsus's cult as well as his literary production; one of the many unfinished projects to be found in Burriel's papers is a compilation on the cult of Ildefonsus in late medieval and early modern Spain.[43]

[38] Martín Sarmiento, *Sistema de adornos del Palacio Real de Madrid*, ed. Joaquín Álvarez Barrientos and Concha Herrero Carretero (Madrid: Sociedad Estatal de Conmemoraciones Culturales, 2002).

[39] Madrid, Biblioteca del Palacio Real, II/483, f. 3rv. See Boynton, *Silent Music*.

[40] Ildefonsus of Toledo. *Ildefonsi Toletani Episcopi De virginitate Sanctae Mariae*, ed. Valeriano Yarza Urquiola, Corpus Christianorum. Series Latina 114A (Turnhout: Brepols, 2007), 147–263.

[41] On this portrait see Susan Boynton, "Writing History with Liturgy," in *Representing History, 900–1300: Art, Music, History*, ed. Robert A. Maxwell (University Park, Pa.: Penn State Press, 2010), 196 and fig. 60.

[42] Toledo became the capital of the Visigothic kingdom during the reign of King Wamba (672–80) and was declared the primatial see at the Twelfth Council of Toledo in 681. See Roger Collins, *Early Medieval Spain: Unity in Diversity, 400–1000* (London: MacMillan, 1995), 70–71.

[43] Burriel's notes on the liturgy of Saint Ildefonsus are preserved in Madrid, Biblioteca Nacional de España, MS 13062.

Like Burriel's liturgical studies, Palomares's numerous hand-drawn copies of Old Hispanic chant manuscripts all remained in manuscript form—except for one small sample that was mechanically reproduced in Burriel's treatise on Spanish paleography. The *Paleografía Española* was first published in 1755 as part of a Spanish translation of a popular French encyclopedia, *Le spectacle de la Nature* by Nöel-Antoine Pluche (1688–1761).[44] Burriel's text replaced a treatise on French paleography that had formed a part of Pluche's original work.[45]

Although Burriel's treatise has not been cited by musicologists, it contains the earliest printed image of an Old Hispanic chant with neumes.[46] One of the engraved plates reproduces a drawing by Palomares of an antiphon for Vespers of Saint Stephen, "Liberabo eum dicit dominus alleluia alleluia."[47] The choice of Toledo, Biblioteca Capitular, MS 35.7 for this one tiny sample of Mozarabic chant was not happenstance. As noted earlier, Burriel considered the manuscript the earliest Toledan liturgical book. Furthermore, he apparently believed that Ildefonsus of Toledo himself had set the liturgical texts to music. Burriel expressed this opinion in his *Paleografía Española* and in the preface to the facsimile of Toledo, Biblioteca Capitular, MS 35.7.[48] The illustration from the manuscript, like the facsimile of the entire source that he commissioned from Palomares, show Burriel's interest in the music of the Old Hispanic chant.

The two reproductions of Toledo, Biblioteca Capitular, MS 35.7 made under the aegis of the Commission on the Archives differ significantly in intention as well as in presentation. The full-color complete facsimile created for Ferdinand VI would have been an ideal tool for scholarly study, but it was a luxury presentation volume for a single patron whose interest in the object was probably more personal than historical. By contrast, the brief excerpt from one chant in Burriel's *Paleografía Española* has been widely available since its publication, but it is not a substantial enough example to have promoted study of Visigothic neumes.

[44] *Espectaculo de la Naturaleza, o conversaciones a cerca de las particularidades de la historia natural, que han parecido mas a proposito para exercitar una curiosidad util, y formarlas la razon a los Jovenes Lectores: parte septima, que contiene lo que pertenece al hombre en sociedad*, trans. Estevan de Terreros y Pando, 13 (Madrid: Gabriel Ramirez, 1755), 201–360. The *Paleografía Española* was also printed as a separate volume in 1758.

[45] *Le spectacle de la nature* was first published in eight volumes in Paris from 1732–50.

[46] There are no Iberian examples among the many engravings of chant notation in Martin Gerbert, *De Cantu et Musica Sacra a Prima Ecclesiae Aetate usque ad Praesens Tempus*, 2 vols. (Sankt Blasien, 1774); reprint edition with indices by Othmar Wessely (Graz: Akademische Druck- u. Verlagsanstalt, 1968).

[47] Burriel, *Paleografía Española*, plate 15 (fourth item), reproducing Toledo 35.7, f. 73r.

[48] Burriel, *Paleografía Española*, 117; Madrid, Palacio Real, Biblioteca, II/483, f. 4r.

Figure 3. Burriel, Paleografía Española, *plate 15*

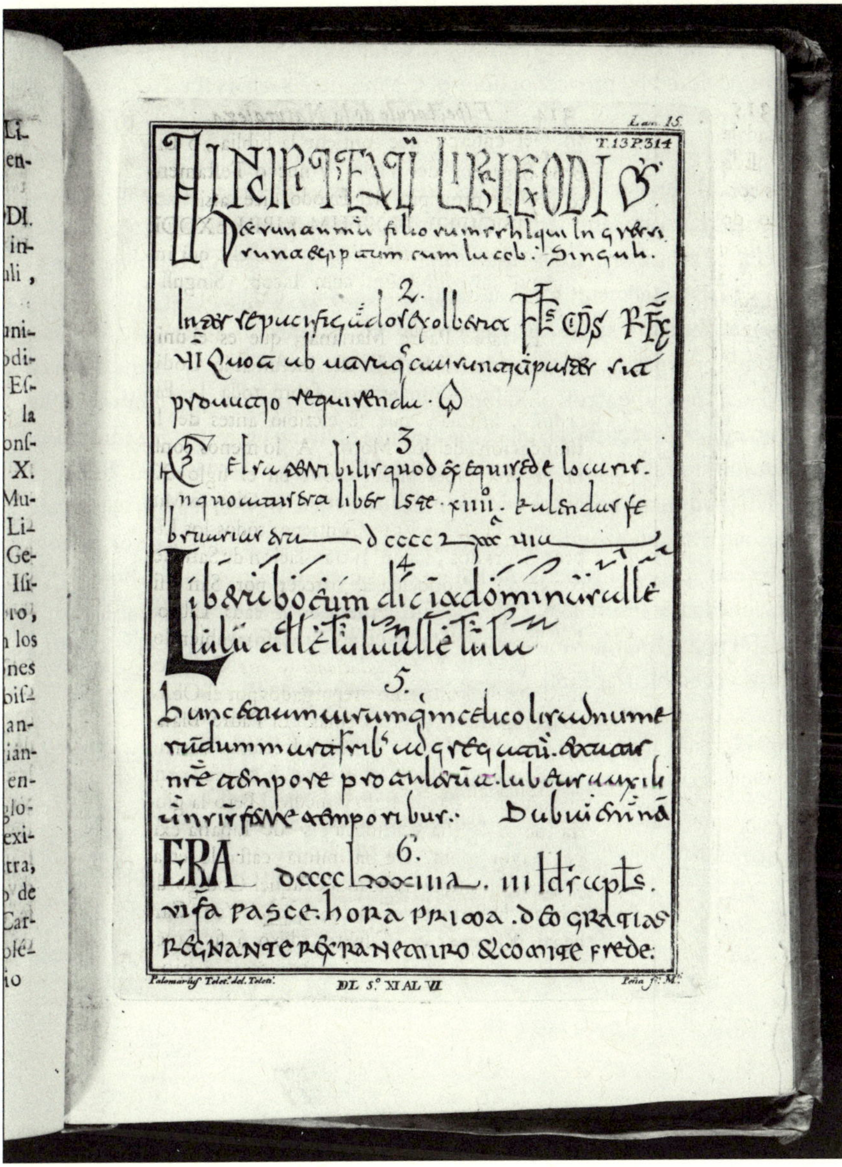

For Burriel and Palomares, reproducing the appearance of manuscripts was a way to understand the past and a way to project contemporary ideas onto the Middle Ages. To copy these historically significant manuscripts was not only a method of study and analysis, but also an interpretation of Spanish history colored by preoccupations of the moment such as the ascendancy of the Bourbon dynasty in Spain. The Jesuit and the calligrapher both emphasized music and liturgy in their respective constructions of Spanish national identity. The music that so fascinated them was, for them, inevitably silent, which perhaps explains why they found it intriguing. The graphic representation of the music in manuscripts as marks on the page was their only access to the Old Hispanic melodies (a situation that has not changed very much since the eighteenth century). Although we are accustomed to conceiving of music as sound, primarily as sounding object and only secondarily in the form of its visual trace, the work of Palomares and Burriel reminds us of how crucial the manuscript record can be in the absence of living performance traditions. They did not envision a revival of any of the music they studied, but they understood its importance as historical evidence. In this regard, they were unusual; most eighteenth-century scholars who dealt with liturgy or paleography considered only texts. As Palomares stated in his treatise, he hoped that someone in the future would decipher the neumes of the Old Hispanic chant. We still maintain the same hope of someday reaching a better understanding of this venerable tradition.[49]

[49] The text of this article was finalized in 2010; a few footnotes were updated in 2012. A fuller exposition appears in Boynton, *Silent Music*.

Part IV

Origins of Forms and of Ideas

Ways of Singing Hexameter in Tenth-Century Europe

ANDREAS HAUG

THE PRIMARY LANGUAGE of early medieval music was the Latin of the translated Bible. Its form was prose, albeit prose that was considered to be resulting from translations unfaithful to the verse form of the original texts.[1] The linguistic features of that prose have for a long time been recognized as a formative factor for the shaping of the melodic idiom of Roman chant. This idiom represents a form of "prose music" or "musical prose," historically significant as an initial stratum of Western music and at the same time as a lasting idiom of reference for any musical production prior to the emergence of mensural music.

When, during the ninth and tenth centuries north of the Alps, that body of Roman chant distributed by the Carolingians was extended by new Frankish forms of singing, another Latin idiom entered the realm of music: the language of Latin classical verse, belonging to a literary heritage that the cultural efforts of Carolingian reformers had made accessible. This was a different language, more artful and more artificial, more distinguished in cultural terms, and more challenging in technical terms than the *sermo humilis* of the Bible with its syntactically straightforward prose. These two languages met in music. Whenever antiphons composed in metrical verse were linked to psalms, or, conversely, whenever metrical tropes were attached to antiphons

[1] The notion that metrical forms of the Greek or Hebrew original were lost in the Latin translation of biblical texts is reflected, for instance, around 800 in the famous *Libri Carolini*, lib. II, cap. 30, ed. Ann Freeman, *Opus Caroli regis contra synodum (Libri Carolini)*, Monumenta Germaniae Historica, Concilia II, Supplementum I (Hanover: Hahn, 1998), 313–14.

in prose, these combinations brought about an idiomatic contrast or even an idiomatic conflict, not just on the textual level. When metrical texts were set to music, moreover, this led to an encounter between the features of music genuinely shaped for prose and the complex features exhibited by text in metrical verse.[2] This encounter might have been an incentive for the emergence of a melodic syntax with intricacies beyond the ones we find in the melodic syntax of Roman chant.

Yet how strongly the structural contrast between verse and prose was perceived in oral delivery depends upon the way Latin metrical verse was read, heard, and sung subsequent to the linguistic change in spoken language during the late classical period that is labeled as the "loss of syllable quantities." This fundamental transformation of the prosodic preconditions had a vital impact both on the making of metrical verse and on its oral performance and aural reception. Augustine is the most prominent and most often quoted contemporaneous witness for that process. The date of origin of his *De musica* provides evidence for its completion no later than around 390.[3] At that time retention of quantitative distinction in Latin pronunciation had become a question of education; it had become an attribute of what has been described as a *Bildungsaussprache* and as a *Schulaussprache*.[4] In Augustine's time the linguistic basis of metrical versification, the "dimensio syllabarum," had to be reconstructed,

[2] On the idiomatic difference between "Biblical" chant and tropes in the "Classical" style and on the different linguistic traditions they represent, see Ritva Jonsson and Leo Treitler, "Medieval Music and Language: A Reconsideration of their Relationship," in *Studies in the History of Music I: Music and Language* (New York: Broude, 1983), 16.

[3] Augustinus, *De musica*, lib. II, cap. 2, and, some forty years later, *De doctrina christiana*, lib. IV, cap. 10. See Hermann Koller, "Die Silbenquantitäten in Augustinus' Büchern De musica," *Museum Helveticum* 38 (1981), 262–67, and Jürgen Leonhardt, *Dimensio syllabarum: Studien zur lateinischen Prosodie- und Verslehre von der Spätantike bis zur frühen Renaissance* (Göttingen: Vandenhoeck & Ruprecht, 1989), 61–66.

[4] That is how Leonhardt (*Dimensio syllabarum*, 63–64) reads Augustine's well-known statement in *De doctrina christiana* (written around 430) and a corresponding remark by the Roman grammarian Consentius (around 500), that "Afrae aures de correptione vocalium vel productione non iudicant" (*De doctrina christiana*, lib. IV, cap. 10) and that wrong pronunciation of vowel quantities is a "vitium Afrorum familare" (Heinrich Keil, ed., *Artium scriptores minores*, Grammatici latini, vol. 5 [Leipzig: B. G. Teubner, 1855–80], 392); i.e., that the statement does not indicate that the change in spoken language had taken place earlier in Africa than at Rome, but that Africans were less educated than the Romans were. As to the question of whether a *Bildungsaussprache* retaining quantitative distinctions had been practiced by the educated Roman upper class, one finds different opinions. For instance, Tore Janson, *Mechanisms of language change in Latin* (Stockholm: Almqvist & Wiksell International, 1979), 27, is skeptical, and Roger Wright, "Speaking, reading and writing late Latin and early Romance," *Neophilologus* 9 (1976), 178–89 and *idem, Late Latin and early Romance in*

taught and learned;[5] prosody needed to be included as an additional subject in the textbooks of *ars metrica*.[6] When, beginning in the Carolingian period, Latin metrical poetry was set to music, it had already turned into a matter of erudition and of school practice.

How Latin hexameter was read under these conditions, that is, to what extent distinctive features of the meter were rendered in its recitation, has been a matter of debate among Latinists for a long time.[7] Now and again they have expected supporting arguments from an analysis of melodies of sung hexameter. Certainly, this expectation is not without foundation: we might suppose that when verse was sung it was sung the same way it was read; or at least, that the melodic setting was not unrelated to, or incompatible with, the way verse was recited outside music; that written records of the melodies can be read as visual traces or tracks of the sounding verse; and that the "soundtrack" of notation would preserve at least some distant echo of common modes of verse articulation, reverberating in the fabric of the melodies.

Spain and Carolingian France (Liverpool: F. Cairris, 1982), rejects the idea, while Leonhardt, *Dimensio syllabarum*, 65–66 *et passim*, provides substantial evidence for it.

[5] Augustine speaks of the *ars grammatica* as a "custos historiae," protecting distinction of quantities (*De musica*, lib. II, cap. 1); at about the same time the grammarian Servius demands a cultivation of classical pronunciation: "studeamus pronuntiationi" (Heinrich Keil, ed., *Probi Donati Servii qvi fervntvr de arte grammatica libri*, Grammatici latini vol. 4, 423). These passages were discussed in Leonhardt, *Dimensio syllabarum*, 63–64.

[6] Beginning with Priscianus in his *Institutio grammatica* (around 500), followed by medieval writers such as Aldhelm in his *Epistula ad Acicium*, Beda in his *De arte metrica* (both around 700), and Hrabanus Maurus in his *Excerptio de arte grammatici Prisciani* (around 800). The testimony of these writings and the process of inclusion of prosody into the teaching of metrics have been described in detail by Leonhardt, *Dimensio syllabarum*, 56–86; see also his summary 182–86.

[7] The (unanswered) question of how Latin (metrical) verse was read *before* the feeling for quantitative distinction had evaporated is beyond the topic of the present paper; what has most fervently been disputed among experts is the existence or non-existence of a verse *ictus* (or verse accent) in classical Latin poetry. See Dag Ludvig Norberg, "Mètre et rythme entre le Bas-Empire et le Haut Moyen Age," in his *Au seuil du Moyen Age II: Études linguistiques, métriques et littéraires, 1975–1995*, ed. Ritva Jacobsson and Folke Sandgren (Stockholm: Kungl. Vitterhets, historie och antikvitets akademien, 1998), 84–86, with references to contributions of other scholars in notes 11–13; Jan M. Ziolkowski, *Nota bene. Reading Classics and Writing Melodies in the Early Middle Ages* (Turnhout: Brepols, 2007), 126–30, with further references in note 56. Both Aage Kabell, "Wie die Verse gelesen wurden," in his *Metrische Studien* (Uppsala: Lundquistska bokhandeln, 1960), vol. 2, 25–31, and Wilfried Stroh, "Kann man es lernen, lateinische Verse zu sprechen?" in his *Apocrypha: Entlegene Schriften*, ed. Jürgen Leonhardt und Georg Ott (Stuttgart: Steiner, 2000), 245–61, dispute the idea of an *ictus* in classical verse.

On closer inspection, the overall question, "How was hexameter read?" can be broken down to several more specific questions, which, for the sake of clarity, should remain separate:

(1) Were *caesuras*, that is, word endings within a verse foot, made perceptible as pauses in the delivery? That is, did an obligatory break within the verbal fabric of the verse cause a true, audible stop in declamation? Modern experts, such as Giovanni Orlandi, have confessed their agnosticism about the effect of such a break.[8] Nevertheless, as caesuras cause metrical partitions of the verse regardless of units of syntax or sense,[9] any pause in reading or in singing within such a unit will be heard by the listener as an audible signal of the metrical construction of a text.

(2) Were the different *quantities of syllables* that determine the patterns of the verses perceived as different durations?

(3) Was the *verse ictus* enhanced by some sort of vocal stress on the beginning of each verse foot? That is, was there an audible "beat" on metrically marked positions?

Of these three questions the last one appears to be the most crucial and most controversial one.[10] The scant evidence provided by the small number of sources is ambiguous.[11] Only post-Classical authors used the expression "scandere versus" for a reading "foot by foot" that enhanced the ictus by vocal means.[12] When Quintilianus mentions a phenomenon called "ictus" he still has in mind a marking of the meter "pedum et digitorum ictu" ("with a stroke of the hand or the foot") but not by way of vocal stress.[13] The earliest witness for a marking of metrical positions merely by means of the voice is the third-century grammarian Sacerdos; he states, "quod versus percutientes, [id est scandentes], interdum accentus alios pronuntiamus quam per singula verba

[8] Giovanni Orlandi, "The Hexameter in the Aetas Horatiana," in *Latin Culture in the Eleventh Century*, ed. Michael W. Herren et. al. (Turnhout: Brepols, 2002), vol. 2, 244.

[9] This is at least the common view held also by Orlandi, "The Hexameter," 245, note 20.

[10] For a recent discussion of the controversial problem see Ziolkowski, *Nota bene*, 126–30.

[11] The relevant sources have been identified by Paul Klopsch, *Einführung in die mittellateinische Verslehre* (Darmstadt: Wissenschaftliche Buchgesellschaft, 1972), 1–4, Dag Ludvig Norberg, in the chapter titled "Comment a-t-on récité le vers," of his study *Les vers latins iambiques et trochaiques au Moyen Age et leurs répliques rythmiques* (Stockholm: Almqvist & Wiksell International, 1988), 13–16, and in "Mètre et rythme entre le Bas-Empire," 84–86, and Jürgen Leonhardt, *Dimensio syllabarum*, 24–71.

[12] Norberg, "Mètre et rythme entre le Bas-Empire," 84, quotes Sergius in Keil, *Probi Donati Servii*, Grammatici latini vol. 4, 522.

[13] Marcus Fabius Quintilianus, *Institutiones oratoriae libri XII*, ed. Helmut Rahn (Darmstadt: Wissenschaftliche Buchgesellschaft, 1995), book 9, cap. 4.51, 386.

ponentes."[14] This is evidence both for different positions of verse accent and normal word accent and for a similar quality of their sound. A fifth-century commentary on Donatus sheds light on the nature of that sound, saying that, "the syllable having the accent" sounds stronger, owns more sonority, more intensity, than the others ("illa syllaba plus sonat in toto verbo, quae accentum habet, . . . quasi habet maiorem potestatem.")[15]

Whereas some modern experts, among them Paul Klopsch, took such statements as support for their opinion that the ictus was stressed by vocal means when metrical verse was recited by medieval readers,[16] others, among them Dag Norberg, did not. Norberg did not discount that ictus was made audible *when* verse was scanned, but he held that this was not done in normal pronunciation.[17] He considered scansion as exceptional, as a kind of analytical mode of pronunciation limited to school practice, where it served as a means for teaching the patterns of verse and the prosody of Latin words. Thus, it only emerged when the spontaneous feeling for the quantity of Latin vowels had become lost in late antiquity and a verse form governed by such quantities had to be demonstrated in an artificial way, as compensation for the loss of quantitative distinction. Conversely a "normal" reading, in Norberg's terms, preserved the normal prose accent.[18] He finds support for his opinion in the *Ars lectoria* of Aimericus of Gastinaux (1086) and in the *Poetria nova* of Geoffrey of Vinsauf (around 1200). Aimericus plainly postulates a reading "non scandendo sed enuntiando."[19] Geoffrey claims that a syllable "non est aliter accentuanda in metro quam extra metrum."[20] Thus, there seem to have been two different medieval ways of performing hexameter: a "regular" and a "didactic" mode; a reading "enuntiando" (where accents were the same "in metro" as "extra metrum") and a reading "scandendo" (where verse accent, in

[14] Heinrich Keil, ed., *Scriptores artis metricae,* Grammatici latini vol. 6, pt. 2, 448.

[15] Keil, *Artium scriptores minores,* Grammatici latini vol. 5, 126.

[16] Klopsch, *Einführung in die mittellateinische Verslehre,* 1–3. See also *idem,* "Der Übergang von quantitierender zu akzentuierender lateinischer Dichtung," in *Metrik und Medienwechsel = Metrics and Media,* ed. Hildegard L. C. Tristram (Tübingen: G. Narr 1991), 95–106.

[17] Norberg mentions the testimony of two Carolingian grammarians of Irish origin: Cruindmelus, who claims in his *Ars metrica* that no one gets to know the quantity of vowels "nisi ex scandendis versibus discere stuedeat" (Johann Huemer, *Cruindmeli sive Fulcharii ars metrica* [Vienna: Alfred Hölder, 1883], 5), and Dicuil, who recommends his treatise *De primis syllabis* to those wishing "scire pedes et scandere versus" (Ernst Dümmler, ed., *Poetae Latini aevi Carolini (II),* Monumenta Germaniae Historica, Poetae II [Berlin: Weidmann, 1884], 667).

[18] See Norberg's above-mentioned chapter, "Comment a-t-on récité le vers," 13–16.

[19] Harry F. Reijnders, "*Aimericus, Ars lectoria* (3) (finis)," *Vivarium* 10 (1972), 127–76 at 172.

[20] Edmond Faral, *Les arts poétiques du XIIe et du XIIIe siècle* (Paris: Champion, 1924) 319.

fact, *was* different from word accent).[21] Either of these opposite modes might be reflected in the melodies, when hexameters were sung.

Little had been written on the peculiarities of such melodies and their notation before a joint study was undertaken by the Latinist Gunilla Björkvall and myself twenty years ago.[22] Moreover, there was an important earlier article by Ritva Jonsson and Leo Treitler, whose authors summarized their analysis of a West-Frankish hexameter trope as follows: "The one feature of the trope verses that has no influence whatsoever on the melodic structure is their metrical structure." They find this assessment "not contradicted by the reflection of the caesuras in the melodies, for caesura is a function of both metre and word-content, and it is the word-content that is consistently projected by melody. Only those aspects of text-structure that relate to the sense of the text were constraints on the melodies."[23] The question I am asking in this paper is whether this statement, based on a single trope, allows for generalization.

But before we turn to issues of performance, let us remember the form and some structural features of what has been described as the "medieval" type of hexameter by Paul Klopsch, or as the typical hexameter of the tenth and eleventh century (the so-called "Aetas Horatiana") by Giovanni Orlandi.[24] Figure 1 demonstrates some of these particular features. The percentages have been

[21] Jan Ziolkowski seems to support Norberg's opinion when he concludes his detailed discussion of the question like this: "On the whole the evidence seems strong that at the latest by late antiquity accentual reading would have been the normal way of reading, while 'scanning' would have constituted the exception" (*Nota bene*, 129–30.)

[22] The jointly authored articles in the study are: "Primus init Stephanus. Eine Sankt Galler Prudentius-Vertonung des zehnten Jahrhunderts," *Archiv für Musikwissenschaft* 48 (1992), 57–78, followed by "Musik und lateinischer Vers im frühen Mittelalter," in *Musik als Text: Bericht über den Internationalen Kongreß der Gesellschaft für Musikforschung, Freiburg 1993*, vol. 2, ed. Hermann Danuser and Tobias Plebuch (Kassel: Bärenreiter, 1999), 234–40; "Zum Verhältnis von Verslehre und Versvertonung im lateinischen Mittelalter," in *Artes im Mittelalter*, ed. Ursula Schaefer (Berlin: Akademie, 1999), 309–23; "Performing Latin Verse: Music and Text in Early Versified Offices," in *The Divine Office in the Latin Middle Ages*, ed. Rebecca A. Baltzer and Margot Fassler (Oxford: Oxford University Press, 2000), 278–99. Ewald Jammers's article, "Grundsätzliches zur Erforschung der rhythmischen Neumenschriften" in *Schrift, Ordnung, Gestalt: Gesammelte Aufsätze zur älteren Musikgeschichte*, ed. Ewald Jammers (Bern: Francke, 1969), 9–24, contains analyses of medieval hexameter settings and their notation, yet does not contribute to an understanding of how the verse was read. To Jammers it appeared as a fact *that* hexameter was scanned, understandably, as his article was first published in 1942/43, before Medieval Latinists had started to deal with the problem.

[23] Ritva Jonsson and Leo Treitler, "Medieval Music and Language: A Reconsideration of their Relationship," in *Studies in the History of Music I: Music and Language* (New York: Broude Brothers, 1983), 1–23.

[24] Klopsch, *Einführung*, 64; Orlandi, "The Hexameter," 240–58.

Figure 1. Structural features of "medieval" hexameter

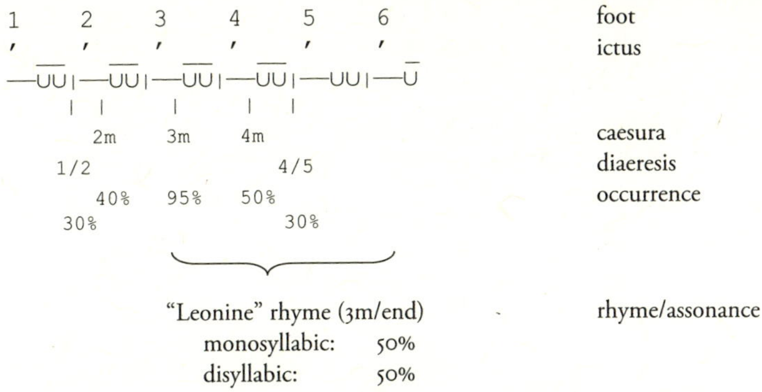

taken from Orlandi's study and rounded up slightly.[25] His data have been gathered from non-liturgical and non-musical verse. The pattern of dactylic and/or spondaic feet is not different from what medieval poets found in their models from antiquity, whereas the frequent caesura in the third foot (designated as 3m in the Figure), which is often enhanced by rhyme, is a non-Classical feature. This medial break dividing the line into two nearly equal parts reflects the medieval notion of the hexameter as a bipartite verse. Such a particular "medieval" type of hexameter emerged once Carolingian poets regained command of the classical art of metrical verse through the ninth century, and it gave way to an again more "classicist" form from the twelfth century on.[26]

Let us now examine a number of settings from the oldest layer of hexameter melodies and ask which way of reading they reflect. The examples are taken from tenth-century manuscripts originating from different places, both monasteries and episcopal churches.

The first example is—in terms of evidence for a specific mode of recitation—perhaps the most striking one. The pair of hexameters shown in Figure 2 form the opening element of a trope in the famous troper from Reichenau, copied in

[25] Orlandi, "The Hexameter," Appendix II: 256–57.

[26] Klopsch, *Einführung*, 64: "Nachdem der Prozeß der Wiedergewinnung der antiken Verskunst abgeschlossen war, etwa seit der Mitte des 9. Jh., begannen die Dichter den Hexameter nach und nach freier zu behandeln. . . . Diesem 'mittelalterlichen' Typus trat bei erneuter Rückorientierung an den antiken Vorbildern, besonders also im 12. Jh., ein 'antikisierender' gegenüber, der sich von den neuen Errungenschaften freihielt."

Figure 2. Reichenau troper, Ecclesiae sponsus

Ecclésiae spónsus, cúnctis iam géntibus órtus,
– UU|– –|– –|– – |– UU|– U
| | | |
2m 3m 4m 4/5

totíus órbis hónor, baptísmatis ípse sacrátor,
– UU|– U U|– –|– UU|– UU|–U
| |
3m 4/5

Ecclésiae spónsus, cúnctis iam géntibus órtus, *"enutiando"*
totíus órbis hónor, baptísmatis ípse sacrátor,

Écclesiáe sponsús, cunctís iam géntibus órtus, *"scandendo"*
tótius órbis honór, baptísmatis ípse sacrátor,

Prose version: Ecclesiae sponsus,
illuminator gentium,
baptismatis sacrator,
orbis redemptor

1001.[27] When read "enuntiando," the lines are stressed as: "Ecclésiae spónsus, cúnctis iam géntibus órtus, / totíus órbis hónor, baptísmatis ípse sacrátor," but, when read "scandendo" as: "Écclesiáe sponsús, cunctís iam géntibus órtus, / tótius órbis honór, baptísmatis ípse sacrátor."

Since the only melodic record of this trope is in staffless notation, an analysis of its melodic shape demands an examination of a related, more fully notated version. The trope is a reworking of a renowned and very widespread trope in prose, which is presumably older than its verse paraphrase. The prose version is also contained in the same manuscript from Reichenau.[28] This text divides in four units of syntax and sense: "Ecclesiae sponsus, | illuminator gentium, | baptismatis sacrator, | orbis redemptor." The Reichenau trope is a transformation of these prose lines into hexameters, with a minimal amount of change of meaning and wording. The opening phrase "Ecclesiae sponsus" matches the first part of a hexameter and could thus be kept, whereas "baptismatis sacrator" matches the second half of a hexameter only; it had to be removed and completed by the filling word "ipse." Both resulting verse lines have a caesura 3m; the break is highlighted by monosyllabic (assonance) rhyme.

[27] Bamberg, Staatsbibliothek, Msc. Lit. 5, f. 43v; *Corpus Troporum* 1 (1975), 85 (Epiph intr 59).

[28] Bamberg, Staatsbibliothek, Msc. Lit. 5, f. 41v; *Corpus Troporum* 1 (1975), 85 (Epiph intr 15). The common prose version of the Epiphany trope has been used (as elsewhere) "IN EPIPHANIA," the unique hexameter version "IN OCTAVA EPIPHANIAE." Photos: Gerald Rabb.

Figure 3a. Bamberg 5, f. 41v, Ecclesiae sponsus, *prose version*

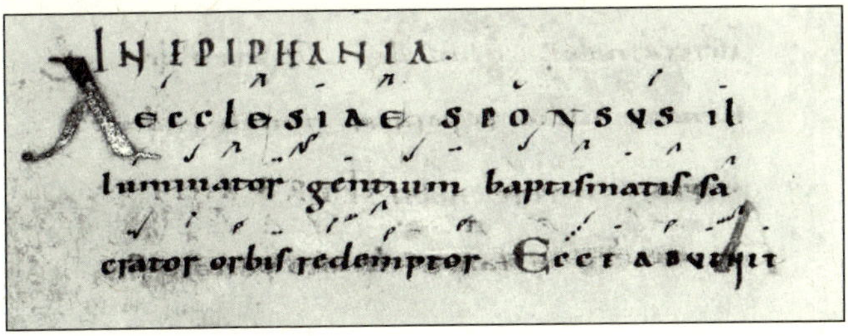

Figure 3b. Bamberg 5, f. 43v, Ecclesiae sponsus, *verse version*

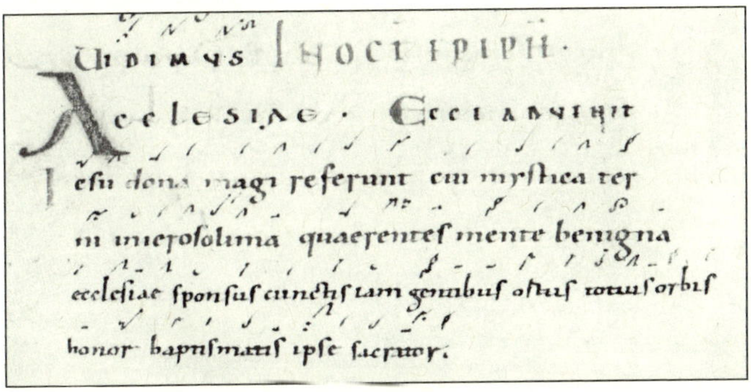

As can be seen in Figure 3, where the texts are the same, the notations are the same as well, and a closer comparison will substantiate the assumption that, as a sort of contrafactum, the hexameter paraphrase was sung upon the existing melody of the original prose text. Some later manuscripts in staff notation for the prose version allow a fairly reliable reconstruction of the tenth-century melody as it appears in the neumatic notation of the Reichenau troper. Samples of staff versions from German manuscripts are given in Example 1 with a reconstruction of the melody from the Reichenau source given in the upper line.[29] Based on the supposition that similar notational signs refer to similar melodic movements in the two versions, a melodic reconstruction of the hexameter version is possible as well. Such a reconstruction is shown in Example 2, together with the original prose version of the trope.

[29] Information on the sources is given in Andreas Haug, *Troparia tardiva: Repertorium später Tropenquellen aus dem deutschsprachigen Raum* (Kassel: Bärenreiter, 1995) [=TT], Bamberg: Bamberg, Staatsbibliothek, Mscr. 12, f. 46v (TT 006), Würzburg: Würzburg, Universitätsbibliothek, M p th f 165, f. 16v (TT 088), Salzburg: Salzburg, Bibliothek der Erzabtei Sankt Peter, Ms. a VII 20, f. 22 (TT 060), Minden: Wolfenbüttel, Herzog-August-Bibliothek, Codex 528, f. 17v (CT 086), Utrecht: Utrecht, Biblioteek der Rijksuniversiteit, Cod. 417, f. 45v (TT 072).

Example 1. Reichenau prose reconstruction and comparison

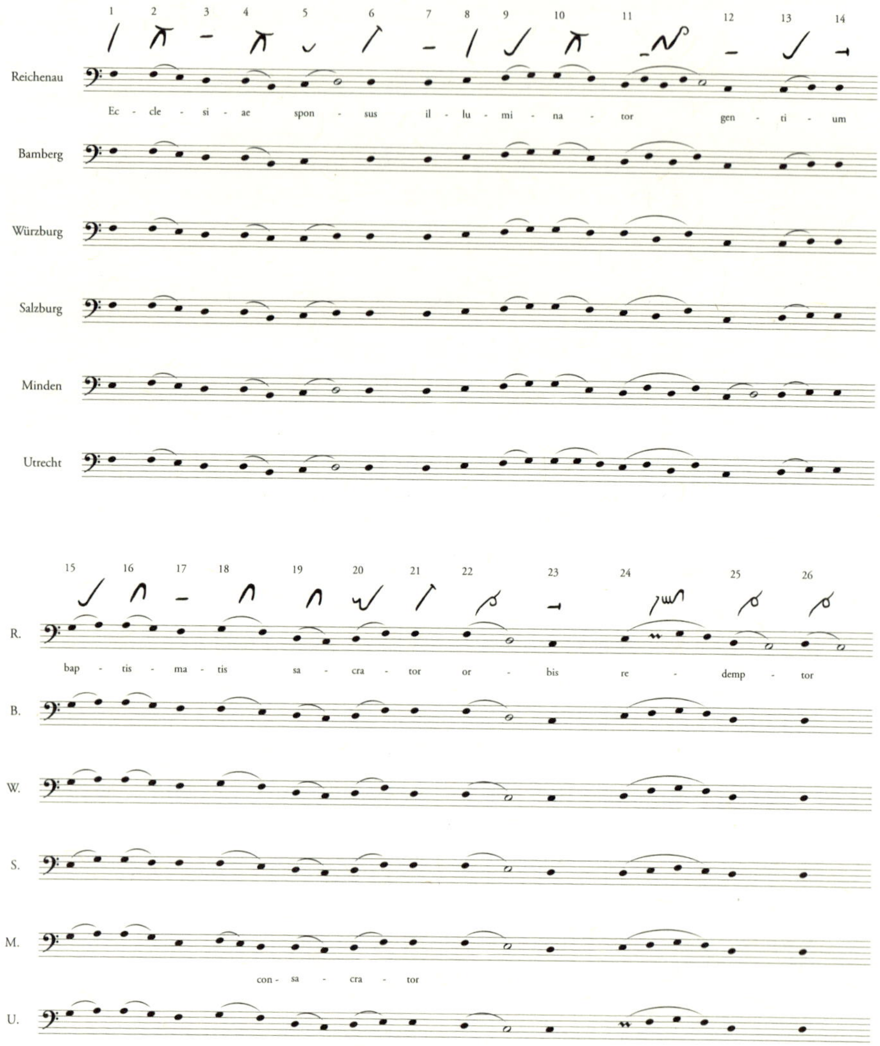

A melodic comparison between the versions will reveal the criteria for the reworking. Let us focus on syllables 15 to 20. The phrases "baptismatis sacrator" in the prose version and "totius orbis honor" in the verse version are of exactly equal length, both comprising seven syllables. Hence, the creator of the hexameter version could easily have proceeded in the same way he did at the beginning and simply adapt the verse text to the existing melody without any further change. This possible solution is suggested in Example 3. As with

Example 2. Reichenau prose and verse versions reconstructed

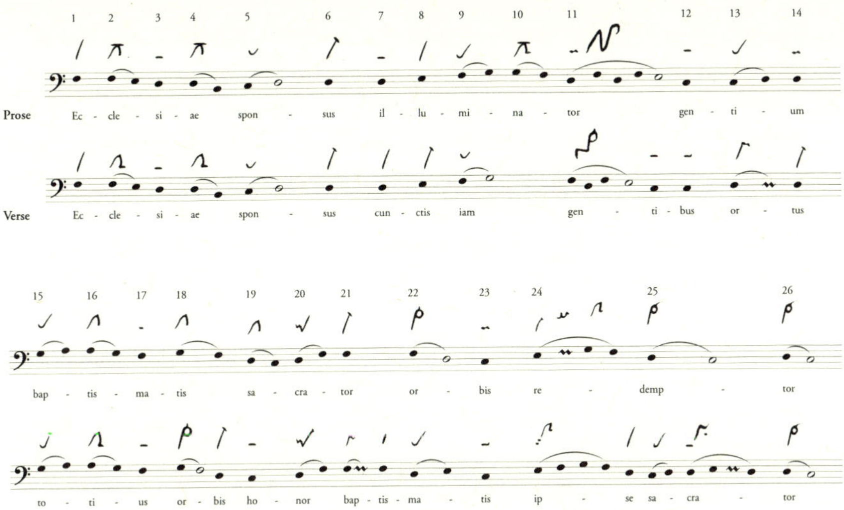

Example 3. Possible solution to prose syllables 15–20

"baptísmatis sacrátor," one might have read and sung the same tones with the same distribution for "totíus orbis hónor." The rising two-tone group on syllable 20, an ascent producing a melodic accent enhancing the prose accent of the word "sacrátor" would have matched the prose accent on "hónor" as well. But that is not what has been done. Instead, the descending two-tone group on syllable 19 of the prose version was split, and the single tones were distributed on the syllables 19 ("-bis") and 20 ("ho-") of the hexameter. Thereby the position of the melodic stress is removed from the penultimate to the ultimate syllable of "honor." Since no other motivation for this manipulation can be discerned, the intention must have been to remove the rising movement in order to obtain a melodic stress rendering the verse ictus on the ultimate syllable of "honór."

The neumes might provide some hints on the duration of single tones in the performance, as for instance, by so-called episemas indicating prolongation. Such episemas occur in the prose version on syllables 2, 4, 6, 10, 21, and 23, whereas they are lacking in the hexameter version on syllables 2 and 4. Conversely, in the hexameter version additional episemas occur on syllables 8 and 15. The shifting positions of episemas can be explained when we presume that the hexameter was performed in a way that matches features of its metrical form: syllable 2 was expanded only in the prose version, where the prolongation enhances the word accent "ecclésiae," but not in the verse version, where that word accent seems to have disappeared in favor of a verse ictus on the initial syllable of the same word. Syllable 8 was expanded in the verse version, where an expansion of the final syllable of "cunctís" both renders the ictus and causes a pause at the caesura (4m), but not in the prose version. As this caesura does not coincide with the end of a sense unit, unlike the caesura after syllable 6 (3m), the expansion indicated by the episema relates to an aspect of the meter, not to the sense of the text. Syllable 15 was expanded only in the verse version, where the initial syllable of "tótius" coincides with the ictus, but not in the prose version, where the word accent "baptísmatis" was to be enhanced. However, none of the prolongations indicated by episemas appears to render the quantity of syllables, as one might expect. There is in fact an episema on syllable 8 (which is long), but there are no episemas on syllables 1, 7 and 23 (which are all long), and the episema on syllable 25 (which is short) has not been omitted.[30]

Since there is no further instance as obvious as this among the great number of hexametric tropes from Reichenau[31] of a mode of singing "scandendo, non enuntiando," this hexameter paraphrase must be regarded as an exception, explained by the wish of the poet, the singer, and the scribe to make the effort of metrification worthwhile and exhibit its audible effect in performance and notation.

Let us now reconsider a case from a neighboring monastery of Reichenau: the verses *Primus init Stephanus* by Prudentius, as transformed to a trope for Saint Stephen and set to music at Saint Gall, likely during the tenth century.[32] A transcription of the melody, based on a later source with staff notation, is given in Example 4.[33] If one inspects the melodic profile of these hexametric lines in the light of the observations on the more-or-less contemporary trope

[30] The prolongation of that short syllable renders the (so-called "bucolic") diaeresis (4/5), which is a common feature of both hexameters of the trope, and which occurs in about 30% of the verses analyzed by Orlandi (see Figure 1).

[31] See Michael Klaper, *Die Musikgeschichte der Abtei Reichenau im 10. und 11. Jahrhundert: Ein Versuch* (Wiesbaden: Steiner, 2003), 95–104.

[32] The relationship between verse and music in this trope has previously been examined by Gunilla Björkvall and myself in "Primus init Stephanus," 68–74.

[33] Einsiedeln, Stiftsbibliothek, Codex 610, 610. This is a single leaf from a lost fourteenth-century troper with square notation on four lines. See Haug, *Troparia tardiva*, 26–27 (TT 014), and Björkvall and Haug, "Primus init Stephanus," 58–61.

Example 4. Einsiedeln 610, Primus init Stephanus

from Reichenau, one becomes aware of the melodic ascents in line 2 (syllables 6 and 8) and line 3 (syllables 6 and 8). Both verses have caesuras 3m and 4m, and at three of these breaks the melodic rise is on the ultimate syllable of a word, thus rendering the ictus, not the word accent ("lapidúm," "christúm," and "rogát"). This indicates again a liturgical performance of a metrical trope perhaps not rigidly "scandendo," but still affected by a "didactic" rather than by a "normal" mode of recitation.

Generally, the melodic treatment of the syllable before a caesura can serve as a basic test point in any hexameter that is set to music. Since a caesura by definition implies a word ending, the syllable preceding the caesura will always be simultaneously the last syllable of a word and the first syllable of a foot. As the last syllable of a word it will never have a word accent, but as the first syllable of a foot it will always have the ictus. Thus, if there is any indication for some kind of melodic stress on that syllable, this is relatively unambiguous evidence for a melodic setting based on scanning rather than on a reading of the verse as prose.

As to the question of whether the quantity of the syllable is rendered by the duration of its tones, a short look at the two oldest neumatic records of the trope in Figure 4 will show that this is not the case.[34] Without getting into the issue of explicit and implicit information provided by additional signs like episemas or letters (such as "c" for "celeriter"), we can observe that an explicit indication of a longer melodic duration of prosodic length is rarely given in

[34] Saint Gall, Stiftsbibliothek, Codex 484, 21–22 and Codex 381, 207. As Susan Rankin has demonstrated, both manuscripts have been copied by the same scribe. See the facsimile edition of the two oldest tropers from Saint Gall, Wulf Arlt and Susan Rankin, eds., *Stiftsbibliothek Sankt Gallen, Codices 484 und 381* (Winterthur: Amadeus, 1996).

Figure 4. Primus init Stephanus *from two Saint Gall manuscripts*

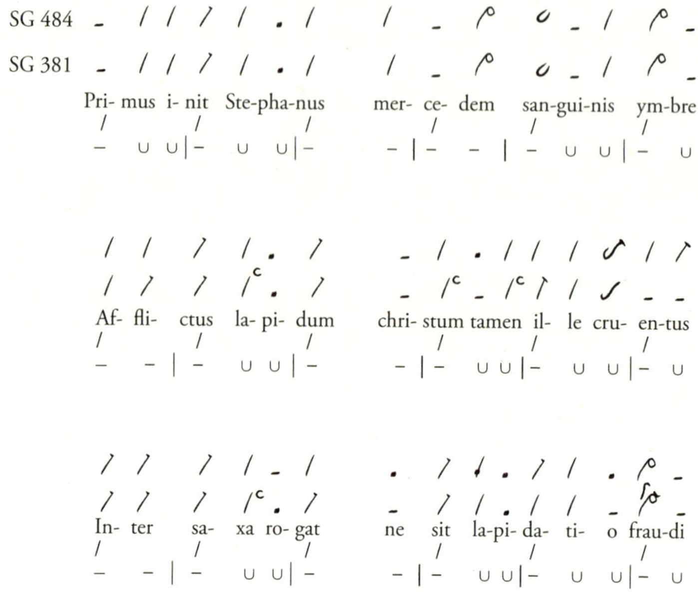

cases where the long syllable does not at the same time carry the ictus. The "c" for "celeriter" on the first syllable and the episema on the last syllable of "lapidum" in line 2, suggests the verse accent "lapidúm" instead of the prose accent "lápidum." Thus, although the use of episemas and additional letters does not seem consistent in these two notations, at Saint Gall also the main concern of the scribe appears not to have been the rendering of prosodic length, but rather the indication of differences between verse accent and word accent.

Figure 5 shows the first half of some lines from the poem *O mortalis homo* by Eugenius of Toledo as transcribed from the neumes within the song collection of Bern, Burgerbibliothek, MS 455, f. 22.[35] John Contreni has shown that this book—copied in central France around the middle of the ninth century—was used at the cathedral school of Laon between 860 and 930.[36] There, during

[35] An edition of the text appears in Friedrich Vollmer, ed., *Fl. Merobaudis reliquiae/Blossii Aemilii Dracontii Carmina/Eugenii Toletani episcopi Carmina et epistulae,* Monumenta Germaniae Historica. Auctores antiquissimi XIV (Berlin: Weidmann, 1905), 233–34.

[36] John J. Contreni, *The Cathedral School of Laon from 850 to 930* (Munich: Arbeo, 1978), 159–61 and 44, note 20.

Figure 5. O mortalis homo, *excerpts*

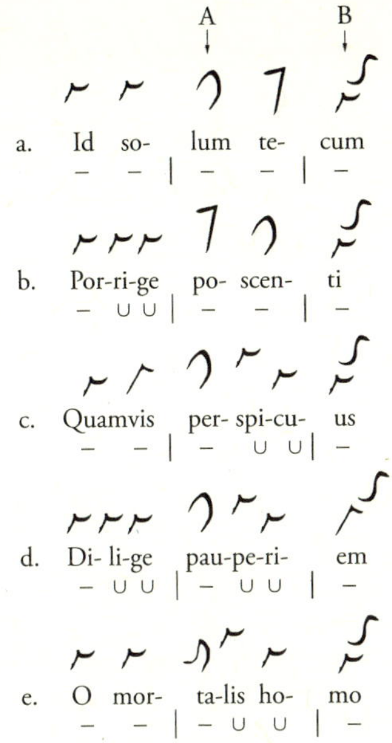

this period, and apparently in the very context of a school, notation was added sporadically and by several hands.[37] The notation of *O mortalis homo* suggests that its couplets have been perceived as stanzas sung on a repeated melody.[38]

All hexameter lines have the caesura 3m not marked by rhyme. At one place there is a melodic ascent on a single syllable discernible from the staffless notation: the rising group of two tones on the syllable before the main caesura, emphasizing the verse ictus. But there is stronger evidence for scansion in this case. Due to the shifting patterns of dactyls and spondees the number of syllables varies between five and seven up to the medial break. As one can see from Figure 5, the additional syllable in the first foot is sung on an additional tone, indeed on the same pitch presumably. That allows the syllable carrying the ictus at the beginning of the second foot to remain in the same, melodically stressed position. The additional syllable in the second foot is sung on the lower tone of the descending two-tone group, which for that purpose has

[37] On that school context see Björkvall and Haug, "Zum Verhältnis von Verslehre und Versvertonung," 312–14.

[38] This example and the following have been discussed previously in Björkvall and Haug, "Musik und lateinischer Vers," 75–77.

Figure 6. Gloria, laus et honor, *excerpts*

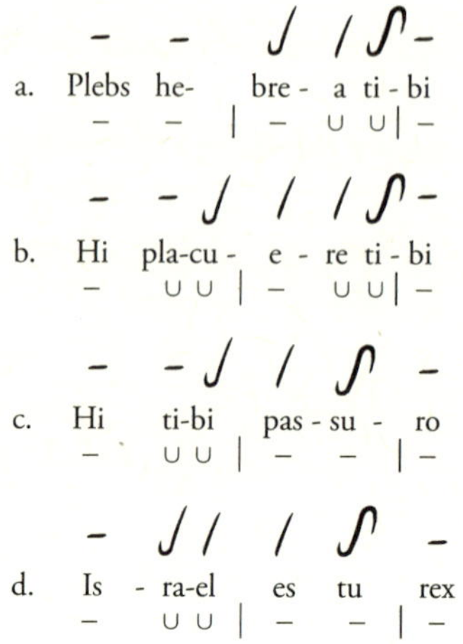

been dissolved into two single tones. Again, that allows the syllable preceding the break to remain in the melodically stressed position.

This strategy of distributing a shifting number of syllables over a flexible sequence of pitches is an obvious precondition for a stable relationship between verse ictus and melodic stress profile (or, as one might put it, for a treatment of metrical feet as musical bars). The presence of this strategy indicates scansion, whereas in other cases its absence almost proves the opposite, that is, a prose-like delivery of the sung verse.

For one such other case we might have a short look at another record from Saint Gall: Figure 6 shows the notation of the processional hymn *Gloria, laus et honor* by Theodulf of Orléan, in a tenth-century manuscript copied at the abbey.[39] Again it will suffice to look only at selected lines and only up to the caesura. The first rising gesture in the hexameter line (actually a leap of a fifth) is connected to the third syllable, regardless of whether that happens to be the ultimate, short syllable of a first dactylic foot or the opening, long syllable of the following foot. In a similar way, the rising and falling gesture on the penultimate syllable before the break is never moved from this melodic position, regardless of whether it falls on the ultimate, and always short, syllable of a dactylic foot or on the ultimate, and always long, syllable of a spondaic

[39] Saint Gall, Stiftsbibliothek, Codex 18, 33. See Anton von Euw, *Die Sankt Galler Buchkunst vom 8. bis zum Ende des 11. Jahrhunderts* (Saint Gall: Klosterhof, 2008), 502–3 (Number 144). Text edition in Ernst Dümmler, ed., *Poetae Latini aevi Carolini (I)*, Monumenta Germaniae Historica, Poetae I (Berlin: Weidmann, 1881) 558–59.

Example 5. Brussels 14650–59, Solicitus plebis

one. In both places a melodic stress moves in relation to the ictus, while at the second place it remains stable in relation to the prose accent of the word before the break. This strongly suggests singing with prose accent. Singing with verse accent is almost excluded. This must have been the regular way of performing Theodulf's elegiacs, as it is reflected in a great number of records from numerous places throughout medieval Europe. The hexameter structure did not influence the melody on the level of declamation, but rather on the level of construction. This seems to be due not to the preferences of a single place or in a single region, but to the function of the metrical poem as a liturgical strophic song.

The next example belongs to yet another genre. It is an antiphon from the Lambertus office by Stephen of Lièges, composed around 900 and copied in a contemporary manuscript.[40] There is a transcription in Example 5.[41] Neither the quantity nor ictus of these hexameters seems to have been influential on the melodic fabric. That (as Example 6 demonstrates) the first half of line 2 and the second half of line 4 have exactly the same melodic shape—without regard to their entirely different metrical patterns and positions—supports that statement.

[40] Brussels, Bibliothèque Royale, MSS 14650–59, f. 38.

[41] Based on the notation in Utrecht, Rijksuniversiteit, MS 406, f. 167rv, a twelfth-century antiphonary from Utrecht.

Example 6. Solicitus plebis, *excerpts*

1 2 3
Con - fir - man - do fi - dem *(line 2*
– – | – ∪ ∪ | – *first half)*

5 6
a - ma - ve - rit un - um *(line 4*
| – ∪ ∪ | – – *second half)*

The only feature of the meter that the music made perceptible to singers and listeners is the consistent marking of both the endings and the caesuras of the verse lines. The cadence-like effect of the melodic figures marking the internal incision is only slightly weaker than that of the figures at the end of lines, and sometimes (as in the case shown in Example 6) even just as strong. None of the internal breaks coincides with the end of an obvious unit of syntax and sense, and therefore the melodic partition of the lines must be determined by the metrical construction only. This is the bipartite construction of the medieval hexameter. Related to music the strong division of the line provides both an option and a problem: the option of a period-like melodic syntax, a sequence of antecedent and consequent sections set apart by a melodic cadence; the problem is that the melodic division frequently will be in conflict with the continuity of meaning. This is a frequent problem, because many medieval hexameters comply with a demand, which Beda Venerabilis formulated in his *Ars metrica* regarding hexameter, that in the "optima forma carminis" words belonging together grammatically ought not follow to each other, but should rather be distributed on the two halves of the verse line.[42] This entails that any melodic break of the line will disconnect related elements of syntax and thus disrupt the continuity of sense.

This is the case in my final example, an introit trope for Saint Peter,

[42] Beda Venerabilis, *Opera*, pars I, Corpus Christianorum, Series Latina, vol. CXXIII (Turnhout: Brepols, 1955), 114.

Example 7. Two basic versions of Angelico fretus

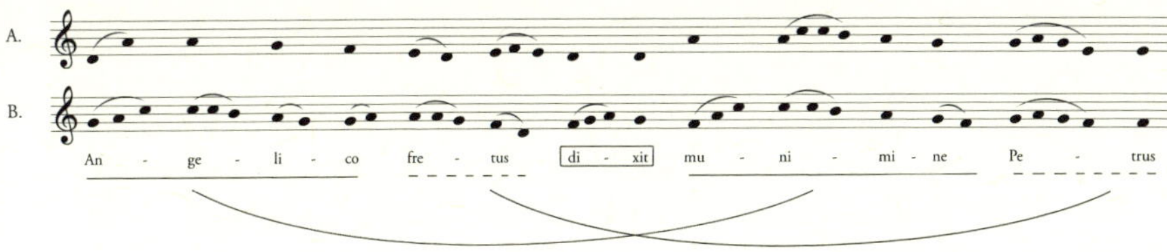

widely transmitted in West-Frankish manuscripts.[43] Example 7 shows two basic versions of its melody, a very widespread one contained in a great number of French, English and Aquitaine manuscripts (labeled as version A in the example)[44] and one occurring only in a few sources from Autun, Nevers, and Apt (version B).[45] The entangled word order "Angelicus fretus dixit munimine Petrus"—instead of, for example, "Angelico munimine fretus Petrus dixit" ("Relying on the protection of the angel, Peter said")—does not easily divide into self-contained units at any point. Syntactical segments that belong together are separated and distributed over the two halves of the verse around the verb that is positioned in the center. Wherever a pause is made, or wherever a melodic cadence is placed, it will interfere with both syntax and sense. The two melodic versions of the trope react differently to this problem.

Version A displays a bipartite melody. The cadential figure on "dixit" is a quite frequent formula in the melodic idiom of tropes, often used at the end of trope elements, and often where direct speech is announced by *verba dicendi* like "dicens," "dixit," "dicentes," or "infit." When the same figure that one is accustomed to hear in such "colon situations" appears in the trope *Angelico fretus* on "dixit," it interrupts the melodic line, suggesting a textual "colon situation" where there is none, and thus causing a semantically inappropriate,

[43] *Analecta hymnica*, vol. 49, 143.

[44] Transcription based on Provins, Bibliothèque municipale, MS 12, f. 186v from Chartres. A selective list of further sources: Cambridge, Corpus Christi College, MS 473 (from Winchester), f. 36; ParisBN lat. 13252 (from Paris, Saint-Magloire), f. 12v; ParisBN lat. 1240, f. 35v; lat. 1120, f. 41v; lat. 1121, f. 26v; lat. 909, f. 40 (all from Saint-Martial de Limoges); ParisBN lat. 1084 (from Aurillac), f. 76v.

[45] Transcription based on ParisBN nouv. acq. lat. 1235, f. 229, from Nevers. Further sources: Paris, Bibliothèque de l'Arsenal, MS 1169 (from Autun), f. 44v; ParisBN lat. 9449 (from Nevers), f. 59v; and Apt, Archives de la Basilique Sainte-Anne, MS 18 (from Apt), f. 62v.

nonsensical division of the verse. From this it seems rather obvious why the more widely used melodic version B of the trope avoids any clear division, thus preventing a foreseeable misconstruction of the meaning. Moreover, by placing similar, rising melodic arches at "Angelico" and "munimine," and by placing "fretus" and "Petrus" (which are related to each other by the sound of the "Leonine rhyme") both in a lower register, the melody highlights and links words that are distanced in the verse line but belong together grammatically. The melodic linkages function so to say as sounding construe marks, as they support a semantic understanding of a hexameter, displaying the "optima forma" of that verse in its construction, but articulate it like prose, that is, with melodic emphasis rendering the word accents on "Angélico," "frétus," "díxit," and "munímine."

* * *

Let me draw some conclusions from what we have observed.

At the outset, the perceptibility of the meter in musical performance of hexameters was by no means limited to a rendering of ictus. Verse form was made audible in various ways: by rendering the verse endings; (frequently) by rendering the caesura; (occasionally) by rendering the ictus; but not, as far as I can see, by rendering the vowel quantities through duration.

The observation that melodic rendition of the caesura was common is significant with regard to the history of verse: when cadence-like melodic figures cause stops that are as strong after the first half of the line as they are at its ending—even at places were such an internal break is inconvenient from the semantic point of view—medieval settings corroborate the medieval concept of hexameter, that is, the notion of both halves of the verse as half verses.

The lack of evidence for a rendition of quantity by duration might either indicate that this was not an option for non-mensural monodic music, or that this idea was foreign to the early Middle Ages, emerging only in humanist circles around 1500.

That the ictus has been rendered in some instances, and in so many others not, might indicate that medieval melodies actually reflect the difference Norberg has described between a "didactic" reading of metrical verse enhancing the ictus, and a "regular" reading with prose accent. When the melodic setting was made for a didactic purpose in the first place, as might be the case in a school manuscript like the one from Laon, one might expect that the ictus will be enhanced. And when a melody serving liturgical purposes was shaped under the influence of a didactic reading, as might be the case at places like Saint Gall or Reichenau, we do get to hear what I have called a distant echo of readings "non enuntiando, sed scandendo," reverberating in the fabric of the melodies.

On the other hand, that musical evidence for a rendition of ictus is so rare must not mean that "regular" articulation of metrical verse "in canto" was not different from an articulation "extra metrum"; it might only indicate that scansion has been avoided when hexameter was sung in church, perhaps because scansion was conceived as a sound affected by an aftertaste of school practice, inappropriate for a liturgical context. A twelfth-century hexameter setting to which Wulf Arlt has called attention might then be an exception confirming the rule. The opening verse of Ovid's *Metamorphoses*, as it was used as a trope line at the cathedral of Beauvais, was sung in a way straightforwardly reflecting its scansion, marking the ictus with a higher pitch in a mechanical way.[46] Within a liturgical celebration so closely related to the world of schoolboys as the New Year's Office from Beauvais, the sound of scansion might have been intended as a kind of winking hint toward the context from which the classical verse was known, to the cathedral school.

What might have been considered a "regular" pronunciation "in canto" outside both school and church, that is, in functional contexts that are neither didactic nor liturgical, is difficult to tell, because few hexameter melodies circulating outside the church are known. Most widespread was a number of settings of passages from Vergil's *Aeneis*. The corpus of these melodies has recently been edited and examined by Gundela Bobeth in a pioneering study.[47] Regarding the influence of meter on the melodic formulation, her results reveal a very differentiated picture: there are instances where verse ictus is enhanced, but this was not the rule in this corpus either.[48]

Still, any generalization of the statement that "metrical structure had no influence whatsoever on the melody" and that "only those aspects of

[46] Wulf Arlt, *Ein Festoffizium des Mittelalters aus Beauvais in seiner liturgischen und musikalischen Bedeutung* (Cologne: Volk, 1970), Editionsband, 46 (Number 5c). The melodic stresses fall on the following positions, "Ánte mar(e) ét terrás et quód tegit ómnia célum."

[47] Gundela Bobeth, *Vergil, Statius, Lucan und Terenz in der Vertonung des Mittelalters. Interpretatorische Erschließung von Neumierungen in Handschriften des 9.–12. Jahrhunderts* (PhD dissertation: University of Basle, 2004). A printed version of this study is forthcoming as *Antike Verse in mittelalterlicher Vertonung: Neumierungen in Vergil-, Statius-, Lucan- und Terenz-Handschriften,* Monumenta monodica medii aevi. Subsidia 5, ed. Andreas Haug, David Hiley, and Karlheinz Schlager (Kassel: Bärenreiter).

[48] See especially the chapter "Grundlagen der musikalischen Formulierung I: Zum Einfluss des Metrums."

text-structure that relate to the sense of the text were constraints on the melodies" would ignore the plurality of musical approaches to meter at different places, under different cultural conditions, and in different functional contexts, and underestimate both the experimental mentality and the intellectual and artistic ambitions of those producing new music during the Post-Carolingian period, as well as the potential of monophonic music for interpreting and performing Latin text in a differentiated manner.

Beyond the Boundaries of Roman-Frankish Chant

Alcuin's de laude Dei *and Other Early Medieval Sources of Office Chants*

SUSAN RANKIN

> "To the most holy father and high priest, Bishop Arn, the humble deacon Alcuin, greeting. . . . Theirs is an angelic life on earth, who rejoice in praising God, and take delight in sacred psalmody with a pure heart. No mortal can fully explain the virtue of the psalms."[1]

ALCUIN'S LETTER TO Arn, Bishop of Salzburg, written *ca.* 801, consists of a long exposition on the seven penitential psalms, about which Alcuin also composed an independent commentary.[2] In that commentary Alcuin explained his preoccupation with the psalms in a way that binds his intellectual activity with the daily practice of singing: "Song elevates labors and takes away weariness from the spirit."[3] Yet the evocation of the last judgment with which his letter to Arn ends is drawn not from the psalms but from the gospel of

[1] "Sanctissimo patri et summo pontifici Arnoni episcopo humilis leuita Alchuinus salutem . . . nullus mortalium uirtutem psalmorum pleniter explicare poterit," Alcuin Ep. 243, *Monumenta Germaniae Historica, Epistolae*, 4, *Karolini Aevi*, 2, ed. Ernst Dümmler (Berlin: Weidmann, 1895), 388–92.

[2] Alcuin, *Expositiones in Psalmos poenitentiales, Psalmum CXVIII et Psalmos graduales, Patrologia latina* 100, cols. 575–638.

[3] "Cantus enim supereleuat labores et aufert animo taedium." Alcuin, *Expositiones in Psalmos poenitentiales, Patrologia latina* 100, col. 604.

Matthew: "Venite benedicti patris mei percipite regnum quod uobis paratum est ab origine mundi."[4] This version of the gospel passage "Venite benedicti" does not match any now traceable form of the Latin bible—certainly not the Vulgate text reproduced in the many Tours bibles springing from Alcuin's abbacy of Saint Martin's in Tours that read, "Venite benedicti patris mei possidete paratum uobis regnum a constitutione mundi (Matthew 25:34)."[5] But this was not sloppiness on Alcuin's part: his memory simply took him to another familiar source—the liturgy. For his words directly match the form of this text used in several Mass and Office chants, including the Introit antiphon for Wednesday after Easter.[6]

Such a transposition, from biblical to liturgical versions of scriptural passages, is not unusual in Alcuin's writings:[7] it is witness to a widespread practice of the absorption and regurgitation of the liturgy in Christian texts, a phenomenon evidently related to the high dependence on memory in the late antique and early medieval periods, not only for retention of texts but as a basis for creation of new texts.[8] Reliance on liturgical texts as a source for spiritual meditation is rendered fully explicit in a devotional florilegium compiled by Alcuin probably while still at York (thus before 786).[9] The collection *de laude Dei et de confessione orationibusque sanctorum* ("from the praise of God and from the confession and prayers of the saints") is divided into four books, the first three comprising extracts from the psalms, from the Old and New Testaments, from patristic writers, and from Christian poets. The fourth book, headed "de antiphonario," is drawn largely from a book of chants for the divine office:

[4] "Come ye blessed of my father, seize the kingdom which has been prepared for you since the beginning of the world."

[5] As, for example, in Saint Gall, Stiftsbibliothek 75, 707; this is one of the two oldest extant Alcuin bibles from Saint Martin's in Tours.

[6] In the late eighth-century gradual, Brussels, Bibliothèque Royale 10127–10144, the Introit antiphon for the Wednesday after Easter Day is copied with this text: "Venite benedicti patris mei percipite regnum alleluia quod uobis paratum est ab origine mundi alleluia alleluia alleluia" (f. 103r).

[7] Donald Bullough, *Alcuin: Achievement and Reputation*, Education and Society in the Middle Ages and Renaissance 16 (Leiden: Brill, 2004), 187ff.

[8] This way of using memory is one of the main themes in Mary Carruthers, *The Craft of Thought: Meditation, Rhetoric, and the Making of Images, 400–1200* (Cambridge: Cambridge University Press, 1998).

[9] For a comprehensive presentation of this florilegium, including discussion of its possible models as well as of the contents of its separate parts, see Bullough, *Alcuin*, 177–204, and *passim*; also, David Ganz, "Le *De laude Dei* d'Alcuin," in *Alcuin. De York à Tours. Écriture, pouvoir et réseaux dans l'Europe du haut moyen âge*, ed. Philippe Depreux and Bruno Judic, Annales de Bretagne et des pays de l'ouest 3 (2004), 387–91.

it opens with the full Gloria text (with the rubric "Carmen Augustini") and the Constantinopolitan Creed ("Simbolum"), followed by a selection of some ninety chant texts and excerpts from hymns and canticles ("de hymnis").[10] That these chant texts were copied in the order of the liturgical year, from Advent through Christmas, Epiphany, Purification, Lent, Holy Week, rogations before Ascension, Ascension, and Pentecost, followed by a series of chants in honor of Mary,[11] underlines the close relation between Alcuin's work of extracting passages that interested him and an actual book of chant. Alcuin's florilegium has survived in two early medieval manuscripts, both continental: the earlier, copied in southern France in the third quarter of the ninth century, is now in the Escorial Library;[12] a later source was copied in the early eleventh century in Mainz and is now in Bamberg.[13] Textually the two sources are close and relate to a common exemplar, but the transmission they represent is more complex than a simple bifurcation.[14]

Most of the *de laude Dei* chant texts are drawn from the liturgy of the divine office. According to the Benedictine Rule, this consisted of eight daily offices, beginning with Matins and Lauds, continuing with the four "little hours," then Vespers, and at the end of the day, Compline. Evidence for the conduct of office liturgy in England before the Benedictine reform is scarce in comparison, and, according to Sarah Foot, "there is not . . . sufficient evidence relating to any one house to determine how many offices were celebrated by its congregation each day."[15] Nevertheless, that a daily cycle of offices would have been celebrated in York in Alcuin's time is not in doubt. In contrast to

[10] Apart from "Carmen Augustini," which appears in only one of the two early medieval sources (see notes 12 and 13 below), these rubrics are common to both sources.

[11] The occasions when the Marian chants were to be sung remain unidentified, yet they attest to "a well-nourished cult of the Blessed Virgin Mary at York in the later eighth century": see Bullough, *Alcuin*, 199.

[12] El Escorial, Real Biblioteca del monasterio de San Lorenzo B.IV.17, ff. 93r–108r: on the date and place of copying see Bernhard Bischoff, *Katalog der festländischen Handschriften des neunten Jahrhunderts I: Aachen–Lambach, II: Laon–Paderborn* (Wiesbaden: Harrassowitz, 1998–2004), vol. 1, 252.

[13] Bamberg, Staatsbibliothek Patr.17 (B II 10), ff. 133r–157v. On the place and date of copying, see Hartmut Hoffmann, *Buchkunst und Königtum im ottonischen und frühsalischen Reich*, Schriften der Monumenta Germaniae Historica 30 (Stuttgart: Hiersemann, 1986), vol. 1, 232–33.

[14] Ganz, "Le *De laude Dei* d'Alcuin," 388.

[15] Sarah R. I. Foot, "Anglo-Saxon Minsters A.D. 597–*ca.* 900: The Religious Life in England before the Benedictine Reform" (PhD dissertation, University of Cambridge, 1989), 196. On the celebration of the divine office in Anglo-Saxon England, see also Jesse Billett, *The Divine Office in Anglo-Saxon England, 597–c.1000*, Henry Bradshaw Society Subsidia Series (Woodbridge: Boydell and Brewer, forthcoming).

the eucharistic Mass liturgy, the office liturgy was essentially meditative in structure, the reading of scripture and the singing of psalms (and, in some liturgies, hymns) its main constituents. Associated with the readings were a class of elaborate chants called responsories, while the psalms were accompanied by the simpler antiphons. Although not rubricated, most of Alcuin's chant texts appear to belong to these two categories of chant.

In this study I shall explore what Alcuin's *de laude Dei*, set beside other early medieval sources for office chants, indicates about the York liturgy, the relation of York practice to Roman liturgy in the second half of the eighth century, and the broader picture of transmission and reception of office chants on the continent in the period of the Carolingian reforms. I do not intend to pursue what *de laude Dei* reflects of Alcuin's own concerns, since an extremely informative survey of the material has been made by Donald Bullough, and I can only attempt to add detail to his general picture. In view of the small number of early medieval sources for chants of the divine office, the fact that several include Advent chants is fortuitous, since it allows many direct comparisons. Exploration of the biblical basis of chant texts for Advent and Christmas in *de laude Dei*, and comparison with parallel texts in other early sources and later chant books, has therefore formed the basis of my work on the *de antiphonario* section. The texts of the chants in this part of *de laude Dei* were edited from the Bamberg source by Constantinescu, with notes referring to various liturgical sources.[16] In Appendix 2 below, texts for the Advent and Christmas seasons (roughly half the total number in *de laude Dei*) are edited from both sources, thus including the occasional longer readings in the Escorial manuscript, and are provided with a commentary that draws on a wider, and at the same time, more securely identified, range of liturgical books than Constantinescu's work.

From what kind of source did Alcuin read? Given the lack of extant chant books from this period and the many references in Bede's *Ecclesiastical History* to the provision of cantors who could teach the chant, doubts about the form in which texts were transmitted in the eighth century may legitimately arise. Nevertheless, I am sure that Alcuin worked from a book, evidently identifiable by him as an "antiphonarium."[17] That conclusion can be drawn from

[16] Radu Constantinescu, "Alcuin et les 'Libelli Precum' de l'époque carolingienne," *Revue de l'histoire de la spiritualité* 50 (1974), 17–56.

[17] Among the various uses of this word in sources of the eighth and ninth centuries, reference to books of chants for the mass is as common as reference to books of office chants. What is clear is that an *antiphonarium* contains chant texts (or, later, chant texts and melodies), and is therefore a book for the cantor. For early references see Cyrille Vogel, *Medieval Liturgy. An Introduction to the Sources*, rev. and trans. William G. Storey and Niels Krogh Rasmussen (Washington: Pastoral Press, 1986), 166, 357–58 and 363–66; on Alcuin's use of the term see Bullough, *Alcuin*, 194, n. 195.

the arrangement of chants, since this reproduces the peculiarities of extant (albeit later) chant books in placing Advent chants first. This is in contrast to Gregorian sacramentaries, which begin at Christmas. A second argument for Alcuin's use of a chant book of some kind is more specific, and concerns the placing of the "O" antiphons (Appendix 2, nos. 18–27). These were sung with the Magnificat from 17 to 24 December and consist of a series of poetic texts that celebrate abstract qualities of the long-awaited savior. In the early Gregorian antiphoners, the "O" antiphons were always copied together, never mingled with the Sundays or weekdays of Advent. Alcuin followed the same practice, copying a corpus of "O" antiphons in an order close to the most common,[18] and placing them immediately before Christmas, without interpolation of other Advent chant texts (which all precede the "O" antiphons). This I take as another hint that his compilation was made not from memory, but from an actual book.

The relation between what liturgical chants Alcuin knew, what was in his York exemplar, and his intentions for the devotional florilegium (material for meditation and prayer) is hard to assess. Appraisal of his choice need not be limited by the absence of possible sources, however. Older layers of Advent sermons and prayers show this liturgical season to have concentrated on Old Testament prophecies (above all, from Isaiah) and preparation for the first and second comings, associating "ideas of fasting and preparation."[19] By the eighth century, the development of Advent liturgy to include the prophecies of John the Baptist and the annunciation to Mary was well advanced, in Roman as well as other liturgies.[20] A list of chant incipits in Lucca, Biblioteca capitolare, MS

[18] On the "O" antiphons in *de laude Dei* see Susan Rankin, "The Liturgical Background of the Old English Advent Lyrics," in *Learning and Literature in Anglo-Saxon England,* ed. Michael Lapidge and Helmut Gneuss (Cambridge: Cambridge University Press, 1985), 317–40. Alcuin's ordering of the "O antiphons" matches the most common order of the seven standard "O" antiphons (by which the initials of the opening words produce the backwards acrostic "erocras," "I will be with you") except in one respect: *O rex gentium* sits not as the fourth, but as the sixth in the series, which therefore reads 1 2 3 5 6 4 7.

[19] Margot E. Fassler, "Sermons, Sacramentaries and Early Sources for the Office in the Latin West: The Example of Advent," in *The Divine Office in the Latin Middle Ages*, ed. Margot E. Fassler and Rebecca A. Baltzer (Oxford: Oxford University Press, 2000), 15–47 at 21; this study presents a wide-ranging introduction to the liturgy of Advent, following its development in the various strands of the liturgy (sermons, prayers, chants) up to the mid-ninth century.

[20] Fassler brings together information about the gospel readings used in Rome *ca.* 645, in the Romano-Frankish liturgy after 750, and the scriptural sources of various sets of homilies for Advent ("Sermons, Sacramentaries," Table 1.1, 29–30). The gospel passages dealing with John the Baptist's prophecies can be traced as the basis of Gregory the Great's homilies for the second and first Sundays before Christmas (thus, in a four-week Advent scheme, the third

490 includes the responsories *Missus est Gabriel* and *Ave Maria gratia plena*, both virtually direct quotations from Luke 1, as well as several other Marian texts.[21] And a large repertory of Advent antiphons and responsories included in an Irish/Gallican fragment, ParisBN nouv. acq. lat. 1628 (hereafter BnF 1628) ff. 1–4, contains the same Marian texts as Lucca 490.[22] It is highly likely that some such chants were included in the York books known to Alcuin. But in the Advent selection for the *de laude Dei* he omitted Marian chants: here the only references to the annunciation are in *Dominus ueniet* (no. 7: "et Gabrihel archangelus annuntiauit *nobis* [my italics] ihesum") and *O ioseph* (no. 27: "quem gabrihel annuncians christum esse uenturum"); neither of these texts actually names Mary.[23] Besides the absence of the figures of John the Baptist and Mary, the other notable missing element from the Advent texts is the holy city, in the form of Jerusalem or Sion—that is, excepting an "O" antiphon addressed directly to Jerusalem: "O hierusalem ciuitas dei summi leua in circuitu oculos tuos et uide dominum deum tuum" (no. 26). The holy city was invoked with a great deal more frequency in the Advent chants listed in Lucca 490 and in the BnF 1628 chants. Indeed, this latter has a series of long, mainly scriptural, texts addressed to Sion that I have been unable to trace elsewhere. In the Gregorian repertory established by the late ninth century, the chants of

and fourth Sundays of Advent): all the later sources for Rome as well as the Frankish north retain the same scheme for those Sundays. Equally the annunciation passage from Luke 1:26–38 appears as the chosen gospel reading for Wednesday in the week before Christmas at Rome in the seventh century, in the eighth-century Romano-Frankish gospel-reading scheme, and as the basis of Paul the Deacon's sermon for that day.

[21] Lucca, Biblioteca capitolare, MS 490 (hereafter Lucca 490), ff. 30r–31r. On this manuscript see Luigi Schiaparelli, *Il codice 490 della Biblioteca capitolare di Lucca e la scuola lucchese (sec. VIII–IX): contributi allo studio della minuscola precarolina in Italia* (Rome: Presso de la Biblioteca Vaticana, 1924), and Bischoff, *Katalog*, vol. 2, 131; on the liturgical list in particular, see Michel Huglo, "Die Adventsgesänge nach den Fragmenten von Lucca (8. Jh.)," *Kirchenmusikalisches Jahrbuch* 35 (1951), 10–15; and Jacques Froger, "Le fragment de Lucques (fin du VIIIe siècle)," *Études grégoriennes* 18 (1979), 145–55.

[22] "Ave Maria gratia plena" (Luke 1:28, 35) as a Responsory; "Ave Maria gratia plena" (Luke 1:28) as a Responsory verse; "Missus est Gabriel angelus" (Luke 1:26–27, 31–32) as a Responsory. On ParisBN lat. 1628 see below 240 ff. and note 45.

[23] Nor could the absence of such material from the Advent selection be explained through its having been moved to sit with the Marian passages at the end of the *de antiphonario* section. Here the annunciation is the basic theme of one text, but this (like the other Marian texts among which it sits) is quite different from anything recorded in ninth- and tenth-century sources of chant: "Salve sancta parens gratia plena Maria . in quo decus angelicae integritatis cunctis venerandum praefulget." (Here the words "Salve sancta parens" are drawn from Sedulius, *Carmen Paschale*, II, line 63.) On the idiosyncrasies of the *de laude Dei* Marian chants see Mary Clayton, *The Cult of the Virgin Mary in Anglo-Saxon England*, Cambridge Studies in Anglo-Saxon England 2 (Cambridge: Cambridge University Press, 1990), 38–40.

the second Sunday of Advent were woven around the theme of Jerusalem, both as holy and as fallen city.[24]

Alcuin restricts himself to narrower themes and images: the need for preparation, expectation of the Lord's coming, what the advent of the savior will bring, and, above all, invitations and petitions: "Veni domine," "Visita plebem tuam," "Visita nos," "Ex alto ueni," "Accelera," and so on. The biblical sources of those texts that rely on scripture are dominated by the psalms (as is typical of the whole chant repertory at this time). Set in the context of other early sources of chant, Alcuin's concentration on expectation and preparation has a very particular flavor, an aspect of the earlier part of the collection consistent with the penitential tone of the chants for Lent, Holy Week, and the rogations that follow. Without more knowledge of devotional practices I can only point to the likely connection between his choice and the intention of the florilegium. It would be interesting to examine the choices of scriptural and patristic texts in the first three books of the *de laude Dei* to know if parallels exist. More significant for the concern with early chant repertories addressed here would be consideration of the rest of the chant texts in *de laude Dei*, and above all, why the Easter feast is unrepresented in this selection.

As an example of chant texts for the divine office documented in an eighth-century record, the *de laude Dei* material is extremely isolated; this is true for both insular and continental liturgies. Very little material dealing with office chants copied before the late-eighth century remains extant, rendering Alcuin's florilegium a key source of evidence for what was being sung, in one locality at least, in the second half of the eighth century. The significance of Alcuin's extracts can be more fully appreciated by comparing the likely date of its first compilation in the 780s with that of the earliest extant full book of chants for the liturgy of the divine office, now ParisBN lat. 17436. This antiphoner was copied in the circle of Charles the Bald for Compiègne in the 870s.[25] The significance of the dates lies not only in the ninety-year gap between the sources, but also in the placing of their compilation more or less before and after the

[24] For this see René-Jean Hesbert, *Corpus Antiphonalium Officii* (hereafter CAO), Rerum ecclesiasticarum documenta, Series Maior, Fontes 7–12 (Rome: Herder, 1965–79), I and II, no. 3a.

[25] On this manuscript and its dating see *Die karolingischen Miniaturen* 5: *Die Hofschule Karls des Kahlen*, ed. Wilhelm Koehler and Florentine Mütherich (Berlin: Deutscher Verlag für Kunstwissenschaft, 1982), 47–51, 127–31. The office liturgy in ParisBN lat. 17436 is edited, with that of other early office antiphoners using the "cursus romanus" for psalm singing (thus, not "cursus monasticus"), in Hesbert, *Corpus Antiphonalium Officii*, I. See also Marie-Noël Colette, "Séquences et *versus ad sequentias* dans l'antiphonaire de Charles le Chauve (ParisBN lat. 17436)," *Revue de musicologie* 89 (2003), 5–29; *eadem*, "The Place and Function of Music in a Liturgical Context: the Earliest Witnesses of Sequences and *versus ad sequentias* in the Antiphoner of Charles the Bald and Other Early Sources," in *Sapientia et Eloquentia. Meaning and Function in Liturgical Poetry, Music, Drama, and Biblical Commentary in the Middles Ages*, ed. Gunilla Iversen and Nicolas Bell (Turnhout: Brepols, 2009), 59–93.

period of Carolingian liturgical reform. The state of the liturgy following that refashioning is much more easily comprehended, since larger numbers of books containing it still survive, and, more significantly, because the centralizing ambitions of the reformers led to greater convergence of liturgical practice in different centers.

* * *

For the earlier period, before the mid-ninth century, substantial sources of office chants are few in number, comprising just seven, copied over a period of 200 years and in places as far distant as Bangor in Ireland, Visigothic Spain, and Lucca in northern Italy:[26]

1 Antiphons included in the "Bangor Antiphonary"[27]	late 7th c.
2 Incipits of 400 or so antiphons in a Visigothic prayer collection[28]	early 8th c.
3 The collection *de antiphonario* in Alcuin's *de laude Dei*	780s
4 List of chant incipits for Advent masses and offices in a Lucca Ms[29]	*ca.* 800
5 Amalarius of Metz, *Liber de ordine antiphonarii*[30]	*ca.* 830
6 Trier, Stadtbibliothek 1245/597: list of chant incipits for the antiphoner[31]	860s
7 The Metz Tonary[32]	ca. 869

[26] For an overview of the history of antiphons in pre-Gregorian sources, see Edward Nowacki, "Antiphonal Psalmody in Christian Antiquity and Early Middle Ages," in *Essays on Medieval Music in Honor of David G. Hughes*, ed. Graeme M. Boone, Isham Library Papers 4 (Cambridge: Harvard University Department of Music, 1995), 287–315. A list of office antiphoners, including fragments, copied before *ca.* 1000, is provided in Jürg Stenzl, "Das Admonter Antiphonar-Fragment aus Cod. 285 *(A-Frag)*," *Anzeiger der philosophisch-historischen Klasse* 141 (2006), 117–58.

[27] Text and facsimile edition in Frederick Edward Warren, ed., *The Antiphonary of Bangor*, 2 vols., Henry Bradshaw Society 4, 10 (London: Harrison and Sons, 1893, 1895); see also Michael Curran, *The Antiphonary of Bangor and the early Irish Monastic Liturgy* (Blackrock: Irish Academic Press, 1984).

[28] Verona, Biblioteca capitolare 89; this "Orationale" is believed to have been copied before 732; it is edited in D. José Vives, *Oracional Visigótico*, Monumenta Hispaniae Sacra, Series Liturgica 1 (Barcelona: Consejo Superior de Investigaciones Científicas, Escuela de Estudios Medievales *[etc.]*, 1946).

[29] Lucca 490, see note 21 above.

[30] Jean Michel Hanssens, ed., "Liber de Ordine Antiphonarii," in *Amalarii episcopi opera liturgica omnia*, III, Studi e Testi 140 (Vatican: Biblioteca Apostolica Vaticana, 1950), 13–224. No surviving antiphoner follows the choices and order of chants advocated by Amalarius. For discussion of the relation between his revision and extant antiphoners see especially René-Jean Hesbert, "L'antiphonaire d'Amalaire," *Ephemerides liturgicae* 94 (1980), 176–94.

[31] On this list see Petrus Siffrin, "Der Collectar der Abtei Prüm im IX. Jahrhundert," in *Miscellanea liturgica in honorem L. Cuniberti Mohlberg*, 2 vols. (Rome: Edizioni liturgiche 1948–49), vol. 1, 223–44; Michel Huglo, *Les Tonaires. Inventaire, Analyse, Comparaison* (Paris: Société française de musicologie, 1971), 77.

[32] Ed. in Walther Lipphardt, *Der karolingische Tonar von Metz*, Liturgiewissenschaftliche Quellen und Forschungen 43 (Münster in Westfalen: Aschendorff, 1965).

These sources are not easily compared, since they reflect a plethora of types: the Bangor Antiphonary and the Visigothic Orationale represent more fluid collections of liturgical texts than those encountered in the ninth century—in both cases the texts included are for priests as well as cantors. Lucca 490 consists of a simple (and abbreviated) list of chant incipits; Amalarius's *Liber de ordine antiphonarii* was intended to introduce a revised antiphoner into the Carolingian realm, but evidently never made it into official usage; the Trier antiphon list remains unedited; and the Metz Tonary presents a modal rather than a liturgical classification of chants, and these only in incipit. Moreover, these sources may have very little specifically in common, given the diversity of liturgical practice they represent ("Celtic," "Mozarabic," "Roman," "Roman-Frankish"): between the two geographically most closely placed sources—the Bangor Antiphonary and Alcuin's *de laude Dei*, for example—there are no shared chant texts, beyond the *Gloria*.

A further group of sources is of considerable interest, even if consisting of fairly small fragments (Appendix 1). All of these sixteen fragments—representing fifteen books—come from books of chants made for cantors, and all contain material which, in some way, relates to Roman practice. Only the Munich/Vienna fragments have been edited. The earliest of these fragments—Saint Gall, Stiftsbibliothek 1399.a.2, consisting of five strips that make up most of two folios—quickly demonstrates why this material deserves to be studied.[33] Here, in a pre-Caroline script replete with ligatures, the work of a named scribe can be identified and dated in the third quarter of the eighth century. The activity of Winithar of Sankt Gallen is represented in seven extant codices[34] in addition to these fragments; he either wrote or signed a series of charters,[35] from which it is evident that he was *decanus* of the abbey in 765. His main work was in the

[33] For reproductions see Alban Dold, *Neue St. Galler vorhieronymianische Prophetenfragmente der St. Galler Sammelhandschrift 1398b zugehörig*, Texte und Arbeiten: Beiträge zur Ergründung des älteren lateinischen Christlichen Schrifttums und Gottesdienstes 31 (Beuron i. Hohenzollern: Beuroner Kunstverlag, 1940), plates set at the end of the volume, as "Die auf S.80 gebotenen neuen Winitharfragmente."

[34] On Winithar see Karl Löffler, "Die St Galler Schreibschule in der 2. Hälfte des 8. Jahrhunderts," in *Palaeographia latina* 6 (1929), ed. W. M. Lindsay, 52–65; Peter Ochsenbein, "Sonderling im Galluskloster: Winitharius - der erste Schriftsteller des Klosters St. Gallen," in *Cultura sangallensis. Gesammelte Aufsätze zu seinem 60. Geburtstag. Peter Ochsenbein*, ed. Ernst Tremp (St. Gall, Klosterhof, 2000), 148–53; Anton von Euw, *Die St. Galler Buchkunst vom 8. bis zum Ende des 11. Jahrhunderts*, 2 vols. (St. Gall, Klosterhof, 2008), I, 33–37, 297–304.

[35] For the charters see Michael Borgolte, Dieter Geuenich, and Karl Schmid, *Materialen und Untersuchungen zu den Verbrüderungsbüchern und älteren Urkunden des Stiftsarchivs St. Gallen*, Subsidia Sangallensia 1 (St. Gall, Staatsarchiv, 1986), 337–40; a useful summary is in von Euw, *Die St. Galler Buchkunst*, 299.

collection of biblical and patristic texts, but in the tiny fragments of Saint Gall 1399.a.2 he copied texts of office antiphons and responsories.

Among these texts are several that cannot be identified in later Gregorian sources, besides versions that were evidently altered in later liturgical revisions. For a famous Marian text, translated from the Greek, Winithar provided a text that (leaving aside its Merovingian Latin readings) is closest to what is preserved in later mass books as a processional antiphon:

St Gall 1399.a.2	*Brussels 10127–10144*
Adorna talamum tuum sion	Adorna thalamum tuum Sion ·
et sus[ci]pe regem christum	et suscipe regem christum ·
amplectare Maria qui est celestis porta ·	amplectere Mariam · quae est celestis porta ·
ipsa enim portat regem gloriae	ipsa enim portat regem glorie ·
nobis luminis subsistit uirgo	nouo luminis subsistit uirgo ·
adducit in manibus filium ante luciferum	adducens in manibus filium ante luciferum ·
quem accipiens simion in ulnis suis ·	quem accipiens Symeon in ulnis suis ·
predicauit populus domini esse	predicauit populis · dominum eum esse ·
uite mor[tis et sa]luatorem mundi	uite et mortis · et saluatorem mundi ·[36]
V [Acci]piens simeon pue[rum in m]anibus	
gracias agens [benedix]it dominum ·	
Quem uirgo adduc[it]	

Later books of office chants—including the Hartker antiphoner made at Saint Gall—have a much reduced form of this text for the responsory (and then the same verse text):[37]

> R. Adorna thalamum tuum Sion et suscipe regem Christum
> quem uirgo concepit uirgo peperit uirgo post partum quem genuit adorauit.
> V. Accipiens Symeon puerum in manibus gratias agens benedixit dominum.
> Quem uirgo

[36] In Brussels, Bibliothèque royale 10127–10144, f. 95v, these Latin phrases are each preceded by their Greek equivalents, transcribed in Latin letters. The texts in the ninth-century books ParisBN lat. 12050 (Corbie) and ParisBN lat. 17436 (Compiègne) are very similar, although without the Greek phrases, but both have the readings "nouo lumine" and "ulnas suas."

[37] This is found already in BnF lat. 17436; it is in the Hartker book as a responsory (Saint Gall, Stiftsbibliothek 390, 116) and, without the verse, as an antiphon (Saint Gall 390, 115).

Through the survival of Winithar's fragment, the Gregorian office responsory is revealed as a secondary transmission of the Greek text, probably shortened by a Carolingian editor.

Knowledge of the history of chant in northern continental Europe in the eighth and ninth centuries can be usefully built around certain documentary references, first appearing in relation to Pippin III's contacts with Rome in the mid-eighth century, but above all, Charlemagne's insistence in the *Admonitio generalis* of 789 that Roman chant be used for the mass and divine office. Such an assertion would not have been necessary, had Charlemagne and his advisors not desired consistency—a consistency surely sought after not for its own sake, but because the singing of chant, as also the reading of scripture, had to be correct in order to be efficacious in the liturgy. Late-eighth-century attempts to achieve that correctness and consistency did not bear immediate fruit. That, at least, is the lament of the well-known reformer Amalarius of Metz, writing circa 830,[38] and of an earlier reviser of the office liturgy, Helisachar, to whom Amalarius pays tribute in the Prologue preceding his study on the office antiphoner.[39] Abbot of St. Albinus in Angers, and later archchancellor in the palace of Louis the Pious, Helisachar oversaw a substantial project of revision of office chants. From a letter addressed to Bishop Nibridius of Narbonne (dated between 814 and 822 by Edmund Bishop), we learn of Helisachar's concern with the responsories of the night office:[40] he found that, in the books he was able to gather, the texts of the chants were rarely in agreement with each other, continuing: "Some things in them are corrupted by the fault of scribes, some are removed by the wish of the unskilled, some are even mixed up."[41] As a result, he went on to make (or to organize) a careful collation of the antiphoners, and of the readings of their texts, eventually rejecting those antiphons and responsories that "were lacking in authority and reason, and

[38] "Prologus de Ordine Antiphonarii," *Amalarii episcopi opera liturgica omnia*, ed. Hanssens, I, 361–63.

[39] On the commentary of these reformers of office liturgy see Michel Huglo, "Les remaniements de l'antiphonaire grégorien au ixe siècle: Hélisachar, Agobard, Amalaire," in his *Les Sources de plain-chant et de la musique médiévale* (Aldershot: Ashgate, 2004), no. XI.

[40] On Helisachar's letter see Edmund Bishop, "A Letter of Bishop Helisachar," in his *Liturgica historica: Papers on the Liturgy and Religious Life of the Western Church* (Oxford: Clarendon Press, 1918), 333–49; for further discussion, with an English translation of the letter, see Kenneth Levy, "Abbot Helisachar"s Antiphoner," in his *Gregorian Chant and the Carolingians* (Princeton: Princeton University Press, 1998), 178–86.

[41] "quoniam quaedam in eis scriptorium uitio deprauata, quaedam imperitorum uoto ablata, quaedam etiam sunt admixta."

were not able to be sung fittingly in the praises of God."[42] Helisachar therefore rejected what was unsuitable and set about replacing it. He also had to ensure that those antiphons and responsories which appeared in some books, but were not known to his own singers, could be sung by them. For this he "called for teachers of the study of the art of melody" from whom the singers could "most eagerly learn these things."[43] Finally he ensured the production of a correct written version, and this revised antiphoner was sent on to Nibridius:

> So what was in some places corrupted by the fault of scribes or the inexperience of the singers, or taken out or added by the lack of skill of some people, is corrected by the study of art and polished by the file of rectitude . . . I humbly beg that it may be received in a kindly way by your paternity and may be used most devotedly in the praises of God. Give this work to those who have a mind to transcribe it carefully.[44]

Those kinds of problems remarked on by Helisachar in the 810s can be seen on one level in the Winithar fragment—in this case in its grammatically questionable forms of expression—and on another entirely different level in the texts preserved in two bifolia written by an Irish hand on yellowed, low-quality parchment at some time in the late eighth century—now ParisBN nouv. acq. lat. 1628.[45] The place of origin of these two bifolia is unknown: one page has a medieval ex-libris of Fleury,[46] but there is no record of Irish scribes

[42] "antiphonas et responsoria quae erant auctoritate et ratione carentia, quae etiam digne in Dei laudibus cantari nequibant, respuimus."

[43] "Unde nostri fuit studii quosdam melodiae artis magistros aduocare, a quibus uestri nostrique ea auidissime didicere."

[44] "Quodque uitio scriptorum, insolentia cantorum, aliquibus in locis deprauatum erat aut quorundam imperitorum demptum uel additum fuerat, artis studio corrigeretur limaque rectitudinis poliretur . . . humiliter exoro, ut a paternitate uestra benigne suscipiatur et in Dei laudibus deuotissime utatur. His uero quibus animo sedet ad diligenter transcribendum hoc opus commodate."

[45] The chant texts on these bifolia were edited by Dom Germain Morin, "Fragments inédits et jusqu'à présent uniques d'antiphonaire gallican," *Revue bénédictine* 22 (1905), 329–56. See also Fernand Cabrol, "Gallicane (Liturgie)," *Dictionnaire d'archéologie chrétienne et de liturgie*, ed. Cabrol (Paris: Letouzey et Ané, 1907–53), cols. 493–96.

[46] I note that Peter Jeffery has recently suggested that the *ex libris* inscription reads not "Liber sancti Be[nedicti]" but "Be[nigni]." See his "Eastern and Western Elements in the Irish monastic prayer of the hours," in *The Divine Office*, 99–143, at 130–32.

working at Fleury in the eighth and ninth centuries.[47] The bifolia were bound up by Libri with four other fragments, none of which reveals any direct association with them.[48] In reality, we do not know whether we are dealing with a book copied for an Irish or for a continental house; if the latter, it must surely have been for a house where Irish script was in routine use. Nor do we know with what kind of liturgy we are dealing—a rite practiced in Ireland or on the continent (thus "Gallican"). Beyond Bischoff's suggestion of a date in the ninth century ("wohl 9. Jh.," reported by Gamber), we do not know when these leaves were copied.[49] Nevertheless, in a situation in which comparison of the *de laude Dei* chant texts with those of the Roman-Frankish tradition codified by the late ninth century leads inevitably to the observation that these differ considerably, the provision on the first bifolium of the Irish/Gallican fragments of a rich collection of Advent chants renders it peculiarly useful for comparison with the *de laude Dei* selection; whatever their origin, the bifolia represent another non Roman-Frankish source and contain a chant repertory that shows no sign of having been subject to Carolingian reform.

The first bifolium of this fragment (ff. 1–2) includes Advent, Christmas and Epiphany chants of two kinds:[50] short texts laid out in groups of five of the kind shown below, and longer texts preceded by short verses, rubricated "T" (for the verse) and "R" (for the longer text).

Ecce ego uenio et habitauo in medio tui dicit dominus.
Ecce ueniet dominus et inluminabit abscondita tenebrarum.
Ecce ueniet dominus et perient gentes a faciae eius.
Ecce iam uenit plenitudo temporum in quo misit dominus filium suum in terris.
Ecce filius hominis in nube caeli ueniet.
(BnF 1628, f. 1r, col. 2)

[47] See Bernhard Bischoff, "Irische Schreiber im Karolingerreich," in *Jean Scot Erigène et l'histoire de la philosophie*, Colloques internationaux du CNRS 561 (Paris: Centre national de la recherche scientifique, 1977), 47–58; reprinted in Bernhard Bischoff, *Mittelalterliche Studien: ausgewählte Aufsätze zur Schriftkunde und Literaturgeschichte*, 3 vols. (Stuttgart: Hiersemann, 1966–1981), vol. 3, 39–54.

[48] On Libri's activities with manuscripts see Léopold Delisle, *Catalogue des manuscrits des fonds Libri et Barrois* (Paris: H. Champion, 1888).

[49] Klaus Gamber, *Codices liturgici latini antiquiores* 1,1, Spicilegii Friburgensis Subsidia (Freiburg im Sch., 1968), no. 428.

[50] Ff. 3–4 contain chants for Purification and Lent.

Each of these text types appears in a series: thus, thirteen groups each of five short texts are followed by twenty-six responsories with verses. Although there is no rubric in this fragment to specify "antiphona," and no musical notation to show in what way the short texts were sung, in Roman usage such texts are used for office antiphons, that is, chants associated with the singing of psalms. That, combined with the hypothesis that the longer texts with verses represent a type of responsorial chant (in which the short verse will be sung congregationally, answered by the cantor, singing the longer text), indicates that this bifolium preserves chants for the liturgy of the offices rather than the mass—as in *de laude Dei.*

Typically, office antiphon texts consisted of scriptural extracts, quoted verbatim, or in slightly altered form; some office antiphons use original texts composed for singing in the early centuries of the church's history. Comparison of the five *Ecce* texts shown above with scriptural sources and with office antiphons of the Roman-Frankish (i.e. Gregorian) tradition illustrates how scriptural texts were modeled for use as chants:

1

Zach 2:10	Ecce ego uenio et habitabo in medio tui ait dominus
Paris	Ecce ego uenio et habitauo in medio tui dicit dominus
Gregorian	Gaude et laetare filia Sion quia ego uenio et habitabo in medio tui dicit dominus[51]

2

I Corin 4:5	. . . ueniat dominus qui et inluminabit abscondita tenebrarum
Paris	Ecce ueniet dominus et inluminabit abscondita tenebrarum
Gregorian	Veniat dominus et non tardabit ut illuminet abscondita tenebrarum[52]

3

Ps. 9:4	. . . et perient a faciae tua[53]
Paris	Ecce ueniet dominus et perient gentes a faciae eius

(no Gregorian parallels)

4

Gal 4:4	at ubi uenit plenitudo temporis misit deus filium suum
Paris	Ecce iam uenit plenitudo temporum in quo misit dominus filium suum in terris
Gregorian	Ecce iam ueniet plenitudo temporis in quo misit deus filium suum in terris[54]

[51] The Gregorian texts are cited here from Hesbert, *Corpus Antiphonalium Officii*, III and IV. *Gaude et laetare* is CAO 2921.

[52] Continues "et manifestauit se ad omnes gentes alleluia." (CAO 5337)

[53] The whole verse reads: "in convertendo inimicum meum retrorsum infirmabuntur et perient a facie tua."

[54] CAO 2519.

5

Dan 7:13	et ecce		cum nubibus caeli	quasi filius hominis	ueniebat	
Paris		Ecce filius hominis	in nube caeli		ueniet	
Gregorian		Ecce	in nubibus caeli	filius hominis	ueniet	alleluia[55]

In western liturgies, the word *Ecce* belongs above all to chants of the Advent season: few chants for other parts of the church year begin this way, and it is common to find series all beginning "Ecce" in liturgies of varied origin, such as the Mozarabic or Milanese uses. In the case of the first antiphon here, *Ecce ego uenio*, the word *Ecce* is carried over from the biblical model, which is retained without major alteration. In the second antiphon the *Ecce* opening has been added to a text from I Corinthians. In the third antiphon the words of a psalm verse have been altered, and its voice changed from second to third, but the sense of the verse has been retained. For the fourth, *Ecce iam uenit*, a close scriptural basis can be found, although "Ecce" is again added, as well as the words "in terris," introduced to make sense of the rest. In the fifth antiphon, a text from Daniel (itself referred to in Luke 21) is simplified: rather than Daniel's prophecy (which refers to a figure coming "quasi filius hominis"), we find the direct and present "Ecce filius hominis."

But what of the relation of these "Irish" or "Gallican" *Ecce* antiphons to the Roman-Frankish repertory? What can be discovered about the origin of BnF 1628? The results of comparison indicate both association and distance. Typically, its textual versions do not match biblical texts as closely as the Gregorian, suggesting that the Irish/Gallican fragment texts depended on another, pre-Vulgate, recension of the bible. In this context, it is worth remembering Helisachar's appeal for the closer linking of chant texts to their biblical models. In the matter of choice of scriptural passages, again there are important similarities and differences. In *Ecce iam uenit* the textual alterations to the scriptural text are shared, suggesting a direct connection between the Irish/Gallican and Gregorian versions. In the case of three others (*Ecce ego uenio*, *Ecce ueniet dominus et inluminabit*, and *Ecce filius hominis*), the textual comparison is inconclusive: these may indicate connections between the Irish/Gallican chants and the foundations of the Gregorian repertory, but equally, the same scriptural passages may have been independently chosen. Finally, *Ecce ueniet dominus et perient gentes* has no parallel in the Gregorian repertory (other than the standard singing of the psalter). Germain Morin, who edited this fragment in 1905,[56] concluded that it preserved part of an antiphoner in use in an unidenti-

[55] CAO 2516.

[56] See note 45 above.

fied church in Gaul, before the adoption of Roman liturgy. More recently, Peter Jeffery has described the fragment as a witness to "the Irish encounter with the Roman office," stressing, on the one hand, the arrangement of the psalms as "close to that of the Roman and Benedictine Psalters," and, on the other, the number of textual concordances between these chant texts and the Gregorian repertory.[57] In other words, a strong relation between the liturgy represented in the fragment and Roman practice is not really at issue, but the detail of what chants are in the fragment, their relation to a systematized use, under umbrella terms like "Celtic," "Gallican," or "Frankish," and how closely tied to Rome this liturgy might be, are matters of considerable interest. If, as Morin argued, this collection of texts for singing does represent Gallican practice, then we find useful corroboration of Helisachar's comments, at a series of textual levels, that is, not only in the readings of single words, but also in the closeness (or distance) between these phrases and those of the Vulgate.

Helisachar's letter highlights Carolingian concern with the establishment of correct texts and melodies. There are many Carolingian references which indicate that what was sung had to display authority, and should thus be expressed in correct language and make grammatical sense. Despite Helisachar's eloquence in regard to his procedures, however, his letter does not specify from where his books or skilled singers came. When Amalarius came to work on the chants of the divine office, also in the time of Louis the Pious, he set off for Rome to find appropriate books, only to be told that Pope Gregory IV had given all that he had to Abbot Wala of Corbie. Amalarius's story is also one of revision, even more fundamental than Helisachar's. For when he did catch up with the Roman books, he found them to differ largely from those in use in Metz. He then set about making a new antiphoner, combining the best of both. The results of his work, couched in considerable discussion of the material, appear in his *Liber de ordine antiphonarii*, but no extant example of an antiphoner using Amalarius's recommended liturgy has been identified.

Interesting as the commentaries of Helisachar and Amalarius on the state of office chants may be, what we learn of the divine office from surviving fragments of antiphoners cannot be directly mapped back onto them. The comparison of Amalarius's preface with extant Gregorian books has two clear results: first, what Amalarius proposed in *de ordine antiphonarii* in relation to the ordering of chants is hardly reflected in the later books,[58] and second, in the books that follow the Compiègne antiphoner, copied in the 870s, the choice

[57] Jeffery, "Eastern and Western elements," 131.

[58] Hesbert, "L'antiphonaire d'Amalaire."

and ordering of chants, as well as detail of their texts, are fairly consistent—to a degree that merits the designation of these books as belonging to a "Gregorian" tradition, itself the result of hybridization of Roman and Frankish practice. Whatever the relation of Amalarius's work to what at some point became an established tradition—and it may have been very little—the process of correction put into train already in the eighth century had not achieved the desired results by the 830s but seems much more evident in books made after the 870s. This implies that the process of correction continued after Amalarius's engagement with the material. Just to reinforce that chronological limitation, I mention briefly another fragment from an office book. Cologne, Historisches Archiv Fragm. B.140 and B.141 consists of a fragment of a bifolium, with one of the leaves largely preserved, and the other cut down to about a quarter of its original size.[59] Here the use of "ab script" determines a date for the host book between the late eighth century and 825.[60] These surviving pages contain antiphons and responsories that mainly correspond to later Gregorian versions, but not in all cases. As an example, responsories for the feast of St. Sebastian include one that disappears from common northern use, but that is found here and in the Roman book San Pietro B79:[61]

> R Quos in parabolis premiis quem accepit palmam martyrii Sebastianus dei famulus gloriosam possedit hereditatem
> [V] Christo cotidie exhibebat officio erat enim uerus dei cultor. Sebastianus

It is possible that the work of revision carried out in different centers through the initiative of individuals such as Helisachar, Wala, and Amalarius, was at some point brought together centrally, as a way of achieving greater consistency. That, at least, is one way of interpreting what appears as a fairly uniform transmission of Gregorian office chants after the late ninth century—but it is not a necessary requirement for later consistency.

* * *

[59] Bischoff, *Katalog*, vol. 1, no. 1955.

[60] On this script see T. Alan M. Bishop, "The Scribes of the Corbie *a–b*," in *Charlemagne's Heir: New Perspectives on the Reign of Louis the Pious (814–840)*, ed. Peter Godman and Roger Collins (Oxford: Clarendon Press, 1990), 523–36; David Ganz, *Corbie in the Carolingian Renaissance*, Beihefte der Francia 20 (Sigmaringen: Jan Thorbecke, 1990), 48–56.

[61] Facsimile edition as *Biblioteca Apostolica Vaticana, Archivio S. Pietro B 79: antifonario della basilica di S. Pietro (Sec. XII)*, ed. Bonifacio Giacomo Baroffio and Soo Jung Kim (Rome: Edizioni Torre d'Orfeo, 1995), f. 57r. The *Cantus* database (http://www.cantusdatabase.org) lists two other sources, one Spanish, one Italian.

Set against this rather sketchy panorama, the chants of the Irish/Gallican fragment and of *de laude Dei* need to be treated as representing local practices of the kind that must have existed before the more uniform tradition of the later Gregorian antiphoners. But now the more critical question concerns the extent to which such local practice was itself based on Roman models. For the situation in England, so few sources of insular office liturgy survive that it is difficult to establish any clear picture of how this was conducted before the eleventh century;[62] thus the path from Alcuin's York chants to later insular sources cannot easily be described. How far then did the liturgies represented in Alcuin's exemplar and in the Irish/Gallican fragment conform to more widespread usage, and how prominent in this was the chant sung in Rome? The question has a special significance for York, since references to Rome in the writings of Bede and Egbert, and the record of the Council of Clovesho (747), encourage the idea that books from York had a close relationship to Roman practice.[63] Such views of the close relation of insular to Roman practice cannot be taken at face value, however: they represent a specific trend in historiographical rhetoric, prominent in England as well as on the continent in the mid-eighth century, and intended to produce conformity and unification through projection back to an authoritative situation—in England the arrival from Rome of Gregory's disciple Augustine at Canterbury in 597.[64] For evidence of what chants were actually sung we need to consult those sources of chant that do survive, however dispersed and limited: in this sense the sixteen fragments listed in Appendix 1 constitute a precious resource. Which chants were sung at Rome but not in Francia in the eighth century cannot now be readily identified, except on those few occasions when Amalarius mentions that a specific chant was in the old Roman books but not in those of Metz. Therefore, although comparison with the later Gregorian repertory represents but a crude approach to finding the relation between the *de laude Dei* chants, or those in the Irish/Gallican fragment and Rome, it is really only through the

[62] Two studies of insular office liturgy will help to shape the current very hazy picture: for the situation after 1100, the "Cursus" project led by David Chadd at the University of East Anglia catalogued chants in monastic sources of office liturgy. For the sources copied before 1100, see Billett, *The Divine Office*.

[63] On Bede's references to Roman liturgical practice in England see Rankin, "The Liturgical Background," 319–22; on Egbert's views, and on the records of the Council of Clofesho, see Catherine Cubitt, *Anglo-Saxon Church Councils ca. 650–ca. 850* (London: Leicester University Press, 1995), 142ff.

[64] On the growth of a sense of Roman tradition in relation to insular liturgy see Cubitt, *Anglo-Saxon Church Councils*, 150–52.

Table 1. Advent chants in de laude Dei, *compared to the Gregorian transmission*

	de laude Dei chants	Gregorian chants
1	Expectamus te dominum deum nostrum	——
2	Intuemini quantus sit iste	CAO 6983
3	Letentur celi	CAO 7068
4	Ecce dominus conteret	no precise match
5	Veni domine salvum fac	——
6	Visita plebem tuam	no precise match
7a	Dominus ueniet	no precise match
7b	cuius uultum desiderat	no precise match
7c	Quem prophete prædixerunt	no precise match
8	Credimus saluatorem	——
9	Expectamus te christe	——
10	Expectamus deum	no precise match
11	Visita nos domine	no precise match
12	Ex alto ueni	——
13	Emitte lucem tuam	no precise match
14	Acelera uisita nos	——
15	Veni domine	CAO 5320
16	Veniat deus meus	no precise match
17	Solius domini	no precise match
18	O sapientia	CAO 4081
19	O adonai	CAO 3988
20	O radix iesse	CAO 4075
21	O rex gentium	CAO 4078
22	O clavis dauid	CAO 4010
23	O oriens splendor	CAO 4050
24	O emanuhel rex	CAO 4025
25	O uirgo uirginum	CAO 4091
26	O hierusalem	CAO 4034
27	O ioseph	——
28	Veni et ostende	Introit Adv IV fer III
29	Excita potentiam tuam	no precise match

parallels between the early sources, and between them and the later Gregorian repertory, that their relation to Rome can be tested.

For the Advent to Epiphany chants in *de laude Dei*—representing about half of the section "de antiphonario"—the relation to chants in later Gregorian books is about as close as that between the Irish/Gallican fragment and the same Gregorian books. In Table 1 the twenty-nine Advent chants of *de laude Dei* are listed, with information about Gregorian concordances: either the same text appears in the Gregorian transmission, or something like it (indicated by "no precise match"), or there is no closely related text ("——"). The same holds for the eighteen Christmas and Epiphany chants, listed in Table 2. Combining the chants in both tables, about half of the *de laude Dei* chants are found in the Gregorian repertory, including long responsory texts such as

Table 2. Christmas and Epiphany chants in de laude Dei, *compared to the Gregorian transmission*

de laude Dei chants		Gregorian chants
30	Gaude nouo partus	——
31	Gaudet exercitus	no precise match
32a	Laudate celi	——
32b	Ex nostra natura	——
33	Te laudent	——
34	Benedictus qui uenit de celis	——
35	Benedictus qui uenit in nomine	CAO 6251
36	Redemptionem misit dominus	CAO 4587
37	Exortum est in tenebris	CAO 2794
38	Apud dominum	CAO 1466
39	Gloria et laus deo	——
40	O ammirabile comercium	CAO 3985
41	Adorabunt eum	CAO 6044
42	Omnes gentes	CAO 4125
43	Lux de luce	CAO 3649
44	Ante luciferum	CAO 1434
45	Fontes aquarum	CAO 2888
46	Te qui in spiritu	CAO 5122
47	Gloria tibi Christe	——

Intuemini quantus sit iste, *Laetentur caeli*, and the famous Epiphany antiphons based on Greek models *Te qui in spiritu* and *Fontes aquarum*.[65] There are also shorter antiphons shared with the Gregorian repertory. There is evidence here that Alcuin did not always reproduce the whole of a specific chant text, but only part (as in other passages of *de laude Dei*, where he drew excerpts from psalms, from hymns, and so on): the Christmas text *Gaudet exercitus angelorum* (n. 31) represents the second part of a responsory that may have already circulated in this early period in the longer form present in the later Gregorian books, that is, given its prominence in the night office of Christmas day: [66]

> Hodie nobis caelorum rex de uirgine nasci dignatus est, ut hominem perditum ad regna caelestia reuocaret. Gaudet exercitus angelorum quia salus aeterna humano generi aduenit. V. Gloria in excelsis deo et in terra pax hominibus bone uoluntatis

[65] Alcuin's citation of *Te qui in spiritu* throws into doubt the story related by Notker Balbulus of this and other Epiphany antiphons having been translated from the Greek at Aachen *ca.* 802. On these antiphons and their relation to Notker's report see Jacques Handschin, "Sur quelques tropaires grecs traduits en latin," *Annales musicologiques* 2 (1954), 27–60; for further bibliography and the counter case see Bullough, *Alcuin*, 196.

[66] CAO 6858: in all of the CAO sources, this is the first responsory of the night office on Christmas day.

But what is especially striking about the pattern of parallels between Alcuin's texts and the Gregorian repertory is the comparative lack of matches for Advent chants (thirteen out of twenty-nine), in contrast to a high frequency of parallelism between *de laude Dei* and Gregorian chants for Christmas and Epiphany (eleven out of eighteen). That is certainly worth exploring further, in consideration of the fact that Advent liturgy developed at Rome rather later than that for the Christmas and Epiphany seasons: Alcuin's exemplar may relate to Roman books made before Advent chants became as fixed as those for Christmas and Epiphany.

In another way, the York *de laude Dei* chants bear witness to a process of editorial intervention in chant texts. Apparently texts for singing were made and remade, only becoming set texts at some time after the florilegium had been made (but before the late ninth century).

Ps 54:9	Expectabam	eum	qui	saluum me fecit a pusillo animo
de laude Dei	Expectamus	deum	qui nos saluos faciet	a pusillo animo · et a tempestate ·
Greg	Exspectabo	dominum		saluatorem meum, et praestolabor eum dum prope est, alleluia[67]

A small number of the *de laude Dei* texts represent direct scriptural quotation, while others combine texts from different biblical passages. Most alter the scriptural model in some way, for example, by changing verbs from singular to plural or otherwise altering biblical language. In no. 10, "Expectamus dominum qui nos saluos faciet," a psalm text expressed in the singular has been made plural, and in no. 9, "Expectamus te Christe," a text from Paul's Epistle to Titus has been simplified to clarify the image of Christ's triumphal advent. But it is the comparison of Alcuin's texts with other parallel texts that suggests editorial intervention on more than one occasion before the Gregorian recension was settled.

Exodus 15:2	iste deus meus et glorificabo	eum deus patris mei et exaltabo eum
de laude Dei 16	Veniat deus meus et honorificabo	eum deus patris mei et exaltabo eum.
Greg	Ecce deus meus et honorabo	eum deus patris mei et exaltabo eum.[68]

In the York version of *Veniat deus meus,* the beginning of the scriptural passage "Iste" has been altered to "Veniat," and "glorificabo" has become "honorificabo." In the Gregorian version, the typical Advent opening "Ecce" is imposed, and the already altered "honorificabo" becomes "honorabo" (retaining the same sense and future tense, but using the more classical verb form

[67] CAO 2805.

[68] CAO 2503. I note that "honorificabo" is the reading in the Roman Psalter.

“honorare”). Of course these alterations to the scriptural text may have been made independently.

In the case of the York text *Ecce dominus conteret*, a whole series of versions, all working with the same material, can be collected from other liturgies: among the six versions set out here, three are drawn from the Irish fragment and two from the Gregorian tradition.

Paris 1	Ecce dominus noster cum uirtute ueniet	
Greg 1	Ecce dominus noster cum uirtute ueniet	
Paris 2	Ecce rex	ueniet dominus terrae
Greg 2	Ecce rex	ueniet dominus terrae
de laude Dei 4	Ecce dominus	
Paris 3	Salvator cito	ueniet

(continued)	*Paris 1*	et ipse	conteret iugum captiuitatis uestrae
	Greg 1	et ipse	conteret iugum captiuitatis nostrae
	Paris 2	et ipse	auferet iugum captiuitatis uestrae
	Greg 2	et ipse	auferet iugum captiuitatis nostrae
	de laude Dei 4		conteret iugum captiuitatis nostrae
	Paris 3	et	conteret iugum captiuitatis terrae

Five of these six texts open with the typical “Ecce”; all versions share the central words “iugum captiuitatis,” but lead to them in a variety of ways; the “yoke of captivity” is then variously linked with “nostrae,” “uestrae,” and “terrae.” The version in *de laude Dei* also has a long extra phrase (“et ipse liberauit nos a peccatis nostris”). In such cases it is clear that there is a common idea on which all versions have drawn, but it is equally plain that each version presents an individual design.

That may provide a useful model for perceptions of the relation between local and Roman usages before the ninth century. Texts such as Alcuin’s “Veni domine salvum fac populum tuum a peccatis eorum” or “Visita plebem tuam sedentem in tenebris et umbra mortis” do not turn up in exactly matching forms in other uses but nevertheless present themes that are found in other uses expressed in similar language. This could be explained if there was shared understanding about the themes relevant to the liturgical season and which passages of scripture were suitable for use in singing, but no strong central control of textual expression.

For knowledge of early office chants, and their relation to Rome, perhaps the most noteworthy aspect of the comparison of chant texts preserved by *de laude Dei* to those of other uses is what *disappears* from the later Gregorian tradition. For informative examples of this I return to the Irish/Gallican fragment.

T Tollite portas principes uestras et eleuamini portae aeternales.
R Gaudete in domino semper et iterum dico gaudete modestia uestra nota sit omnibus hominibus dominus prope est nihil solliciti sitis sed in omni oratione cum gratiarum actione petitiones uestrae innotescant apud dominum. Gloria

T Vox clamantis in diserto parate uiam domini rectas facite semitas dei nostri.
R Credimus saluatorem nostrum uenturum esse cum gloria et uos estote parate suscipere regnum dei.

(BnF 1628, f. 2v, col. 2)

These are two of the longer texts from BnF 1628, probably corresponding to the responsories of the Gregorian office liturgy. Where in Gregorian books such texts would be written with the longer part first, followed by a shorter verse—indicating the performance order Responsory, Verse, Responsory (part repeat)—here they are presented with the shorter part, representing a scriptural verse first.[69] The responsory *Gaudete in domino* was mentioned by Amalarius: he had not found it in the Metz antiphoner, but in the Roman antiphoner, where it was placed first among the responsories of the night office on the third Sunday of Advent.[70] That is also where it appears in the list copied into Lucca 490. But *Gaudete in domino* did not become the standard first responsory of the night office for Advent III in the Gregorian tradition, and indeed, did not become a commonly used chant in the office repertory at all.[71] In fact, the place where *Gaudete* appears in the Gregorian tradition is in the mass liturgy of the same day, as the Introit antiphon on the third Sunday of Advent: the wish not to duplicate between mass and office might explain the exclusion of the responsory from that part of the Romano-Frankish tradition that had been centrally designed and shaped before the end of the ninth cen-

[69] "Tollite portas": Psalm 23:9; "Gaudete in domino": Phil. 4:4–6 (ending "apud deum"); "Vox clamantis": Isaiah 40:3 (ending "facite in solitudine semitas dei nostri"); also Mark 1:3, Luke 3:4 (both ending "facite semitas eius").

[70] "In metensi antiphonario quem legi, non continetur responsorius 'Gaudete in Domino', sed de romano transtuli illum in nostrum." Amalarius, "Liber de Ordine Antiphonarii," X.1.

[71] The responsory *Gaudete in domino* is cited in CAO for three of the twelve edited sources (Verona, Silos, and Benevento), and in the *Cantus* indices for sources from Toledo, Marseille, St Vaast, and Rome; in this latter—the twelfth-century "Old Roman" antiphoner—it is placed as the first responsory of the night office, directly in accordance with Amalarius' description of Roman practice. In the other sources, while usually sung in the night office of the third Sunday of Advent, the place of the responsory varies. For studies of the use and ordering of Advent responsories in Gregorian books see René-Jean Hesbert, "Les séries de répons des dimanches de l'Avent," *Les questions liturgiques et paroisalles* 39 (1958): 299–326; also the fifth and sixth volumes of Hesbert, *Corpus Antiphonalium Officii*, which are entirely dedicated to the Advent responsories; also Knud Ottosen, *L'antiphonaire latin au Moyen-Age: Réorganisation des séries de répons de l'avent classés par R.-J. Hesbert*, Rerum ecclesiasticarum documenta (Rome: Herder, 1986).

tury. *Gaudete* apparently represents an office responsory with a considerable pre-ninth-century history, known in Rome, known to the makers of the Irish/Gallican book, known in Lucca—but not present in northern office books made after the Carolingian reforms.

The following piece in BnF 1628, *Credimus salvatorem*, also suffered a checkered history. Apparently it does not appear in any of the 800 Gregorian antiphoners collated by Hesbert.[72] But the text does have two concordances, both of considerable interest: a version of the text is used as an Introit in the Milanese mass liturgy,[73] and a precise parallel is in *de laude Dei* (no. 8). Unlike *Gaudete in domino*, *Credimus salvatorem* does not represent a scriptural quotation. Parts of the text can be recognized: "uenturum esse cum Gloria" recalls the creed, while "uos estote parati" is used in the gospels of Matthew and Luke, in both cases associated with the same thought, "for in such an hour as ye think not the son of man cometh."[74] In the chant the warning to be prepared is linked with "receiving the kingdom of God." In the Irish/Gallican and Alcuin versions, it is necessary to imagine the first part as spoken by the prophets of Christ, who then address the words "et uos estote parati" to those on earth awaiting the advent of Christ. If the text had been scriptural, a parallel between the Irish/Gallican fragment and the *de laude Dei* could have been assessed as coincidental. As it is, their sharing of the text points to their drawing on a common source, one also available to the compilers of the Milanese liturgy. We cannot say whether that source was Roman or Gallican (or something else), so much have the traces of the liturgical practice of this early period disappeared under the force of Carolingian liturgical projects.

For the first half of the *de laude Dei* chant series there are two other significant concordances for texts not found in the later Gregorian repertory. The Christmas chant, *Te laudent montes* (no. 33) is also found in a book of Mozarabic chant, copied for Léon Cathedral in the early tenth century;[75] there is nothing like this in Gregorian books. The other non-Gregorian concordance is again with the Irish/Gallican fragment. The first piece in Alcuin's *de antiphonario* collection, "Expectamus te," turns up there as "Exultavimus te":

[72] In the study of Advent responsories in CAO V, this text has no entry.

[73] "Credite saluatorem nostrum uenturum esse cum gloria et uos estote parati suscipere regnum dei": used as the Ingressa for the first (of six) Sundays of Advent in a twelfth-century book of Ambrosian mass liturgy. See Appendix 2, no. 8.

[74] For the scriptural sources, see Appendix 2, no. 8.

[75] Léon, Cathedral 8: see Appendix 2 for the edition.

Micah 7.17-18		dominum deum	nostrum desiderabunt	et timebunt te
de laude Dei 1	Expectamus	te dominum deum	nostrum	et timemus te
Paris	Exultauimus	te dominum	nostrum	et timemus

Micah	quis deus	similis tui
de laude Dei	quia non est	similis tibi in diis
Paris	quia non est	similis tibi

Micah		qui aufers	iniquitatem et transis	peccatum	reliquiarum hereditatis tuae.
de laude Dei		deus auferens	iniquitatem et mundans	peccata.	
Paris	domine	deus auferens	iniquitatem et mundans	peccata	reliquorum israhel.

Comparison with the passage from Micah indicates how both *de laude Dei* and the Irish source arrange this text in similar ways, implying that this is a genuine rather than coincidental concordance. And again, there is nothing quite like it in Gregorian Advent liturgies.

Finally, there is one example of a chant copied by Alcuin that has a reverse history to that of *Gaudete in domino. Benedictus qui uenit* (no. 35) appears in a series of non-Gregorian sources: besides *de laude Dei*, in the twelfth-century Old Roman antiphoner and in the Milanese rite. According to Amalarius, he found *Benedictus qui uenit* in the Roman antiphoner he consulted, but not in the Metz antiphoner.[76] Yet this chant did make the leap into Gregorian repertories and is found everywhere as a responsory for Christmas day.

Thus, comparison of the *de laude Dei* chants with those in other early medieval sources of office chants leads, even if only indistinctly, to a view of certain chants as in wide circulation, but not necessarily fixed use, in European liturgies before the end of the eighth century: regional repertories such as the Old Roman, Milanese, and Mozarabic may preserve elements of this older use, even if recorded in later sources. Between these regional repertories and sources such as *de laude Dei* and the Irish/Gallican fragment in BnF 1628, there are significant elements of agreement that are *not* shared with the later Gregorian repertory. Study of the *de laude Dei* chants therefore exposes the "renewal" of liturgical chant instigated by Pippin in the 750s as leading not only to the wide establishment in northern Europe by the late ninth century of a stable office liturgy, but also to the virtual obliteration in the northern books of material shared by earlier liturgies.

* * *

[76] "Liber de ordine antiphonarii," LXXX.1–2. Since Amalarius is dealing here with the responsories of Vespers, this reference to *Benedictus qui uenit* may indicate a different and shorter text than the great responsory for the Night Office.

Of the structure of the office practiced in York in the second half of the eighth century very little is known, yet it is more likely to have resembled Roman than Irish practice, if contemporary documentary evidence is set with the evidence of chant text concordances: there are plenty between *de laude Dei* and Rome but none with the Bangor Antiphonary. As for the precise relation between the liturgies of York and Rome in the eighth century, it is a nut that cannot easily be cracked.[77] Some of the chants recorded in *de laude Dei* and other non-Roman uses were once sung in Rome also. Yet Alcuin's antiphoner also included many chant texts for which there are *no* concordances elsewhere, and some of these probably represent local York usage. The fact that the chants in *de laude Dei* represent a record of actual rather than inferred practice, witnessing a diversity of expression that disappears from the later sources, is surely their most valuable quality.

The eclectic state of early medieval chant repertories exposed by the *de laude Dei* florilegium can usefully be juxtaposed with the less divergent state of later Gregorian repertories. An important consequence of this contrast is a warning: to extrapolate an earlier history of office chants directly from those later books—tracing the core of their content directly to Rome in earlier centuries—is to falsify even the small amount of historical knowledge we can gain from extant sources, for it ignores the work of selection and formulation undertaken by the Carolingians before those later books were made. That work was far from complete in the early years of the ninth century, and may eventually have depended on a series of initiatives, rather than one campaign in one center. I close therefore with a central musical question raised by all of this textual archaeology: if the texts that eventually formed the basis of the Gregorian repertory were subject to this much revision, to what extent can we imagine the Gregorian melodies handed on from the Carolingian period as reflections of Roman practice?

[77] On the shape of the office in Anglo-Saxon England, with a useful presentation of what is known of the Roman and Gallican offices before the period of Carolingian reform see now Jesse Billett, "The Liturgy of the 'Roman' office in England from the Conversion to the Conquest," in *Rome Across Time and Space: Cultural Transmission and the Exchange of Ideas, c. 500–1400*, ed. Claudia Bolgia, Rosamond McKitterick, and John Osborne (Cambridge: Cambridge University Press, 2011), 84–110.

APPENDIX 1. FRAGMENTARY SOURCES OF BOOKS OF OFFICE CHANTS (NOT INCLUDING MARGINALIA OR THE OFFICE OF THE DEAD)

		Date	Catalogue listing
1	Berlin theol.lat.oct.159	s.ix 2/3	B 486
2	Cologne HA Fragm. B140-141	s.viii ex/s.ix in	B 1955
3	Darmstadt 749 (palimpsest)	s.ix	CLLA 1305
4	Disentis Stiftsarchiv Fragm. 22	s.ix 2/4	B 1022
5	Hildesheim DB 651	s.ix ex	B 1535
6	Laon 136	s.ix 4/4	B 2087
7	Leiden BPL 25	s.ix 3/4	B 2135
8/9	Munich, Cgm 6943 + Vienna 3645	s.ix 4/4	B 2918
10	Munich, Clm 29316/1	s.ix ex/s.x in	B 3421
11	Nuremberg Ger. Natm. K.Kab. Kapsel 536/SD 2815-6	before 846	B 3644
12	Oxford Auct F.4.26	s.ix 2/4	B 3773
13	St Gall 1397, 13–16	ix 4/4	(Bischoff's notes)
14	St Gall 1399.a.2	760s	CLLA 1301
15	Vienna 612	s.ix 3/4	Bischoff, *Schreibsch.*, II
16	Zurich Rheinau 26	s.ix 3/4	CLLA 1309*

B = Bischoff, *Katalog*
CLLA = Gamber, *Codices Liturgici Latini Antiquiores*
Bernhard Bischoff, *Die südostdeutschen Schreibschulen und Bibliotheken in der Karolingerzeit*, 2 vols. (Wiesbaden: Harrassowitz, 1960–80).

APPENDIX 2. THE *DE LAUDE DEI CHANT TEXTS* "*DE ANTIPHONARIO*": *ADVENT TO EPIPHANY*

The texts for the period from Advent to Epiphany in the section "de antiphonario" of Alcuin's *De laude dei* are transcribed here from El Escorial, Real Biblioteca MS B.IV.17, ff. 128v–133v *[Esc]*, and Bamberg, Staatabibliothek Patr.17 (B.II.10), ff. 149r–150v *[Bam]*. Punctuation (only the *distinctio*) and capitalization follow El Escorial; variants in Bamberg are shown in square brackets. Variant spellings such as "ae/e," "nl/ll," "dm/mm" are not reported. The numbering follows Constantinescu's edition.

For each entry, scriptural sources are cited, followed by citations from sources of office chants dated before the second half of the ninth century, further followed by citations from later sources that represent regional chant repertories (Gregorian, Mozarabic, Milanese). For two of the sources of office chants listed above, the Bangor Antiphonary and the Metz Tonary, there are no concordances with *de laude Dei*. The sources collated are indicated as follows:

Bible	*Biblia sacra iuxta vulgatam versionem*, ed. Robert Weber, 2 vols. (Stuttgart:Wurttembergische Bibelanstalt, 1969); but for the Psalter, *Le Psautier romain et les autres anciens psautiers latins: édition critique*, ed. Robert Weber (Vatican: Abbaye Saint Jérôme, 1953)
Oracional	*Oracional Visigothico*, ed. Vives; see note 28 above
Lucca	Lucca, Biblioteca capitolare, 490, ff. 30r–31r (incipits only); see note 21 above
BNF 1628	ParisBN nouv. acq. lat. 1628, ff. 1–2; see note 45 above
Amal	Amalarius, *Liber de ordine antiphonarii*, *Liber officialis*, ed. Hanssens (incipits only); see note 30 above

Greg René-Jean Hesbert, *Corpus Antiphonalium Officii*; see note 24 above

Moz León Cathedral 8 (s.x), ed. in *Antifonario visigotico mozarabe de la Catedral de León*, 2 vols., Monumenta Hispaniae Sacra, Serie Liturgica V.1, ed. Louis Brou & José Vives (Barcelona, 1953–59)

Mil LondonBL Add. 34209 (s.xii), ed. in *Paléographie musicale* V/VI (Solesmes: Abbaye Saint Pierre, 1896, 1900)

A: antiphon, R: Responsory

1 Expectamus te dominum deum nostrum · et timemus te · quia non est similis tibi · in diis deus · auferens iniquitatem · et mundans peccata ·

Bible: Dominum Deum nostrum desiderabunt et timebunt te quis Deus similis tui qui aufers iniquitatem et transis peccatum reliquiarum hereditatis tuae (Micah 7:17-18; cf. Luke 12:30; Psalm 85:8; Isaiah 6:7).

BNF 1628, f. 2r: [V] Ecce dominator dominus cum uirtute ueniet et brachium eius cum dominatione. [R] Exultauimus te dominum nostrum et timemus quia non est similis tibi domine deus auferens iniquitatem et mundans peccata reliquiorum israhel.

Moz, f. 117r: Desideramus te dominum deum nostrum et timemus te quoniam quis deus similis tibi auferens iniquitates et mundans peccata reliquiarum israhel.

See Bullough, *Alcuin*, 194–95, n.196.

2 Intuemini quantus sit iste qui ingreditur ad saluandos populos · ipse est rex iusticie · cuius generatio non habet finem ·

Lucca, f. 30v: R for adv IV.

Amal, de ordine ant XI: R for adv IV.

Greg: R for adv IV, populos: gentes (CAO 6983).

Mil: R for second Sunday before Christmas ("ad saluandum populum").

3 Letentur celi et exultet terra · iubilate montes laudem · quia dominus noster ueniet · et pauperum suorum miserebitur · et nomen eius replet uniuersam terram ·

Bible: Psalm 95:11; Isaiah 49:13 (but not "et nomen eius . . . terram").

Lucca, f. 30r: R for adv I.

Amal, de ordine ant X: for adv III.

Greg: R for adv I, but not "et nomen eius . . . terram" (CAO 7068).

4 Ecce dominus conteret iugum captiuitatis nostre · et ipse liberabit [*Esc*: liberauit] nos · a peccatis nostris ·

Bible: cf. Hier. 30:8 (but no direct biblical source).

BNF 1628, f. 1r: Ecce Dominus noster cum uirtute ueniet et ipse conteret iugum captiuitatis uestrae. Also in two other versions: see above [250].

Greg: Ecce Dominus noster cum uirtute ueniet et ipse conteret iugum captiuitatis nostrae (A fer. II ante nat.dni: CAO 2507). Also: Ecce rex ueniet Dominus terrae et ipse auferet iugum captiuitatis nostrae (Fer II hebd II adv: CAO 2543).

5 Veni domine · saluum fac populum tuum · a peccatis eorum ·

Bible: cf. Psalm 27:9, 79:3 (but no direct biblical source).

No other liturgical sources, but cf. *Te Deum*, "saluum fac populum tuum."

6 Visita plebem tuam · sedentem in tenebris · et umbra mortis ·

Bible: Visitauit nos oriens ex alto inluminare his qui in tenebris et in umbra mortis sedent (Luke 1:78).

BNF 1628, f. 1r: Habitantibus in regione umbrae mortis lux orta est eius (Is 9.2).

Greg: Visita, Domine, plebem tuam, alleluia (CAO 5467); Visita, Domine, plebem tuam, et libera eam a tenebris et umbra mortis, sicut locutus est (CAO 5468); Visita, Domine, plebem tuam, sicut locutus es, Deus Israel (CAO 5469); Visita et libera plebem tuam, Domine (CAO 5470): all A *ad Benedictus*, recorded in the Compiègne antiphoner.

7a Dominus ueniet · occurrite illi dicentes · magnum principium et regni eius non erit finis · Dominus [Bam: "deus"] fortis dominator · princeps pacis. [*Bam*: omit "pacis"]

Lucca, f. 31r: A hebd ante nat.dom.

Greg: A adv IV, 'deus fortis' (CAO 2423).

Mil: second Sunday before nat.dom. (as CAO 2423).

7b cuius uultum desiderat uniuersa terra ·

Greg: Rex pacificus magnificatus est cuius uultum desiderat uniuersa terra (A vig.nat. dni: CAO 4657).

7c Quem prophete prædixerunt · et gabrihel archangelus annuntiauit nobis ihesum · esse uenturum ·

Cf. no. 27 below: "O Ioseph . . . quem Gabrihel annuncians Christum esse uenturum."

8 Credimus saluatorem nostrum uenturum esse cum gloria · Et uos estote parati suscipere regnum dei ·

Bible: et uos estote parati quia qua hora non putatis filius hominis uenit (Luke 12:40) and Matthew 24:44.

BNF 1628, f. 2v: "parete," with "[V] Vox clamantis in diserto parate uiam domini. . . ."

Mil: Credite saluatorem nostrum uenturum esse cum gloria: et uos estote parati suscipere regnum Dei (Ingressa adv VI)

9 Expectamus te christe · triumphum glorie tue pietate replendum ·

Bible: Expectantes beatem spem et aduentum gloriae magni Dei et saluatoris nostri Iesu Christi (Titus 2:13).

No other liturgical sources.

10 Expectamus deum qui nos saluos faciet a pusillo animo · et a tempestate ·

Bible: Expectabam eum qui saluum me fecit a pusillo animo (Psalm 54:9).

Greg: Exspectabo Dominum Saluatorem meum, et praestolabor eum dum prope est, alleluia
(A fer V hebd I adv: CAO 2805).

11 Visita nos domine in salutari tuo · ad uidendum in bonitate · electorum tuorum ·

Bible: Psalm 105:4–5e

Greg: Visita nos, Domine, in salutari tuo (A sabbato per annum: CAO 5471).

Greg: Memento nostri, Domine, in beneplacito populi tui: uisita nos . . . (Introit adv IV).

Moz: Visita nos domine in salute tua.

Mil: Visita nos, Domine, in salutari tuo.

12 Ex alto ueni domine omnipotens · libera nos · de camino ignis ·

Bible: emitte manum tuam de alto eripe me et libera me (Psalm 143:7); uisitauit nos oriens ex alto (Luke 1:78); cf. Daniel 3:17.

No other liturgical sources.

13 Emitte lucem tuam · et ueritatem tuam domine. [*Bam*: omit "domine"] ut cognoscamus in terra uiam tuam ·

Bible: Emitte lucem tuam et ueritatem tuam (Psalm 42:3); ut cognoscamus in terra uiam tuam (Psalm 66:3).

Greg: Ut cognoscamus, Domine, in terra uiam tuam in omnibus gentibus salutare tuum (A adv III: CAO 5290).

Mil: as *Greg*.

Moz: Emitte lucem tuam, Domine, et ueritatem tuam.

14 Acelera · Visita nos · deus noster ·

No biblical or liturgical sources.

15 Veni domine · et noli tardare. relaxa [*Bam*: relexa] facinora plebi tue ·

Oracional: A.

BNF 1628, f. 2r (as a R verse)

Greg: A fer. VI ante nat.dom., "tuae Israel" (CAO 5320). Also as a R verse (CAO 6728).

Moz: continues "et reuoca dispersos in terram suam."

Mil: as CAO 5320.

16 Veniat deus meus · et honorificabo eum · deus patris mei · et exaltabo eum ·

Bible: iste deus meus et glorificabo eum Deus patris mei et exaltabo eum (Exodus 15:2–3).

Greg: Ecce Deus meus et honorabo eum, Deus patris mei et exaltabo eum (A fer V ante nat.dom: CAO 2503).

17 Solius domini nomen exaltatum est · Confessio eius · super celum et terram ·

Bible: quia exaltatum est nomen eius solius confessio eius super caelum et terram (Psalm 148:13–14).

Greg: Sanctum nomen domini in cruce exaltatum est super cælum et terram, alleluia alleluia. (A Exalt.S.Crucis: CAO 4769).

Mil: as *Greg*

18 O sapientia · quae ex ore altissimi prodisti · attingens a fine · usque ad finem fortiter suauiter disponensque omnia · ueni ad docendum nos · uiam prudentie ·

Amal: *de ordine ant* XIII

Greg: CAO 4081

Mil: uiam scientiae.

19 O adonai et dux domus israel · qui moysi in flamme ignis rubo apparuisti · et ei in sina legem dedisti · ueni ad redimendum nos · in brachio extento ·

Amal: *de ordine ant* XIII

Greg: in igne flammae rubi (CAO 3988).

Mil: in brachio excelso *[sic]*.

20 O radix iesse · qui stas in signum populorum · super quem continebunt reges hos suum · quem gentes deprecabuntur · ueni ad saluandum nos domine deus noster ·

Amal: *de ordine ant* XIII

Greg: ueni ad liberandum nos, iam noli tardare (CAO 4075).

Mil: as *Greg*

21 O rex gentium · et desideratus earum lapisque angularis · qui facis utraque unum · ueni salua hominem · quem de limo formasti ·

Amal: *de ordine ant* XIII

Greg: CAO 4078

Mil: quem de limo plasmasti

22 O clauis dauid et sceptrum domus israel · qui aperis et nemo claudit · claudis et nemo aperit · ueni · et educ uinctum [*Bam*: uinctos] de domo carceris · sedentem [*Bam*: sedentes] in tenebris · et umbra mortis ·

Vita Alcuini, 24, records Alcuin singing this

Amal: *de ordine ant* XIII

Greg: "uinctum"/"uinctos" both widespread; the same is true of "sedentem"/"sedentes" (CAO 4010).

Mil: omits "qui"; vinctos ; sedentes

23 O oriens splendor lucis eterne · et sol iusticie · ueni et illumina · sedentes in tenebris · et umbra mortis ·

Amal: *de ordine ant* XIII

Greg: CAO 4050

Mil: ueni et illumina in te credentes.

24 O emanuhel · rex · et legifer noster · exspectatio gentium · et saluator earum · ueni ad saluandum nos · iam noli tardare ·

Amal: *de ordine ant* XIII

Greg: ueni ad saluandum nos Domine Deus noster (CAO 4025).

Mil: as Greg

25 O uirgo uirginum · quomodo fiet istud · quia nec primam simile uisa es [*Bam*: prima te similis uisa est] · nec habere [*Bam*: habebis] sequentem · filie hir[u] salem · quid me ammiramini · diuinum est misterium · hoc quod cernitis ·

Amal: *de ordine ant* XIII

Greg: similem uisa est/es (CAO 4091).

Mil: as Bam

26 O hier[u]salem ciuitas dei summi · leua in circuitu occulos tuos · et uide dominum deum tuum · ecce iam ueniet soluere [*Bam*: soluere te] a uinculis [*Bam*: uinculo] ·

Greg: ecce iam: quia iam; soluere te (CAO 4034).

27 O ioseph qui modo [*Bam*: quomodo] credidisti · quod ante ea [*Bam*: antea] expauisti · Quod enim · in ea natum est · de spiritu sancto est · quem gabrihel annuncians christum esse uenturum ·

No other liturgical sources.

28 Veni et ostende nobis faciem tuam domine · qui sedes super cherubim · et salui erimus ·

Bible: ueni ut saluos facias nos . . . et ostende faciem tuam et salui erimus (Psalm 79:3–5); qui sedes super Cherubin appare coram Effrem et Beniamin et Manasse (Psalm 79:2).

Lucca, f. 30r: R for adv I.

Greg: Veni et ostende nobis faciem tuam, Domine, qui sedes super Cherubim: et salui erimus (Introit adv IV fer III).

29 Excita potentiam tuam et ueni ·

Bible: excita potentiam tuam et ueni (as 28 above; Psalm 79:3).

Missale Gallicanum vetus (BAV pal. lat. 493): the *Missa de adventu domini nostri Iesu Christi* begins: Excita potentiam tuam, domine, et ueni, et quod ecclesiae tuae usque in finem saeculi promisisti, clementer operare (ed. Mohlberg, 1958).

Greg: this psalm text is commonly used in chants, but not in this exact form.

Moz: Excita potentiam tuam Domine alleluia et ueni ut saluos nos facias alleluia alleluia (sabb in hebd IV adv).

Mil: Excita potentiam tuam, et ueni Domine, ut nos saluos facias.

30 Gaude nouo partus [*Bam*: partu] seclis clarissima uirgo · Gloria summo deo · teneant terrestria pacem · Lux noua enituit · celorum gloria terris · plenus honor uerbi Deus · et caro gloria plena est · Agia regnantis saluet nos sophia patris · [*Bam*: omit "plenus . . . regnantis"]

No other liturgical sources.

31 Gaudet exercitus angelorum · quia salus aeterna humano generi aduenit ·

Greg: R nat.dom.: Hodie nobis cælorum rex de uirgine nasci dignatus est, ut hominem perditum ad regna cælestia reuocaret. Gaudet . . . (ends "apparuit"; CAO 6858).

Mil: as Greg, but ends "aduenit" (R nat.dom.).

32a Laudate celi et exultet terra · quia homo OCYωN patri · ante secula natus · Idem ipse ad nos · ex uirginali utero · homo natus aduenit ·

Not in Bamberg

Bible: Laudate celi et exultet terra (Isaiah 49:13).

No other liturgical sources.

32b Ex nostra natura passibilis et in sua · miraculis · coruscabat · et refulsit deus ·

See Bullough, *Alcuin*, 195

33 Te laudent [*Bam*: laudant] montes · et omnes colles · Te laudent [*Bam*: laudant] reges · et omnes populi · Te laudent [*Bam*: laudant] principes et omnes iudices terre · Omnes angeli te conlaudent [*Bam*: conlaudant] dominum ·

Bible: cf. Psalm 148:9, 11

Moz: Te laudant montes et omnes colles te laudant principes et omnes iudices terre omnes populi te conlaudant domine (A feria II Quad. II).

34 Benedictus qui uenit de celis · ouem perditam requirere in terris ·

No liturgical sources

35 Benedictus qui uenit in nomine domini · deus dominus· et inluxit nobis ·

Bible: Psalm 117:26–7.

Amal: *de ordine ant* LXXX.

Greg: R nat.dom (CAO 6251).

Mil: R dom. post nat.dom.

36 Redemptionem misit dominus · in [*Bam*: omit "in"] populo suo ·

Bible: Psalm 110:9 (without "in").

Greg: without "in"; continues: mandauit in aeternum testamentum suum (A nat.dom.: CAO 4587).

Mil: as *Greg*

37 Exortum est in tenebris lumen rectis corde ·

Bible: Psalm 111:4

Greg: continues: misericors et miserator et iustus dominus (A nat.dom.: CAO 2794).

38 Apud dominum misericordia est et copiosa apud eum redemptio ·

Bible: Psalm 129:7

Greg: A nat.dom. (CAO 1466).

39 Gloria et laus deo · uirtus · honor · et imperium in seclis ·

Greg: cf. Ecce aduenit dominator Deus et regnum in manu eius, et potestas et imperium in aeternum, alleluia (A nat.dom.: CAO 2489, also Introit antiphon for Epiphany).

40 O ammirabile comercium creator generis humani animatum corpus sumens · de uirgine natus · et procedens homo · sine semine · largitus est nobis suam deitatem ·

Amal: *Liber off* IV, 32, 7 (A oct.nat.dom.).

Greg: de uirgine nasci dignatus est (A oct.nat.dom.: CAO 3985).

Mil: as *Greg* (Nat. dom.)

41 Adorabunt eum omnes reges terre · omnes gentes seruient ei ·

Bible: Psalm 71:11

Greg: R and V (Omnes), Epiphany (CAO 6044).

Mil: A nat.dom.

42 Omnes gentes quascumque fecisti · uenient · et adorabunt coram te domine ·

Bible: Psalm 85:9

Greg: A Epiphany (CAO 4125).

43 Lux de luce apparuisti christe · cui magi munera offerunt ·

Greg: A Epiphany (CAO 3649).

44 Ante luciferum genitus et ante secula dominus saluator noster [*Bam*: omit] mundo apparuit ·

Greg: hodie mundo apparuit (A Epiphany: CAO 1434).

45 Fontes aquarum sanctificate sunt · christo apparente in gloria · orbi terrarum · haurite aquas de fontibus [*Bam*: fonte] saluatori · sanctificauit enim nunc omnem creaturam christus deus noster ·

Greg: santificati; fonte; saluatoris (A oct.Epip.: CAO 2888).

46 Te qui in spiritu · et igne purificas humana contagia · deum et redemptorem omnes glorificamus ·

Amal: *Liber off* IV, 34

N.B. Notker on the *Veterem hominem* antiphons (but see Bullough, *Alcuin*, 196).

Greg: A oct.Epip. (CAO 5122).

47/48 Gloria tibi Christe · teque benedicimus ihesu · qui sedes ad dexteram patris · christe fili dei · miserere nobis ·

No other liturgical sources.

Part V

French Music in the Middle Ages

Un fragment de tropaire aquitain peu connu

(ParisBN, nouv. acq. lat. 2444, ff. 5–6)

MARIE-NOËL COLETTE

Le recueil de fragments conservé sous la cote Nouvelles acquisitions latines 2444 à la Bibliothèque nationale de France se compose de défaits de reliure étrangers les uns aux autres. Certains sont notés. Il en est un, numéroté f. 5–6, qui a attiré notre attention par des formes rares de sa notation, de type aquitain.[1] Il s'agit d'un tropaire qui, comme le montre l'organisation des chants qui ont été sauvés, conforme à celle d'autres tropaires aquitains, devait être complet, ou tout au moins comprendre l'ensemble des tropes de l'ordinaire. Il ne s'agit donc pas d'un choix de pièces, en dépit des similitudes de texte trouvées dans les deux Kyrie. Ce bifolio ne paie pas de mine, il est très abîmé, rempli de taches. Il a été collé dans la largeur des deux folios aplatis, de sorte que les deux premières lignes des ff. 5 et 6v sont recouvertes d'un papier et que leur contenu ne peut qu'être deviné par transparence. Des trous marquent la place d'anciennes attaches. Des mains ultérieures ont ajouté ça et là, dans une encre très foncée, quelques essais de plume, principalement des citations de psaumes.

La marge du haut a été tronquée mais il ne manque que quelques notes, la marge inférieure faisant 20 mm, on peut compter que ce manuscrit de parchemin mesurait environ 195 x 130 mm, avec une justification de 155 x 85 mm,

[1] Ce fragment ne semble pas avoir, jusqu'à présent, retenu l'attention qu'il mérite, bien qu'il fût cité dans les répertoires de Margaretha Landwehr-Melnicki, *Das einstimmige Kyrie des lateinischen Mittelalters* (Erlangen : Gustav Bosse, 1955)[cité Melnicki], et de Peter Josef Thannabaur, *Das einstimmige Sanctus* (München : W. Ricke, 1962)[cité Thannabaur].

Exemple 1. ParisBN, nouv. acq. lat. 2444, f. 6

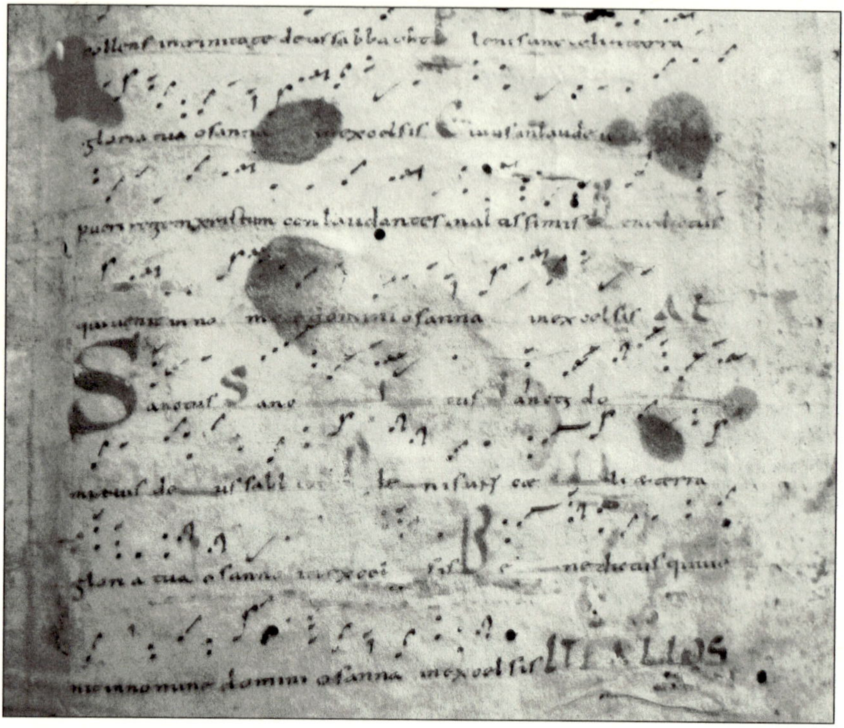

à 14 longues lignes, et un interligne de 12 mm. Une double ligne de réglure verticale souligne les marges de chaque côté. Estampille de la Bibliothèque nationale. Les neumes et le texte sont de même couleur brune. Aucune ligne n'a été réservée pour la notation. Celle-ci est donc placée entre les lignes et aucun guidon ne précise la lecture. La notation incite à dater ce tropaire de la fin du Xème ou du début du XIème siècle, datation confirmée par la couleur rouge-orangée des rubriques.[2]

Le f. 5 comporte deux Kyrie tropés, et le f. 6 deux Sanctus tropés et deux non tropés. Ces deux folios, faisant partie d'un même fragment de parchemin ne se suivent pas et donc ne constituaient pas le centre d'un cahier. Contrairement à d'autres tropaires aquitains, les Sanctus non tropés sont placés dans la suite des autres et non à la fin. On constate certaines hésitations dans la copie : phrase oubliée ou ajoutée à la fin d'un folio, quelques erreurs ou variantes de texte.

[2] Je remercie Marie-Thérèse Gousset (Bibliothèque nationale de France, Centre des Manuscrits Enluminés) pour l'examen de ce fragment.

CONTENU DU FRAGMENT

f. 5 <Kyrie Clemens rector aeterne . . .

Sabbaoth> agie semper rege eleison, Criste.

Criste eleison.

Trine et une, sedulas nostras preces, rex, suscipe.

Criste leison. (*phrase omise*) Christe.[3]

Respice nobis omnibus, inclite, fer opem de excelsis et nostras, redemptor orbis terre, voces iugi, angelorum carmina adiunge, eleison.

Kirrie leison.

Cunctipotens sophie tue lumen nobis infunde.

Kirrie leison.

Tripertite et une domine,[4] qui manes in aeternum cum patre, te ore, te corde atque mente, psallimus, nunc tibi, o benigne, Ihesu bone te precamur omnes assidue eleison.

Kirrie leison.[5]

AL V PROSAS[6]

<O> theos alme, tibi vota precum, poscentes cunctis pie eleison.

Kirrie leison.

5v <S>alva (Salve *ms*) sancte Kirrie familiam, benigne, eleison.

Kyrrie leison.

Polorum qui et rector angelorum creator turme tuae eleison.

Kirrie <leison>.

Nunc, nunc iam te submissis vultibus, te ore te corde poscimus te, eleison.

Criste leison.

Atque clementissime, agie, salva nosmet tuos, Christe eleison.

[3] Je rends X par Ch. On remarquera les deux manières d'écrire Christe : Criste ou Xriste. De plus, une certaine constante gouverne l'écriture du mot *eleison* : lorsqu'il vient dans le texte de la prosule, le mot est écrit en entier, s'il vient après Kyrie ou Christe, la première syllabe de *eleison* n'est pas écrite. Le chant est ainsi unifié autour d'une même vocalise.

[4] 'Domine' pour 'Kyrie', variante suivie aussi par ParisBN, lat. 1120 et 887.

[5] Ed. Guido-Maria Dreves, *Analecta hymnica Medii Aevi.*, t. XLVII (Leipzig : O.R. Reisland,1905), 56 n°6 [cité AH] ; Melnicki, 105 n°102. Transcription David A. Bjork, *The Aquitanian Kyrie Repertory of the Tenth and Eleventh Centuries*, ed. Richard L. Crocker (Aldershot, Ashgate, 2003), 290–2. Nombreux manuscrits, principalement de l'Ouest : les tropaires de Winchester (Cambridge, Corpus Christi College 473 ; Oxford, Bodleian Library, Bodley 775, éd. Alejandro Enrique Planchart, *The Repertoty of Tropes at Winchester*, 2 vols. [Princeton : Princeton University Press, 1977]), le tropaire d'Autun (Paris, Bibliothèque de l'Arsenal 1169), pour les aquitains : ParisBN, lat. 1084, 1120, 887 f. 47 etc., quelques italiens.

[6] Après AL, avec L barré, espace et rubrique très effacée, V surmonté d'un signe d'abréviation : 'Versus' ou 'Si volueris' ?

Christe leison.
Auge tuae humili katerve (*sic*) per secla spem veram doxam perennem, eleison.
Criste <leison>.
Sistit en ecce cohors, ratha trine deum unum adorat te (adorate *ms)*, eleison.
Kyrrie leison.
Kyrrie, Ihesu bone, lucide, (lucidus *ms)* caeli chorum coetus laudat diatim pulchre, eleison.
Kyrrie leison.
Aethereae hyskirros flamine sancto et illustra (illustrat *ms)*, redemptosque tuos perfer, in axe poli regnans (regnat *ms*) per heon.
Kyrrie leison.[7]

ALIOS
f. 6 <Sanctus Ante saecula deus
In principio cum patre manens natus> patris natique spiritus et ipse.
Deus sabbaoth.
Pleni sunt caeli et terra gloria tua.
Osanna in excelsis.
Nos, cernui tui famuli, de tuo adventu gratulantes dicimus
Benedictus qui venit in nomine domini,
Osanna in excelsis.[8]

ALIUS
Sanctus Pater ingenitus
Sanctus Orbis redemptor filius
Sanctus dominus,
Vivificans spiritus pollens in trinitate
Deus sabbaoth,
Pleni sunt celi et terra gloria tua,
Osanna in excelsis
Cuius in laude voces dabant pueri
regem Christum conlaudantes in altissimis
Benedictus qui venit in nomine domini
Osanna in excelsis.[9]

[7] AH 47, 109 n°43 ; Melnicki, 99 n°68 : seulement ParisBN, lat. 887, f. 48v ; nouv. acq. lat. 2444, f. 5. Transcription Bjork, *Aquitanian Kyrie Repertory*, ed. Crocker, 279–81. Mélodie de Kyrie XIV, *Graduale Triplex* (Solesmes, 1979), 757, var. : *Iesu redemptor.*

[8] Cf. Gunilla Iversen, *Corpus troporum* VII, Tropes du Sanctus (Stockholm, Almqvist & Wiksell International, 1990, 74 n°6 [cité CT] ; Thannabaur n° 223. Trope universel qui est rapporté dans les plus anciens tropaires de l'Est et de l'Ouest. Pour l'Ouest, citons au moins les tropaires de Winchester cités ci-dessus et pour l'Aquitaine, ParisBN, lat. 909, 1120, 887 etc.

[9] CT VII n° 97 ; Thannabaur n° 216. Nombreux manuscrits, principalement de l'Ouest :

AL
Sanctus non tropé[10]

ITEM ALIOS
f. 6v Sanctus Sanctus
Sanctus dominus deus sabbaoth.
Conlaudemus dominum eia.
Pleni sunt caeli et terra gloria tua
Omnes, tua gratia quos a morte redemisti perpetua[11]
Morte tua ius mortis cum principe proculcans vite nos reparans
Deo patri dans carum te pro nobis precium et vivam hostiam.[12]
Tecum nos resuscitans, tecum in celis collocans et regni largiris consortia
Te ergo deposcimus ut cum iudex adveneris <advenerit *ms*> cunctorum discernere merita,
Nos cum angelis et sanctis socia <saciat *ms*>
Cum quibus tibi canimus Osanna in excelsis
Gloria, victoria et salus aeterna sit deo nostro
Benedictus qui venit in nomine domini,
Osanna in excelsis.[13]

ITEM COTIDIANIS FESTIS
Sanctus non tropé.[14]

Le Kyrie *Clemens rector* et les tropes de Sanctus *Ante secula deus* et *Pater ingenitus* sont assez bien répandus, en particulier dans le domaine Ouest et Aquitain. On remarquera cependant qu'ils ne se trouvent pas dans les plus anciens tropaires et que nous avons peut-être ici une des plus anciennes copies de ces tropes, ainsi que des Kyrie non tropés, copiés par J.P. Thannabaur d'après le manuscrit ParisBN, lat. 1132, plus récent que notre fragment.

citons les tropaires de Winchester mentionnés ci-dessus, et pour les aquitains : ParisBN, lat. 1120, 909, 887, etc.

[10] Cf. CT VII 289 : Ce Sanctus est rapporté dans le tropaire ParisBN, lat. 887, f. 64v, où il figure après les Sanctus tropés, au début de la série des Sanctus non tropés. Voir Thannabaur, 193 n°196 d'après ParisBN, lat. 1132, f. 112.

[11] Nous ne présentons pas ces prosules en strophes comme dans le CT VII, 139, n° 80 III, mais en phrases car dans le manuscrit chaque phrase est suivie du mélisme, de même que dans le manuscrit ParisBN, lat. 887.

[12] Renvoi, cette phrase a été ajoutée en bas du folio.

[13] CT VII, 139 n° 80 III : ParisBN, lat. 887.

[14] CT VII, 298 : ParisBN, lat. 887, f. 64v ALIOS MINORES. Voir Thannabaur, 210, n° 229 d'après ParisBN, lat. 1132.

Deux tropes ne se trouvent dans le même état que dans le tropaire attribué à Limoges ou Aurillac, ParisBN, lat. 887. Ce tropaire possède tous les tropes mentionnés dans notre fragment, avec très peu de variantes. Comme dans Nouv. acq. lat. 2444, aucune ligne n'y a été réservée pour la notation, et les mélismes sont notés après chaque phrase de la prosule d'Osanna. Cependant quelques différences entre ces manuscrits sont évidentes, la présentation, la notation, les couleurs rouges des rubriques, la présence du guidon, qui font de lat. 887 un manuscrit plus récent que le fragment. Le format les distingue encore, lat. 887 est nettement plus grand : au f. 63, 270 x 190 mm, justification 182 x 132, 11 longues lignes espacées de 20 mm. Le format de notre fragment le rapprocherait davantage des tropaires de Saint Martial (ParisBN, lat. 1240, 1120, 1136).[15]

La notation est atypique. Elle n'est pas encore conforme aux normes des manuscrits aquitains du XIe siècle, avec des points au début de toutes les formes, avec les graphies bien définies de *clivis, porrectus, oriscus* que l'on connaît. Ce n'est pas non plus une notation protoaquitaine avec ses *virgas* et *pes* courbés, l'*oriscus* descendant bien caractéristique que l'on trouve dans le fragment de Montpellier (B.M.4), dans l'antiphonaire d'Albi (Médiathèque Pierre Amalric, 44), la plus grande partie du tropaire de Saint-Martial de Limoges (ParisBN, lat.1240), dans le fragment du manuscrit provenant de Saint-Martial (ParisBN, lat.13220, f. 135 ; exemple 2) et même encore dans le manuscrit BAV, Reg. lat. 1127, f. 165v.[16] Elle ne comporte pas non plus le *pes stratus* à forme messine, en crosse, des séquences de ParisBN, lat.1240, qui par sa forme rapproche de manière la plus évidente les notations protoaquitaines des notations messines. Les ductus de ces deux familles de notation présentent en outre des analogies que nous avons, en d'autres occasions mises en évidence. Mais avec le manuscrit ParisBN, nouv. acq. lat. 2444 nous tenons d'autres signes messins repris tels quels dans un manuscrit aquitain.

LES NEUMES DU MANUSCRIT PARIS BN, NOUV. ACQ. LAT. 2444 FF. 5–6

Le *punctum* est rond ou étalé en forme incurvée, forme messine qui se retrouve dans d'autres manuscrits aquitains du IXème au XIème siècle, comme, par exemple, dans les séquences du manuscrit latin 1979.[17] La *virga*, d'une forme

[15] Cf. les relevés des dimensions externes des tropaires-prosaires par Michel Huglo, *Les Livres de chant liturgique* (Turnhout : Brepols, 1988), 125, et de manuscrits aquitains par Gisèle Clément-Dumas, *Le Processionnal en Aquitaine* (Thèse dactylographiée, Tours, 2001), t. I , 199.

[16] Ed. Henry Marriott Bannister, *Monumenti vaticani di Paleografia musicale latina*, Codices e Vaticanis selecti, vol. XII (Leipzig : Harrassowitz, 1913 ; repr. Weastmead : Gregg International Publishers, 1969), t. I, 111, n°298 ; t. II, tav. 63.

[17] Marianne Besseyre, Marie-Noël Colette, Sumi Shimahara, "Le manuscrit Paris, BnF, latin

Exemple 2. ParisBN, lat. 13220, f. 135

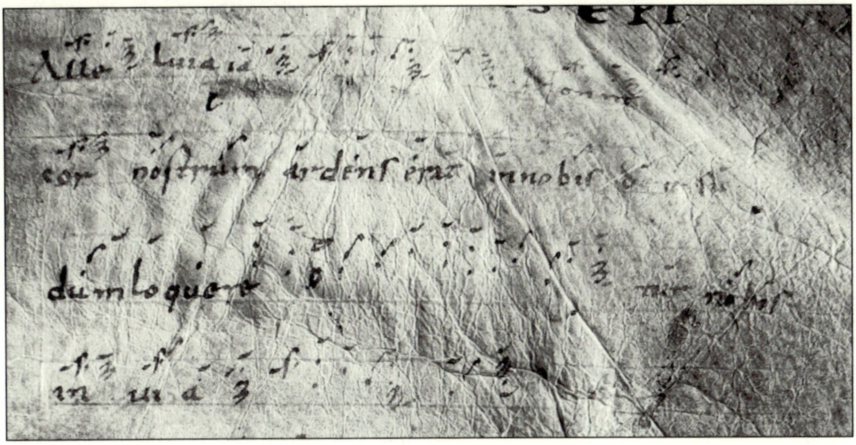

droite très légèrement appuyée en son sommet, comme on peut la trouver dans des manuscrits messins encore au XIIe siècle, présente aussi des formes aquitaines ultérieures : *virga* habituelle avec son renflement à la base et au sommet sur la droite, *virga* semi-circulaire. La *virga* cornue a ici une forme très particulière : grand trait surmonté d'un demi-cercle à gauche du sommet. La *clivis* est souvent aquitaine, mais parfois de forme messine avec départ horizontal ou en *oriscus* messin. Le *porrectus* suit deux traditions : f. 5v, il est messin et se termine par la forme crochue de la *virga* (f. 5v) ; au f. 6, il serait vraiment aquitain si ses angles aigus et son sommet final tourné à gauche ne lui donnaient une allure bien française.

L'*oriscus* est particulièrement caractéristique de l'influence messine, servant en *oriscus* simple, ou pour former le *pressus*, (*oriscus* suivi d'une note plus basse), ou encore le *pes stratus* dont le sommet retrouve la forme aquitaine du XIème siècle. Cet *oriscus*, avec ou sans ses dérivés, est emprunté à la notation messine, dans une particularité graphique qui rappelle singulièrement celle des manuscrits de Reims : BAV, Reg. lat. 1000a, f. 3v ; Reg. 466, f. 80v, 102v,[18] et surtout une addition du Xème siècle dans l'évangéliaire de Saint-Thierry de Reims.[19]

1979, entre héritage carolingien et pré-roman aquitain" (à paraître).

[18] *Ibid.*, t. I, 101, n°275 ; 102–3, n° 276–77 ; t. II, tav. 57–58. Nous remercions David Hiley pour la mise en ligne de cet inestimable ouvrage, et de bien d'autres, dans le site de Regensburg (http://www-app.uni-regensburg.de/Fakultaeten/PKGG/Musikwissenschaft/Cantus/Bannister/index.htm), auquel nous renvoyons le lecteur.

[19] Reims, Bibliothèque municipale, ms. 7, IXème s., f. 13v. Cf. Bruno Stäblein, *Schriftbild der einstimmigen Musik.* (Leipzig : Deutscher Verlag fur Musik, VEB, 1975), Abb. 63.

Une autre forme de *pes stratus*, avec un sommet ascendant et très étendu, est issue des notations françaises. Un *torculus* à forme de boucle large (f. 5) est emprunté à la notation paléofranque.

Une *clivis* d'apposition démarre en pointe ou à l'horizontale et descend avec une longue queue ; proche d'une *clivis* bretonne, elle se trouve aussi dans le manuscrit martialien ParisBN, lat. 1154, à fonction de liquescence comme dans quelques manuscrits aquitains ultérieurs. Le *cephalicus,* en forme de virgule, est utilisé dans les Kyrie même au sein d'un mélisme, là où la prosule exigerait une liquescence. L'*epiphonus* marque la cadence ascendante *eleison.* Enfin, l'addition de la lettre *e* (*equaliter*) de correction est visible, f. 5, au-dessus du mot *redemptor.*

Quelques-uns de ces neumes, signes *d'oriscus* ou de *pressus* se trouvent aussi en Aquitaine, dans quelques pages du tropaire de Saint-Martial (ParisBN, lat. 1240), entre les ff. 17v et 35, et entre les ff. 92 et 97[20]. Encore ne s'y trouvent-ils que sporadiquement (ff. 17–18v). Même si les dimensions, en particulier une justification de 155 x 108 ne sont pas très éloignées, il ne semble donc pas que nous ayons ici le complément du tropaire du manuscrit ParisBN, lat. 1240. Il s'agirait plutôt d'un tropaire aquitain (auvergnat ou limousin ?) encore inconnu, selon une notation qui n'est pas tout à fait inconnue puisqu'elle est très proche de celle des derniers folios du manuscrit ParisBN, lat. 1120, ff. 217 –19, pour l'office de saint Valéry.

LES FEUILLETS 217–219 DU MANUSCRIT PARIS BN, LAT. 1120

Ces quelques pages, à l'aspect étranger au reste du manuscrit font cependant partie de son dernier cahier, qui se présente comme un quaternion si l'on inclut les onglets apparents : 216, 217 [onglet 217 bis], 218, centre du cahier, 219, 220, 221 [onglet 221 bis].[21]

Le cahier, commençant au f. 216, continue l'office de la Nativité de la Vierge (ff. 215v–216v).

Ff. 217–219 : Office de saint Valéry noté, f. 217–218 dans une notation proche de celle de notre fragment ; au f. 219 deux antiennes non notées, et à la fin une antienne, dans une notation aquitaine banale.

Ff. 219v–220 : De Pentecosten, Prosa *Ad te summe celsa*, non notée, mais copiée sur un interligne de même dimension que celui du f. 219. Cette prose

[20] Tropaire-prosaire de Saint-Martial de Limoges, ParisBN, lat. 1240, Xème s. Cf. le facsimilé en ligne http://gallica.bnf.fr/ark:/12148/btv1b6000528g.r=1240.langFR

[21] ParisBN lat. 1120; cf. le facsimilé en ligne, http://gallica.bnf.fr/ark:/12148/btv1b84323135/f443.image.r=1120.langFR

bénéficie de rubriques colorées comme le reste du manuscrit mais la présentation et la main sont différentes.

F. 220v : Texte sans notation avec tout petit interligne : *Coetibus angelicis* (aucune notation prévue).

Neumes, textes et initiales des ff. 217–219 sont de même couleur brune, sans rubriques.

Si le tropaire nouv. acq. lat. 2444 présente une notation très proche de ces pages du manuscrit lat. 1120, ses dimensions ne sont pas exactement les mêmes puisque le manuscrit 1120 mesure 220 x 100 mm avec une justification de 152 x 65, à 15 longues lignes et un interligne de 12 mm.

INFLUENCES ET RELATIONS

Par conséquent, proche de lat. 887 par son répertoire, entre lat. 1240 et lat. 1120 pour ses dimensions et l'usage de signes identiques, il s'agit d'un tropaire aquitain encore inconnu, ce qui confère à ces pages, si fragmentaires soient-elles, tout leur intérêt. En outre, le mélange de signes témoins d'influences diverses offre des indications sur la réflexion qui a présidé à la constitution des notations aquitaines telles qu'on les trouve à peu près stabilisées, au moins dans leur structure, au milieu du XIe siècle. Y aurait-il un rapport entre l'*oriscus* en forme de *m* et ces trois formes d'*oriscus* : *m* couché protoaquitain d'Albi (Médiathèque Pierre-Amalric, ms 44) et du tropaire-prosaire de Saint-Martial (ParisBN, lat.1240), longue queue partant d'un trait horizontal, *oriscus* à forme messine, ces deux derniers ayant bien pu évoluer vers la forme de *m* couché protoaquitain, lui-même redressé au XIème siècle ? *L'oriscus* aquitain n'est pas toujours facile à distinguer du *pressus* messin lorsque les boucles supérieures de ce dernier sont resserrées. Qu'y a-t-il de commun entre la *virga* cornue dont la corne est dessinée à droite de la haste de la *virga*, et la virga couchée de nouv. acq. lat. 2444 et lat. 1120 avec sa corne à gauche de la haste. Le *pes stratus* à long plateau représenterait-il une transition entre le *pes stratus* à forme messine en crosse de lat. 1240 et le *pes stratus* à forme plus proche des manuscrits allemands et français que l'on trouve dans les manuscrits aquitains, mais qui semble plutôt résulter de la jonction d'une *virga* semi-circulaire avec le trait qui la suit ? La réflexion a peut-être au contraire été mêlée d'hésitations dont seraient témoins des signes qui ne se retrouvent pas dans les manuscrits aquitains ultérieurs.

L'influence des notations messines, de Compiègne, de Laon, a été évoquée en d'autres occasions. Mais s'il s'agit plus précisément de manuscrits rémois de la fin du Xème siècle, la référence à Gerbert d'Aurillac ne peut être passée sous silence. Gerbert, grand érudit, parfait connaisseur de son quadrivium, était alors archevêque de Reims et entretenait une correspondance avec l'abbaye où, selon ses propres termes, il avait été 'nourri et formé'. [22] Des lettres attestent de ces relations en particulier avec Ayrard, moine d'Aurillac à qui il avait déjà en 983, de Bobbio, demandé la copie de quelques manuscrits.[23] Il ne s'agissait pas de manuscrits notés, mais rien n'empêche qu'il se fût intéressé aussi à la copie de manuscrits liturgiques, car aucun pan de la culture de son temps ne lui échappait, et certainement pas les questions relatives au culte et à sa transmission. Rappelons que l'attribution du manuscrit ParisBN, lat. 887 reste incertaine entre Saint-Martial et, justement, Aurillac. Evidemment, dans cette affaire, et en l'absence de plus amples renseignements, la référence à Gerbert et à ses relations avec la grande abbaye d'Aurillac ne peut aller au-delà d'une hypothèse suggérée par une coïncidence de temps et de lieux. Cependant, même si Gerbert lui-même avait à Reims d'autres soucis que la notation musicale, il ne faudrait pas s'étonner que les allers-retours de moines d'Aurillac entre leur abbaye et l'archevêché de Reims, suscités par la présence de Gerbert, eussent laissé quelques traces, à Aurillac ou même dans un périmètre plus large car le tropaire ParisBN, lat. 1084 n'est pas le témoin le plus proche de notre fragment dont il ne comporte pas les signes spéciaux. Rappelons, afin de faciliter des recherches ultérieures, que les plus proches parents de ParisBN, nouv. acq. lat. 2444 sont, pour la notation, quelques pages de lat. 1240 et de lat. 1120, et pour le répertoire, lat. 887, dont l'attribution est encore incertaine.

De tels fragments, sortis de l'ombre des grands monuments contemporains, élargissent le pan de nos connaissances, les remettant en question ou éclairant certaines positions acquises en ce qui concerne l'écriture musicale d'une région. C'est dire leur intérêt, et l'immense valeur qu'ils prennent lorsqu'ils ont été relevés en si grand nombre comme l'a fait dans sa monumentale édition des fragments bénéventains Thomas Kelly[24], à qui je suis heureuse de dédier cette modeste monographie sur deux pages d'un tropaire aquitain.

[22] Gerbert d'Aurillac, *Correspondance*, éd. Pierre Riché et Jean Pierre Callu, 2 vol. (Paris : Les Belles Lettres, 1993), t. I, 113, lettre 45.

[23] *Ibid.*, t. I, 15, lettre 7.

[24] Thomas F. Kelly, *Les témoins manuscrits du chant bénéventain*, Paléographie musicale, XXI (Solesmes : Abbaye Saint-Pierre, 1992).

The Topography of Music Theory in Paris, 900–1450[1]

MICHEL HUGLO† AND BARBARA HAGGH
WITH LEOFRANC HOLFORD-STREVENS

In an important article published in 1973, Lawrence Gushee urged musicologists to consider the genres through which medieval writers on music transmitted their knowledge, in order to interpret those writings more accurately.[2] His call for better interpretations of medieval thought on music came in a period when the topic of "medieval music theory" evoked the new postwar series of its editions, the *Corpus scriptorum de musica*, and of the translations published by Colorado College. Today, with most Western theory and even a good part of the dictionary of its vocabulary online,[3] and a substantial number

[1] Michel Huglo wrote the first draft of the text in French and also provided his notes on manuscripts and bibliography. Barbara Haggh suggested the topic to him initially, researched manuscript and published book lists in Paris and the volumes of the RISM project, compiled the list of manuscripts from St. Victor, translated the text into English, revised it, and edited it. Leofranc Holford-Strevens translated the first part of the epistle from Muris to Vitry (Appendix 2). Haggh thanks the University of Maryland, College Park and Lindsey Carlson for assistance with this project.

[2] Lawrence Gushee, "Questions of Genre in Medieval Treatises on Music," in *Gedenkschrift Leo Schrade*, ed. Wulf Arlt et al. (Bern: Francke, 1973), 365–433.

[3] See *Thesaurum musicarum latinarum*, dir. Thomas Mathiesen, http://www.chmtl.indiana.edu/tml/ and *Lexicon musicum latinum medii aevi*, dir. Michael Bernhard http://www.lml.badw.de, *Musiktheorie des Mittelalters, Texte im Internet* by Christian Meyer.

of interpretative studies of theory of the kind Gushee advocated in print,[4] we can move away from the texts themselves to consider their original homes in manuscripts as part of a culture of books and of their keepers and users.

Following the theme of this volume, by using the RISM volumes on sources of music theory[5] and published and unpublished library catalogues, now conveniently inventoried in the 1987 CNRS publication, *Bibliothèques de manuscrits médiévaux en France*,[6] we have sought to identify the location of medieval music theory treatises in Paris, effectively preparing a provisional topography of music theory in this major city.[7] We have chosen 1450 as the

[4] See Christian Meyer, *Les traités de musique*, Typologie des sources du Moyen Âge occidental 85 (Turnhout: Brepols, 2001), and studies on individual genres, such as Michel Huglo, *Les tonaires* (Paris: Heugel, 1971) and Michael Bernhard, "Die Überlieferung der Neumennamen im Lateinischen Mittelalter," in *Quellen und Studien zur Musiktheorie des Mittelalters*, ed. Michael Bernhard, vol. 2 (Munich: Verlag der Bayerischen Akademie der Wissenschaften, 1997), 13–91, or on intended audiences, such as Joseph Dyer, "Chant Theory and Philosophy in the Late Thirteenth Century," in *International Musicological Society Study Group Cantus Planus, Papers Read at the Fourth Meeting, Pécs, Hungary, 3–8 September 1990*, ed. László Dobszay (Budapest: Institute for Musicology, Hungarian Academy of Sciences, 1992), 99–118, or broader historical surveys of theorists and the scope of their writings, such as Bonnie Blackburn, "Music Theory and Musical Thinking after 1450," in *The New Oxford History of Music: Music as Concept and Practice in the Late Middle Ages*, vol. 3/1, ed. Reinhard Strohm and Bonnie Blackburn (Oxford: Oxford University Press, 2001), 301–45.

[5] Joseph Smits van Waesberghe, Pieter Fischer, Christian Maas, Michel Huglo, Christian Meyer, Nancy C. Phillips, Elżbieta Witkowska-Zaremba, Karl-Werner Gümpel, Cesarino Ruini, Giuliano Di Bacco, Pia Ernstbrunner, Alexander Rausch, eds., *The Theory of Music from the Carolingian Era up to c. 1500. Descriptive Catalogue of Manuscripts* (*RISM B/III/1–6*) (Munich: G. Henle Verlag, 1961–2003). RISM citations are abbreviated as follows: RISM B/III/1, 100 = RISM 1:100; RISM B/III/6, 20=RISM 6:20.

[6] Anne-Marie Genevois, Jean-François Genest, Anne Chalandon, eds., *Bibliothèques de manuscrits médiévaux en France* (Paris: Editions du CNRS, 1987), though its citations of secondary literature are sometimes inaccurate. Still useful is Léopold Delisle, *Le Cabinet des manuscrits de la Bibliothèque nationale*, 3 vols. (Paris: Imprimerie Nationale, 1868–81; reprinted Hildesheim: Olms, 1978). On the early library catalogue as a genre of book, see Albert Derolez, *Les catalogues de bibliothèques*, Typologie des sources du Moyen Âge occidental 31 (Turnhout: Brepols, 1979). The first major survey of the history of Parisian libraries is Alfred Franklin, *Les anciennes bibliothèques de Paris: églises, monastères, collèges, etc.*, 3 vols. (Paris: Imprimerie Nationale, 1867–73).

[7] A poster-sized map of Paris in 1380, reconstructed by Jacqueline Leuridan and Jacques-Albert Mallet was published by the Service géographique du CNRS in Paris in 1991; cf. the smaller reproductions in Jacques Verger, "L'Université de Paris et ses collèges au temps de Jerôme de Moravie," in *Jerôme de Moravie, un theoricien de la musique dans le milieu intellectuel parisien du XIIIe siècle*, ed. Christian Meyer (Paris: Créaphis, 1992), 15–31, at 18, and in Michel Huglo, "Recherche sur la personne et l'œuvre de Francon," *Acta musicologica* 71 (1999), 1–18, at 3. A map of Merovingian Paris is reconstructed in *La Neustrie. Les pays au nord de la Loire, de Dagobert à Charles le Chauve (VIIe–IXe siècle)*, ed. Patrick Périn and Laure-Charlotte Feffer (Paris: Musées et Monuments départementaux de Seine-Maritime, 1985), 334–35.

limit for our study because it marks a watershed when other universities, such as those in Cologne and Leuven, began to compete with Paris, and when musical knowledge and tastes changed dramatically. In what follows, after a short introduction, we trace the evidence for writings on music from the libraries of the oldest Parisian monasteries to those of the cathedral of Paris, the universities, and their colleges, and finally to two of the secular churches from which evidence survives. We also consider briefly some aspects of the question of who read and taught from these manuscripts, with case studies of Aristotle's *Problemata* and Plato's *Timaeus*, and we end with recommendations for future research. Our study does not consider the content or interpretation of the theory,[8] or the issue of what music or if music was taught at the University of Paris, the subject of important recent scholarship.[9] Instead, we concentrate on the accessibility and diffusion of theory within the city through what we can learn about it from the then-available or surviving manuscripts. In Appendix 1, surviving manuscripts of music theory of Parisian origin or provenance are listed in a series of tables, ordered by their home libraries. Appendix 2 presents Leofranc Holford-Strevens's translation and analysis of the first part of Johannes de Muris's letter to Philippe de Vitry, written in 1343, most likely in Paris, to accompany Muris's *Quadripartitum numerorum*, one of many of his treatises available for consultation at the Abbey of St. Victor.

WHAT IS "MUSIC THEORY"?

The term "music theory" here covers not only treatises of *musica plana* and *musica mensurabilis*, but also *musica speculativa*, or music within the four liberal arts of the quadrivium, and music within a wide range of other writings by philosophers, theologians, and instrument makers. Initially, the RISM

[8] See F. Alberto Gallo, "Philological Works on Musical Treatises of the Middle Ages: A Bibliographical Report," *Acta musicologica* 44 (1972), 78–101, and Michel Huglo, "Bibliographie des éditions et études relatives à la théorie musicale du Moyen Age (1972–1987)," *Acta musicologica* 60 (1988), 229–72.

[9] On the place of music in the texts known in Paris and of the study of speculative music at the University of Paris, see Joseph Dyer, "The Place of Musica in Medieval Classifications of Knowledge," *The Journal of Musicology* 24 (2007), 3–71; and *idem*, "Speculative 'Musica' and the Medieval University of Paris," *Music & Letters* 90 (2009), 177–204. Both studies provide comprehensive bibliographies on their subjects. See also Nan Cooke Carpenter, *Music in the Medieval and Renaissance Universities* (Norman, Okla.: University of Oklahoma Press, 1958), 46–69. Michel Huglo, "L'enseignement de la musique dans les universités médiévales," in *Atti del XIV Congresso della Società Internazionale di Musicologia*, 3 vols. (Turin: Edizioni di Torino, 1990), vol 1, 30–37; and Olga Weijers, "La place de la musique à la Faculté des Arts de Paris," in *La musica nel pensiero medievale*, ed. Letterio Mauro (Ravenna: Longo, 2001), reviewed by Sandrine Thieffry in *Scriptorium* 56 (2002), 88*, no. 233.

catalogues of music theory manuscripts deliberately omitted the treatises on speculative music, but later volumes, and especially volume six, do include some manuscripts of Boethius's *De institutione musica*. Since it became clear that medieval theorists used not only Boethius, but also other speculative writings,[10] here we include all of the old "encyclopedias" of the liberal arts, such as Martianus Capella's *De nuptiis Philologiae et Mercurii*, composed in Carthage by 439 and reaching Gaul in the next century.[11] It is cited by Gregory of Tours in the last chapter, written in 594, of his *History of the Franks*.[12] The second encyclopedia is that of Cassiodor, composed beginning in 540 under the title *Institutiones humanarum litterarum*, because it followed the *Institutiones divinarum litterarum*, that is, the study of the Bible.[13] The section on music includes mention of the writers on music Censorinus, Martianus Capella, and Augustine, but not Boethius.[14] Another is Isidore of Seville's monumental *Etymologiae*, with a chapter on music mostly taken from Cassiodor, but without the Greek modes. Isidore's texts in the *Etymologiae* on the liberal arts were ordered alphabetically in the *Liber glossarum*, an eighth-century dictionary probably compiled by the nuns of Chelles in the region northeast of Paris.[15] The entry "Musica" in this dictionary consists of two chapters on the origins of music probably due to Varro, which Isidore apparently did not consider worth reproducing. The version of the *Liber glossarum* that was reviewed and brought up to date by Papias in the mid-eleventh century under the title of

[10] See Michael Bernhard, "Überlieferung und Fortleben der antiken lateinischen Musiktheorie im Mittelalter," in *Geschichte der Musiktheorie*, ed. Thomas Ertelt and Frieder Zaminer, vol. 3 (Darmstadt: Wissenschaftliche Buchgesellschaft, 1990), 7–35, and Michel Huglo, "Grundlage und Ansätze der mittelalterlichen Musiktheorie von der Spätantike bis zur Ottonischen Zeit," in *Geschichte der Musiktheorie*, ed. Thomas Ertelt and Frieder Zaminer, vol. 4 (Darmstadt: Wissenschaftliche Buchgesellschaft, 2000), 21–102.

[11] See the list of manuscripts in Claudio Leonardi, "I codici di Marziano Capella," *Aevum* 34 (1960), 1–99.

[12] See Serge Antès, "Témoignages précarolingiens sur Martianus Capella: Cassiodore, le Pseudo-Cassiodore et Grégoire de Tours," in *Hommage à Jean Cousin: Rencontre avec l'Antiquité Classique*, ed. Membres de l'Institut Félix Gaffiot (Paris: Les Belles Lettres, 1983), 289–97, at 291–93.

[13] On the date, see Alain Galonnier, *Anecdoton Holderi ou Ordo generis Cassiodororum. Éléments pour une étude de l'authenticité Boécienne des Opuscula sacra* (Louvain-Paris: Peeters, 1997), xi–xv. The work is edited by Roger Aubrey Baskerville Mynors in *Cassiodori Senatoris Institutiones*, 2nd ed. (Oxford: Clarendon Press, 1937).

[14] This effective guide for the constitution of a library was copied in Auxerre, Reims, Corbie, south of the Loire, and at Chartres, so around Paris, but has not been found in a Parisian manuscript.

[15] Michel Huglo, "Les arts libéraux dans le 'Liber glossarum,'" *Scriptorium* 50 (2001), 3–33.

Elementarium was quite widely diffused in France from the eleventh to the thirteenth century, with ninety known manuscripts of which twenty-five are now at the Bibliothèque nationale de France in Paris. We also consider as "music theory" the translation and commentary on Plato's *Timaeus* written by Calcidius, which replaced an early translation by Cicero, because Calcidius's commentary is supported by three diagrams of harmonics and many others of astronomy and geography.[16] This commentary was known in the circle of Alcuin and to Remigius of Auxerre, Hucbald of St. Amand, Sedulius Scottus, Gerbert of Reims, and Abbo of Fleury, among others. Of 140 manuscripts with this commentary, fifteen are at the ParisBN).

EARLY PARIS: THE CATHEDRAL OF ST. ÉTIENNE

The *civitas Parisiorum*, first limited to the Île de la Cité and later extended by the Romans to the left bank of the Seine, counted approximately 135 churches and oratories served by secular clergy or monks at the end of the Merovingian period.[17] The first cathedral—dedicated to St. Stephen, with five naves and now buried under the *parvis Notre-Dame*—was recognized in the sixth century by Venantius Fortunatus, bishop of Poitiers, as a model for performing psalmody and liturgical chant.[18] The influential teaching of music theory in Paris by Remigius of Auxerre at the end of the ninth century, most likely in the cathedral school since he was not a monk, set the model for his successors, who taught mainly the glosses to such "encyclopedias" on the liberal arts as Martianus Capella's *De nuptiis Philologiae et Mercurii*,[19] Macrobius's

[16] Michel Huglo, "Recherches sur la tradition des diagrammes de Calcidius," *Scriptorium* 62 (2008), 185–230 and plates 23–27.

[17] Grégoire Poras, "Recherches sur les conditions du chant liturgique pendant le haut Moyen Âge," *Études grégoriennes* 21 (1986), 23–26, at 23.

[18] See Michel Huglo, "*Les versus* de Venance Fortunat pour la procession du Samedi-Saint a Notre-Dame de Paris, " *Revue de musicologie* 86 (2000), 119–26, at 124 and note 30. The text of Fortunatus is edited by Bruno Krusch in *Monumenta Germaniae Historica, Auctorum Antiquissimorum*, vol. 4 (Berlin: Weidmann, 1881), 37–39 (*Opera poetica*, book II, no. 9).

[19] See Jean-Paul Migne, *Patrologia latina*, vol. 133, cols. 45, 52 (Life of St. Odo, second abbot of Cluny, who was taught by Remigius of Auxerre): "Deinde apud Parisium dialectica musicaque a Remigio doctissimo viro est instructus [. . .]," cited by Carpenter, *Music in the Medieval and Renaissance Universities*, 47, note 3. The glosses of Remigius of Auxerre on Martianus Capella's *Marriage of Philology and Mercury* survive in two French sources: ParisBN lat. 8674 (10th c.), probably from the Loire region or from south of the Loire (omitted by Claudio Leonardi, *I codici di Marziano Capella* [Milan: Vita e pensiero, 1959–60], but see RISM 1:111, and RISM 6:211–12), and ParisBN lat. 13026 (early 10th c.), the latter from the library of the abbey of St. Germain-des-Prés (Leonardi, no. 170). Cf. the editions and discussion in Cora Lutz, *Remigii Autossiodorensis Commentarium in Martianum Capellam* (Leiden: Brill, 1962–1965) and Mariken Teeuwen, *Harmony and Music of the Spheres* (Leiden: Brill, 2002).

commentary on the *Dream of Scipio* from Cicero's *De republica*,[20] and, to a lesser degree, the first three books of the *Etymologiae* of Isidore of Seville.[21] The *De institutione musica* of Boethius, which was reserved for "philosophers," according to Guido of Arezzo,[22] was apparently not taught in the cathedral school of Paris (see Appendix 1, Table A, which lists music treatises kept at St. Étienne and later at Notre Dame), but only at schools in the monasteries of the city, and, of course, later at the University.

The oldest inventory of books ever to have been associated with Paris is ParisBN lat. 943. Once thought to describe the library of the cathedral of Notre Dame, this eleventh-century manuscript's origin has recently been located, with some hesitation, at the abbey of Chelles. The catalogue lists an unidentified *liber Isidorii*,[23] a copy of Plato's *Timaeus*,[24] one book by Martianus Capella, one book of *Etymologiae* (presumably Isidore's), and one quaternion with a commentary on music by an unknown author, perhaps a commentary on Martianus Capella. As we shall see, *De nuptiis* was always available to potential commentators in medieval Paris, perhaps evidence of the continuing fame of Remigius's teaching.

[20] See ParisBN lat. 6370 (9th c.), with diagrams added by Lupus of Ferrières himself, and ParisBN lat. 18421 (12th c.). On the interest of Macrobius's writings for the theory of consonances, see Christian Meyer, "La théorie des *symphoniae* selon Macrobe," *Scriptorium* 53 (1999), 82–107.

[21] Chapters 15–23 of Book III concern music. See Charlotte Denoël, "Le fonds des manuscrits latins de Notre-Dame de Paris à la Bibliothèque nationale de France," *Scriptorium* 58 (2004), 131–73, at 171. Two manuscripts with Isidore's *Etymologiae* were part of the library of Notre Dame in the seventeenth century, but their prior history is not known: ParisBN lat. 17875 (12th c., including the book *De numeris* by Isidore on f. 226r) and ParisBN lat. 17876 (12th c.).

[22] Stated by Guido of Arezzo in the last sentence of his *Epistola de ignoto cantu*: "Qui autem curiosus fuerit, libellum nostrum, cui nomen Micrologus est, quaerat; librum quoque Enchiridion, quem Reverentissimus Oddo Abbas luculentissime composuit, perlegat, cuius exemplum in solis figuris sonorum dimisi, quia parvulis condescendi, Boetium in hoc non sequens, cuius liber non cantoribus, sed solis philosophis utilis est." See Dolores Pesce, ed., *Guido d'Arezzo's Regule Rithmice, Prologus in Antiphonarium, and Epistola ad Michahelem* (Ottawa: Institute of Mediaeval Music, 1999), 530–31.

[23] On ParisBN lat. 943, ff. 154v–155r, see Anne-Marie Turcan-Verkerk, "Ouvrages de dames? A propos d'un catalogue du XIe siècle jadis attribué à Notre-Dame de Paris," *Scriptorium* 61 (2007), 286–347, and Birger Munk Olsen, *L'étude des auteurs classiques aux XIe et XIIe siècles*, vol. 3/1 (Paris: Éditions du CNRS 1987), 290.

[24] The section of this treatise pertaining to music is translated into English by Francis Cornford and edited by Thomas Mathiesen in *Strunk's Source Readings in Music History*, revised edition ed. Leo Treitler (New York: W.W. Norton, 1998), 19–23.

THE LIBRARIES OF THE MONASTERIES

Among the oldest Parisian monasteries was the abbey of St. Denis north of the city, initially a basilica built on the tomb of St. Denis around 475, which had its own monastic rule *ca.* 650.[25] Its library, which includes some books from the end of the eighth century, had an especially great number dating from the reign of Charles the Bald (843–877). There is no extant medieval catalogue of this library, just two modern reconstructions.[26] From these, we learn that before 1200 it included a copy of only the book on astronomy in Martianus Capella's *De nuptiis*, Boethius's *De institutione musica*, excerpts from Macrobius's commentary on Cicero's *Dream of Scipio* (the latter cited by Dúngál as at the abbey already by 811),[27] Calcidius's commentary on Plato's *Timaeus*, and two tonaries, as Table B of Appendix 1 shows. Peter of St. Denis, author of a *Tractatus de musica* in two parts following the *Notitia artis musicae* of his contemporary, Jean de Muris, is very likely the same individual as "Anonymous VI." He is thought to be associated with the abbey of St. Denis only in name, however.[28]

On the right bank of the Seine, but outside the wall built by King Charles V, the abbey of St. Pierre-des-Fossés, founded *ca.* 640 by the archdeacon of the Church of Paris, already had a collection of manuscripts by 868 when it was renamed after St. Maur upon the arrival of his relics that year. This library was further developed when Maieul, abbot of Cluny, reformed the abbey in 988 and 989. By the twelfth century, the abbey owned 150 manuscripts, including liturgical books, most of which were transferred in 1716 to the library of the abbey of St. Germain-des-Prés.[29] The twelfth-century catalogue lists a copy of

[25] Anne Walters Robertson, *The Service-Books of the Royal Abbey of Saint-Denis* (Oxford: Clarendon Press, 1991), 5, 16.

[26] Donatella Nebbiai-Dalla Guardia, *La bibliothèque de l'Abbaye de Saint-Denis en France, du IXe au XVIIIe siècle* (Paris: Éditions du CNRS, 1985). Additions and corrections by Dom Daniel Misonne in "L'histoire des manuscrits de Saint-Denis," *Revue bénédictine* 98 (1988), 21–30. Also see Robertson, *The Service-Books*, 356–438.

[27] *Epistolae Karolini Aevi*, vol. 4, ed. Ernst Duemmler and Ernst Perels, *Monumenta Germaniae Historica* (Berlin: Weidmann, 1974), 570.

[28] Robertson, *The Service Books*, 335–36. The treatise by Peter of St. Denis is transmitted in three Italian manuscripts, in Siena, Biblioteca Comunale, L.V.30 (RISM 2:120–23, and RISM 6:604), Chicago, Newberry Library, Case Ms. 54.1 (RISM 4:152–55; RISM 6:725), and Washington, D.C., Library of Congress, Music Div ML 171 J 6 Case (RISM 4:191–96; RISM 6:731–32).

[29] Charlotte Denoël, "Un catalogue des manuscrits de Saint-Maur-des-Fossés au XIIe siècle," *Scriptorium* 60 (2006), 186–205.

Isidore's *Etymologiae* (no. 49) and two tropers (nos. 144, 145), all now lost, but a late eleventh-century copy of Boethius's *De institutione musica* and a tonary from St. Magloire with additions made at St. Maur-des-Fossés do survive as ParisBN lat. 7361, ff. 57r–103v (no. 94) and ParisBN lat. 13252, respectively.[30] (See Appendix 1, Table B.)

The priory of St. Martin des Champs *intra muros*, near St. Martin's Gate, also belonged to Cluny. Its prior, Yvo, had the library built *ca.* 1180. About 150 manuscripts are listed in the early thirteenth-century catalogue,[31] and they include a copy of Isidore's *Etymologiae* and of Martianus Capella's *De nuptiis*.

Further north on the right bank is the priory of St. Magloire, whose manuscripts came to the Bibliothèque du Roi in the seventeenth century.[32] Only one tonary survives from this priory, which is found at the end of the troper-proser of St. Magloire from *ca.* 1020, ParisBN lat. 13252. It includes the echemata *Noeane/Noeagis*, as well as additions that were made later at the abbey of St. Maur-des-Fossés.[33]

On the left bank of the Seine, the oldest abbey is that of St. Germain-des-Prés, founded in 542 by Childebert I, the son of Clovis, when he returned from Spain with the tunic of St. Vincent.[34] Childebert's remains would rest next to those of St. Germain (496–576), that bishop of Paris who was famously buried with a north-Italian psalter written in silver letters on purple parchment, an early witness to responsorial psalmody.[35] In 1026, the abbey became part of the Congregation of St. Bénigne of Dijon, led by Guillaume of Volpiano, and in 1631, of the Congregation of St. Maur.

[30] Ibid., 202–5.

[31] Delisle, *Le Cabinet*, vol. 2, 235–38, at 236–37.

[32] Unpublished catalogue in ParisBN nouv. acq. fr. 5473 (Genevois et al., *Bibliothèques de manuscrits*, no. 1393).

[33] Denoël includes ParisBN lat. 13252 in her list of manuscripts at the Abbey of St. Maur-des-Fossés (Denoël, "Un catalogue," 205).

[34] Cf. the history of the office of St. Vincent as discussed by Pieter Mannaerts in "A Collegiate Church on the Divide: Chant and Liturgy at the Church of Our Lady of Tongeren (10th–15th Century)," PhD dissertation, Katholieke Universiteit Leuven, 2008, and in "A New Source for the Liturgical Office of St. Vincent," in *Papers Read at the Thirteenth Meeting of the IMS Study Group "Cantus Planus," Dobogókő, Hungary, August 2009*, ed. Barbara Haggh and Debra Lacoste (Vancouver: Institute of Mediaeval Music), forthcoming.

[35] ParisBN lat. 11947, described in Elias Avery Lowe, *Codices latini antiquiores*, Part 5: *France: Paris* (Oxford: Clarendon Press, 1950), no 616. Cf. Michel Huglo, "Psalmody in the Ambrosian Rite: Observations on Liturgy and Music," in *Ambrosiana at Harvard: New Sources of Milanese Chant*, ed. Thomas Forrest Kelly and Matthew Mugmon (Cambridge, Mass.: Houghton Library of the Harvard College Library, 2010), 97–124.

The library of St. Germain-des-Prés was surely the richest in the region of Paris in manuscripts with writings about music, although after the twelfth century the abbey of St. Victor had a better library of what were then more recent works. In the seventeenth-century inventory of St. Germain-des-Prés,[36] we find three copies of Isidore's *Etymologiae*, two copies of Boethius's *De institutione musica* along with his other treatises on the quadrivium, an anonymous treatise *Id est de liberalibus artibus*, and the treatise *De proprietatibus rerum* of *ca.* 1245 by a Franciscan scholar at the University of Paris, Bartholomeus Anglicus (d. *ca.* 1272).[37] This treatise ends with a list of instruments, which Klaus-Jürgen Sachs suggests is a commentary on Isidore's discussion of instruments (*Etymologiae* III, 21, and XVIII, 4). It surely includes instruments Bartholomeus saw in Paris. The library also contained one complete and three incomplete books of Martianus Capella and glosses to *De nuptiis* by both an anonymous author and Remigius of Auxerre.[38] An eleventh-century manuscript written at St. Germain-des-Prés of the commentary of Macrobius, now Copenhagen, Det Kongelige Bibliotek Slotsholmen Ny kgl. S. 218, includes at its end, on f. 50r, a large diagram of musical intervals representing the octave plus fifth (= 3/1), elaborated with the numbers from Calcidius's commentary on Plato's *Timaeus*. A manuscript of Capella's *De nuptiis* from the ninth or tenth century was lost during the French Revolution.[39] The manuscripts with writings on music from St. Germain-des-Prés are listed in Appendix 1, Table C.

The Augustinian abbey of St. Geneviève, which became important when Abelard began teaching there *ca.* 1120, also had a notable library, from which books were lent. A fragment of a thirteenth-century catalogue includes Isidore's *Etymologiae* (no. 12), Macrobius's commentary on the *Dream of Scipio* (no. 104), and a *Boecius de consonancia* (no. 105).[40] Later, the abbey acquired Paris, Bibliothèque Sainte-Geneviève 2284, from the early thirteenth century, the unique manuscript of the Cistercian *Regule de musica* ascribed to a certain

[36] ParisBN nouv. acq. fr. 5782. The manuscripts cited here are listed on pages 30, 36, 67, 122, 128, 130, 135, and 144 in this paginated source. There is no music theory in the fragmentary thirteenth-century catalogue from St. Germain-des-Prés published by Delisle, *Le Cabinet*, vol. 2, 515.

[37] See Klaus-Jürgen Sachs, "Bartholomeus Anglicus, O.F.M.," *Die Musik in Geschichte und Gegenwart*, ed. Ludwig Finscher, vol. 2 (Kassel: Bärenreiter, 1999), cols. 334–35.

[38] ParisBN lat. 13026. See note 19 above.

[39] Delisle, *Le Cabinet*, vol. 2, 55 (no. 1096).

[40] ParisBN lat. 16203, ff. 71v–72r (a thirteenth-century catalogue of St. Geneviève). See Delisle, *Le Cabinet*, vol. 2, 513–15, and on this catalogue, Rouse, "The Early Library," 69–71. Cf. note 36 above.

"Abbot Guido" and attributed to Guy d'Eu by Claire Maître, which prescribed the reforms to be made to Cistercian chant.[41] Although Abelard often cited Plato's *Timaeus*, the catalogue does not include it.[42]

Like the abbey of St. Geneviève, the abbey of the regular Augustinian canons of St. Victor, founded in 1113 by Guillaume de Champeaux, housed a lending library.[43] Its intellectuals played an important role in the establishment of the University of Paris. They included Hugh of St. Victor, the leading theologian of his time and author of the much read *Didascalicon*.[44] The abbey's extensive library served the region of Paris, as had that of St. Germain-des-Prés, but its manuscript collection had more recent books, from the twelfth century and later. The extensive catalogue compiled in 1514–15 (ParisBN lat. 14767) includes numerous books by musicians and about music, many identified among extant manuscripts in the magisterial catalogue by Gilbert Ouy, conservator of manuscripts at the Bibliothèque nationale in the 1960s. These include not only the familiar writings by Martianus Capella, Macrobius, Boethius, and Isidore, but also treatises of the thirteenth and fourteenth century from Paris and Germany. Many of the treatises on composing discant are anonymous; those on music as part of the quadrivium or on other speculative topics are often by named authors (see Appendix 1, Tables D1–D3). This library housed many treatises by Johannes de Muris on the quadrivial arts, as well as a lengthy letter in dactylic hexameters on mathematical topics, which he addressed to Philippe de Vitry (English translation in Appendix 2).[45]

[41] See Claire Maître, *La réforme cistercienne de plain-chant.* Étude d'un traité théorique (Brecht: Abdij Nazareth, 1995), and reviews by Christian Meyer in *Scriptorium* 51 (1997), 193–95, and Michel Huglo, *Revue de musicologie* 83 (1997), 146–48. This manuscript was not copied by a Cistercian scribe, however.

[42] Abelard's citations of the *Timaeus* are listed in Lawrence Moonan, "Abelard's Use of the *Timaeus*," *Archives d'histoire littéraire et doctrinale du Moyen Age* 56 (1989), 7–90.

[43] Gilbert Ouy, *Les manuscrits de l'abbaye de Saint-Victor. Catalogue établi sur le répertoire de Claude de Grandrue (1514)*, vol. 1: *Introduction, Concordances, Index*, vol. 2: *Texte*, Biblioteca Victorina 10 (Turnhout: Brepols, 1999).

[44] See Joseph Dyer, "Speculative 'Musica,'" 180–81; Thilo Offergeld, ed., *Hugo de Sancto Victore, Didascalicon de studio legendi*, Fontes Christiani 27 (Freiburg im Breisgau: Herder, 1997); Jerome Taylor, trans., *The Didascalicon of Hugh of St. Victor: A Medieval Guide to the Arts* (New York: Columbia University Press, 1961); and Hugh of St. Victor, *Didascalicon de studio legendi*, ed. Charles Henry Buttimer, CUA Studies in Medieval and Renaissance Latin 10 (Washington, D.C.: The Catholic University Press 1939).

[45] See note 175 below and the discussion under "Jewish and Arabic Writings, Mathematics and Music" below.

THE LIBRARIES OF NOTRE DAME II AND III

The state of the library of the cathedral chapter is only known from the thirteenth century on, from catalogues and lists of bequests.[46] The first catalogue of books at Notre Dame dates from 1297, but a document shows that the abbess of Yères donated service books, some notated, to the cathedral in 1268, and that the bishop of Paris, Étienne Tempier (d. 1279), also left books to the cathedral at his death, including *unum troperium*.[47] The early catalogues name books of the Bible, with or without glosses, and the treatises of St. Augustine or of Richard of St. Victor, and general works on the liberal arts, detailed below, but no liturgical books, because those books were kept in the choir or sacristy. In later centuries, a substantial number of books came from canons of the Cathedral, such as Claude Joly (1607–1700), cantor at Notre Dame and author of a *Traité historique des écoles épiscopales et ecclésiastiques* (Paris, 1678) (identified by Craig Wright) and of other works. Joly had inherited the collections of his grandfather, Antoine Loisel (1536–1617), a prominent Parisian lawyer.[48] We include these books in Appendix 1, Table A below.

The main cathedral library, which was divided into thirteen sections, was not only open to the canons of the chapter but also to students, as was the case at the abbey of St. Victor. Craig Wright identified the books that were used to educate musicians at Notre Dame, books of grammar, as well as of the quadrivium.[49] This library would also serve the canons of the nearby Sainte-Chapelle. In the early fifteenth century, its treasurer received permission from the chapter of the cathedral to keep a key to the library of Notre Dame.[50]

As for books about music, a seventeenth- to eighteenth-century catalogue of the library of Notre Dame, ParisBN lat. 10397, ff. 171r–184v, includes a *Ptomolomaei [sic] harmonica*,[51] two copies of Isidore's *Etymologiae*, one of

[46] A brief history of the construction of Notre Dame Cathedral is in Craig Wright, *Music and Ceremony at Notre-Dame of Paris, 500–1550* (Cambridge: Cambridge University Press, 1989), 4–9.

[47] Franklin, *Les anciennes bibliothèques*, vol. 1, 7–13.

[48] Denoël, "Le fonds," 131–73 : on Loisel and Joly see 150–54. The *liber glossarum* of Corbie (ParisBN lat. 11529, described in Lowe, *Codices latini antiquiores* 5, 611, is not cited in the list of manuscripts of Claude Joly (Denoël, "Le fonds," 163), because he offered it to the Abbey of St. Germain-des-Prés (see Huglo, "Les arts libéraux," 19).

[49] Franklin, *Les anciennes bibliothèques*, vol. 1, 20; Wright, *Music and Ceremony*, 174–80. ParisBN lat. 17487, with didactic works by Gerson, is described in Appendix 1, Table E below.

[50] Franklin, *Les anciennes bibliothèques*, vol. 1, 22–23.

[51] Not an early work, but a Latin translation published in Venice in 1562.

which is signed by Joly,[52] a *Horattus [sic] cum notis*,[53] one glossed Martianus Capella on vellum and another with glosses on parchment, a Macrobius with marginal notes, another Macrobius signed by Joly, and another—twelfth-century—Martianus Capella donated by Joly.[54] There is no trace of any more recent writings on music, though it is possible that the library housed the Parisian manuscript of the "Vatican organum treatise," which describes how organum should be improvised.[55]

THE FORMATION OF THE UNIVERSITY OF PARIS

The increasing number of students and teachers in Paris at the end of the twelfth and beginning of the thirteenth century, and the intellectual activity at the abbeys of St. Geneviève and St. Victor and at the Cathedral school of Notre Dame, led to the formation of an association of Parisian schoolmasters and students with the status of *clerc*. A letter of 1215 from the papal legate, Robert de Courçon, an Englishman who had studied in Paris, is addressed to *universis magistris et scholaribus parisiensibus*. Nowhere does it mention music in the curriculum, but it prescribes the logical works of Aristotle, grammar, rhetoric, and ethics, and notes that the quadrivium may be taught on feast days. Joseph Dyer concludes that "the traditional programme of instruction in the *artes liberales* had not been marginalized."[56] The relationship between the professors and students was described further *ca.* 1230 in the non-official *De disciplina scolarium*, published under the name of Boethius.[57]

[52] ParisBN lat. 17875 and lat. 17876. See note 21 above and Appendix 1, Table A below.

[53] See Silvia Wälli, *Melodien aus mittelalterlichen Horaz-Handschriften. Edition und Interpretation der Quellen* (Kassel: Bärenreiter, 2002), and Jan Ziolkowski, *Nota bene: Reading Classics and Writing Melodies in the Early Middle Ages* (Turnhout: Brepols, 2007), the latter reviewed by Michel Huglo in *Scriptorium* 61 (2007), 290*, no. 672, and by Charles M. Atkinson in *Speculum* 85 (2010), 212–14.

[54] ParisBN lat. 18530.

[55] BAV Ottoboni lat. 3025. Although RISM 2:106 and RISM 6:576 have "Origine inconnue" for this manuscript, its Parisian origin was confirmed to Michel Huglo by Gilbert Ouy on his return from a trip to the Vatican *ca.* 1970 to study the manuscripts of St. Victor. The treatise was edited by Frieder Zaminer, *Das Vatikanische Organum-Traktat (Ottob. lat. 3025): Organum-Praxis der frühen Notre Dame-Schule und ihrer Vorstufen* (Tutzing: Schneider, 1959). Cf. the English manuscript source and its progeny described by Michael Bernhard in "Eine neue Quellen für den Vatikanischen Organum Traktat," in *Quellen und Studien zur Musiktheorie des Mittelalters*, vol. 3, ed. Michael Bernhard (Munich: Verlag der Bayerischen Akademie der Wissenschaften, 2001), 175–190.

[56] See Dyer, "Speculative 'Musica,'" 183–84.

[57] Pseudo-Boèce, *De disciplina scolarium*, ed. Olga Weijers (Leiden: Brill, 1976). One manuscript was in the library of Notre Dame of Paris, the fourteenth-century ParisBN lat. 18424 (described in ibid., 80–81).

SMALL COLLEGES AND THEIR LIBRARIES

Before 1250, there was no college for the students, so they stayed in the vicinity of Notre Dame Cathedral and of the abbeys of St. Victor and St. Geneviève. At this time, the Chancellor of the University was responsible for books and libraries.[58]After 1250, the students lived in colleges named after the their "nations" of origin, such as the College of Four Nations, College of Picardy, and College of Navarre, the latter near the abbey of St. Geneviève and endowed with an important library.[59] Other students stayed in the colleges established by their dioceses of origin, such as those of Autun, Tours, Reims, and Cambrai. The principal religious orders also had houses of study for the young who had just taken their vows: the College of Cluny, College of St. Bernard,[60] the College of the Praemonstratensians, and the College of the Recollets, for example. The libraries of each of these colleges normally had liturgical manuscripts conforming to the *ordo* of the designated diocese or religious order, which served the students who would participate in regular liturgical services in the college chapel.[61]

The smaller college libraries also had many books of philosophy and theology, but books of music theory or even on the liberal arts were exceedingly rare. The list of books dated 14 May 1330 from the Collège des Dix-Huit does not contain music theory, but instead grammar, philosophy, and small liturgical books for private use, including an office of St. Catherine and an office of the dead.[62] The College of Dormans-Beauvais, founded by Jean Dormans, bishop of Beauvais in 1370, had a few music books, as well as liturgical books that were kept in its chapel. In 1389, the College bought a manuscript

[58] Franklin, *Les anciennes bibliothèques*, vol. 1, 3 and 7.

[59] Delisle, *Le Cabinet*, vol. 2, 252–55; Isabelle Chavassa-Gouron, *Les lectures des maîtres et étudiants du Collège de Navarre: Un aspect de la vie intellectuelle à l'Université de Paris (1380–1520)*, Position des thèses soutenues par les élèves de la promotion de 1985 (Paris: École des Chartes, 1985), 31–37.

[60] See Edmond Kwanten, "Le collège Saint-Bernard a Paris, " *Revue d'histoire ecclésiastique* 43 (1948), 443–72. Students read mainly scripture and the writings of the Church Fathers (ibid., 444).

[61] Cf. Beth Anne Lee-De Amici, "*Ad sustentacionem fidei Christiani*: Sacred Music and Ceremony in Medieval Oxford" (PhD dissertation, University of Pennsylvania, 1999); and *eadem*, "Academic Colleges in the Oxford Community, 1400–1560," in *Music and Musicians in Renaissance Cities and Towns*, ed. Fiona Kisby (Cambridge: Cambridge University Press, 2001), 94–105.

[62] For an interesting discussion of the origin and organization of the College, see Érnest Coyecque, "Notice sur l'ancien Collège des Dix-Huit (1180–1529)," *Bulletin de la Société de l'histoire de Paris et de l'Île de France* 14 (1887), 176–86.

with Aristotle's *Problemata* from a doctor in Montpellier for one *solidus* (no. 431). Circa 1402, the college received a copy of Macrobius's commentary on the *Dream of Scipio* (no. 164) from Jean de Neuilly-Saint-Front, today Bern, Burgerbibliothek ms. 436, the only evidence of writing on speculative music at this college.[63] The College of Laon was founded in 1324 by Guy de Laon at the bottom of mount St. Geneviève. Recently, Shin Nishimagi suggested that the early-twelfth-century manuscript Milan, Biblioteca Ambrosiana M. 17 sup., with the treatises of Guido of Arezzo, Berno of Reichenau, and the fragment of the *Dialogus de musica*, as well as a collection of measurements and texts on music, was donated to this college in the fifteenth or sixteenth century.[64] The compilation also contains two versions of *Ad organum faciendum*, one in prose, the other in verse, and has glosses on chapters fifteen and sixteen of the *Micrologus*. If this manuscript was indeed in Paris, then it is the only source with the treatises of Guido of Arezzo to have any association with that city. The library of the College d'Autun was inventoried several times in the Middle Ages. The inventory made in 1615, Paris, Bibliothèque de l'Université, ms. 397, lists 253 volumes.[65] Numbers 4–5 are two volumes of unidentified works by Jean Scot; no. 54 is Martianus Capella's *De nuptiis* "cum aliis tractatibus de artibus liberalibus," and no. 223 is Plato's *Timaeus* with Calcidius's commentary in a compilation including Aristotle's *Predicamenta* and Simplicius's commentary on it.[66] The library also included some music books, but mostly Church Fathers, isolated liturgical books, dictionaries, grammars, Classics, and French literature.[67]

Opposite from the cathedral of Notre-Dame, still on the left bank, but in back of the Port St. Bernard, was the College of St. Bernard, where the *Bernardins*, young Cistercians who had taken their vows, continued their study of theology at the University of Paris. Their library included fifty-seven

[63] Elisabeth Pellegrin, "La bibliothèque de l'ancien Collège de Dormans-Beauvais," *Bulletin philologique et historique du Comité des travaux historiques et scientifiques* (1944–45), 99–164 at 122 (*Problemata*) and 132 (Macrobius).

[64] Shin Nishimagi,"Les gloses sur les chapitres XV et XVI du *Micrologus* de Guy d'Arezzo dans Milano, Biblioteca ambrosiana, M. 17 sup. (début du XIIe s.)," *Bulletin of the Institute for Mediterranean Studies* 7 (2009), 81–96 at 82.

[65] It was not possible for us to consult the inventories of 1462 and 1467, cited in Genevois et al., *Bibliothèques de manuscrits*, 151. The inventory of 1615 is edited in Charles Beaulieux, "Un fragment de l'histoire de la bibliothèque du Collège d'Autun à Paris. Deuxième article," *Revue des bibliothèques* 22 (1912), 334–51.

[66] Cf. the letter of the Faculty of Ars to Thomas of Aquinas, discussed below.

[67] Beaulieux, "Fragment de l'histoire." The music books are no. 120: *Cancionero de todas las obras de Juan del Enzina*, and no. 134: *Manipulus florum Thomae de hymnis*.

manuscript books from the abbey of Clairvaux.[68] No books on the liberal arts were part of this collection, nor did the Bernardins keep a copy of the Cistercian *Regule*. This work was destroyed along with the liturgical books of the first reform, once the second reform had been completed.

At this point we must also mention the library of the Dominicans of St. Jacques. Here the exemplar of the Dominican chant books was copied in 1254 under the direction of the Dominican master general, Humbert of Romans, now Rome, Curia Generalizia dei Domenicani (Santa Sabina), Ms. XIV L 1, and a portative book for the use of the Master General was also copied, LondonBL Add. 23935. Both include tonaries, and the late-thirteenth-century Scottish musician, Jerome of Moray, later wrote a commentary on the Dominican tonary in his treatise,[69] which was chained in the chapel of St. Ursula of the Sorbonne.[70] Most inventories of this library, however, are very late.[71] One other

[68] Barbara Haggh and Michel Huglo, "Gilles de Roye, Abbé de Royaumont (1454–1458) et David de Bourgogne" *Miscellanea in memoriam Pierre Cockshaw (1938–2008)*, ed. Frank Daelemans and Ann Kelders, vol. 1 (Brussels: Bibliotheque Royale de Belgique, 2009), 195–205 (I. Régent du Collège des Bernardins à Paris), based on Caroline Obert-Piketty, "Les maîtres et étudiants du Collège Saint-Bernard à Paris, de 1224 à 1494" (PhD dissertation: École nationale des Chartes, 1987). Also see Delisle, *Le Cabinet*, vol. 2, 255–56.

[69] Christian Meyer, "Le tonaire des Frères Prêcheurs," *Archivum fratrum praedicatorum* 76 (2006), 117–56. Throughout this article, we consider Hieronymus de Moravia to be Jerome of Moray from Scotland, based on the research of Michel Huglo, for several reasons. First, relations between Paris and Scotland were more significant in the thirteenth century than relations between Paris and Central Europe, the latter increasing only in the fourteenth century. Second, the diocese of Moray was among the most important in Scotland. Established in the early twelfth century by David I of Scotland, this diocese was led by many early bishops identified as *de Moravia* (see Cosmo Innes, ed., *Registrum episcopatus moraviensis* [Edinburgh: n.p., 1837]). Third, a young Dominican from that region wanting to study with the greatest Dominican theologians would naturally travel to the well-established Dominican *studium* in Paris, even though there was a flourishing Dominican school in Oxford soon after the Dominican house was founded there in 1221, which was made a *studium generale* by the General Chapter of the Order in Paris in 1246 (letter from Father Bede Bailey, O.P. at Blackfriars, London, to Michel Huglo, 10 November 2000).

[70] The manuscript ParisBN lat. 16663 was bequeathed to the Sorbonne by Pierre de Limoges, master of arts and professor in the Faculty of Arts, whose annotations appear in this manuscript. See Michel Huglo, "La place du *Tractatus de Musica* dans l'histoire de la theorie musicale du XIIIe siècle: étude codicologique," in *Jérôme de Moravie, un théoricien de la musique dans le milieu intellectuel parisien du XIIIe siècle*, ed. Christian Meyer (Paris: Créaphis, 1992), 33–42, at 35–37.

[71] A first inventory is Paris, Bibliothèque de l'Arsenal MS 6492, ff. 150–74 from 1790, with 167 manuscripts. A second inventory is ParisBN nouv. acq. fr. 5416–17, made in 1815–1848, containing a list of manuscripts from the convent of St. Jacques that entered the French imperial library during the Revolution. See Nicole Guibout-Chagué, "Les manuscrits des Jacobins de la rue St Jacques d'après les inventaires révolutionnaires dressés pour les dépôts

small library is that of the Benedictine monks in Paris who were known as "Celestines." They owned a *Didascalicon* of Hugh of St. Victor, according to a fifteenth-century catalogue.[72] The manuscripts with writings on music in these smaller libraries are listed in Appendix 1, Table F.

THE COLLEGE OF THE SORBONNE AND ITS LIBRARIES

The best-known college and the richest in books, however, was that founded in 1257 by Robert of Sorbon, canon of the chapters of Cambrai Cathedral and of Notre Dame of Paris, with assistance from King Louis IX. Like Notre Dame cathedral, the Sorbonne received numerous books by gift and bequest, the largest of which was the donation of 300 manuscripts, many of patristic writings, by Gérard d'Abbeville (d. 1272), archdeacon of Ponthieu and canon of Cambrai cathedral, leader of the struggle of the canons against the mendicant orders and associated with Robert of Sorbon. Dozens of these manuscripts had once belonged to the poet, physician, and chancellor of the cathedral of Amiens, Richard de Fournival. At his death in 1260, his library passed to Gérard d'Abbeville and at the latter's death in 1272 to the Sorbonne. Gérard stipulated in his will that his books should be available to other secular masters and to the arts faculty.[73] One-hundred-eighteen manuscripts bequeathed by Gérard d'Abbeville survive at the ParisBN,[74] but some are located in other libraries.

The oldest known catalogue from the Sorbonne is a fragment dated by Richard Rouse as from "soon after 1274."[75] It describes a collection dominated by patristic works and without any music theory, many of which are the books offered in 1260 by Gérard d'Abbeville.

littéraires," École nationale des Chartes, Positions des thèses (1978), 63–68, and the review by Geneviève Grand in *Scriptorium* 34 (1980), 154*, no. 765. See also Franklin, *Les anciennes bibliothèques*, vol. 1, 195, note 2.

[72] Albert Derolez, "Fragment d'un catalogue médiéval de la bibliothèque des Céléstins de Paris," *Scriptorium* 40 (1986), 184–201, at 196. See also Delisle, *Le Cabinet*, vol. 2, 248–51.

[73] See Richard H. Rouse, "Manuscripts belonging to Richard de Fournival," *Revue d'histoire des textes* 3 (1973), 253–69 and plates XIX–XXIV; *idem*, "The Early Library of the Sorbonne," *Scriptorium* 21 (1967), 42–71, 227–51, at 47–51; and Genevois and others, *Bibliothèques*, 177, no. 1434.

[74] Listed in Delisle, *Le Cabinet*, vol. 2, 148–49.

[75] Rouse, "The Early Library," edits this fragmentary list on pages 245–46 (ParisBN lat. 16412, ff. 323r–324v, first edited by Palémon Glorieux in *Aux origines de la Sorbonne* 1: *Robert de Sorbon* [Paris: Vrin, 1966], 240–53). See Rouse, "The Early Library," 52–53 on its date and further discussion on pages 54–55.

A second catalogue, of what was later termed the *parva libraria*, was that drawn up *ca.* 1290, which counted 1,017 books; the catalogue survives only in its revision made in 1338.[76] As Rouse explains, his reconstructed 1290 catalogue corresponds to the formal establishment of a library of chained books at the Sorbonne in 1289, which was, in his opinion, a new addition to an already present general library. After 1290, the two libraries took on different names: the unchained collection was called the *parva libraria* and its books were kept in *armaria*, and the chained library was called the *libraria communis* and later the *magna libraria*.[77] Before 1290 there were no chained books, but by 1338 there were some noted in the catalogue. A comparison between Rouse's reconstructed early catalogue and the 1338 catalogue shows that the number of books increased from 1,017 volumes *ca.* 1290 to 1,722 volumes *ca.* 1338, or 705 more than had been present in 1290.[78]

In the catalogue of 1338 but perhaps not of 1290, which listed fewer books, the library is divided into 59 sections by subject. According to Rouse, it describes the books as they were taken out of the *armaria*:[79] in section 23, there are two copies of Isidore's *Etymologiae* (nos. 2 and 7); in section 37, no. 27 is the *Didascalicon*; in section 38, no. 7 is a copy of Plato's *Timaeus;* in section 42 (*Libri ecclesiastici officii*), among the missals and breviaries, one notices no. 4, a *Liber de cantu organico* donated by Étienne d'Abbeville, and no. 10, a second *Liber de cantu organico*, beginning on f. 2 with *Viderunt*. In section 51 (*Libri Tullii et Boecii*), we find two copies of *Musica Boecii* bequeathed by Gérard d'Abbeville (no. 4 and no. 29) and a third *Musica Boecii* (no. 39).[80] In section 52, among the "Libri Socratis, Platonis, Ciceronis, Valerii, Solini, Cassiodori, Plini et aliorum auctorum," there is, among the gifts from the same canon, the translation of Plato's *Timaeus* by Calcidius, preceded by the dedicatory letter to Osius (ParisBN lat. 16579) among three copies of the

[76] Rouse, "The Early Library," 63–64. Rouse thinks that the 1338 catalogue largely transmits earlier catalogues and that none was made in 1321 (ibid., 231). The catalogue is transcribed from its only manuscript source, ParisBN nouv. acq. lat. 99 (*olim* Paris, Bibliothèque de l'Arsenal MS 1223) in Delisle, *Le Cabinet*, vol. 3, 9–72, and also in Glorieux, *Aux origines*, vol. 1, 245–46.

[77] Rouse, "The Early Library," 60–61.

[78] See Rouse, "The Early Library," 227–51, especially 241–44, at 242.

[79] Rouse, "The Early Library," 67, and see Delisle, *Le Cabinet*, 3, 36, 40, 41, 54, 61–63, 67–68.

[80] The two Boethius manuscripts are ParisBN lat. 16201 and ParisBN lat. 16652. See Appendix 1, Table E.

Timaeus (nos. 8, 9, and 19).[81] Section 53, no. 14 is a large compilation with a *Timaeus*, a glossed Macrobius, and much else, and no. 23 (ParisBN lat. 16093) is a copy of Bartholomeus Anglicus's *De proprietatibus rerum*. In section 56 (*libri quadruviales*), the books of music theory are less numerous than the books of astronomy: in addition to a Macrobius (no. 6) and the unidentified *Musica Milonis* (no. 13), we notice a *Quidam totatus*[?] *exponens Thimeum Platonis* (no. 20),[82] and also a *Musica Guidonis* (no. 27), by either Guido of Arezzo or Guido of St. Denis,[83] two Martianus Capellas (nos. 36 and 45), and a *Timaeus* (no. 37).

The third catalogue, dated *ca.* 1321 by Rouse, lists codices chained to 26 benches in the *libraria communis* or *grande librairie*.[84] At this time, between 312 and 340 manuscripts were chained. This list includes a Martianus Capella (P), Macrobius commentary (P), *Musica fratris Jeronimi* (V), Calcidius commentary (AB), *De proprietatibus rerum* (AB), and Aristotle's *Problemata* (AD, the thirteenth-century manuscript that is now ParisBN lat. 16633).

The fourth catalogue, the "Répertoire méthodique de la Grande Librairie," also dated by Rouse as *ca.* 1321, is an analytical catalogue of manuscripts in the same *magna libraria* that was the work of one individual, named "Johannes." This catalogue carefully limited entries to books that were confirmed to be present by checking them, sometimes incorrectly, against older catalogues.[85] Indeed, we find some of the same books in this list, at the same location, but often with new books alongside them. The list includes the same *Problemata*, now two Macrobius commentaries instead of one, one with further glosses, the same *Timaeus*, the same Calcidius commentary, the same Martianus Capella and another volume with glosses to Martianus Capella, the same *Musica fratris Jeronimi*, then two new books with anonymous treatises: *Commentum super*

[81] This manuscript was prepared with much room for glosses, which include borrowings from the commentary by Calcidius and also by Bernard of Chartres. The manuscript is related to two other translations of the *Timaeus* with commentary by Calcidius: ParisBN lat. 6280 and ParisBN lat. 6281. See Beatrice Bakhouche, "Marginalia et histoire du texte: L'exemple du manuscrit Paris BnF latin 16579," *Revue d'histoire des textes*, nouvelle serie 4 (2009), 157–77.

[82] Delisle also cites ParisBN lat. 15685, but it is a manuscript of Bede.

[83] The treatise by the latter was composed after 1301, as is shown by Guido's reference to a quodlibet by Peter of Auvergne given in that year. The script and the decoration of the only surviving manuscript, LondonBL Harley 281, link it to Paris and the first quarter of the fourteenth century (from an email from Elizabeth A. R. Brown to Barbara Haggh, November 2009).

[84] Transcribed in Delisle, *Le Cabinet*, vol. 3, 72–79, and in Glorieux, *Aux origines*, 248–87.

[85] Transcribed in Delisle, *Le Cabinet*, vol. 3, 79–114, and in Glorieux, *Aux origines*, 247–351.

musicam (whose incipit is given as *Quoniam musica non solum*)[86] and *Item de musica* (with the incipit given as *Musice tria sunt genera;* that is, the *Ars nova* of Philippe de Vitry),[87] and a large compilation with *Musica Augustini* and *Ysidori*, Bernard of Clairvaux (*Cantum quem*), and a *Quid est cantus*, followed by a Cistercian tonary.[88] Finally, there is a manuscript with excerpts from Isidore's *Etymologiae*.[89]

Rouse claims that both of these catalogues, i.e. the third and the fourth, neither of which are complete, date from after 1318 and before the late 1320s, and are contemporary with the initiatives of which the statutes of 1321 were a part. Those statutes sought to bring order to the chaos ensuing from insufficient supervision of booklending.[90]

The descriptions of twenty-eight of the chained books in the second catalogue could not be read by the fourth cataloguer, who wrote "*Deficit quia cathenatus.*" Léopold Delisle identified some of these books, however, such as no. 64, *Musica fratris Jeronimi*. This music treatise, now ParisBN lat. 16663, is by the Scottish Dominican, Jerome of Moray, and contains traces of the ring to which the chain was attached on its inside cover.[91] Therefore, this manuscript, in which Jerome's treatise is followed by four "positions" written by a Dominican concerning the polyphony of Notre Dame, was not kept at the convent of

[86] Johannes de Muris wrote a "Commentum super musicam," but it does not survive. See Wathey, "Philippe de Vitry's Books," 150. We have not been able to identify this incipit.

[87] While this is also the incipit of the treatise by the Anonymous ex trad. Garlandia IV, in fact the only source of that treatise, BAV Barb. lat 307, which also includes part of Vitry's *Ars Nova*, is of Italian origin. Vitry's *Ars Nova* survives in ParisBN lat. 14741, a manuscript from the Abbey of St. Victor, meaning that the Sorbonne copy is lost or has not been identified.

[88] ParisBN lat. 16662. The text by Bernard of Clairvaux is edited in Francis J. Guentner, *Epistola sancti Bernardi de revisione cantus cisterciensis. Tractatus scriptus ab auctore incerto cisterciense 'Cantum quem'*, Corpus scriptorum de musica 24 (Rome: American Institute of Musicology, 1974).

[89] Delisle, *Le Cabinet*, vol. 3, 83, 87, 89, 90, 103. The unidentified *Item quadripertitum glosatum*, beginning "Scire et intelligere gloriosum est," at shelfmark AD.b. (Delisle, *Le Cabinet*, vol.3, 89, col. 1) is not Muris's treatise, but rather *Ptolemaei Geographi Opus quadripartitum*.

[90] Rouse, "The Early Library," 232–41, especially 236 and 240 on the date, and 228–32 on the 1321 statutes.

[91] On this manuscript, see Appendix 1, Table E below, and Delisle, *Le Cabinet*, vol. 2, 168. It appears in the inventory of books of the *Grande Librairie* at the twentieth bench, given the letter "V" (Delisle, *Le Cabinet*, vol. 3, 77). This is not a *pecia* manuscript, as has been claimed (see note 114). Also see Laura Weber, "A Translation and Commentary on Jerome of Moravia's *Tractatus de musica*" (PhD dissertation, Yale University, 2009); C. Meyer et al., eds., *Hieronymous de Moravia, Tractatus de musica*, CCCM 250 (Turnhout, 2013).

St. Jacques, but rather at the College of the Sorbonne.[92] Nevertheless, chapter 21 of Jerome's treatise is a commentary on the Dominican tonary.[93]

The presence of three copies of Boethius's *De institutione musica* and of two copies of Boethius's *Arithmetica* (nos. 43 and 44 of the second catalogue) in the *parva libraria* of the Sorbonne provides a context for the work of the musician Johannes de Muris, a master of arts at the university living at the Sorbonne beginning in 1321. His *Musica speculativa* was completed at the Sorbonne: "Explicit musica speculativa secundum Boethium abbreviata Parisius in Sorbona anno Domini 1323."[94] Muris's *Notitia artis musice* is based on the third book of Boethius's *De institutione musica*[95] and the first part of his *Quadripartitum numerorum* is derived from Boethius's *Arithmetica* and Euclid's *Elements.*[96]

The lending registers of the library of the Sorbonne from 1402–1536 include few music books, but most of those lent out were centuries out of date: Plato's *Timaeus* (eleven times), Macrobius (twelve times), Martianus Capella (fourteen times), Boethius's *musica* (three times), Isidore's *Etymologiae* (once), Hugh of St. Victor's *Didascalicon* (once), an unidentified Johannes de Muris *Liber* (once),[97] and an unidentified *Liber de cantu* (four times). The most sought-after books were the works of theology; the least requested were

[92] See note 70 above.

[93] See Meyer, "Le tonaire."

[94] Ulrich Michels, ed., *Johannis de Muris. Notitia artis musicae et Compendium musicae practicae. Petrus de Sancto Dionysio Tractatus de musica*, Corpus scriptorum de musica 17 (Rome: American Institute of Musicology, 1972), 8. Also see Olga Weijers, *Le travail intellectuel à la Faculté des Arts de Paris: Textes et maîtres (ca. 1200–1500)*, vol. 5 (Turnhout: Brepols, 2003), 129: this treatise figures in ParisBN lat. 7207 (Italy) and ParisBN lat. 7369 (Florence), but not in ParisBN lat. 7378A (*ca.*1350–1400, possibly of Parisian origin, RISM 1:107–08, RISM 6:206–07), which also includes on ff. 58rv a brief anonymous passage on speculative music (cf. RISM 6:206). To this list, one must add the manuscript in Berlin described by Christian Meyer, "Une source inconnue de la *Musica speculativa* de Jean de Murs: Berlin, Staatsbibl. Preuss. Kulturbesitz, Ms. lat. fol. 600,"*Revue d'histoire des textes* 11 (1981), 415–18 (RISM 6:260, a French manuscript of the first quarter of the 15th century of Parisian provenance).

[95] On this, see Nicolas Bell, "Readings and Interpretations of Boethius's *De institutione musica* in the later Middle Ages," in *Sapientia et eloquentia. Meaning and Function in Liturgical Poetry, Music, Drama, and Biblical Commentary in the Middle Ages*, ed. Gunilla Iversen and Nicolas Bell (Turnhout: Brepols, 2009), 365–80, at 376–78.

[96] Ghislaine L'Huillier, *Le Quadripartitum numerorum de Jean de Murs: Introduction et édition critique*, Mémoires et documents de l'École des Chartes 32 (Geneva: Droz, 1990), 12.

[97] A book of Muris with second folio "sinunt in exteriori" and last folio "M C." See Jeanne Vieilliard, "Le Registre de Prêt de la bibliothèque du Collège de Sorbonne au XVe siècle," in *The Universities in the Late Middle Ages*, ed. Jozef Ijsewijn (Leuven: Leuven University Press, 1978), 276–92, following Paris, Bibliothèque Mazarine 3323.

the treatises on arithmetic, computus, geometry, the outdated *Etymologiae* and Boethius's music treatise.[98]

THE LIBRARY OF THE COLLEGE OF NAVARRE

Another substantial library also augmented with donations of books was that of the College de Navarre, founded by Queen Jeanne I of Navarre in 1305. An inventory of 1741 lists an overwhelming majority of books by patristic authors and of more recent theology, but also, in the midst of a series of grammar books, we find an anonymous *De musica liber.* The library also had a copy of Isidore's *Etymologiae,* possibly the fourteenth-century Paris, Bibliothèque Mazarine 609 with the *Etymologiae* and interpolations found in Visigothic manuscripts.[99] This book was donated to the college by Master Alexander, doorman at the College and probably the student in grammar, Joannes Alexandri, who matriculated in 1376.[100] From other evidence, we can trace to this College a *De institutione musica* of Boethius (ParisBN lat. 18514) and a thirteenth-century Papias. (See Appendix 1, Table E.) We now know that the composer Philippe de Vitry was one of two exterior governors of the College of Navarre in his capacity as bishop of Meaux. He was thus responsible for allocating bursaries at the College between 1351 and when he died in 1361.[101]

THE COLLEGE LIBRARIES, UNIVERSITY INSTRUCTION, AND PRIVATE BOOKS

It now remains to determine the place of such manuscripts of music theory in the framework of oral instruction at Parisian monastic and cathedral schools, if not at the Faculty of Arts of the University of Paris. From the ninth to the beginning of the thirteenth century, the teaching of the liberal arts in the schools was accomplished by a "reader," that is, a qualified master who read

[98] Vieilliard, "Le Registre de Prêt," 276.

[99] On these interpolations, see Michel Huglo, "The *Musica Isidori* Tradition in the Iberian Peninsula," in *Hispania Vetus,* ed. Susana Zapke (Madrid: Fundación BBVA, 2007), 63–92 with many color facsimiles of the diagrams; *idem,* "The Diagrams Interpolated into the Musica Isidori and the Scale of Old Hispanic Chant," in *Western Plainchant in the First Millennium. Studies in the Medieval Liturgy and its Music,* ed. Sean Gallagher et al. (Aldershot: Ashgate, 2003), 243–260; *idem,* "Die Interpolationen von Texten und Diagrammen in der Musica Isidori," in *Quellen und Studien zur Musiktheorie des Mittelalters,* ed. Michael Bernhard (Munich: Verlag der Bayerischen Akademie der Wissenschaften, 2001), 1–17.

[100] Emile Châtelain, "Les manuscrits du Collège de Navarre en 1741," *Revue des bibliothèques* 11 (1901), 362–411, at 381, 389, and 401.

[101] Pascale Duhamel, "L'enseignement de la musique à l'Université de Paris d'après le manuscrit BnF lat. 7378A," *Acta musicologica* 79 (2007), 263–89, at 283.

the text by an authority aloud and commented on it, phrase by phrase. A reader with less of a flair for teaching could make use of a manuscript filled with marginal or interlinear glosses. The works on music that were most often glossed were, of course, the ninth book of Martianus Capella's *De nuptiis*,[102] and, above all, Boethius's *De institutione musica*.[103] Calcidius's commentary on the *Timaeus* of Plato had also been glossed frequently, so that it could be taught in the schools, notably in Chartres and later at the University of Paris.[104] While the glossing of these musical texts had all but ended by 1200, no doubt because fewer copies in large format with room for glosses were made, the production of commentaries continued, especially for Boethius.[105]

Another way of presenting music theory in Paris was by means of the *question disputée*. Joseph Dyer points out that musical questions within this genre often concern classification and are general, requiring no specialized knowledge of speculative music, yet some do address music as a natural phenomenon. As Pascale Duhamel explains, *questions disputées* were copied in groups, but, as Dyer reminds us, without answers.[106] Duhamel, in her study of those in the compilation ParisBN lat. 7378A, copied in Paris in the second half of the fourteenth century, edits and discusses its 32 *questions disputées* (f. 85rv), all of which explore the relationships between sound and nature and the senses as well as some purely musical questions.[107] They demonstrate the continuing

[102] Ten anonymous or named glossators contributed to this collection of glosses, but Book 9, entitled *De harmonia*, and often modified to read *De musica* in the ninth century, is not always glossed. Cf. Paul Oskar Kristeller and Edward Cranz, *Catalogus translationum et commentariorum*, vol. 2: *Martianus Capella* (Washington, D.C.: Catholic University of America, 1971).

[103] Michael Bernhard and Calvin M. Bower, *Glossa maior in institutionem musicam Boethii* (Munich: Beck, 1993–2009), 3 vols. and index.

[104] Margaret Gibson, "The Study of the Timaeus in the Eleventh and Twelfth Centuries," *Pensiamento* 25 (1969), 183–94; Bakhouche, "Marginalia et histoire du texte"; Anna Somfai, "The Brussels Gloss: A Tenth-Century Reading of the Geometrical and Arithmetical Passages of Calcidius's Commentary (*ca.* 400 AD) to Plato's *Timaeus*," in *Scientia in margine: études sur les marginalia dans les manuscrits scientifiques du Moyen Age à la Renaissance*, ed. Danielle Jacquart and Charles Burnett (Geneva: Droz, 2005), 139–169; *eadem*, "Transmission and Reception of Plato's *Timaeus* and Calcidius's *Commentary* during the Carolingian Renaissance" (PhD dissertation, Cambridge University, 1998).

[105] Cf. Dyer, "Speculative 'Musica,'" 187, which notes that Michael Bernhard associates the end of glossing with the rise of the universities. It is true that the changes in page preparation of university manuscripts effectively left no room for glosses. Thirteenth-century university manuscripts have little space in margins, cramped writing, and are usually heavily abbreviated.

[106] See Dyer, "Speculative 'Musica,'" 193–99, on *questions disputées*.

[107] See Duhamel, "L'enseignement." Other questions and their manuscript sources are listed

study of Boethius's *De institutione musica*, but also of Jean de Muris's *Notitia artis musicae* and *Musica speculativa*. The manuscript was probably used by Thémon Juif for writing his works and teaching; he was the procurator of the English Nation in Paris in 1355–56 and then its receiver until 1361. Scholars represented in the manuscript include Dominique de Clavasio, Nicolas Oresme, Campanus de Novara, Gerard of Cremona's translation of Archimedes and of Ibn al-Haytham, Euclid, Jordan of Nemours, Jean de Muris (*Musica speculativa libri duo*, *Notitia artis musice*, and his Prognostication on the conjunction of Saturn, Jupiter, and Mars), Jean de Lignères, Levi ben Gerson (*Tractatus de harmonicis numeris*), Firmin de Beauval, Pierre de Maricourt, Jean Pecham, and Pseudo Masha'allah. A different dialectical method of objection and response, which is described in the anonymous treatise, *De modo opponendi et respondendi*, seems not to have been applied to problems of music theory.[108]

At the university, oral teaching could be remembered if students took notes or *reportationes*. At question is whether the *reportationes* on music necessarily represented official university teaching. Such examples include the *Ars nova* of Philippe de Vitry, transmitted in an early-fourteenth-century fascicle within the Parisian compilation, ParisBN lat. 7378A, which survives only as *reportationes* taken *ca.* 1320 by a student.[109] The *Gaudent brevitate moderni* is a summary of Franco of Cologne's teaching perhaps made for a similar purpose.[110] Furthermore, Christian Meyer argued that the four versions of the *musica plana* of Johannes de Garlandia are *reportationes* of Garlandia's teaching, but Joseph Dyer found evidence that this teaching was part of official lectures.[111] Dyer's point is important: the procedure of taking notes may well have been learned at the university, but only applied by students learning music in ecclesiastical or private locations.

in Pascale Duhamel, "Les questions disputées de musique de l'Université de Paris (XIIIe–XIVe siècles)," *Bulletin de l'Association Les amis de l'I.R.H.T.* (Octobre 2005), 1–3.

108 Lambert M. De Rijk, *Die mittelalterliche Traktate "De modo opponendi et respondendi": Einleitung und Ausgabe der einschlägigen Texten* (Münster in Westfalen: Aschendorff, 1980). The edition is based on two manuscripts from the Sorbonne, ParisBN lat.16617 and ParisBN lat. 16390. These manuscripts are partially in the script of Pierre de Limoges, who owned the main manuscript source of Jerome of Moray; see Madeleine Mabille, "Pierre de Limoges, copiste de manuscrits," *Scriptorium* 24 (1970), 244–52.

109 Sarah Fuller, "A Phantom Treatise of the Fourteenth Century? The *Ars nova*," *Journal of Musicology* 4 (1985), 23–50.

110 Huglo, "Recherches," 15.

111 See *Musica plana Johannis de Garlandia*, ed. Christian Meyer, Collection d'études musicologiques 91 (Baden-Baden: V. Koerner, 1998), and Dyer, "Speculative 'Musica,'" at 192–93 on *reportationes*.

A characteristic method of distributing copies of texts to university students was the system of *pecia*, by which personal copies of works of philosophy and theology were made from a duly corrected exemplar that had been deposited at an accredited stationer. This procedure was not used for music theory, but only for philosophy and theology. Works that discuss music in passing, such as Aristotle's *Problemata* and Thomas of Aquinas's *Sententia libri de caelo et mundo*, were sometimes copied by *pecia*, however.[112] And stationers did have music books available. Nan Cooke Carpenter cites a list of books from 1304 with stationer's prices for each. That list includes Macrobius's commentary and the *Problemata*.[113] The manuscript containing the treatise of Jerome of Moray, ParisBN lat. 16663, for example, was not the product of the *pecia* system, despite its gathering structure and foliation with Arabic numerals, since it was copied by a scribe who was not a professional.[114]

Music treatises were frequently recopied in full, however, not just for local Parisian use, but because many foreigners in Paris brought what they had found back to their homelands, whether intentionally or not. The major treatises on Parisian polyphony by Johannes de Garlandia (*ca.* 1275) and by the Anonymous of 1279, who was acquainted with the canon of Notre-Dame, Henri Tubeuf, and with Franco of Cologne (*ca.* 1280), are known to us only from manuscripts taken from Paris to distant regions or copied far from Paris from Parisian models.[115] The treatise derived from that of Franco of Cologne, *Gaudent brevitate moderni*, in ParisBN lat. 15139, is also found in the late-thirteenth-century Regensburg manuscript, Munich, Bayerische Staatsbibliothek

[112] Giovanna Murano, *Opere diffuse per exemplaria e pecia* (Turnhout: Brepols, 2005) lists 920 titles treated this way between 1228 and 1457, including no. 884 *Sententia* (ParisBN lat. 16144); on the state of the *pecia* question, see Pieter Beullens and Pieter De Leemans, "Aristote à Paris: le système de la pecia et les traductions de Guillaume de Moerbeke," *Recherches de théologie et philosophie médiévales* 75 (2008), 87–135 (reviewed by Pierre Hamblenne in *Scriptorium* 63 (2009), 9*–10*, no. 20). They demonstrate that Aristotle's *Problemata* were copied by *pecia* in Paris.

[113] Carpenter, *Music in the Medieval and Renaissance Universities*, 50.

[114] Huglo, "Le Tractatus," 33–42; *idem*, "Recherches," 1–2; and cf. Dyer, "Speculative 'Musica,'" 186–87.

[115] Jeremy Yudkin, ed., *De musica mensurata: The Anonymous of St. Emmeram* (Bloomington: Indiana University Press, 1990). Its only manuscript source, Munich, Bayerische Staatsbibliothek clm 14523 (RISM 3:113–16; RISM 6:335–36), copied in Freising probably on a Parisian model, reached the Benedictine Abbey of St. Emmeram in Regensburg by the mid-fourteenth century. Two hockets cited in this treatise and on the flyleaves of Dijon, Bibliothèque municipale 447, a manuscript whose main texts were probably written at the College of St. Bernard in Paris, may have circulated in Paris as well, even though such hockets were severely criticized by Aelred of Rievaux. See Mary Wolinski and Barbara Haggh, "Two Thirteenth-Century Hockets on *Manere* Recovered," *Early Music* 38 (2010), 43–57.

Clm 5539, ff. 24–27.[116] The most striking case of this kind is that of the *Musica speculativa* of Jean de Muris, Master of Arts in 1321, which exists in numerous copies, mostly of German or Polish origin.[117] Muris's writings also influenced many Flemish and Italian theorists.[118] Other foreigners who studied in Paris and later wrote about their contact with music there included Jan of Jenstein, Adelhard of Bath, Master Gossouin (whose encyclopedia, the *Image du monde*, has a chapter, no. 12, on music), Robert Grosseteste, Robert Kilwardby, and Alan of Lille (who discusses music as part of the seven liberal arts in book III of his *Anticlaudianus*).[119]

Foreign works also traveled to Paris. Sankt Paul im Lavanttal (Austria), Stiftsbibliothek Cod. 264/4, from *ca.* 1394–1400, is a French manuscript including Parisian treatises (works of Muris and of a pupil of Muris, Arnulph of St. Ghislain,[120] as well as part of Franco's *Ars mensurabilis musicae*), but also a *Summa music*e, which Christopher Page places in Würzburg *ca.* 1200.[121]

There were exceptions to the rule of widely diffused treatises in smaller, personal manuscripts. The *Speculum musicae* by Jacobus de Ispania, who arrived in Paris in 1280, had limited diffusion, as far as we know, perhaps because it is an encyclopedic monument, not a university work. Its only source is an Italian manuscript of large size and illuminated, which are unusual features in a theory manuscript.[122] Another unusually large and fastidiously decorated Parisian theory manuscript is Madrid, Fundación Lazaro Galdiano Inv. 15554, measuring 353 x 263 mm., with the treatise of Bartholomeus Anglicus. It was illuminated by the Atelier of Paris "Maestro of 1402" and belonged to the Duke of Berry before it traversed Europe and eventually arrived in Madrid.[123]

This evidence also points to the important role of the private study and

[116] See RISM 1:122 and RISM 6:224 (ParisBN lat. 15139 from the Augustinian abbey of St. Victor), and RISM 3:91–94 and RISM 6:328 (Munich, Bayerische Staatsbibliothek clm 5539, origin Regensburg, provenance Augustinians of Diessen).

[117] Elżbieta Witkowska-Zaremba, *Musica Muris and [the] Speculative Trend in the Medieval Musicography*, Studia Copernicana 32 (Warsaw: Polska Akademia Nauk, 1992).

[118] Carpenter, *Music in the Medieval and Renaissance Universities*, 66–68. She observes that Coussemaker's Anonymous V calls Muris by name and then "magister meus."

[119] Carpenter, *Music in the Medieval and Renaissance Universities*, 49–55.

[120] We now know that St. Ghislain near Mons was the birthplace of the composer Johannes Ockeghem *ca.* 1410.

[121] *Summa musice. A Thirteenth-Century Manual for Singers*, ed. and trans. Christopher Page (Cambridge: Cambridge University Press, 1991; paperback ed. 2007), 12.

[122] Karen Desmond, "Behind the Mirror: Revealing the Contexts of Jacobus's *Speculum musicae*" (PhD dissertation, New York University, 2009), 5–6 and 20–24 on his stay in Paris.

[123] RISM 5:88–89; RISM 6:685.

teaching of music theory in the shadow of the university, and to personal book ownership. Books owned by Philippe de Vitry and Johannes de Muris have been identified, for example.[124] Of interest here is Reims, Bibliothèque municipale Ms. 1092, a copy of Papias's *Elementarium*, which Andrew Wathey identified as belonging to Philippe de Vitry and having glosses by him. It was in the library of the convent of St. Jacques in Paris before Vitry acquired it, whereafter it stayed in Paris into the early fifteenth century.[125] Jerome of Moray cited a definition of *celeuma* (song of sailors) from either a *Papias* or a *Liber glossarum*,[126] and could conceivably have used the Papias at St. Jacques before Vitry acquired it. Also owned by Vitry was BAV Ottoboni lat. 1521, an early fourteenth-century copy of a thirteenth-century commentary on Aristotle's *Libri naturales*.[127] The books belonging to Johannes de Muris also include his handwriting. One manuscript, now Escorial O.II.10, includes on f. 225v a list of books that were loaned to Philippe de Vitry: Muris's own *Commentum super musicam* (a commentary on Boethius's *De musica*?) and Hugh of St. Victor's *Didascalicon*. Near the end of the list one can read, "Dominus J. de Navarra[128] habet [. . .] in papiro de fructibus numerorum," that is, Muris's treatise, *Quadripartitum numerorum*.[129] An anonymous musician's personal compilation of slightly later date is the so-called "Berkeley Manuscript," written with care in Paris.[130] The third treatise in the compilation, which is on mensural notation, is dated 1375 and attributed to Goscalcus of Paris by the scribe of the manuscript. A treatise on instruments in the same manuscript may be the work of the composer, Jean Vaillant, according to Christopher Page.[131]

[124] See Andrew Wathey, "Philippe de Vitry's Books," in *Books and Collectors, 1200–1700, Essays Presented to Andrew Watson*, ed. James P. Carley and Colin G. C. Tite (London: British Library, 1997), 145–52, and Lawrence Gushee, "Jehan de Murs and his Milieu," in *Musik- und die Geschichte der Philosophie und Naturwissenschaften im Mittelalter: Fragen zur Wechselwirkung von'musica' und 'philosophia' im Mittelalter*, ed. Frank Hentschel (Leiden: Brill, 1998), 339–71, especially 352–60 on Muris's books, of which some have his handwriting in them.

[125] Wathey, "Philippe de Vitry's Books," 149. The manuscript was acquired by a graduate of the University of Paris who became *scholarius* in Reims in 1421 and bequeathed it to that cathedral's library in 1461.

[126] Cserba, *Hieronymus*, 154, line 11, and observation made by Michel Huglo.

[127] Wathey, "Philippe de Vitry's Books," 149.

[128] An unidentified individual, not Muris, since Muris has written the list.

[129] Wathey, "Philippe de Vitry's Books," 150; L'Huillier, *Le Quadripartitum numerorum*, 11.

[130] RISM 5:466–71.

[131] Berkeley, University of California Music Library, ms. 744 (*olim* Phillipps 4450): RISM 4:142–44 and RISM 6:724. The treatises are edited in Oliver B. Ellsworth, *The Berkeley Manuscript: University of California Music Library, ms. 744 (olim Phillipps 4450)* (Lincoln:

MUSICIANS READ BOETHIUS AND ARISTOTLE

Returning to the University of Paris, in the mid-thirteenth century, two important events changed how the quadrivium was taught: the Statutes of the Faculty of Arts dated 19 March 1255, and the appearance of the mathematical works by Jordanus of Nemours around 1260.[132] The statutes of 1215 had forbidden university teachers to lecture on Aristotle's *Metaphysics* and natural philosophy or on commentaries of them,[133] but this changed with the statutes that were promulgated as the quarrels about the translations of Aristotle's treatises into Latin were being resolved.[134] They prescribed the minimum time to be assigned to the teaching of Boethius's *Logica vetus*, the grammarian Priscian's *Institutiones*, Aristotle's *Logica nova* and *Libri naturales*, and some ten other minor treatises. There is no question of the teaching of music in these statutes, probably because the *Problemata physica*, 11: *De voce* and 19: *De harmonia*, which were attributed to Aristotle in the third century, were only translated by Bartholomew of Messina several years after the Statutes were proclaimed. They arrived in Padua *ca.* 1280 and only later in Paris.[135] Indeed, Joseph Dyer recently concluded that although quadrivial music was part of the educational program of the liberal arts, notably Boethius, music had no official place in the instructional program of the university of Paris — no place in the magisterial lecture or the formal academic dispute.[136]

University of Nebraska Press, 1984). Carpenter, *Music in the Medieval and Renaissance Universities*, 53 notes that Vaillant "tenoit a Paris escolle de musique." See also Christopher Page, "Fourteenth-Century Instruments and Tuning: A Treatise by Jean Vaillant (Berkeley Ms. 744)," *The Galpin Society Journal* 33 (1980), 17–35.

[132] Listed in Weijers, *Le travail intellectuel*, 192–96.

[133] Dyer, "Speculative 'Musica,'" 183–85; See Leonard Johnston, trans. of Fernand Van Steenberghen, *Aristotle in the West. The Origins of Latin Aristotelianism* , 2nd ed. (Louvain: Nauwelaerts, 1970), 66–77. A useful table of the dates of medieval Latin translations of works by Aristotle and Pseudo-Aristotelian works is found in Bernard G. Dod, "Aristoteles latinus," in *The Cambridge History of Later Medieval Philosophy*, ed. Norman Kretzmann, Anthony Kenny, and Jan Pinborg (Cambridge: Cambridge University Press, 1982), 45–79, at 74–79.

[134] On the 1255 statutes, see Michel Huglo, "The Study of Ancient Sources of Music Theory in the Medieval University" (trans. Fabian Lochner), in *Music Theory and its Sources*, ed. André Barbera, (Notre Dame, Ind.: University of Notre Dame Press, 1990), 150–72, especially 152–58.

[135] F. Alberto Gallo, "Greek Text and Latin Translations of the Aristotelian *Musical Problems*: A Preliminary Account of the Sources," in *Music Theory and its Sources. Antiquity and the Middle Ages*, ed. André Barbera (Notre Dame, Ind.: University of Notre Dame, 1987), 190–96, including a list of manuscript sources of the Greek and Latin versions.

[136] Dyer, "Speculative 'Musica,'" 202–4.

The exceptional use of Boethius's *Musica* by musicians must be remembered. In Paris, as in Chartres and later in Oxford, the teaching of Boethius's *De institutione musica* was limited to the first two books, which are less complex than the last three.[137] Jacobus de Montibus explains that he made his compilation, the monumental seven-book *Speculum musicae*, by sometimes excerpting or abbreviating, or supplementing texts from Boethius, because he was afraid he might forget what he had learned from it while a student in Paris. In his treatise, he writes that he "heard" Boethius in Paris.[138] Muris also used Boethius, as we mentioned elsewhere.

Even if the statutes make no mention of music, the writings of Aristotle were clearly read by music theorists. Jean de Muris, in his *Notitia artis musicae* from 1319 or 1321, begins his prologue by naming Aristotle the "prince of philosophers."[139] Claire Maître, using the *Lexicon musicum latinum*, identified 207 citations from Aristotle and 30 mentions of the philosopher in Latin music theory from 1260–1500.[140] Most writers on mensural music in the late thirteenth century were influenced by Aristotle, for example. The *Musica* of Johannes de Grocheio of *ca.* 1300 was modeled on Albert the Great's edition of Aristotle's monumental *De animalibus*.[141]

Musicians especially read Aristotle's *Problemata*, a work divided into twenty-seven sections, each section consisting of a list of questions under a particular topic. Sections 11 on the voice and 19 on *harmonia* are the only sections exclusively on music. Nevertheless, musicians also cited the others. Cited nine times is Problem 18 ("the taste for letters"); twice is Problem 13 ("bad odors"), and only once are Problems 3 ("the use of wine and drunkenness"), 10 ("summary of natural science"), 17 ("living beings"), 21 ("wheat, les pâtes etc."), 28, and 32. It is

[137] Christian Meyer, "Un abrégé universitaire des deux premiers livres du *De institutione musica* de Boèce," *Archives d'histoire doctrinale et littéraire du Moyen Age* 65 (1998), 91–121. On the reception of Boethius, see Dyer, "Speculative 'Musica;'" 179, 180, 187, 190–204; and Bell, "Readings," Cf. Calvin M. Bower, "The Role of Boethius' *De institutione musica* in the Speculative Tradition of Western Musical Thought," in *Boethius and the Liberal Arts: A Collection of Essays*, ed. Michael Masi (Bern: Lang, 1981), 157–74.

[138] Desmond, "Behind the Mirror," 6, note 10, and 313.

[139] See Lawrence Gushee's review of Christoph Falkenroth, *Die "Musica speculativa" des Johannes de Muris* in *Music & Letters* 76 (1995), 275–80, at 275.

[140] Claire Maître, "La place d'Aristote dans l'enseignement de la musique à l'Université de Paris," in *L'enseignement des disciplines à la Faculté des Arts (Paris et Oxford, XIIIe et XVe siècles)*, ed. Olga Weijers and Louis Holtz (Turnhout: Brepols, 1997), 217–33, and the review by Isabelle Draelants in *Scriptorium* 55 (2001), 206*, no. 450.

[141] John Haines, "Proprietas and Perfectio in Thirteenth-Century Music Theory," *Theoria* 15 (2008), 5–29, at 6.

surprising that the theorists do not cite Problems 11 ("On the voice"), 15 ("questions concerning mathematics"), or, especially, 19 ("about harmonics").

Three versions of the *Problemata* are known, but only two survive in Parisian manuscripts. The first version, that of Bartholomew of Messina (1258–1266), was used by Engelbert of Admont during his studies in Padua from 1271 to 1281.[142] This version, which quickly reached Paris, survives in the thirteenth-century ParisBN lat. 16633, which Gérard d'Abbeville bequeathed to the Sorbonne.[143] The second version is that of George de Trébizonde (1452–1454). Only one of its many manuscript sources is Parisian, ParisBN lat. 6328. The third version is that of Theodore Gaza, a contemporary of George of Trebizonde, but no French manuscripts survive. Finally, a commentary on the *Problemata* was written by Pietro d'Abano at the University of Padua in 1310. His text was brought to the University of Paris by Marsilius of Padua, where it was revised by Jean de Jandun. It survives in ParisBN manuscripts lat. 6540, 6541, 6541A, 6543, 6740, to which one must add ParisBN lat. 15454 of the fifteenth century.[144] The eleven manuscripts with Jean de Jandun's text include Paris, Bibliothèque de l'Arsenal 723; Paris, Bibliothèque Mazarine 3520; and ParisBN lat. 6542.

THOMAS AQUINAS READS PLATO'S TIMAEUS

While Aristotle represented the avant-garde of the time, Plato still continued to be read, especially the *Timaeus*, as we have seen from the numerous manuscripts of this work and its commentaries in Paris not to mention Chartres. Most interesting is the evidence we have of a request that Thomas Aquinas write a commentary on Plato's *Timaeus*. On Wednesday, 2 May 1274, the Faculty of Arts of the University of Paris wrote to the General Chapter of the

[142] Pia Ernstbrunner, *Der Musiktraktat des Engelbert von Admont* (Tutzing: Schneider, 1998), who lists citations of the *Problemata* from Admont, Benediktinerstift, Cod. 345 (f. 79 ff.).

[143] Former shelfmarks "ZS" and "NZ 7" (on the back cover); "850," with the "wheel" of the stamp of the Sorbonne (f. 1); "1205" (f. 1v). Estimated cost of borrowing: 30 solidi. This manuscript is described in the third Sorbonne catalogue listing the chained books in the *parva libraria* of the Sorbonne as attached to bench AD (Delisle, *Le Cabinet*, vol. 3, 79: "Probleumata Aristotelis et liber de coloribus"). In the fourth catalogue, there is mention of a "Liber ejusdem de problematibus, habens particulas [gatherings?] xxxviij [with incipit:] *Propter quid magnae superhabundancie egritudinales*" (Delisle, *Le Cabinet*, vol. 3, 83, first column at AD.b.). This was not necessarily ParisBN lat. 16633, because the chained books do not always reappear in the new classification made in 1338. Gallo, "Greek Text," 195–96, lists fifty manuscripts of the first version of the *Problemata*, but George Lacombe et al., *Aristoteles latinus: Codices* (Rome: Libreria dello Stato, 1939–61), cites sixty manuscripts (vol. 2, 1345).

[144] See Gallo, "Medieval Latin Translations," Christian Meyer is preparing an edition of Book 19, *De harmonia*.

Dominicans, which was to take place in Lyon during the Octave of Pentecost. In their letter, they asked:

> Ceterum sperantes quod obtemperetis nobis cum effectu in hac petitione devota humiliter supplicamus ut quaedam scripta ad philosophiam spectantia, Parisius inchoata ab eo, quae in suo recessu reliquerit imperfecta, et ipsum credamus, ubi translatus fuerat, complevisse, nobis benivolencia vestra cito communicari procuret, (et specialiter commentum Simplicii super librum *de celo et mundo*, et **expositionem Timei Platonis**, ac librum *De aquarum conductibus* et ingeniis erigendis) de quibus nobis mittendis speciali promissione fecerat mentionem. Si qua similiter ad logicam pertinentia composuit—sicut quando recessit a nobis humiliter petivimus ab eodem—ea vestra benignitas nostro communicare collegio dignetur.[145] (*emphasis ours*)

> Finally, hoping that you will effectively follow up on this pious request, we ask you humbly to send us as soon as is possible by your benevolence several writings concerning the philosophy begun by him [Thomas] in Paris, but remaining unfinished because of his departure [for Naples] which nevertheless in our opinion he must have finished there: especially the commentary of Simplicius on the *De caelo et mundo* [of Aristotle], and **the exposition on Plato's *Timaeus***, as well as the book [of Archimedes] on water conduits and engines for lifting, which he [Thomas] had mentioned to us with the formal promise to send it. If similarly he has composed something pertaining to logic—as we had humbly asked him to do when he left us—would your kindness deign to communicate it to our college?[146]

[145] This letter is published in Benedictus M. Reichert, *Litterae encyclicae magistrorum generalium Ordinis Praedicatorum ab anno 1233 usque ad annum 1376* (Rome-Stuttgart: LX Typographia Polyglotta, 1900), 104–6, no. XXVIII-*bis* (see Michel Huglo, "L'étude des diagrammes d'harmonique de Calcidius au Moyen Âge," *Revue de musicologie* 91 [2005], 319, note 45) and in Henri Denifle and Émile Chatelain, *Chartularium universitatis parisiensis*, 4 vols. (Paris: Delalain, 1889–97), vol. 1, 505, no. 447, cited here after Pierre-Marie Gy, "Le *Tractatus de musica* de Jérôme de Moravie et le commentaire de saint Thomas sur le *De caelo et mundo* d'Aristote," in *Jérôme de Moravie un théoricien de la musique dans le milieu intellectuel parisien du XIIIe siècle*, ed. Christian Meyer (Paris: Créaphis, 1992), 75–81, at 77.

[146] Authors' translation.

Thomas had left Paris for Naples after Easter Sunday in 1272, promising the students and masters of the Arts Faculty to complete his commentary on Aristotle's *De caelo et mundo* and on the commentary of Simplicius on it, which had been translated by brother William of Moerbeke, bishop of Corinth, and completed on 15 June 1271. In fact, Thomas never finished this commentary, no doubt for lack of time. It ends at the beginning of book three. The projects on which he worked in Naples that were collected after his death by brother Reginald de Piperno were returned to Paris in 1275. Thomas of Aquinas's commentary on *De caelo et mundo* is cited by Jerome of Moray in his *Tractatus de musica*, which reveals at the end a tension between French traditionalists and the foreigners who studied Aristotle.[147]

Thomas had also promised to write a commentary on Plato's *Timaeus* before departing for Naples. The reason why this was asked of him can be explained by the fact that Thomas, in his *questions disputées* as well as in his commentaries on the works of Aristotle, notably *De caelo et mundo* and *De anima*, explicitly cited Plato's *Timaeus* more than thirty times[148] and mentioned the ideas of Plato and the positions of the Platonists in his diverse writings more than eight hundred times.[149] This impressive number of citations results from Thomas's necessary separation of the theories of Plato as they were discussed by Aristotle from his own refutation of the philosopher's thought in his lectures.[150] For example, in Thomas's *question disputée* on the *De anima* of Aristotle, which was to be commented on at the Faculty of Arts for thirty-one to thirty-six weeks,[151] regarding the matter of "harmony, the soul of the world," that is, of the source of the ordered movement of the universe, Thomas summarizes:

> Ita et *Timaeus* qui introducitur a Platone loquens, assignat rationem qualiter anima movet corpus . . . Plato haec verba quae hic ponuntur

[147] On this last observation, see Gy, "Le *Tractatus*," 80.

[148] Roberto Busa, *Index Thomisticus* (Stuttgart-Bad Cannstatt: Frommann-Holzboog, 1974–80), vol. 8, 729. We are most grateful to brother Innocent Smith, O.P., of the Dominican *studium* in Washington, D.C., for helping us with this research on the works of St. Thomas.

[149] Busa, *Index Thomisticus*, vol. 17, 334–39.

[150] Cf. George S. Claghorn, *Aristotle's Criticism of Plato's Timaeus* (The Hague: Nijhoff, 1954).

[151] See the table showing the minimum amount of time to be spent on the works of Aristotle and others, following the Statute of the Arts Faculty of the University of Paris of 19 March 1255, in Michel Huglo, *La théorie de la musique antique et médiévale* (Aldershot: Ashgate, 2005), article 13, 37.

> in *Timaeo* prosequitur loquens de anima mundi . . . Plato dixit quod anima erat composita numeris harmonicis.[152]

> Thus, *Timaeus* was introduced by Plato saying that he assigns a reason for which the soul animates the body. . . Plato follows these words expressed in this way in *Timaeus* by speaking of the soul of the world. . . . Plato said that the soul was composed of harmonic numbers.

In these three short citations, Thomas's students could easily recognize Plato's meaning even without his words: in the *Timaeus*, Socrates (29d)[153] and not Plato invites Timaeus to present his theory of the creation of the material world and of the soul of the world, this soul being the principle of the ordered movement of the body (34a), because it was composed of the numbers creating harmonic proportions, the *numeri harmonici* (35b–36b).[154] It is precisely Plato's notion of movement expressed in *Timaeus* that Aristotle criticizes in his *De anima*.[155] But Thomas returns to this point later in the same lesson (lesson 7, 95). Having briefly commented, according to Boethius,[156] on the legend of the discovery of Pythagoras observing the sounds produced by the hammers of the blacksmith with the proportional weights of 6, 8, 9, and 12, Thomas returns to Plato in these terms:

> Plato dixit quod anima erat harmonia numerorum [. . .] Posuit enim ex his numeris animam constitutum [esse], scilicet I, II, III, IV, VIII,

[152] These three passages are taken from lessons 7 and 9 in *Sancti Thomae Aquinatis in Aristotelis librum De anima commentarium*, ed. Angelo M. Pirotta (Turin: Marietti, 1959), nos. 91, 92, and 136.

[153] See J.H. Waszink, *Timaeus a Calcidio translatus* (London: Warburg Institute, 1975), 22 (29d), 26 (34a), and 27–30 (35b–36b). In the version of the *Timaeus* translated by Cicero, the names (or their initials) of the participants in the dialogue are always omitted. See Marcus Tullius Cicero, *De divinatione, De fato, Timaeus*, ed. Remo Giomini. (Leipzig: Teubner, 1975).

[154] The expression *numeri harmonici,* which replaced the *numeri musici* in the fourteenth century, comes from the treatise *De anima* (I, 8), which is edited by Antonio Jannone and Edmond Barbotin, *Aristote, De l'âme* (Paris: Les Belles Lettres, 2002), 14.

[155] Aristotle, *De l'âme*, I, 8 and I, 14. In a footnote, the editors note that the psychology of Timaeus at 34ff. is understood by Aristotle with extreme literalism (100 and 114, note 1).

[156] Without commentary, Thomas cites Boethius, *De institutione musica*, I, 10, which is copied in its entirety in chapter 3 of Jerome of Moray's *Tractatus de musica*. See *Anicii Manlii Torquati Severini Boetii De institutione arithmetica libra duo: De institutione musica libri quinque: accedit geometria quae fertur Boetii*, ed. Gottfried Friedlein (Frankfurt: Minerva, 1966), 196–97, and *Hieronymus de Moravia. Tractatus de musica*, ed. Simon M. Cserba (Regensburg: Pustet, 1935), 14–16.

> IX, XXVII, in quibus huiusmodi proportiones inveniuntur (Lesson 7, 96). Plato dixit quod anima erat composita numeris harmonicis (Lesson 9, 139). Non enim anima potest dici harmonia (*ibid.*).
>
> Plato said that the soul of the world is a numerical *harmonia* [. . .] It is established thus that the soul was constituted by [certain] numbers, that is to say 1, 2, 3, 4, 8, 9, 27, in which are found the proportions of this kind [3/2, 4/3, 9/8 etc]. Plato said that the soul was composed of harmonic numbers. Truly, one cannot say that the soul can be called harmony.

Thomas here makes mention of the numbers of the *psychogonia* (*Timaeus*, 35–36b; Waszink, 27–30), which are illustrated by the lambdoid diagram found in Latin manuscripts. In the commentary to *De caelo et mundo*, begun in Paris and continued in Naples in 1272, but left unfinished, Thomas of Aquinas cited the *Timaeus* again in the same terms. In Thomas's critical commentaries of Plato's ideas, always expressed with serene objectivity, he could not clash with the traditional French students attached to the study of the *Timaeus* with its glosses and commentaries.

One should ask if Thomas of Aquinas read the *Timaeus* in one of its numerous exemplars that had circulated in the twelfth century, or if he had known it indirectly through the commentaries of Aristotle translated into Latin. In any case, the value of Thomas's explanations of the *Timaeus* led the masters of arts of the university to ask him before his departure for Naples to write a new commentary on the *Timaeus*, which Thomas accepted, but never finished. Nevertheless, we know the tenor of what he would have written, thanks to his numerous remarks dispersed in the *questions disputées* and in his commentaries, such as ParisBN lat. 15078 (see Appendix 1, Table D1), f. 30r, where a brief note appears next to the diagram with three superimposed lambdas: "Quia Plato animam ad similitudinem numerorum disposuit." ("Because Plato presented the soul by showing its resemblance to numbers.") Similar remarks are found in ParisBN lat. 16579, bequeathed to the Sorbonne by Gérard of Abbeville;[157] BAV Reg. lat. 1107, of French origin and use of St. Victor of Paris; and BAV Vat. lat. 3815, of French origin.[158]

[157] Bakhouche, "Marginalia et histoire du texte," 157–77.

[158] See Michel Huglo, "Recherches," 223–26.

JEWISH AND ARABIC WRITINGS, MATHEMATICS AND MUSIC

An increasing interest in arithmetic, and notably the question of proportions, was due to the writings of Jordanus of Nemours from *ca.* 1260[159] and to the translations of Arabic treatises on arithmetic and astronomy.[160] These had as much influence on practice as on theory; thus, the use of Arabic numbers in scientific treatises[161] now reached the workshops where manuscripts were copied by *pecia* more rapidly: increasingly, the quaternions were signed with Arabic numerals. Pierre de Limoges (d. 1307) used Arabic numerals to annotate the *Musica* by Jérôme de Moray, though this was not a *pecia* manuscript.[162] Anonymous IV, a student in Paris in the second quarter of the thirteenth century, in describing the two forms of lozenge employed to notate *currentes*, used the Arabic terms *elmuahim* and *elmuarifa* from the translation of the Euclid's *Elements* into Latin that was attributed to Adalard of Bath of the twelfth century, a source Anonymous IV could have found in the Sorbonne library, now ParisBN lat. 16201.[163] He was also indebted to Jordanus of Nemours's *Arithmetic*.[164] Jerome of Moray, at the beginning of his *Musica*, cites the definition of music of Al-Farabi.[165] But the influence of Arabic thought on the development of Parisian music theory stops there.

[159] The treatise of Jourdain de Nemours, *De elementis arithmeticae artis*, was written *ca.* 1260 and offered to the Sorbonne by the author: see Delisle, *Le Cabinet*, vol. 3, 68 (no. 31 is ParisBN lat. 16644) and 88 (column one, B.b.), *Jordanus de Nemore. De Elementis Arithmeticae artis, A Medieval Treatise on Number Theory*, ed. Hubert L. L. Busard, 2 vols. (Stuttgart: Franz Steiner, 1991), reviewed by Michel Huglo in *Scriptorium* 48 (1994), no. 56, 17*–18*. Busard's critical edition is based on 25 manuscripts, of which two were written in Paris, ParisBN lat. 7364 and ParisBN lat. 16644 (Sorbonne 1758, gift of Gérard d'Abbeville). See also Hubertus L. L. Busard, "Die Traktate *De Proportionibus* von Jordanus de Nemore und Campanus," *Centaurus* 15 (1970), 193–227, and Ron B. Thomson, "Jordanus de Nemore: Opera," *Medieval Studies* 38 (1976), 97–144.

[160] At the same time at the University of Paris the teaching of the quadrivium and of mathematics declined. See Dyer, "Speculative 'Musica,'" 185–86.

[161] Richard Lemay, "The Hispanic Origin of Our Present Numerical Forms," *Viator* 8 (1977), 435–562, with fifteen plates of university manuscripts.

[162] See note 114 above.

[163] Charles Burnett, "The Use of Geometrical Terms in Medieval Music: *Elmuahim* and *Elmuarifa* and the Anonymous IV," *Sudhoffs Archiv* 70 (1986), 198–205. ParisBN lat. 16201 is described in Appendix 1, Table E.

[164] See *Der Musiktraktat des Anonymus IV*, ed. Fritz Reckow (Wiesbaden: Steiner, 1967), 64, at "Unitas est discretio rei per se [. . .]."

[165] Cserba, *Hieronymus*, 9.

One Jewish mathematician's work known at the College de Navarre was more widely distributed, that of Leo Hebraeus, better known as Levi ben Gerson, on the subject of *De numeris harmonicis*, written in 1343 at the request of Philippe de Vitry.[166] Philippe asked Leo to verify that of all of the "harmonic numbers," only the ratios 1/2, 2/3, 3/4, and 8/9 differ in their numerators and denominators by one number, which Leo could prove.

A concern with fractions is exhibited in another work dating from the same year, Johannes de Muris's *Quadripartitum numerorum*, which includes a lengthy four-part epistle in dactylic hexameters throughout, which is addressed to Philippe de Vitry.[167] Although the epistle has been neglected in musicological scholarship, since it concerns mathematics, it contributes to biographical evidence showing Johannes de Muris's respect for the elder Vitry. Most of the *Quadripartitum* is on fractions and is based on *l'Algorismus minutiarum* of Jean de Lignères and on the text of ParisBN lat. 15461.[168] The first of four parts is a short treatise on speculative arithmetic based on Boethius's *Arithmetic* and Euclid's *Elements*;[169] the second part is on practical arithmetic (operations) and presents an introduction to fractions; the third part is concerned with proportions and algebra. At this point, Muris read the *Liber abaci* of Leonard of Pisa (Fibonacci), which prompted him to write a *Semiliber* inspired by the work, and *Questiones* on problems of algebra. Only then did he finish the fourth and final part of the *Quadripartitum*, on diverse subjects and inspired by the *Liber abaci*. Muris intended to include questions on the theme of "*De*

[166] Christian Meyer and Jean-François Wicker, "Musique et mathématique au XIVe siècle. Le De *numeris harmonicis* de Leo Hebraeus [=Levi ben Gerson]," *Archives internationales d'histoire des sciences* 50 (2000), 30–67, at 36–37. Meyer includes an edition based on two surviving manuscripts, of which one is the Parisian ParisBN lat. 7378A, ff. 55v–57v. See also Wolf Frobenius, "Levi ben Gerson," in *Die Musik in Geschichte und Gegenwart*, second edition *Personenteil* (Kassel: Bärenreiter, 1994–2007), with further bibliography; and Frobenius, "*Numeri harmonici.* Die Zahlen der Timaios-Skala in der Mathematik des 14. Jh.," in *Kontinuität und Transformation der Antike im Mittelalter*, ed. W. Erzgräber (Sigmaringen: Thorbecke, 1989), 245–60.

[167] We are grateful to Leofranc Holford-Strevens, who kindly agreed to translate the first part of this very lengthy letter at our request (see Appendix 2), to Shin Nishimagi for consulting the Parisian sources of the letter, and to Christian Meyer for providing bibliography.

[168] L'Huillier, *Le Quadripartitum numerorum*, 47.

[169] There are references to music at the beginning of this part. See L'Huillier, *Le Quadripartitum numerorum*, 136–37.

sonis musicis" in this part, but that text has not been found and is not part of the otherwise completely transmitted *Quadripartitum*.[170]

The epistle to Vitry was initially noticed by Léopold Delisle, who brought it to Coussemaker's attention, but Coussemaker only edited its first four lines, dismissing it as a short treatise on number.[171] It is listed separately among the works by Muris in an early twentieth-century edition of the *Grove Dictionary of Music and Musicians*,[172] but subsumed under the title of the *Quadripartitum* in the present editions of *Oxford Music Online* and *MGG*. It is discussed briefly by Ulrich Michels.[173] Finally, it was edited fully as part of the treatise it once accompanied by Ghislaine L'Huillier.[174]

L'Huillier concluded that Muris wrote the letter when the treatise was nearly finished; it was completed in 1343 at Mezières-en-Brenne. Muris himself dates the treatise to November 13, 1343. The reference to Vitry as bishop of Meaux, which formerly suggested a date of 1351, is found only in ParisBN lat. 14736, the main source for L'Huillier's edition, but there it is a later addition.[175] L'Huillier places the letter before the fourth part of the *Quadripartitum*, as does the Paris manuscript. Part one of Muris's letter to Vitry, for which an English translation by Leofranc Holford-Strevens is given as Appendix 2, gives a list of operations and then discusses the extraction of rational and irrational square roots, then the square root of two determined by using zeros, then the extraction of rational and irrational cubic roots by using zeros. Next, he explains the origin, addition, subtraction, multiplication, and division of fractions, then the extraction of square roots of fractions. Finally, the last three sections explore algebra in operations of multiplication and division, and a great variety of

[170] L'Huillier, *Le Quadripartitum numerorum*, 14.

[171] Edmond de Coussemaker, *Scriptorum de musica medii aevi* (Hildesheim: Olms, 1963), vol. 3, IX.

[172] *Grove Dictionary of Music and Musicians*, 4 vols. and *American Supplement*, ed. John Alexander Fuller-Maitland et al. (London: Macmillan, 1904–20), vol. 2, 320.

[173] Ulrich Michels, *Die Musiktraktate des Johannes de Muris* (Wiesbaden: Franz Steiner Verlag, 1970), 13 and note 52.

[174] L'Huillier, *Le Quadripartitum numerorum*, 89–133 (edition), 12–14 (discussion), and 601–3 (summary).

[175] L'Huillier, *Le Quadripartitum numerorum*, 8 and 13. Andrew Wathey, "Philippe de Vitry's Books," 146–47, notes that part of an unidentified letter addressed to Vitry as bishop of Meaux survives in scraps pasted to BAV Reg. lat. 544, but from the bits of words Wathey has transcribed, this seems to be a different letter.

equations.[176] The concern with ratios and fractions in these works of 1343 by Leo Hebraeus and Johannes de Muris corresponds to interest among musicians in the topics of how breves and tones should be divided.

Numbers are again considered by Johannes Boen, who, in 1358, using a "beautiful tablet" (*tabula pulchra*) he discovered at the College of Navarre, discussed this series of *numeri harmonici*, including the ratio 81/64 for the major third 5/4, in order to safeguard the Pythagorian edifice of *musica ex numeris* in its entirety.[177]

THE CALENDAR AND TOPOGRAPHY OF TEACHING

All of these late medieval treatises situated in the Parisian university milieu prompt us to indulge in some more precise topographical research. For example, if indeed authors, such as Jean de Muris, did teach in well-known colleges such as the Sorbonne or the College of Navarre, one should ask where its Faculty of Arts was situated, with the same question for the Faculty of Law and the Faculty of Theology. The question is not pointless, because in reading the calendar of courses that was distributed to all of the university colleges, one observes that on the days of major feasts, classes were suspended (*non legitur*) in all of the colleges, but on the days of minor feasts, classes were only suspended in certain colleges. The colleges are not named in this document, but—and this is what is of interest—their locations are often given, as Table 1 (next page) reports.

[176] L'Huillier, *Le Quadripartitum numerorum*, 601–3.

[177] Meyer and Wicker, "Musique et mathématique," 36–37.

Table 1. Paris, Bibliothèque Sainte-Geneviève Ms. 1655, Calendar from the "Livre de la Nation de Picardie" at the University of Paris[178]

1. 6. 22. 25. I: 22. VII etc.	Non legitur in aliqua Facultate.
3. I	Non legitur in theologia, nec in decretis; tamen legitur in aliis.
5. I; 7. IX; 24. XI; 5. XII	Non legitur ultra tertiam in vico Straminis, nec in nonis Nostrae Dominae in vico Brunelli.
8. I	Hac die reincipiunt ordinarie[179] magistri in vico Straminis
17. 20. I; 3. II; 15. V etc:	Non legitur in vico Brunelli: legitur tamen in aliis.
30. IV	*Petri Jacobitae et martyris*: Non legitur in aliqua facultate, excepto in vico Straminis ubi tunc legitur cursorie. Et eodem die fit sermo in Jacobitis.
25. VI	*Eligii Noviomensis episcopi*: Non legitur in vico Straminis, nec in vico Brunelli: in aliis tamen legitur.
11. VII	*Translatio sancti Benedicti*: Non legitur in theologia, nec in vico Brunelli: legitur tamen in aliis.
20. VIII	*Bernardi abbatis*: non legitur in aliqua Facultate. Eodem fit sermo in Bernardinis.
27. IX	*Cosmae et Damiani martyrum*: Festive. Et non legitur in decretis in vico Brunelli: legitur tamen in decretalibus.
1. X	*Remigii archiepiscopi*
8. XI	*Mathurini confessoris*: Eodem die legitur cursorie in vico Straminis.
4. XIII	*Sancti Francisci confessoris*: Eodem die non legitur in aliqua Facultate et fit sermo in Cordigeriis [=Franciscans].

From this short excerpt, which should be reconstructed fully as suggested above, one can conclude that the university calendar was closely calibrated with the liturgical calendar of the cathedral of Paris. This relationship is completely normal, given the circumstances of the foundation of the University and of certain colleges, among them that of the Sorbonne. The *nonni*, or poor students attached to the Cathedral of Notre Dame in the thirteenth century, remind us that the books donated to the library of Notre Dame at the beginning of the thirteenth century had been destined in their favor. The *vicus Brunelli*, or small street of the ass, which led directly into the nave of the

[178] Slightly later addition to early fourteenth-century manuscript. Manuscript described in Michel Huglo, *Les manuscrits du processionnal*, vol. 2 (Munich: Henle, 2004), 139, no. F-148/2. The document is transcribed in Denifle and Chatelain, *Chartularium*, vol. 1, 2–11.

[179] *Ordinaria* designates a lesson given by a master, and *cursoria* (27.I; 30.IV; 1.X etc.) a lesson given by a bachelor. On these terms, see Dyer, "Speculative 'Musica,'" 187–89.

Cathedral for the celebrations of the Feast of Fools on the first of January, was thus situated on the Île de la Cité near the cloister of the Cathedral. A more precise study of the calendar and of the cartularies of the University of Paris could determine the location of the *vicus Straminis* (or *ruelle de la Paille*, probably near the *rue de l'Abreuvoir*).[180]

Notice that the calendar also mentions the designated election days for procurators (13. I; 5. V; and 22. IX) and rectors or regents of the different faculties (23. VI and 16. XII). The regent of the Faculty of Arts resided in the college where he taught, as in some Oxford colleges. Wherever these faculties were located, the production of distinguished works in all areas of knowledge during the thirteenth and fourteenth centuries infused Paris with a reputation as an intellectual center of incontestable value.

SECULAR CHURCHES AND OTHER SMALL LIBRARIES

Finally, we come to the secular churches in Paris. Although they were numerous by 1400, the evidence for writings on music from their archives is slim. It nevertheless sheds a ray of light on the understanding of music in these environments, because it confirms that issues of performance took precedence over speculative theory. Thus, an inventory of the church of St. Sépulcre in the *grant rue saint Denis*, dated 1 July 1369, in ParisBN fr. 14490, lists a motet book,[181] but nothing more, and we found no other evidence for music theory books in this or any other secular church.[182] Only the 1480 inventory of the books of the Sainte-Chapelle of Paris, within a long list of liturgical books of every kind, includes "unus liber introductorius de plano cantu incipiens 'eccle[sie]' et fin[is] 'Qui l'entendenit.'"[183]

180 We could not consult the *Dictionnaire des rues de Paris* or the card files of the Bibliothèque historique de la Ville de Paris for this project, which would have been useful.

181 ParisBN fr. 14490 is an inventory made of books at the church of St. Sépulcre in Paris on 1 July 1369. Folio 12r (old foliation) reads, "Ce sont les choses que les clers du sepulcre ont en garde et lesquelx clercs en ont un rolle des choses cy dessoubz contenues par maniere dinventoire." The inventory includes on f. 17r, "Item un livre de motez qui commence Et in terra et fenist alle," (and, later, many processionals), and on ff. 22v–23r, "Ce sont pluseurs viez livres [. . .] quy ne sont pas en la garde des diz clers," with liturgical books, followed by a list of the books kept in each side chapel, i.e. missals, many listed as being "sanz note."

182 A thorough search through account books and other archives would be necessary but was not possible for this study.

183 In ParisBN lat. 9941, an inventory of the Sainte-Chapelle made in July 1480, we find on f. 34v four antiphoners "notati de minuta nota," on f. 35v, "Item tres libri prosarum notati [. . .] Item unum aliud gradalle cum prosis," and then amidst these service books the introduction to chant. On medieval chant theory, which Joseph Dyer often finds to be elementary, see his "Chant Theory and Philosophy in the Late Thirteenth Century," in *International*

CONCLUSIONS

More books about music were found in monasteries and colleges than in secular churches. In the former they were classified either by author or among quadrivial texts; they never merited a separate category of "music book." Older popular books had extremely long shelf lives and continued to be collected, even as new copies diminished in number.[184] In 1763, when the library of the City of Paris was augmented by the acquisition of the library of Sir Bonamy, it included manuscripts of Isidore and Martianus Capella.[185] Yet such books were not only valued and kept for posterity, but continued to be used, as the lending registers of the Sorbonne, in particular, show.[186]

While we cannot be surprised at the presence of certain books in Paris throughout the Middle Ages, other absences are notable. There was no copy of *Musica disciplina*, of Hucbald, or of *Alia musica*. Although Guido of Arezzo's treatise survives in dozens of manuscripts and was the most widely disseminated treatise in the Middle Ages after Boethius's *De institutione musica*, only one possibly Parisian copy of his treatise survives.[187] Johannes de Muris is the preferred author of the fourteenth century, but he is more famous as a mathematician and astronomer than as a musician.[188] Philippe de Vitry is not named in the library catalogues.

Our research on this topic, which can only be considered preliminary, has identified many gaping lacunae in our knowledge. First, a surprisingly

Musicological Society Study Group Cantus Planus. Papers Read at the Fourth Meeting, Pécs, Hungary, 3–8 September 1990, ed. László Dobszay et al. (Budapest: Institute for Musicology, Hungarian Academy of Sciences, 1992), 99–118; and cf. Klaus-Jürgen Sachs, "Musikalische Elementarlehre im Mittelalter," in *Rezeption des antiken Fachs im Mittelalter*, ed. Michael Bernhard (Darmstadt: Wissenschaftliche Buchgesellschaft, 1990), 105–61.

[184] See Figure 4 in Huglo, "The Study of Ancient Sources," 167, which compares the number of copies in circulation of Macrobius, Calcidius, Augustine, and Boethius from the ninth to fifteenth century, Huglo observes that the copying of Boethius, Macrobius, and Calcidius declines in the thirteenth century.

[185] Franklin, *Les anciennes bibliothèques*, vol. 3, 225–28.

[186] See the end of the discussion of the Sorbonne library above.

[187] Christian Meyer, "La tradition du Micrologus de *Guy d'Arezzo*. Une contribution à l'histoire du texte," *Revue de musicologie* 83 (1997), 5–31. None of the manuscripts used by Dolores Pesce in her edition are from Paris; see *Guido d'Arezzo's Regule Rithmice, Prologus in Antiphonarium, and Epistola ad Michahelem*, ed. Dolores Pesce, (Ottawa: Institute of Mediaeval Music, 1999), 221–22. Dyer, "Speculative 'Musica,'" 203 notes that the question of Guido's authority never came up in Parisian academic circles. Also see note 64 above.

[188] According to Carpenter, *Music in the Medieval and Renaissance Universities*, 48 and 140, statutes of Guillaume d'Estouteville of 1452 specified that no one was to be admitted *ad licentiam docendi* unless he had heard certain books including *aliquos libros mathematicales*. This same point had been made in statutes of 1366. This may explain the prominence of Muris's mathematical works—they could be used at the university, while his music treatises could not be.

small number of the music theory manuscripts repertoried in RISM have been assessed by paleographers. For many we barely know their country of origin.[189] The possibility of learning more about what was most likely the handwriting of musicians,[190] and hence their skill and education, should be tempting. Second, few theory manuscripts have been subjected to the codicological scrutiny that has informed us about manuscripts of polyphony. Are there significant patterns in compilations of music theory? Who made such compilations and why? Most worthwhile would be a study of punctuation and of glosses or corrections in such manuscripts, since such markings provide valuable evidence of book use or of reading aloud.[191] For manuscripts such as these, which are rarely decorated and often lack "local" characteristics that could situate them, paleography and codicology are tools of fundamental importance.

Whereas much recent work has improved our understanding of the major existing medieval library catalogues, other evidence for book ownership, notably that in wills and in post-mortem inventories, has not been brought together, except in rare publications.[192] This would be an enormous task for Paris, but one with potentially great consequences.

On a positive note, our research has shown that the study of medieval libraries can provide glimpses of medieval scholars at work.[193] We saw, for

[189] For example, see RISM 2:21, 72, 74, 95, and 118 (manuscripts from "France" or "France or Italy") or RISM 2:102 (BAV Barb. lat. 283, with Hugh of St. Victor's *Didascalicon* and an anonymous treatise), for which no place of origin is given at all.

[190] Lawrence Gushee, "Jehan de Murs and his Milieu," in *Musik – und die Geschichte der Philosophie und Naturwissenschaften im Mittelalter. Fragen zur Wechselwirkung von 'musica' und 'philosophia' im Mittelalter*, ed. Frank Hentschel (Leiden: Brill, 1998), 339–71, especially 352–60 on Muris's books, some of which have his handwriting in them. On Muris's handwriting, see L'Huillier, *Le Quadripartitum numerorum*, 46 and Stephen Victor, "Johannes de Muris's autograph in the *De Arte mensurandi* (ms. Paris latin 7380)," *Isis* 61 (1970), 389–95.

[191] On the term "auditor," see Dyer, "Speculative 'Musica,'" 189–90. The term is used by Franco, Petrus Picardus, and Johannes de Grocheio. The latter was a master.

[192] A model study of this kind is *Corpus catalogorum belgii. The Medieval Booklists of the Southern Low Countries*, ed. Albert Derolez et al., 4 vols. (Brussels: Paleis der Academiën, 1994–2001); Haggh discusses personal libraries in late medieval Brussels and provides further bibliography in her "Music, Liturgy, and Ceremony in Brussels, 1350–1500," (PhD dissertation, University of Illinois at Urbana, 1988), 474–81.

[193] We have not discussed citations here, but the relationship of citations to libraries, as opposed to memory, is an important question. See Barbara Haggh, "Aurelian's Library," in *International Musicological Society Study Group Cantus Planus. Papers Read at the 9th Meeting, Esztergom & Visegrád, 1998*, ed. László Dobszay (Budapest: Hungarian Academy of Sciences, Institute for Musicology, 1998), 271–300; and *eadem*, "Ciconia's Citations in *Nova musica*: New Sources as Biography," in *Citation and Authority in Medieval and Renaissance Musical Culture: Learning from the Learned*, ed. Suzannah Clark and Elizabeth Eva Leach (Woodbridge, Suffolk: Boydell & Brewer, 2005), 45–58.

example, how generations of scholars glossed and commented on the same works. We learned from a library catalogue that Johannes de Muris loaned books and wrote a lengthy letter to Philippe de Vitry, evidence of the former's esteem for the latter. And we saw how intellectual trends shaped the collection and use of books. We thus see library holdings taking a central place in the generation of future thought—sometimes conserving outdated ways of thinking, but also *artes novissimas*.

Table A. St. Étienne and Notre Dame II–III

	Cathedral of St. Étienne	Notre Dame II–III
Plato, *Timaeus*	Ms. cited by Abelard (1114–1116)[194]	
Calcidius, Translation and Commentary on *Timaeus*		BAV Reg. lat. 1804, 13th c.; ParisBN lat. 18104, 13th c., signed by Joly
Martianus Capella, *De nuptiis*, IX: *De musica*	ParisBN lat. 8674, 10th c. (glosses by Remigius of Auxerre)	ParisBN lat. 18530, 12th c.
Macrobius, Commentary on Cicero's "Dream of Scipio"		ParisBN lat. 18421, 12th c., signed by Joly
Liber glossarum, entry: *Musica*		ParisBN lat. 11529, 8th or 9th c., offered by Joly in 1680
Papias, *Elementarium*, entry: *Musica*		ParisBN lat. 17162, 13th c. (A–M) & lat. 17879, 13th c. (N–Z)
Isidorus, *Etymologiarum* (vol. 3, 15–23: *Musica*)		ParisBN lat. 17875 (with *De numeris*), end 12th c.; ParisBN lat. 17876, 12th c., with name of Joly
Ps.-Boethius, *De disciplina scolarium*		ParisBN lat. 18424, 14th c.
Leoninus/Leonius, *Hystorie sacre gestas* (Poem on Old Testament)[195]		ParisBN lat. 18559, 13th c., donated by Joly (RISM 1:120; RISM 6:222)

[194] Huglo, "Recherches," 223–24 and 228.

[195] Wright, *Music and Ceremony*, 285–86; *idem*, "Leoninus, Poet and Musician," *Journal of the American Musicological Society* 39 (1986), 1–36, at 16–28.

Table B. Parisian Monasteries on the Right Bank

	Royal Abbey of St. Denis	**Benedictine Abbey of St. Maur-des-Fossés**
Capella, *De nuptiis*	BAV Reg. lat. 309, 9th c. (VIII: *De astronomia* only)	
Macrobius, Commentary	Berlin, Staatsbibliothek Phillipps 1784, 9th c., origin St. Remi of Reims, provenance St. Denis; BAV Reg. lat. 309, 9th c. (excerpts)	
Calcidius, Commentary	Valenciennes, Bibliothèque municipale MS 293, 9th c. (copied at Reims by monks from St. Denis)	
Isidore, *Etymologiae*		Library catalogue, 12th c., no. 49
Tonary	ParisBN lat. 17296, antiphoner *ca.* 1140–50, with added *differentiae* (Robertson, *The Service Books*, 394).	ParisBN lat. 13252, end 11th c., for St. Magloire (Huglo, *Les Tonaires*, 314–15; RISM 1:118; RISM 5:143–44; RISM 6: 218); ParisBN lat. 12584, 12th c. gradual/antiphoner/ tonary (RISM 1:118, RISM 6:217)
Boethius, *De institutione musica*	ParisBN lat. 7199, late-10th c., origin northern Italy, provenance St. Denis, with glosses (RISM 6:185)	ParisBN lat. 7361, *Musica*, 11th or 12th c. (RISM 1:106; RISM 6:198), could be from St. Maur[196]
Guido of St. Denis, *De tonis*[197]	Original lost; later copy, at end of Ms., is LondonBL Harley 281, 14th c. (RISM 4:771, RISM 6: 394)	

[196] Charlotte Denoël, email sent to Michel Huglo, 9 October 2009

[197] Robertson, *The Service-Books*, 334–35.

Table C. On the Left Bank: Abbey of St. Germain-Des-Prés[198]

Isidore, *Etymologiae*	Leiden, Rijksuniversiteit Bibliotheek Voss. lat. F 82[199] early 9th c., Caroline minuscule, origin Paris, at St. Germain-des-Prés by beginning of 10th c; ParisBN lat. 14085, 10th c., from Corbie[200]
Boethius, *De institutione musica*	ParisBN lat. 13020, *ca.* 850–75, from Corbie (RISM 6:218); ParisBN lat. 13908, last third 9th c., from Northern France, then at Corbie (RISM 6:218–19); ParisBN lat. 13955, *ca.* 850–75 to 11th c., from Corbie, with glosses (RISM 1:119; RISM 6:219); ParisBN lat. 14080, *ca.* 850–75, from Corbie, with glosses (RISM 6:220)[201]
Cassiodore, *Institutiones*	ParisBN lat. 12963, first half of 10th c. (Mynors, *Cassiodori*, xxxiii); ParisBN lat. 13048, ff. 59–82, 9th c. (Mynors, *Cassiodori*, xxxiii); ParisBN lat. 12958, last quarter of 9th c., from Corbie[202]
Macrobius, Commentary	Copenhagen, Det Kongelige Bibliotek Slotsholmen Ny kgl. S 218 4°, 11th c., with large diagram of octave plus fifth[203]
Capella, *De nuptiis*, book IX	ParisBN lat. 13026, 9th c. (excerpts); ParisBN lat. 12410, 11th c.; ParisBN lat. 12117, 11th c.
Musica enchiriadis (excerpt)	ParisBN lat. 13955 (see above, Boethius)
Measurements of organ pipes	ParisBN lat. 12949, 9th–13th c., provenance St. Germain-des-Prés (RISM 1:118; RISM 6:217)
De nominibus cordarum [sic] sive tonorum	ParisBN lat. 12958, 9th or 10th c., provenance Corbie (RISM 1:118; RISM 6:218)
Troper with Tonary	ParisBN lat. 13252, second half 9th c., from St. Magloire (RISM 1:118; RISM 6:218)
Treatise on bells, cymbals, and pipes (*fistule*)	ParisBN lat. 14069, 12th c., provenance St. Remi of Reims (RISM 1:119; RISM 6:219–20)

198 Provenance indicated for a manuscript preceded its arrival at St. Germain-des-Prés.

199 Described in E.A. Lowe, *Codices latini antiquiores*, vol. 10 (Oxford: Clarendon Press, 1963), no. 1581; Bernhard Bischoff, *Katalog der festländischen Handschriften des neunten Jahrhunderts*, ed. Birgit Ebersperger (Wiesbaden: Harrassowitz, 2004), vol. 2, no. 2203.

200 Charlotte Denoël, email sent to Michel Huglo, 9 October 2009.

201 On all of these manuscripts, see David Ganz, *Corbie in the Carolingian Renaissance* (Sigmaringen: Thorbecke, 1990), 172–73.

202 Ganz, *Corbie*, 79.

203 Ellen Jørgensen, *Catalogus Codicum Latinorum Medii Ævi Bibliothecæ Regiæ Hafniensis* (Copenhagen: Gyldendals Forlag, 1926), 332.

Table D1. Abbey of St. Victor: Pre-Carolingian Authors[204]

Plato, *Timaeus*	ParisBN lat. 15078, late 12th c., with a diagram copied from a manuscript at St. Denis (see Huglo, "Recherches," 223) [FFF26, O505]; BAV Reg. lat. 1107, early 12th c. [HHH22, O535–36]; ParisBN lat. 15124, second half 12th c. [HHH25, O537–38]; ParisBN lat. 14716, 15th c., glosses on *Timaeus*[205] [LLL15, O582]
Aristotle, *Problemata*[206]	ParisBN lat. 14382, late 13th c. [G12, O60]; ParisBN lat. 14725, 14th c. [LLL7, O578]; ParisBN lat. 15081, 13th c. [LLL8, O579]
Calcidius, Commentary	Lost [HHH26, O538]
Macrobius, Commentary	ParisBN lat. 15170, mid-12th c. (ff. 71–125) [KKK18, O563–64]; lost book [Perd. 15., O631]
Capella, *De nuptiis*	ParisBN lat. 14753, 12th c. (not in Ouy; Delisle, *Inventaire des manuscrits de l'Abbaye de Saint-Victor conservés à la Bibliothèque impériale, sous les numéros 14232–15175 du fonds latin, Paris, Durand et Pedone-Lauriel, 1869,* 46); ParisBN lat. 14754, mid-12th c., with commentary by Remigius of Auxerre [FFF4, O484]
Augustine, *De musica*	ParisBN lat. 14294, late 13th c. [CC5, O199–200]; Paris, Bibliothèque de l'Arsenal 350, mid-15th c. [DD11, O217–18]; ParisBN lat. 14477, mid-13th c. [DD17, O222–23]
Fulgentius[207]	Lost [Perd. 15, O631]
Boethius, *De institutione musica*	Lost [GGG8, O512]
Isidore, *Etymologiae*	ParisBN lat. 14743, late 12th c. [FF3, O237]; ParisBN lat. 15009, late 12th c. [HH6, O260–61]; Bern, Burgerbibliothek Ms. 392, 12th c. [BBB7, O443]; ParisBN lat. 15007, 11th c. [CCC3, O450–51].

[204] In this and the next two tables, manuscript content and current shelfmarks are followed by entries in square brackets identifying its place in the original library, the page number of Ouy's description (O*xxx–yyy*), and page numbers of descriptions in RISM volumes, if the manuscript in question was included in RISM.

[205] On the manuscripts with diagrams, see Michel Huglo, "Recherches," 185–230: 222–23 (ParisBN lat. 15078) and 226 (BAV Reg. lat. 1107).

[206] The editions of the texts concerning music are old: James Green, *Aristotle's Musical Problems: A New Edition with Philological Notes* (Worcester, Mass.: C. Hamilton, 1903); F. A. Gevaert and J. C. Vollgraff, *Les Problèmes musicaux d'Aristote: Texte grec avec traduction française, notes philologiques, commentaire musicale et appendice* (Ghent: A. Hoste, 1903; reprinted Osnabrück: Biblio Verlag, 1977).

[207] On this writer, see Huglo, "Bibliographie des éditions," 237; *Fabii Planciadis Fulgentii V.C. Opera*, ed. Rudolf Helm (Leipzig: Teubner, 1898, reprinted Stuttgart: Teubner, 1970); and the useful annotated bibliography at http://people.virginia.edu/~bgh2n/fulgbib.html, maintained by Gregory Hays.

Table D2. Abbey of St. Victor: Writings by Medieval Musician-Authors

Remigius of Auxerre	Commentary on Martianus Capella's *De nuptiis*: ParisBN lat. 14754, mid-12th c., cf. above [FFF4, O484]
Hermannus Contractus	Especially Paris, Bibliothèque de l'Arsenal 831 [FFF29, O507; MMM19, O599–600], but no treatises on music. Instead: *De astrolabio* [FFF26], *Pars cuiusdam libri astrologiae* [KKK26], *Compotus* [T2], *Ludus rigmachiae [sic]* [FFF29, MMM19].
Raoul of Laon	Treatise on the abacus, then treatise on the semitone:[208] ParisBN lat. 15120, 13th c. [FFF28, O506] (RISM 1:120; RISM 6:222)
Hugh of St. Victor, *Didascalicon*	Paris, Bibliothèque Mazarine 717, *ca.* 1200 [HH1, O256–57]; ParisBN lat. 15009, late 12th c. [HH6, O260–61]
Leoninus/Leonius, *Hystorie sacre gestas* (Poem on Old Testament) and eight of his own poems[209]	ParisBN lat. 14759, 13th c. (Léopold Delisle, *Inventaire des manuscrits de l'Abbaye de Saint-Victor*, Paris, Durand et Pedone-Lauriel, 1869, 47)
Speculum divinorum quod edidit Henricus de Mallinis (Malines/ Mechelen) *quondam cantor leodiensis*	Lost [M5, O98]
Quedam de musica (by Johannes Boen) in which he argues against the Moderns to defend Pythagoras	ParisBN lat. 7371, second half 14th c., origin Paris [GGG11, O514–17] (RISM 6:204)

(Continued next page)

208 This was a much-discussed topic at this time. See Frank Hentschel, "Die Unmöglichkeit der Teilung des Ganztones in zwei gleiche Teile und der Gegenstand der musica sonora um 1300," in *Musik und die Geschichte der Philosophie und Naturwissenschaften im Mittelalter: Fragen zur Wechselwirkung von musica und philosophia im Mittelalter*, ed. Frank Hentschel (Leiden: Brill, 1998), 39–60, at 39–40. On divisions of the tone in the treatise of Jacques de Liège, see Desmond, "Behind the Mirror," 92–95. See also Bruno Bouckaert, ed., *CANTUS 21: Memoires du chant. Le livre de musique d'Isidore de Séville à Edmond de Coussemaker* (Neerpelt: Alamire/Lille: Ad fugam, 2007), 154–55 (facsimile and description by Christian Meyer of the twelfth-century Cambrai, Bibliothèque municipale, Ms. B 490, ff. 110v–112r: "Dicta magistri Symonis de semitonio platonico").

209 Wright, *Music and Ceremony*, 286.

Table D2 continued

Johannes de Muris	*Reformatio kalendarii anno 1345 papae Clementi directa* (written with Firminum de Bellavalle) [FFF24, O503–04][210] = ParisBN lat. 15104, mid-14th c.; *Theorica numerorum libri IV sive Quadripertitum* [sic] *numerorum* [GGG1, 1]; *Epistula metrica ad Philippum de Vitriaco*[211] [GGG1, 87] = ParisBN lat. 14736, ff. 87r–98r (main source for L'Huillier edition), paper manuscript written probably in the 1430s by Simon de Plumetot, *conseiller-clerc* of the Parliament of Paris, who died in 1443 and left his library to the Abbey of St. Victor (L'Huillier, 67–70); *De arte mensurandi*[212] [GGG1, 111] = ParisBN lat. 14736; *Theorica proportionum musicalium per magistrum Johannem de Muris . . . Item proportiones magistri Thome Anglici* [Thomas Bradwardine] plus works of Jourdain de Nemours [GGG2, O508–09] = ParisBN lat. 14737, ff. 3–11, early-15th c.; *Compendium musicae practicae* (complete) and *Notitia artis musicae* (excerpt) = ParisBN lat. 14741, 14th–15th c., Muris not named in catalogue [GGG12, O517–18] (RISM 6:220–22)
Philippe de Vitry	*Ars nova* (fragment, Vitry not named in catalogue) = ParisBN lat. 14741, 15th c. [GGG12] (RISM 6:220–22)
Jean Gerson	Pedagogical writings about music: ParisBN lat. 14905 [NN9, O329–31][213]

[210] Christine Gack-Scheiding and Johannes de Muris, *Epistola super reformatione antiqui kalendarii. Ein Beitrag zur Kalenderreform im 14. Jahrhundert*, Monumenta Germaniae Historica, Studien und Texte, 11 (Hannover: Hahn, 1995).

[211] See above, note 175.

[212] Johannes de Muris, *De arte mensurandi. A Geometrical Handbook of the Fourteenth Century*, ed. H.L.L. Busard (Stuttgart: Franz Steiner Verlag, 1998).

[213] We thank Shin Nishimagi for signaling this manuscript to us.

Table D3. Abbey of St. Victor: Anonymous Writings about Music

Item *liber dictus Trop*[ar]*ius cantoris parisiensis incomplete*[us] *cuius deest inicium. Item tractatus eiusdem cantoris de figuris, versus de eiusdem figuris; item et septem regule Thiconii*	ParisBN lat. 14414, in lost end of manuscript, probably early 13th c. like surviving folios [E17, O44]
Pseudo-Petrus de Cruce, *Ars musicae mensurabilis*, also *Gaudent brevitate moderni* (summary of Franco of Cologne's treatise, probably for young listeners)[214]	ParisBN lat. 15129, *ca.* 1300 [FFF21, O500–501] (RISM 1:121–22; RISM 6:223; CSM 15)
De punctis, instantibus et momentis	Lost; from Simon de Plumetot [GGG6, O510–11]
Quedam de arte dictaminis and *Quedam de discantu*	Paris, Bibliothèque de l'Arsenal 763, 14th c. [GGG7, O511–12] (RISM 6:172–73)
Circa musicam de tonis	ParisBN lat. 11412, lost part of compilation, probably early 13th c. [GGG9, O513] (not in RISM)
Quedam artis musice ut sciatur contrapunctus (in compilation including *Extracta quedam de libris sancte Hildegardis prophetisse*)	Lost [GGG10, O513–14]
Practica quedam artis musice ad cantandum diversis vocum consonancijs et partibus	Lost [GGG13, O518]
Quedam de arte canendi	ParisBN lat. 15128, 14th c. Germanic cursive script [JJJ23, O550–51] (RISM 1:120–21; RISM 6:223)
Compendium artis metrificate and *ars discantandi*	Lost [JJJ24, O551–52]
Quedam liber cantus sub quo quidam libellus in gallico de arte discantandi = "St. Victor Manuscript"	ParisBN lat. 15139, 13th–14th c. [KKK22, O566–67] (RISM 1:122; RISM 6:224; CSM 36)
Quedam communia concernentia septem artes liberales	ParisBN lat. 15121, 13th c., origin unknown [KKK24, O569] (RISM 1:120; RISM 6:222)

[214] Huglo, "Recherches," 14–15.

Table E. University of Paris: Colleges of the Sorbonne and Navarre

	College of the Sorbonne	College of Navarre
Plato, *Timaeus* (on flyleaf only)	BAV Reg. lat. 72., 12th c., not of Parisian, gift from Fournival then Gerard of Abbeville (RISM 2:111; RISM 6:531; Delisle, *Le Cabinet*, vol. II, 530; Rouse, "Manuscripts," 261)	
Calcidius, Commentary	ParisBN lat. 16579, second half 12th c., with dedicatory letter to Osius, gift from Fournival then from Gerard of Abbeville (Delisle, *Le Cabinet*, vol. 3, 62, no. 19); BAV Reg. lat. 1572, 13th c., origin English, chained book from Fournival (Rouse, "Manuscripts," 266)	
Augustine, *De musica*; Isidore, *Etymologiae*; *Tonale sancti Bernardi*	ParisBN lat. 16662, 13th c., monastic origin, bequest from Fournival then Gerard of Abbeville to Sorbonne (RISM 1:123–24; RISM 6:226; Rouse, "Manuscripts," 262)	
Isidore, *Etymologiae*		ParisBN lat. 17160, 12th c.; Paris, Bibliothèque Mazarine 609, 14th c., with interpolations from Visigothic manuscripts
Capella, *De nuptiis*	BAV Reg. lat. 244, 12th c. (Leonardi, no. 202, 471); BAV Ottoboni lat. 1840, 13th c. with glosses (Leonardi, no. 198, 471); cf. Rouse, "Manuscripts, 267	
Macrobius, Commentary	ParisBN lat. 16677, 9th c., orig. Fleury, prov. Sorbonne (Rouse, "Manuscripts," 266); ParisBN lat. 6367; ParisBN lat. 16680, 13th–15th c., orig. Italy, prov. Sorbonne (RISM 1:124; RISM 6:230)	
Boethius, *De institutione musica*	ParisBN lat. 16652, f. 43, late 13th c., Fournival to Gerard of Abbeville, who bequeathed it (RISM 6:225; Rouse, "Manuscripts," 261); lost manuscript (1338 cat., LI. 4; Delisle, vol. 3, 61); ParisBN lat. 16201, late 12th c., with Hermannus Contractus *De comp. astrolabii* and Adelard's Commentary on Euclid[215] (RISM 1:123; RISM 6:225), possibly consulted by Anonymous IV[216]	ParisBN lat. 18514, late 13th–early 14th c.; *De institutione musica* followed by a *Tractatus de musica collectus ex hiis quae dicta sunt a Boetio supra atque declaratio musicae practicae* (Bower, *Scriptorium* 42/2 (1988), 236, no. 101; RISM 6:231), also Anonymous I in the tradition of Johannes de Garlandia's treatise on *cantus planus*

Table E, continued

Anon. ref. to music and Boethius	ParisBN lat. 16089, 13th–14th c., unknown orig., prov. Sorbonne (RISM 1:123; RISM 6:224)	
Papias, *Elementarium*		ParisBN lat. 17878, 13th c.
Hugh of St. Victor, *Didascalicon*	ParisBN lat. 15256, 13th c. (RISM 1:122; RISM 6:224; Delisle, *Le Cabinet*, vol. II, 146 and vol. III, 40)	
Vincent of Beauvais, *Speculum doctrinale*, book XVII: *De musica*	ParisBN lat. 16100, 13th c., unknown orig., prov. Sorbonne (RISM 1:123; RISM 6:224)	
Jerome of Moray, *Tractatus de musica; Discantus positio vulgaris*, Johannes de Garlandia, Franco of Cologne, *Ars cantus mensurabilis*, Petrus Picardus, *Ars motetorum*	ParisBN lat. 16663,[217] *ca.* 1272–74 (RISM 1:124; RISM 6:226–27), belonged to Pierre de Limoges, master of arts (d. 1306); chained at the Sorbonne.	
Works of Jean Gerson[218]		ParisBN lat. 17487, origin Paris, 1447 (RISM 6:230–31)

[215] On these two manuscripts, see Calvin Bower, "Boethius' *De institutione musica*: A Handlist of Manuscripts," *Scriptorium* 42 (1988), 205–51, at 235, no. 98 (ParisBN lat. 16201) and no. 99 (ParisBN lat. 16652).

[216] See note 164 above.

[217] See notes 70 and 114 above.

[218] The texts are edited in Isabelle Fabre, *La Doctrine du chant du chœur de Jean de Gerson* (Geneva: Droz, 2005), especially 282–84 and 287–89. We thank Shin Nishimagi for this information.

Table F. Other University Colleges and Religious Houses

College	Title	Manuscript
College of St. Bernard	Isidore, *Etymologiae*	Reims, Bibliothèque municipale Ms. 431 (Piketty, see note 68 above)
College of Laon? (see above)	Treatises of Guido of Arezzo, Berno of Reichenau, two versions of *Ad organum faciendum*	Milan, Biblioteca Ambrosiana M. 17 sup., early 12th c. (RISM 2:59–63; RISM 6:518)
University	Notebook of Georg Erber with anon. music treatise	Innsbruck, Universitätsbibliothek Cod. 962, 15th c. (RISM 6:20–22)
Augustinians of St. Geneviève	Cistercian *Regulae*	Paris, Bibliothèque Sainte-Geneviève 2284, early 13th c., not by Cistercian scribe (RISM 1: 127; RISM 6:237)
Convent of *Grands Augustins*	Vincent of Beauvais, *Speculum doctrinale*, XVII[219]	Paris, Bibliothèque de l'Arsenal 1016, 14th c., unknown orig. (continuation of Paris, Bibliothèque de l'Arsenal 1015) (RISM 1:87; RISM 6:173)
Hermits of St. Augustine[220]	Isidore *Etymologiae* and *Liber hymnorum cum Augurismo*[221]	Isidore *Etymologiae* (possibly Paris, Bibliothèque Mazarine 313)
St. Jacques	Johannes de Garlandia, *de musica plana* and *De musica mensurabili*	BAV Vat lat. 5325, ff. 12v–30v, *ca.* 1260 (RISM 2:100–101; RISM 6:571–72)
St. Jacques	Dominican antiphoner with tonary probably from St. Louis de Poissy; Jerome of Moray (excerpt)	ParisBN *Musiques*, Rés. 1531 (RISM 1:87)
Feuillants[222]	Prologue to Cistercian gradual	ParisBN lat. 17328, 12th c., orig. northern France (RISM 6:230)

[219] Gottfried Göller, *Vincenz von Beauvais, O.P. (um 1194–1264) und sein Musiktraktat im Speculum doctrinale*, (Regensburg: Bosse, 1959).

[220] The Augustinian hermits were grouped into a single congregation under Pope Alexander IV (1254–1261).

[221] Eelcko Ypma, *La formation des professeurs chez les ermites de Saint-Augustin de 1256 à 1354* (Paris: Centre d'études des augustins, 1956), 157 and 159. This library's catalogue from *ca.* 1300 is now Paris, Bibliothèque Mazarine 627.

[222] The Feuillants were a reformed Cistercian order practicing rigorous poverty, including a strict diet, remaining bareheaded and barefooted, sleeping very little and on the ground, and valuing silence and manual labor. Although the Cistercian abbey of Feuillant existed in the twelfth century, the house of the Feuillants in Paris was founded in 1587 when Henry III, King of France, constructed for them the monastery of St. Bernard, in the Rue Saint-Honoré. Cf. Delisle, *Le Cabinet*, vol. 3, 251–52.

Table G. Manuscripts Possibly or Certainly from or in Paris

Calcidius, Commentary	Brussels, Bibliothèque Royale Albert 1.er 20782 293v–299r, early 14th c.	Paris?
Boethius, *De institutione musica*	Los Angeles, J. Paul Getty Museum, 15th c. (Christie's, 26/03/03, lot 8, 28–35); formerly London, Coll. Aut. Seilers, Phillipps 1351[223]	Paris
Isidore, *Etymologiae*	ParisBN lat. 7586; ParisBN lat. 7587	Paris
Isidore, *Etymologiae*	Orléans, Bibliothèque municipale, 296 (249); ParisBN lat. 7520, ff. 25–45, first half of 9th c. (Bischoff, *Katalog*, vol. 2, 350, no. 3738)	Region of Paris
Tonary with Greek and Latin modal information (Huglo, *Les tonaires*, 381–82)	Wolfenbüttel, Herzog August Bibliothek 79 Gud. Lat. 2° (cat. 4383), 11th c. (RISM 3:211–12; RISM 6:368)	Origin St. Martial, provenance Paris, Celestines?
Vatican organum treatise, ed. Zaminer	BAV Ottoboni lat. 3025, *ca.* 1225 or later, origin unknown (RISM 2:106; RISM 6:576)	Parisian origin according to Ouy (see above, note 55)
Notes and excerpts on music	Oxford, Corpus Christi College Library 283, 13th c.	Origin in Paris, later in Canterbury (RISM 6:413–14)
Works of Guido of Arezzo and Pseudo-Odo, Cistercian tonary, Johannes de Grocheio, Petrus de Cruce, only surviving source of treatise by Guido of St. Denis (ff. 58v–96v)	LondonBL Harley 281, first quarter 14th c.[224] (RISM 4:74–78; RISM 6:394)	Paris (script and decoration)
Guido of Arezzo writings, Pseudo-Bernolinus, Tonaries	LondonBL Harley 3199, late 11th, 14th c. (RISM 4:81–83; RISM 6:395–96)	French or English? In Paris by 16th c.
Lambertus	ParisBN lat. 11266, *ca.* 1280 (RISM 1:117; RISM 6:216)	Paris?
Boethius, Johannes de Garlandia, Philippe de Vitry	BAV Vat. lat. 5325, first half 14th c. (RISM 2:100–101; not in RISM 6)	Paris?

(Continued next page)

[223] Calvin Bower, "Manuscripts of the *De institutione musica* of Boethius," *Scriptorium* 42 (1988), 205, no. 47.

[224] Elizabeth A.R. Brown, email sent to authors fall 2009.

Table G, continued

Philippe de Vitry, *Ars nova* (*reportatio*)	ParisBN lat. 7378A, 1362 (RISM 1:107–8; RISM 6:206–7)	Paris?
Works of Muris and of Arnulph of St. Ghislain, part of Franco's *Ars mensurabilis musicae, Summa musice*	Sankt Paul im Lavanttal (Austria), Stiftsbibliothek Cod. 264/4, *ca.* 1394–1400 (RISM 4:809–10; RISM 6:55–57)	French, not necessarily Parisian (Christopher Page; see note 121 above)
Muris, *De proprietate* and *Musica speculativa*	Milan, Biblioteca Ambrosiana C 241 inf., 1401 (RISM 2:52; RISM 6:513–14)	Origin in Paris
Works of Johannis de Muris	Berlin, Staatsbibliothek ms. lat. fol. 600, first quarter 15th c. (RISM 3:18–19; RISM 6:260)	
Muris, letter to Vitry and *Quadripartitum numerorum*	ParisBN lat. 7190, ff. 101r–114v, late 15th c.; ParisBN lat. 7191 (L'Huillier, 70–72)	ParisBN lat. 7190 of Parisian origin, copied using ParisBN lat. 14736 from St. Victor; in the 16th c., the end of the treatise was copied into ParisBN lat. 7191, probably by Oronce Fine (d. 1555)
Leo Hebraeus, *De numeris harmonicis*; Muris, *Notitia artis musicae* and other works	ParisBN lat. 7378A, 1362 (RISM 1:107–8; RISM 6:206–7)	Paris?
Goscalc, anon. Ellsworth, treatise on dividing the tone	Berkeley, University of California Music Library Ms. 744, *ca.* 1375 (RISM 4:142–44; RISM 6:724; R. Crocker, *Acta musicologica* 39 (1967), 161–71; Huglo, *Les tonaires*, 433)	Origin in Paris
Reportatio on music teaching and music theory in hand of doctor of Emperor Charles IV	BAV Pal. lat. 1380, 14th c. (RISM 6:579–80)	Origin in Bologna; in Paris after 1366

APPENDIX 2: JOHANNES DE MURIS, LETTER TO PHILIPPE DE VITRY, PART ONE OF FOUR

Translation and Notes by Leofranc Holford-Strevens

Letter from Jean to Philippe: Part I.

Philippe, you venerable one, who can make your wishes commands for me your friend, correct these verses; in dedicating them to you as to the man worthiest of this work in the world.[225] I transfer ownership to you along with the book. Thus work is divided into four parts: one presents the roots, the second gives the marrow, the third bears the blossom, and the fourth tastes the fruit, whereby everything to do with number is connected to everything. Here begins the Four-Part Book of Numbers.

And now that I have learnt that thrice three figures,[226] placed in defined positions, count whatever there has been in the world, by which the art has taught me readily to multiply, then divide, to take all the roots, of which a compendious art is at hand which few care to seek out,[227] calculation is done more properly in numbers, but you will not be able[228] to reach the topmost peak of numbers or things.[229]

So, when you aim at writing down square roots, look at your digits, written in a straight line, and under the one that stands situated in the odd position,[230] find the number that, multiplied by itself, can cancel out whatever is written above it. Take[231] twice that number onto a line by itself and find the number that, multiplied first by that number doubled, then by itself, cancels whatever is written above

[225] In the text, *unus*, as in older English, "one the worthiest." However, the hiatus between *qui* and *unus* encourages me to prefer the reading of MS P (ParisBN lat. 14736), *vivit*, "who lives," i.e. to the person living in the world worthiest of this work. In any case *dignior* is used for *dignissimus*.

[226] I.e., the numbers one to nine.

[227] The period in the edition after *curant* deprives the sentence of a main clause.

[228] There is no subject here. *Poterit* appears to be a mistake for *poteris* (I noticed several such confusions when editing Geffroy de Paris's Latin *dits*).

[229] I.e., they are infinite.

[230] That is, separate the numbers into pairs from right to left and start with the first pair (or the isolated number).

[231] Or "Then take," reading *tunc*.

them, and those preceding, until the first number is cancelled out and departs.[232] Even if that happens only rarely, know that the number set out is a square whose root is known to you. It is the last figure and the half, or even several halves if present, that you will take as the root.[233]

If a number is given that cannot be a square,[234] for the nature of the case will not allow a standstill,[235] at least one must approach as near as possible to the surd roots that are manifest therein. Who shall count the roots of incommensurables? Neither God nor man, if it[236] is one of the things that do not exist, unless we should say that he knows things impossible and knows how the matter stands, but we do not. Therefore be quiet. It is enough for intellect to touch such roots; but[237] if they should exist, there would be a descent to atoms.[238]

Let two have been set forth (as the number) whose root is to be obtained. Put as many zeros as you like in a double row, and the more there are, the more valuable[239] the root will be. Then extract the roots as far as the figures could be so treated; if they are seen to exceed half the number of the zeros, you will put all those that are such in the first part; multiply all the remaining digits by any multiple of ten,[240] and place the result, if they exceed the middle of the zeros, after (those set aside). (Continue) thus, until half the zeros remain. Thus the root will be recognized. The whole numbers will be written first and then their fractions

[232] Having found the square root of the isolated number, double it and write after it the number that, after multiplying the doubled number in tens position and itself as a unit, equals (or most nearly approaches from below) the pair of numbers following the isolated number and the remainder of that number to the square already found (if any); then continue to the end. For example, to find the square root of 97969, first write it as 9|79|69, then find the square root of 9, namely 3, which cancels out the first digit. Multiply 3 by 2, yielding 6, and shift that number to the tens position. Then find the highest value of x such that $x(60 + x) \leq 79$. That number is 1, with a remainder of 18; write after this remainder the remaining pair of numbers, 69, as 1869. Then multiply the first two found numbers written sequentially, 3 and 1 = 31, by 2, yielding 62. Apply the same formula as above, finding the highest value of x such that $x(620 + x) \leq 1869$. Find that $x = 3$ since $1869 = 623 \times 3$. Therefore the square root of 97969 is 313.

[233] In the example given in the last note, the square root is the last digit of the final multiplicand, namely 3, preceded by the halves (31) of the preceding digits (62).

[234] That is, a number other than a perfect square.

[235] I.e., an end to the process; *finem* simplifies the text. The process is infinite since the square root is irrational ("surd").

[236] The number of such roots.

[237] Conjecturing *quod* (*quod si* = "but if," classical French *que si*) for the impossible *quos*.

[238] I.e., very small fractions, cf. book 2, ch. 23 of Muris's *Quadripartitum numerorum*, last paragraph.

[239] More valuable, in that it will be more exact.

[240] An attested meaning of *articulus*; I am not sure I am right here, but the prose text offers no help.

will come after, and will be their decadal denominator, such as 60, if you work thus with it.[241] And if there are more ways, I am content with this one.

This shall remain the rule for cube roots; having written out the digits, see where the thousands are placed and look for a number that when cubed can completely cancel out what is written above it. Place its triple in two places further and look for a figure placed under the next figure such that when you cause it to increase the triple together with the *subtriplum* and the product [of itself and the triple] without the *subtriplum* and also cube it, it cancels out everything written above.. And do not cease to do this until there is no figure left, if this is possible.[242]

[241] For explanation, see book 2, ch. 22, 81–103, which gives the following example. To find the square root of 2, write (for example) six zeros after it: 2000000. Take the square root by the rule given above: it will prove to be 1414. Count three digits (being half the number of zeros) from the right, 414, leaving the residue 1. Let the multiplier be 60; multiply 414 by 60, product 24840. This makes five digits, which are more than three; count three digits from the right, namely 840, put the residue of 24 sixtieths ("minutes") after 1; multiply 840 by 60, product 50400; proceed as before, putting 50 "seconds" after 1 24/60; multiply 24000, count three digits from the right, 000, and put 24 "thirds" after the rest of the root.

[242] Divide the number up into thousands, find the cube of, or highest cube less than, the leftmost segment, bring down the next three digits to follow the remainder, and repeat as necessary. For example, let the given number be 14706125, divide it into thousands, 14|706|125: The first group, 14, is $2^3 + 6$; take the remainder and bring down the next three digits: 6706. Multiply 2 by 3, set it down twice, and look for a whole number such that its product with 6 and 2, the product of its square and 6, and its cube, when accorded their respective place value as hundreds, tens, and units, shall equal 6706 or most nearly approach it from below. That number is 4:

$6 \times 2 \times 4 = 48 \qquad 6 \times 16 = 96 \qquad 4^3 = 64$

$$\begin{array}{r} 48 \\ 96 \\ 64 \\ \hline 5824 \end{array}$$

Now 6706 5824 – 892; bring down the remaining digits, making 892125. Repeat the process: the digits of the root found so far, namely 24, multiplied by 3 make 72. The new number needing to be found turns out to be 5:

$72 \times 24 \times 5 = 8840 \qquad 72 \times 25 = 180 \qquad 5^3 = 125$

$$\begin{array}{r} 8840 \\ 1800 \\ 125 \\ \hline 892125 \end{array}$$

The cube root of 14706125 is thus 245.

$$\begin{array}{l} \;2\quad 4\quad 5 \\ \hline 14|706|125 \\ \underline{8} \\ 6\,706 \\ 5\,824 \\ \hline \quad 892\,125 \\ \quad \underline{\underline{892\,125}} \end{array}$$

Muris calls the digits of the root successively thus found, other than the last, *subtriplum*, because they comprise a third of the multiplier.

But if the number is cubic—such numbers, though rare, are sown numberless in actuality[243]—let your root be the *subtriplum* together with the final digit.

But if the given number cannot be a cube, proceed as with the squares, but group the zeros in threes, exactly following[244] the method that[245] was stated, and thus you will be able to establish the nearest roots, in which the error will belong to nature, but not the art. It is not[246] the whole heaven that may be made into a cube by art and its cube root written, for that would be an error, since it is a ten thousand thousandth part that would endure it, and it is enough for the work that you wish to trust by sense.

And having seen that after the whole numbers nature has provided nothing, and that it is man who conceives of them, the double and half that are always on our lips, in my boyhood I wished to know the art of fractions, which is said to be supreme, very useful, exalted, which I shall write out for you, my corrector, in the treatise following. If you wish to add two fractions, multiply the two numbers that are below by each other, and the denominator will come into being; then multiply one of the numbers above with one below cross-wise,[247] add the results together and place the sum over the denominator, and read off the fraction or the whole numbers with the fractions, if there are any.[248]

But if you wish to subtract, multiply the whole as before, but do not add the crosswise products, but subtract the lesser from the greater. Put the remainder above what you have written and denominated,[249] and let a faint written line keep them apart. There is no one who can take whole numbers from fractions.[250]

But if you want to multiply a fraction by a fraction, multiply the bottom numbers under the bar, and then multiply the upper numbers above the bar. Do nothing more, but read off what you have done. If you wish to multiply fractions by whole numbers, multiply the whole number by the upper fraction,[251] but leave the

[243] That is, they are actually, not just potentially, infinite. The image of *seminantur* is of the sower scattering seed.

[244] Read *observando*.

[245] Read neither *quod* nor *que* but *qui*.

[246] Read *Non*.

[247] Reading *crucis* (cf. 110 *cruce*) for *uncis*, which violates meter, grammar, and sense.

[248] Thus: to add three-fifths to four-sevenths proceed as follows

$$\frac{3}{5} + \frac{4}{7} = \frac{3 \times 7 + 4 \times 5}{5 \times 7} = \frac{21 + 20}{35} = \frac{41}{35} = 1\,\frac{6}{35}.$$

[249] Read *denoqueminatum*, where *que* marks not an addition but an explanation.

[250] Fractions are taken to be vulgar (proper and simple, that is lying between 0 and 1), not compound (as in 1½). Thus, there is no whole number that can be subtracted from a fraction since negative numbers had not been recognized.

[251] I.e., the numerator.

low ones.[252] If there are whole numbers together with fractions, multiply them separately; read off each product. Or multiply them to the same form; then multiply the entire reduction of the fractions as before.[253]

If you wish to divide a fraction, proceed thus: let the numerator that is placed above the divisor multiply the number beneath the dividend,[254] and this becomes the numerator. Let the cross make the other number for you to place below the numerator.[255] Divide whole numbers by fractions thus: multiply the denominator by the whole numbers, divide the product by the numerator; or divide the whole number by the numerator, multiply the answer by the denominator, and either way the division will be done. If you wish to divide fractions by whole numbers, multiply the denominator by the whole numbers, leaving the numerator alone.[256] If dividends consist of whole numbers and fractions, multiply the dividend by each of the denominators, then divide the dividend thus obtained by the numerators.[257] Or proceed the other way round, and let a like fraction result. Then act in accordance with the previous rule.

To seek the (square) roots in all fractions is impossible, for there are many in which no root arises. But when each element of the fraction consists of a square, then it has a root. Sometimes there arrives a numerator that is a square with a denominator that is not, and vice-versa; rarely are both squares. Let the number whose root you wish to find be seven-tenths. Say: "they are three-quarters." Three-fifths, too, have no numerical root other than a surd, in which childhood arithmetic should have instructed you. But now it is established that there are only a few people in the world who wish to live without getting something whence comes

[252] I.e., the denominator.

[253] That is, either multiply the integral and the fractional parts of one number separately by the integral and the fractional parts of the other then add the products, or reduce them to a common denominator and then multiply.

[254] *Descindendum*, here and after, means "the thing to be split," i.e., the dividend; P substitutes the normal term, which will not scan.

[255] I.e., multiply the numerator of the dividend by the denominator of the divisor to obtain the denominator of the quotient.

[256] Read *dimisso*.

[257] That is, reduce the compound fraction to an improper fraction by multiplying the integral part by the denominator (and, not said, adding the numerator of the fractional part), then multiply by the denominator of the divisor and divide by its numerator.

gain:[258] not to count equal numbers[259] but to ride horses.[260] Thus do the arts perish. Yet no art will perish: nature does not wish to be without such practitioners, lest the forms that it preserves in this or in that should perish. Therefore all things are eternal, if God wills this. If not, nothing is eternal except God himself.[261] These are the things without which none of what follows is known.

End of the discourse on fractions.

End of the first part, which is on the roots of numbers.

[258] This is the age-old and world-wide complaint that most people simply want to make money, but expressed very awkwardly.

[259] The text is corrupt: "coins not equal numbers"; P's *numeros* for *nummos* does not even scan. I suspect loose syntax and conjecture *non numeros numerare equos*: "(who do not wish), not to count equal numbers but to ride horses (as a mark of wealth)."

[260] There is a play on *ēquos* (= *aequos*) "equal" and *ĕquos* "horses."

[261] Read *ipse*.

Notes on Contributors
Index to Manuscripts
General Index

Notes on Contributors

PETER BLOOM is author of *The Life of Berlioz* (Cambridge University Press, 1998) and editor of five collections of essays on Berlioz and his era including *Berlioz: Scenes from the Life and Work* (University of Rochester Press, 2008). He is editor of volumes 7 (*Lélio ou Le Retour à la vie*) and 24 (*Grand Traité d'instrumentation et d'orchestration modernes*) of the *New Berlioz Edition* and co-editor of the *Dictionnaire Berlioz* (Fayard, 2003). His study of Berlioz and Shakespeare appeared in volume 11 of *Great Shakespeareans* (Continuum, 2012). He is a member of the editorial board of the *Critique musicale d'Hector Berlioz* (Buchet/Chastel) and is preparing volume 9 of Berlioz's *Correspondance générale* (Flammarion). Bloom is the Grace Jarcho Ross 1933 Professor of Humanities at Smith College, in Northampton, Massachusetts.

SUSAN BOYNTON, Professor of Historical Musicology at Columbia University, has published on medieval liturgy, chant, monasticism, and liturgical drama. She is the author of *Shaping a Monastic Identity: Liturgy and History at the Imperial Abbey of Farfa, 1000–1125* (Cornell University Press, 2006), and of *Silent Music: Medieval Song and the Construction of History in Eighteenth-Century Spain* (Oxford University Press, 2011). She has co-edited *Musical Childhoods and the Cultures of Youth* with Roe-Min Kok (Wesleyan University Press, 2006); *From Dead of Night to End of Day: The Medieval Customs of Cluny* with Isabelle Cochelin (Brepols, 2005); *Young Choristers, 650–1700* with Eric Rice (Boydell and Brewer, 2008); and *The Practice of the Bible in the Middle Ages: Production, Reception, and Performance in Western Christianity* with Diane Reilly (Columbia University Press, 2011).

MARIE-NOËL COLETTE is Directeur d'Etudes emerita, Ecole Pratique des Hautes Etudes (Paris-Sorbonne). Her research focuses on the sources and analysis of early medieval music, more specifically the performance of Gregorian chant based on information from ninth- and tenth-century manuscripts and on practices in oral traditions. She is co-author of *Histoire de la notation du Moyen Âge à la Renaissance* (Paris/Tours, 2003) and editor of *Tropaire Séquentiaire Prosaire Prosulaire de Moissac, Ms. Paris, BnF, N.a.l. 1871* (Paris, 2006). She is currently preparing a catalogue of notated manuscripts from before 1200 held at the Bibliothèque nationale de France (Programme MANNO, http://www.univ-nancy2.fr/MOYENAGE/UREEF/MUSICOLOGIE/MANNO/).

IAIN FENLON is Professor of Historical Musicology in the Faculty of Music at Cambridge University, and a Fellow of King's College. After studies at Reading and Birmingham, Fenlon received his PhD from Cambridge. He has held fellowships at the University of Birmingham, Villa I Tatti in Florence, and King's College, Cambridge. In addition to his time as Lecturer, Reader, and Professor at Cambridge, he has been a visitor at many European and American colleges, including Wellesley College and Harvard University. Fenlon has received the Dent Medal of the Royal Musical Association and is a Fellow of the Society of Antiquaries. In 1981, Fenlon became founding editor of *Early Music History*. His work focuses on music from 1450 to 1650, particularly in Italy. His books include studies of sixteenth-century Mantua, the early Italian madrigal (with James Haar), Italian print culture, the letters and documents of Giaches de Wert, and, most recently, music in the city of Venice.

BARBARA HAGGH is Professor of Music at the University of Maryland, College Park, and past Chair of the International Musicological Society Study Group "Cantus Planus." She has published archival studies on early music in Brussels, Ghent, and Cambrai, and on the Order of the Golden Fleece; editions and analyses of several medieval historiae; an exhibition catalogue of musicalia in Cambrai and Douai; an article on the influence of the Van Eyck polyptych on Burgundian culture; and another, with Michel Huglo, on the manuscript "F" with the repertory of the Magnus liber organi of Paris.

ANDREAS HAUG is holder of the chair in Music in Pre-Modern Europe at the University of Würzburg. After receiving his PhD at the University of Tübingen in 1986, he worked in several capacities, including at the Corpus Troporum center at the University of Stockholm. After his Habilitation at the University of Tübingen in 1999 he was named Professor at the Center for Medieval Studies at the University in Trondheim, and from 2004 to 2008, successor to Fritz Reckow as holder of the chair in Musicology at the University of Erlangen-Nürnberg. He has held visiting professorships at the Universities of Basel and Vienna. Haug's main field of research is monophonic music of the Middle Ages. He is co-editor of the series *Monumenta Monodica Medii Aevi* and, since 2011, editorial head of the long-term project "Corpus Monodicum. Die einstimmige Musik des lateinischen Mittelalters.

DAVID HILEY was lecturer at Royal Holloway College, University of London, from 1976, and has been professor at the Institut für Musikwissenschaft of Regensburg University since 1986. From 1978–90 he edited the *Journal of the Plainsong & Mediaeval Music Society*. He was Chairman of the Study Group "Cantus Planus" of the International Musicological Society 1988–97 and has been co-editor of *Monumenta Monodica Medii Aevi* since 1991. In 1999 he was elected a member of the Academia Europea, and in 2002, Corresponding Member of the American Musicological Society.

LEOFRANC HOLFORD-STREVENS is the author of *Aulus Gellius: An Antonine Scholar and his Achievement* (Oxford University Press, 2003) and *The History of Time: A Very Short Introduction* (Oxford, 2005), co-author with Bonnie J. Blackburn of *The Oxford Companion to the Year* (Oxford, 1999), and co-editor with Amiel D. Vardi of *The Worlds of Aulus Gellius* (Oxford, 2004). He has also published several articles on classical, computistical, and musicological subjects. Having retired as Consultant Scholar-Editor at Oxford University Press, he is working on a new Oxford Classical Text of Aulus Gellius.

MICHEL HUGLO (d. 13 May 2012) was director of research at the Centre national de la recherche scientifique (CNRS) in Paris, adjunct research professor at the University of Maryland, College Park, doctor of letters *honoris causa* of the University of Chicago (1991), corresponding member of the American Musicological Society (1997), honorary member of the International Musicological Society (2007), and fellow of the Medieval Academy of America (2008). After working on the *Graduel critique: Les sources* and *Paléographie musicale* at Solesmes (1949–60), he directed research at the CNRS, where he founded the musicology section of the I.R.H.T., and taught in Paris and Brussels. His publications include *Les tonaires* (1971), *Les livres de chant liturgique* (1988), over 200 articles on western chant, theory, and early organum (many of them reprinted in four volumes of Ashgate's Variorum Series), and three manuscript catalogues (RISM B III 3, B III 4, and B XIV 1–2).

ÁRNI HEIMIR INGÓLFSSON studied music at the Oberlin Conservatory of Music and Harvard University, completing his PhD in 2003 with a dissertation on *tvísöngur*, an Icelandic form of two-part polyphony. He has written extensively on Icelandic music history, including a biography of the composer Jón Leifs (2009). He was Associate Professor of Musicology at the Iceland Academy of the Arts from 2005–08, and now holds a research position at the Árni Magnússon Institute for Icelandic Studies. He is currently writing a comprehensive study on music in Icelandic manuscripts from 1400–1800.

KATARINA LIVLJANIĆ, singer and musicologist, is currently Maître de conferences in medieval music at the Université de Sorbonne Paris IV, where she co-directs a medieval music performance Masters program. She is the founder and director of the vocal ensemble Dialogos. The ensemble has been acclaimed by critics and has toured in most European countries, in the USA, Canada, North Africa, and Latin America, including radio and television broadcasts. Livljanić spent a semester as visiting lecturer and directed a Gregorian chant *schola* at Harvard University. With Benjamin Bagby (of the group Sequentia), she was awarded a Cornille Visiting Professorship at Wellesley College in 2007. She was artist-in-residence at the Flanders Festival *Laus Polyphoniae* in Antwerp in 2012.

MATTHEW PEATTIE is Assistant Professor in Musicology at the University of Cincinnati, College-Conservatory of Music. He completed his PhD at Harvard in 2005 under the direction of Thomas Forrest Kelly with a dissertation on Beneventan music in the South Italian Office. Peattie also holds degrees in musicology from the University of Calgary and Université de Montréal. He served as an Allston Burr Resident Dean in Harvard College from 2004–07, and from 2007–08 he was the Associate Director of the Atkinson Centre at York University in Toronto, where he worked on issues of access to higher education and support for non-traditional students.

ANDREAS PFISTERER studied musicology and Latin philology in Tübingen (M.A., 1998) and Erlangen (PhD 2001; published as *Cantilena Romana: Untersuchungen zur Überlieferung des gregorianischen Chorals*, Paderborn, 2002). In 2009 he completed his Habilitation at Regensburg University ("Studien zur Kompositionstechnik bei Orlando di Lasso: Tonsystem—Tonarten—Satztechnik"), where he now teaches.

SUSAN RANKIN is Professor of Medieval Music at the University of Cambridge, and a Fellow of Emmanuel College. She studied in Cambridge, London, and Paris, with a doctoral thesis on medieval liturgical drama. Since then she has published on early medieval sources and notations, with St. Gall and Winchester as central points of interest. Her current research is on Carolingian musical sources and notations. She was awarded the Dent medal in 1995, and elected a fellow of the British Academy in 2009.

CRAIG WRIGHT received the degree Bachelor of Music in piano and music history at the Eastman School of Music (1966) and a PhD in musicology at Harvard (1972), and since 1973 has taught at Yale University, where he is currently the Henry L. and Lucy G. Moses Professor of Music. He was the recipient of a Guggenheim Fellowship (1983), the Dent Medal of the International Musicological Society (1980), and the Einstein (1976) and Kinkeldey (1990) awards of the American Musicological Society. Among his seven books are *Music and Ceremony at Notre Dame of Paris* (1989), *The Maze and the Warrior: Symbols in Architecture, Theology, and Music* (2001), and *Music in Western Civilization* (2nd edition, 2009). He is presently at work on a volume entitled *Mozart's Brain: Exploring the Nature of Genius*. In 2004 Wright was awarded the honorary degree Doctor of Humane Letters by the University of Chicago and in 2010 was elected to the American Academy of Arts and Sciences.

Index of Manuscripts

Tables are not included in this index. Parenthetical page numbers indicate discussions of manuscripts unnamed in text.

General Index